John Steinbeck:
The War Years,
1939—1945

Other Books by Roy Simmonds

The Two Worlds of William March

William March: An Annotated Checklist

John Steinbeck: The War Years, 1939–1945

Roy Simmonds

Lewisburg
Bucknell University Press
London: Associated University Presses

Associated University Presses
440 Forsgate Drive
Cranbury, NJ 08512

Associated University Presses
16 Barter Street
London WC1A 2AH, England

Associated University Presses
P.O. Box 338, Port Credit
Mississauga, Ontario
Canada L5G 4L8

The paper used in this publication meets the requirements
of the American National Standard for Permanence of Paper
for Printed Library Materials Z39.48-1984.

Library of Congress Cataloging-in-Publication Data

Simmonds, Roy S.
    John Steinbeck : the war years, 1939−1945 / Roy Simmonds.
        p.   cm.
    Includes bibliographical references (p.   ) and index.
    ISBN 0-8387-5317-5 (alk. paper)
    1. Steinbeck, John, 1902−1968. 2. World War, 1939−1945−
Literature and the war, 3. Novelists, American−20th century−
Biography, 4. War correspondents−Europe−Biography.
5. World War, 1939−1945−Journalists.   I. Title.
PS3537.T3234Z8667   1996
813'.54−DC20
[B]   95-41415
                                                                                CIP

PRINTED IN THE UNITED STATES OF AMERICA

This book is dedicated to
Tetsumaro Hayashi
Robert DeMott
John Ditsky
and
Warren French

One may never hope to put his finger on the whole secret of a great writer. That magic is his individual possession, his chrism, his sanctifying grace. Neither God nor nature offer explanations of their mysterious workings. But certain characteristics do fall within the compass of criticism, and certain qualities distinguish if they do not define the genius of Steinbeck.

> —Edmund C. Richards
> "The Challenge of John Steinbeck" (1937)

It will be interesting to see what the war will do to Steinbeck, to his viewpoint, to his selection of subject-matter. In a world changing as rapidly as this, no man could appear to have better qualifications than he for reflecting and interpreting important phases of the picture, regardless of what it is to be.

> —J.S. Noack
> "John Steinbeck" (1941)

Everything the people admires, it destroys.

> —John Steinbeck
> Quoted in John Hersey's "John Steinbeck: 1902–1968" (1970)

Contents

Acknowledgments

THE PROVENANCE OF THIS BOOK CAN BE TRACED BACK TO 1983, WHEN I commenced research for an essay, "Steinbeck and World War II: The Moon Goes Down," which was published the following year in the *Steinbeck Quarterly*. The idea of expanding the essay into a full-length study took wing approximately four years later, and the subsequent writing of the book, not forgetting the vast amount of additional research I had to carry out, could not have been achieved without the advice, help, and encouragement of a number of people, and the assistance and generosity of various libraries both in the United States and in England.

My principal gratitude must be extended to Tetsumaro Hayashi and Preston Beyer. Tetsumaro Hayashi, the distinguished Steinbeck scholar, has been a valued friend and mentor for more than twenty years, and, as President of the International John Steinbeck Society and editor of the *Steinbeck Quarterly*, was responsible not only for the publication of my original 1984 essay referred to above, but also for the first Steinbeck essay I ever wrote – way back in 1971. Preston Beyer, the noted Steinbeck collector and authority, has also been an enduring friend, giving unstinting help, sharing with me his vast knowledge of Steinbeck, the man and the writer, and providing me with archival and research materials that I would never have been able to track down so readily elsewhere. Time and time again, he pointed my researches into fresh and productive areas. It cannot be too strongly stressed that but for his unfailing generosity of spirit in giving of his time in answering my questions, in seeking out information for me, and in keeping the mailman busy delivering fat envelopes to my door this book would not be the work that it is.

A special debt of gratitude is also due to Steinbeck's widow, Mrs. Elaine Steinbeck, and to the Steinbeck Estate and its agents, McIntosh & Otis, Inc., for their generosity in allowing me access to Steinbeck's unpublished letters and manuscripts, and for their permission to quote from such material. At no stage whatsoever were any of my requests denied. In this connection, I wish to express my particular thanks to Mr. Eugene H. Winick and Ms. Julie Fallowfield of McIntosh & Otis, Inc. for their promptness and their invariable kindness in dealing with my correspondence over the years.

I also extend my sincere gratitude to three leading Steinbeck scholars whose support has been essential to me: John Ditsky, who, by way of Transatlantic correspondence, lived through parts of this book with me during its composition, and later read an earlier version of my manuscript, offering many useful, essential, and (for me) face-saving suggestions;

Warren French, with whom I have spent many enriching hours discussing Steinbeck and his work, and who has been generous to a fault in sharing his wisdom and his ideas, and in providing much-needed encouragement; and Robert DeMott, whose level-headed advice, unbounded enthusiasm, and scholarly example have been a spur to me during the whole gestation period of this book, and especially during those happily infrequent periods of self-doubt.

I also wish to record my gratitude to the many people who have contributed directly in a variety of different ways toward the writing of the book. I name them alphabetically, for want of a more appropriate order: Jean Ashton, Rare Book and Manuscript Library, Butler Library, Columbia University in the City of New York; Barbara Begley, Department of Special Collections, Stanford University; Jackson J. Benson; Anne Marie Bridy, John Fitzgerald Kennedy Library, Boston; Stanley W. Brown, Dartmouth College Library; Donna Burkons, Twentieth Century-Fox Film Corporation; Yvonne Burton, Preservation Records, Butler Library, Columbia University in the City of New York; Pascal Covici, Jr., Southern Methodist University, Dallas; Bernard R. Crystal, Rare Book and Manuscript Library, Butler Library, Columbia University in the City of New York; Stan and Alison Dex; James M. Dourgarian; Florence B. Eichin, Penguin USA; Mary Jean S. Gamble, John Steinbeck Library, Salinas; Frances Garner, Mobile College, Alabama; Mimi Reisel Gladstein, University of Texas, El Paso; Howard B. Gottlieb, Special Collections, Mugar Memorial Library, Boston University; John Gross, John Steinbeck Library, Salinas; Bonnie Hardwick, Manuscripts Division, Bancroft Library, University of California, Berkeley; Robert B. Harmon; Constance Hawkes, Periodicals Library, University of London Library; Lee Richard Hayman; Cathy Henderson, Harry Ransom Humanities Research Center, University of Texas at Austin; Jean Holah, Octopus Publishing Group Library; Robert A. Hull and Gregory A. Johnson, Manuscripts Department, University of Virginia Library; Margaret J. Kimball, Department of Special Collections, Stanford University; Kenneth A. Lohf, Rare Book and Manuscript Library, Butler Library, Columbia University in the City of New York; Malcolm M. MacDonald, University of Alabama Press, Tuscaloosa; D. Mesher, San Jose State University; Karen Mix, Special Collections, Mugar Memorial Library, Boston University; Robert E. Morsberger, California State Polytechnic University, Pomona; Michael Mulcay, Periodicals Library, University of London Library; Kiyoshi Nakayama, Kansai University, Japan; Wallace M. Nelson, Steinbeck Center Foundation, Salinas; Louis Owens, University of California at Santa Cruz; Patricia J. Palmer, Department of Special Collections, Stanford University; Pauline Pearson, John Steinbeck Library, Salinas; Michael Plunkett, Manuscripts Department, University of Virginia Library; Estelle

Rebac, Manuscripts Division, Bancroft Library, University of California, Berkeley; Robert and Evelyn Remple; Arthur Ring; Jean Rose, Octopus Publishing Group Library; Carol A. Rudisell and Michael T. Ryan, Department of Special Collections, Stanford University; Susan Shillinglaw, Steinbeck Research Center, San Jose State University; Roger Smith, William Heinemann Ltd.; George H. Spies; Sarah Timby, Department of Special Collections, Stanford University; Catherine Trippett, Reed Consumer Books Ltd.; Walter W. Wright, Dartmouth College; Jack Yaeger, Twentieth Century-Fox Film Corporation; and Elizabeth Ziman, U.S. Library, University of London Library.

I acknowledge my indebtedness to the following libraries and institutions for providing me with photocopies of various research and unique Steinbeck materials: Manuscripts Department, University of Virginia Library; Manuscripts Division, Bancroft Library, University of California, Berkeley; British Library, London; British Newspaper Library, Colindale; Rare Book and Manuscript Library, Butler Library, Columbia University in the City of New York; Harry Ransom Humanities Research Center, University of Texas at Austin; John Fitzgerald Kennedy Library, Boston; John Steinbeck Library, Salinas; Periodicals Library, University of London Library; Special Collections, Mugar Memorial Library, Boston University; Steinbeck Research Center, San Jose State University; Department of Special Collections, Stanford University; Twentieth Century-Fox Film Corporation, Beverley Hills, California; and Westminster Public Library, London.

All who have written about Steinbeck and studied his work since 1984 must be profoundly indebted to Jackson J. Benson for his monumental biography, *The True Adventures of John Steinbeck, Writer*. I am no exception. Benson's work is staggering in its depth, breathtaking in its scope, and penetrating in its perceptions. It has become the fountainhead of the new Steinbeck scholarship.

Finally, but by no means least, I pay tribute to my wife, Joyce, who has not only acted as my initial editor and provided me with unending support but has also demonstrated an immense degree of understanding for the long hours I have remained closeted in my study. The wives of writers surely deserve a special medal.

Permissions

of the Steinbeck Estate through Eugene H. Winick, president of McIntosh & Otis, Inc.

From *Cup of Gold* by John Steinbeck. Copyright 1929, renewed © 1957 by John Steinbeck. Used by permission of Viking Penguin, a division of Penguin Books USA Inc.

From *In Dubious Battle* by John Steinbeck. Copyright 1936, renewed © 1964 by John Steinbeck. Used by permission of Viking Penguin, a division of Penguin Books USA Inc.

From *The Long Valley* by John Steinbeck. Copyright 1938, renewed © 1966 by John Steinbeck. Used by permission of Viking Penguin, a division of Penguin Books USA Inc.

From *The Grapes of Wrath* by John Steinbeck. Copyright 1939, renewed © 1967 by John Steinbeck. Used by permission of Viking Penguin, a division of Penguin Books USA Inc.

From *The Forgotten Village* by John Steinbeck. Copyright 1941, renewed © 1968 by John Steinbeck. Used by permission of Viking Penguin, a division of Penguin Books USA Inc.

From *The Log from the Sea of Cortez* by John Steinbeck. Copyright 1941 by John Steinbeck and Edward F. Ricketts. Copyright renewed © 1969 by John Steinbeck and Edward F. Ricketts, Jr. Used by permission of Viking Penguin, a division of Penguin Books USA Inc.

From *The Moon Is Down* by John Steinbeck. Copyright 1942 by John Steinbeck. Renewed © 1970 by Elaine A. Steinbeck, John Steinbeck IV and Thom Steinbeck. Used by permission of Viking Penguin, a division of Penguin Books USA Inc.

From *Bombs Away* by John Steinbeck. Copyright by John Steinbeck. Renewed copyright © by Elaine Steinbeck, John Steinbeck IV and Thom Steinbeck. Used by permission of Viking Penguin, a division of Penguin Books USA Inc.

From *Once There Was a War* by John Steinbeck. Copyright 1943, 1958 by John Steinbeck. Renewed © 1971 by Elaine Steinbeck, John Steinbeck IV and Thomas Steinbeck. Used by permission of Viking Penguin, a division of Penguin Books USA Inc.

From *Cannery Row* by John Steinbeck. Copyright 1945 by John Steinbeck. Renewed. © 1973 by Elaine Steinbeck, John Steinbeck IV and Thom Steinbeck. Used by permission of Viking Penguin, a division of Penguin Books USA Inc.

From *The Pearl* by John Steinbeck. Copyright 1945 by John Steinbeck. Renewed © 1973 by Elaine Steinbeck, John Steinbeck IV and Thom Steinbeck. Used by permission of Viking Penguin, a division of Penguin Books USA Inc.

From *East of Eden* by John Steinbeck. Copyright 1952 by John Steinbeck. Renewed © 1980 by Elaine Steinbeck, John Steinbeck IV and Thom

Steinbeck. Used by permission of Viking Penguin, a division of Penguin
Books USA Inc.
From *Sweet Thursday* by John Steinbeck. Copyright 1954 by John
Steinbeck. Renewed © by Elaine Steinbeck, John Steinbeck IV and
Thom Steinbeck. Used by permission of Viking Penguin, a division of
Penguin Books USA Inc.
From *Journal of a Novel* by John Steinbeck. Copyright © 1969 by the
Executors of the Estate of John Steinbeck. Used by permission of
Viking Penguin, a division of Penguin Books USA Inc.
From *Steinbeck: A Life in Letters* by Elaine A. Steinbeck and Robert
Wallsten. Copyright 1952 by John Steinbeck, © 1969 by The Estate of
John Steinbeck, © 1975 by Elaine A. Steinbeck and Robert Wallsten.
Used by permission of Viking Penguin, a division of Penguin Books
USA Inc.
From *The True Adventures of John Steinbeck, Writer* by Jackson J.
Benson. Copyright © 1984 by Jackson J. Benson. Used by permission
of Viking Penguin, a division of Penguin Books USA Inc.
From *Working Days: The Journals of The Grapes of Wrath* by John
Steinbeck, Introduction by Robert DeMott. Copyright © 1989 by Elaine
Steinbeck. Introduction copyright © by Robert DeMott. Used by per-
mission of Viking Penguin, a division of Penguin Books USA Inc.
From *Cup of Gold*, *In Dubious Battle*, *The Long Valley*, *The Grapes of
Wrath*, *The Log from the Sea of Cortez*, *The Moon Is Down*, *Once
There Was a War*, *Cannery Row*, *The Pearl*, *East of Eden*, *Sweet
Thursday*, *Journal of a Novel*, and *Steinbeck: A Life in Letters*. Used
also by permission of Reed Consumer Books Ltd.
From *Bombs Away*, *The Forgotten Village*, *The Moon Is Down* (play),
and *The True Adventures of John Steinbeck, Writer*. Used also by
permission of Curtis Brown, London.
From *The True Adventures of John Steinbeck, Writer*. Used also by
permission of Jackson J. Benson.
From *The Outer Shores – Part 1: Ed Ricketts and John Steinbeck Explore
the Pacific Coast. Part 2: Breaking Through*. Used by permission of
Joel W. Hedgpeth & Edward F. Ricketts, Jr.
From article "John Steinbeck Joins the Daily Express." *Daily Express*
(London), 25 June 1943. Used by permission of the *Daily Express*.
From Pascal Covici's unpublished letters. Used by permission of Pascal
Covici, Jr. and Harry Ransom Humanities Research Center, University
of Texas at Austin.
From Steinbeck's unpublished letters to Elizabeth R. Otis, Mildred Lyman,
Carlton A. Sheffield, and Webster F. Street, and the unpublished
holograph manuscripts of *The God in the Pipes* and *Cannery Row*.
Used by permission of the Department of Special Collections, Stanford

University [The John Steinbeck Collection (M 263)].

From Steinbeck's unpublished letters to Pascal Covici, Alfred Katz, and Robert Ballou, and Steinbeck's holograph manuscript draft of the suggested "Introduction" to *The Portable Steinbeck*. Used by permission of the Harry Ransom Humanities Research Center, University of Texas at Austin.

From Steinbeck's holograph draft of his unpublished obituary of Ernie Pyle. Used by permission of the Steinbeck Research Center, San Jose State University.

From Steinbeck's holograph manuscript of *The Grapes of Wrath* and his unpublished letters to Merle Armitage. Used by permission of the Clifton Waller Barrett Library, Manuscripts Division, Special Collections Department, University of Virginia Library [John Steinbeck Collection #6239].

From Steinbeck's unpublished first holograph drafts of *The Pearl* and *The Wizard of Maine*. Used by permission of Steinbeck Archives, Salinas, California.

From Steinbeck's unpublished letters to Gwyn Conger Steinbeck [Gwendolyn C. Steinbeck Collection #71/40c], Ritch Lovejoy [John Steinbeck Letters #70/124c], and Joseph H. Jackson [Joseph Henry Jackson Papers #C-H40, Boxes 10 & 25], and from Steinbeck's unpublished film narrative script for *The Red Pony* [John Steinbeck Collection] and his holograph statement on the Soviet invasion of Finland [Gwendolyn C. Steinbeck Collection #71/40c]. Used by permission of the Bancroft Library, University of California, Berkeley.

From Steinbeck's unpublished letters to Annie Laurie Williams and Oscar Dancigers, and from Steinbeck's unpublished typed statement on *The Moon Is Down*, his unpublished holograph first draft of *The New Order*, and the unpublished *A Medal for Benny* typescript by John Steinbeck and Jack Wagner, all in the Annie Laurie Williams Papers. Used by permission of the Rare Book and Manuscript Library, Butler Library, University of Columbia in the City of New York.

From Steinbeck's unpublished manuscript of *Lifeboat*. Used by permission of Twentieth Century-Fox Film Corporation.

Parts of Chapters 1, 7, and 8 have appeared in somewhat different form in "The Original Manuscript," an essay published in *San Jose Studies* 16 (Winter 1990), a special issue devoted to *The Grapes of Wrath*, and in "Steinbeck's *The Pearl*: Legend, Film, Novel," an essay published in *The Short Novels of John Steinbeck: Critical Essays with a Checklist to Steinbeck Criticism*, ed. Jackson J. Benson (Durham, NC: Duke University Press, 1990).

Abbreviations

Adventures	Jackson J. Benson, *The True Adventures of John Steinbeck, Writer* (New York: Viking Press, 1984)
ALW	Annie Laurie Williams
Astro	Richard Astro, *John Steinbeck and Edward F. Ricketts: The Shaping of a Novelist* (Minneapolis: University of Minnesota Press, 1973)
CAS	Carlton A. Sheffield
Conversations	*Conversations with Steinbeck*, ed. Thomas Fensch (Jackson: University Press of Mississippi, 1988)
CR	John Steinbeck, *Cannery Row* (New York: Viking Press, 1945)
ERO	Elizabeth R. Otis
Fensch	Thomas Fensch, *Steinbeck and Covici: The Story of a Friendship* (Middlebury, Vermont: Paul S. Erikson, 1979)
French 1	Warren French, *John Steinbeck* (Boston: Twayne Publishers, 1961)
French 2	Warren French, *John Steinbeck* [2nd edition, revised] (Boston: Twayne Publishers, 1975)
GOW	John Steinbeck, *The Grapes of Wrath* (New York: Viking Press, 1939)
GC	Gwyndolyn Conger
GS	Gwyndolyn Steinbeck
Hedgpeth	Joel W. Hedgpeth, *The Outer Shores* (Eureka, CA: Mad River Press, Inc., 1978)
JHJ	Joseph H. Jackson
JN	John Steinbeck, *Journal of a Novel: The EAST OF EDEN Letters* (New York: Viking Press, 1970)
Letters	John Steinbeck, *Letters to Elizabeth*, ed. Florian J. Shasky & Susan F. Riggs (San Francisco: The Book Club of California, 1978)
Lifeboat	John Steinbeck, *Lifeboat* (unpublished typescript)
Lisca	Peter Lisca, *The Wide World of John Steinbeck* (New Brunswick, NJ: Rutgers University Press, 1958)
LSC	John Steinbeck, *The Log from the Sea of Cortez* (New York: Viking Press, 1951)
LV	John Steinbeck, *The Long Valley* (New York: Viking Press 1938)

MID   John Steinbeck, *The Moon Is Down* (New York: Viking Press, 1942)

Millichap   Joseph R. Millichap, *Steinbeck and Film* (New York: Frederick Ungar Publishing Company, 1983)

ML   Mildred Lyman

MM   Mavis McIntosh

NO   John Steinbeck, *The New Order* (unpublished holograph manuscript)

NYHT   *New York Herald Tribune*

OTWW   John Steinbeck, *Once There Was a War* (New York: Viking Press, 1958)

PC   Pascal Covici

RL   Ritch Lovejoy

RP script   John Steinbeck, *The Red Pony* (unpublished narrative script)

SC   John Steinbeck & Edward F. Ricketts, *Sea of Cortez* (New York: Viking Press, 1941)

SLL   John Steinbeck, *Steinbeck: A Life in Letters*, ed. Elaine Steinbeck & Robert Wallsten (New York: Viking Press, 1975)

TC   John Steinbeck, *Travels with Charley* (New York: Viking Press, 1962)

TP   John Steinbeck, *The Pearl* (New York: Viking Press, 1947)

WD   John Steinbeck, *Working Days: The Journals of THE GRAPES OF WRATH*, ed. Robert DeMott (New York: Viking Press, 1989)

WFS   Webster F. Street

Wizard   John Steinbeck, *The Wizard of Maine* (unpublished holograph manuscript)

WOD   John Steinbeck, *The Winter of Our Discontent* (New York: Viking Press, 1961)

John Steinbeck:
The War Years,
1939—1945

John Steinbeck:
The War Years,
1939–1945

Introduction

1

IN THE EARLY SUMMER OF 1939, FOLLOWING THE PUBLICATION IN APRIL THAT year of his novel *The Grapes of Wrath*, the volume of critical and popular acclaim accorded Steinbeck's literary career had reached its apogee. In the short period of ten years, he had risen from obscurity to being the most talked-about living American writer of fiction. In 1929, the publication of his first novel, *Cup of Gold*, had passed almost unnoticed, and his second and third published novels, *The Pastures of Heaven* (1932) and *To a God Unknown* (1933), had also received scant attention. It was not until the appearance of *Tortilla Flat* in 1935, *In Dubious Battle* in 1936, and, more particularly, the novel and play versions of *Of Mice and Men* in 1937, that his career had taken flight.

Literary honors began to come his way. In 1936, *Tortilla Flat* was awarded the Gold Medal of the Commonwealth Club of California as the best book of general literature published by a California author in 1935. In 1937, he won the same award for *In Dubious Battle*, and *Of Mice and Men* was selected as a Book of the Month choice. Following the New York Drama Critics Circle Award in April 1938 to *Of Mice and Men* as the best new American play of the season, critics and readers alike eagerly anticipated Steinbeck's next book. *The Long Valley*, a volume of short stories, came out in September 1938, but contained only two works not previously published in America: "Flight" and "The Leader of the People," the latter a meaningful addition to the 1937 three-story cycle *The Red Pony*.[1] Those who had been expecting a new full-length work were disappointed, especially as there had been various newspaper reports in late 1937 and early 1938 that, after gathering material by working as a laborer on ranches up and down the state of California, Steinbeck was writing a new novel, provisionally titled *The Oklahomans*, at his home in Los Gatos.[2] One report in November 1937 even suggested that the book was one-third completed and would run to about one thousand pages.[3] When interviewed by Louis Walther of the *San Jose Mercury-Herald*,

Steinbeck expressed his belief that the current migration of "people from the dust bowl states will profoundly alter the tenor of life in California," and continued:

> Their coming here now is going to change things almost as much as did the coming of the first American settlers. . . . These people have that same vitality that the original Americans who came here had, and they know just what they want. The Californian doesn't know what he does want. He wants things. The Oklahoman knows just exactly what he wants. He wants a piece of land. And he goes after it and gets it. California will be a better state for his coming.[4]

The manuscript on which Steinbeck had then embarked was, however, nothing like the one thousand-page epic mentioned in the newspaper report. *L'Affaire Lettuceburg* was a bitter, satirical novel of approximately sixty thousand words. When he had completed the revision of the first draft in May 1938, he realized with dismay that he had produced a bad, "a smart-alec" book (Lisca 147). He decided to destroy the manuscript and start over. In a tremendous, almost unbelievable, burst of creativity, he had the new, entirely different, book written by the end of the year.

When *The Grapes of Wrath* appeared in the bookstores four months or so later, it was perhaps inevitable that many of the reviewers should have concentrated on Steinbeck's treatment of those economic and sociological matters he had discussed so controversially the previous year in the *San Jose Mercury-Herald* interview, and especially in the series of articles about the plight of the Dust Bowl migrants he had written for the *San Francisco News* under the title *The Harvest Gypsies*. In *The Nation*, Louis Kronenburger, while having some overall aesthetic reservations about the book, admitted:

> No novel of our day has been written out of more genuine humanity, and none, I think, is better calculated to awaken the humanity of others. . . . *The Grapes of Wrath* is a superb tract because it exposes something terrible and true with enormous vigor. . . . One salutes it as a fiery document of protest and compassion, as a story that had to be told, as a book that must be read. It is, I think, one of those books — there are not very many — which really do some good.[5]

Although Steinbeck's bitter exposé of the economic and social climate of those days in both Oklahoma and California is as valid now as it was in 1939, it is a truism that the passage of time is, in most instances, an extremely effective leveler of the passions once engendered by contemporary events. While we are by no means able to subdue feelings of anger and pity, such being the power, vividness, and humanity of Steinbeck's prose, we are today more inclined to assess the book as a work of literature rather than as a sociological indictment. We are not primarily concerned whether the wrongs Steinbeck reveals in this book are the unadulterated truth of the matter, or, as was strenuously claimed in some quarters, are an irresponsible distortion of fact. What does concern us emotionally as readers today is our belief in and our involvement in the plight of the members of the Joad family as they are dispossessed of their home and persuaded by false prophets to embark on their forlorn, make-shift journey toward the mirage of a promised land in the West. Without necessarily having firsthand experience or contemporaneous knowledge of the Joad's cruel predicament, we are unequivocally aware that it requires only change of setting and circumstance, plus a catalystic chain of events, both natural and manmade, to create yet again somewhere in the world the selfsame economic, social, and political atmosphere in which the downtrodden are forced to fight for their very existence. More than a half-century after its publication, *The Grapes of Wrath* has long been established as a masterpiece of twentieth-century American literature, and, as the supreme work of art that it is, an enduring metaphor for the universality of man's inhumanity (and humanity) toward his fellow men.

Harry Thornton Moore, who published the first full-length critical study of Steinbeck's work on the very day *The Grapes of Wrath* was published, and who had been afforded the opportunity of reading the book in galley proof, concluded:

> It is impossible, at the time this is being written, to gauge the public response to *The Grapes of Wrath*, but it is safe to predict—and not solely on the basis of the tremendous advance sale—that *The Grapes of Wrath* will be a long-term best-seller. This despite the fact that almost every passage in the book would ordinarily be considered violently revolutionary and profane by the majority of those who will read it. But the author of *Of Mice and Men* is in vogue now: in America, those in vogue can do little wrong. The vogue will last as long as Steinbeck can hold the public's interest; eventually he may be displaced by writers whom the public will consider more interesting, but such a day seems, at this time, very remote.[6]

2

In some respects, Moore's prognosis was remarkably accurate. *The Grapes of Wrath* did indeed become a long-term best-seller, although Moore certainly could not have foreseen that the book would still be read more than fifty years later as avidly as it had been by its original admirers, and would have been reprinted at frequent intervals in both hardback and paperback editions to satisfy a continuing demand.

Steinbeck, on the other hand, was more pragmatic than Moore, confiding to the critic that he thought it "mathematically predictable that the crowd [would] one day turn on him."[7] If by "the crowd" he was referring to the critical fraternity, he was right. While his popularity with the reading public remained constant, not only in America but across the world, contemporary reviewers and critics did turn against him in increasing numbers, belittling his achievements and his literary importance, and all too often displaying an ongoing indifference toward the work he subsequently produced. If most of the books Steinbeck published during the war years — *The Forgotten Village* (1941), *Sea of Cortez* (1941) (written in collaboration with Edward F. Ricketts), *The Moon Is Down* (1942), and *Bombs Away* (1942) — rated a mainly favorable critical reception no doubt generated in part by an undercurrent of residual respect for the author of *The Grapes of Wrath*, the reviews that greeted his last novel of the war years, *Cannery Row* (1945), and the first novel he published postwar, *The Wayward Bus* (1947), gave ample evidence that whatever self-imposed moratorium some critics may have been observing was now coming to an end. One of the early warning notes was sounded in 1946 by James Gray:

> Steinbeck remains, midway in his career, a variable artist who has made unhappy concessions in his best works and risen to moments of unique excellence in his worst. Perhaps the very fact that he still gropes, and often bungles, will keep him interested in his own talent long after other contemporary writers have lost any impulse to use their better-integrated skills. That has been known to happen.[8]

During the period from the ending of World War II until his death in 1968, Steinbeck published ten new books, both fiction and nonfiction, and two books, *The Log from the Sea of Cortez* (1951) and *Once There Was a War* (1958), that consisted mainly of reprinted work from the war years. Most were greeted with lukewarm praise, downright disdain, or indifference. Only the novella *The Pearl* (1947) seemed to attract anything like universal approval. Certainly, so far as the critics were concerned, Steinbeck was no longer in vogue. The literary darlings were now the exciting new writers — Norman Mailer, Gore Vidal, Vance Bourjaily, John Horne Burns, Truman Capote, William Styron, and Saul Bellow — who had come into prominence during the early postwar years. This was the era of John W. Aldridge's *After the Lost Generation* (1951) and of Maxwell Geismar's *American Moderns* (1958). Consideration of the work done by the writers in the Thirties did not really come within the scope of Aldridge's study, and he mentioned Steinbeck only twice, and very briefly, in passing. Geismar lamented the decline of the "classic moderns" — Dos Passos, Faulkner, Hemingway, and Steinbeck — noting that although two of them had won the Nobel Prize in recent years, not one had produced any fresh or important work since the war. Of Steinbeck, Geismar wrote: "The real question about John Steinbeck is what has happened to John Steinbeck."[9]

The publication of Peter Lisca's pioneering study *The Wide World of John Steinbeck* in 1958 gave another respected critic, Alfred Kazin, the opportunity to survey Steinbeck's career to that date. In *On Native Grounds* (1942), Kazin had already expressed his doubts concerning Steinbeck's work, seeing it as becoming "more and more tenuous and even sentimental," and he referred to Steinbeck as looking still "like a distinguished apprentice."[10] In his 1958 review of Lisca's book, Kazin consolidated his attack. He saw the root of all Steinbeck's more recent failures stemming on the one hand from the writer's postwar detachment from his California heritage, causing him to become "intellectually adrift at that point in his career where every American writer with the same theme has either found new strength or has relapsed into sentimentality," and on the other hand from a dependence on "a vaguely 'non-teleological' biologism which in itself (apart from the beautiful descriptions of the natural world in which it usually comes) is not so much a philosophy as an excuse for not having one."[11]

When Steinbeck was awarded the 1962 Nobel Prize for Literature the critical wolves emerged in a pack, baying for blood. Almost the only leading American newspaper to approve the Nobel Prize Committee's choice was the *New York Herald Tribune*. By the time Steinbeck and his third wife had journeyed to Stockholm for the official presentation, the critical wolf pack was well and truly primed for the kill. In the *New Leader*, Stanley Edgar Hyman registered his "amazement" at the honor bestowed upon Steinbeck. The author's last two books, *Travels with Charley* and *The Winter of Our Discontent*, were, Hyman opined, "clearly the work of a writer who, if he was not always a lightweight, is a lightweight now."[12] Arthur Mizener had been even more scathing in his article the day before in the *New York Times Book Review*:

> Perhaps the time has come around for some American to receive the award, and among Europeans Steinbeck turned out to be, for one or another reason, the most widely read American author, just as Sinclair Lewis was when he received the Nobel Prize in 1930. Neither of these explanations is, I am afraid, very flattering. But it is difficult to find a flattering explanation for awarding this most distinguished of literary prizes to a writer whose real but limited talent is, in his best books, watered down by tenth-rate philosophizing and, in his worst books, is overwhelmed by it.[13]

3

When Steinbeck died on 20 December 1968 his reputation had, in many respects, sunk to an all-time nadir. He had produced no work of fiction since *The Winter of Our Discontent* seven years before, and the only book he had published since becoming the 1962 Nobel Laureate was the large-format volume *America and Americans* (1966), in which his text, fearlessly and lovingly examining and celebrating the multifarious faces and aspects of his native land, was interspersed with glossy pictures by fifty-five leading photographers. Not only had his literary output been virtually nonexistent during the six years preceding his death, but his public support for Lyndon Johnson's policies in pursuing the war in Vietnam—which Steinbeck voiced principally in his notorious, but perhaps misunderstood, dispatches from the war zone in the Long Island newspaper *Newsday*—had resulted in his being accused by many (even by large numbers of his erstwhile admirers) of having betrayed the "little people of the world," who in the past had looked to him as one of their most passionate spokesmen.[14]

The publication of two full-length biographies—Thomas Kiernan's *The Intricate Music: A Biography of John Steinbeck* in 1979, and Jackson J. Benson's monumental *The True Adventures of John Steinbeck, Writer* in 1984—provided the critics and reviewers with the opportunity of either restating past condemnations or of making new and constructive assessments of the Steinbeck canon. The influence of the biologist Edward F. Ricketts on Steinbeck's thinking was considered by two of the reviewers of Kiernan's biography. Roger Sale noted:

> Whatever the merits of Ricketts's ideas on their own, their effect was to shackle Steinbeck because he could usually make use of them only with great awkwardness and see them at work only among emotionally limited and intellectually dim people.

Sale suggested that the only works of Steinbeck's likely to give pleasure in the future were *The Grapes of Wrath*, *Of Mice and Men*, and some of the stories from *The Long Valley*. He added: "The rest, unfortunately, is not silence, but one can be silent about it."[15] John W. Aldridge also saw one of the principal failures of Steinbeck's work as stemming from the conflict between Steinbeck the scientist and Steinbeck the philosophizing romantic allegorist, a conflict that could be resolved only through the creation of characters "without human life ... biological phenomena, specimens confected out of an imaginative vision based not on sympathy or compassion but on a sentimental love affair with the piety of feeling."[16]

Following the publication of Benson's biography five years later, Thomas R. Edwards declared: "It is hard to think of a writer whose reputation has fallen farther than John Steinbeck's." Edwards then posed the question: "Why did such success lead to such failure, and where did the success come from in the first place?" In partial answer, he suggested that

after the success of the stage and movie versions of *Of Mice and Men* [Steinbeck]
conceived and sometimes even wrote (or dictated) most of his fiction as scripts
... and dreamed in vain of success as a playwright. This mingling of genres was
surely unhealthy for his writing.[17]

Scholarly interest in Steinbeck's work has flourished during the years
since his death. In addition to the vast number of bibliographical articles
and critiques of specific works in leading academic journals, a great many
full-length critical studies and collections of critical essays have been
published, reaching a sort of crescendo in conjunction with and subsequent to the celebration in 1989 of the fiftieth anniversary of the
publication of *The Grapes of Wrath*. What all this spate of critical work
over the past quarter-century or so has demonstrated is that Steinbeck
scholarship remains divided into two well-defined camps. On one side,
there are those who maintain that, with the ending of World War II,
Steinbeck's work became locked into disastrous decline. On the other
side, a new generation of scholars, with fresh, unbiased minds, has been
questioning all that had been accepted, by weight of the conventional
approach, as long-established truths.

This new criticism began persuasively to explore the suggestion that
what had upset so many critics and scholars of the old school was the fact
that Steinbeck, with his ever-questing mind, had simply not been content
to rest on his laurels and churn out work in the old, familiar vein, but had
instead elected to embark on a series of literary experiments in search of
new forms and ways of expression. By doing this, of course, he could not
be conveniently categorized. But was it, the proponents of the new
criticism forcibly argued, that the work Steinbeck had been doing since
The Grapes of Wrath had simply not been understood, so that, in consequence, the postwar fiction had been seriously and wrongly undervalued?
Balanced interpretations and judgments at last began to appear of critically
neglected novels like *East of Eden* (so often dismissed as not only a
structural mess, but also a mishmash of fact and fiction, of half-baked
philosophies, and of pretentious religious analogies), and *Sweet Thursday*
(widely regarded as a pale successor to *Cannery Row* and barely rating
critical attention).[18]

The new criticism did not necessarily seek to establish that the postwar
fiction was the equal of the earlier fiction of the 1930s, but rather that it
indicated a radical change over the years in Steinbeck's thinking, and a
brave desire on his part to shuck off the confines of critical categorization.
Certainly, viewed as the expression of Steinbeck's development as a
writer, the postwar books cannot be dismissed out of hand as virtually
worthless, as several critics have claimed and go on claiming. John Ditsky,

one of the staunchest defenders of Steinbeck's later fiction, has applauded the fact that

> Steinbeck criticism has increasingly begun to accept the writer on his own terms, a process no more complicated than the reading closely of what heretofore has been often subjected to a routinely and callously applied imposition of extraneous critical assumptions.[19]

The new criticism makes it clear that in many ways and indeed for the whole of his creative working life Steinbeck remained, as Alfred Kazin dubbed him, "a distinguished apprentice." The label is not applied here in the assumed pejorative sense in which Kazin used it, but in recognition of the fact that Steinbeck's restless mind, combined (if you will) with what some might consider a misdirected artistic courage, meant that he was possibly never able to attain his full potential. The experimenting, of course, did not commence only after *The Grapes of Wrath*. It was very much inherent in that work and in all the work that preceded it. But whereas the artistic, technical, and philosophical experiments he carried out, beginning with *Cup of Gold* in 1929, displayed a continuing upward progression in both quality and assuredness to culminate in 1939 in *The Grapes of Wrath*, the experiments he conducted thereafter never quite seemed to jell. In too many instances, together with a regrettable intermittent failure of language, the results were a good way below Steinbeck's best.

The reality or fiction of Steinbeck's postwar "decline" is a subject endlessly debated among Steinbeck scholars, and the measure of the disagreement is sometimes profound, although, almost without exception, all would concur with the stance adopted by Warren French when he categorically states:

> I cannot agree with those who would write Steinbeck off as not even a serious writer. His failures by no means cancel out his successes.[20]

Even among those who maintain that there was a "decline" there is some confusion as to when the decline commenced. John Ditsky has succinctly and somewhat wryly postulated the problematic nature of the schism:

> A favorite critical guessing game has been the identifying of the precise moment when Steinbeck's powers began to weaken. By 1940? The War's end? 1950?[21]

The dates, of course, are significant. Those who regard 1940 as the watershed year broadly agree with Harold Bloom, who has unequivocally declared that Steinbeck's best novels are those that came early in his career — *In Dubious Battle*, *Of Mice and Men*, and *The Grapes of Wrath* — and that nothing after *The Grapes of Wrath* "bears rereading."[22] Those who hold the view that the beginning of the "decline" coincided with the ending of World War II are those who broadly agree with French, when he opines that in the years following *Cannery Row* Steinbeck never "recaptured the spirit that makes the novel glow like a homing beacon in a drab world,"[23] and that probably in those subsequent years, "in the evening of his talent," Steinbeck "should have stayed with journalism."[24] Those who delay the coming of the decline until 1950 are those who, while accepting and finding much to admire in *The Wayward Bus* and *The Pearl*, finally became disillusioned when *Burning Bright* appeared in 1950 in the van of what they regarded as the chaotic *East of Eden*, the facetious *Sweet Thursday*, the trivial *The Short Reign of Pippin IV*, and the disappointingly artificial *The Winter of Our Discontent*.

4

It is salutary here to remind ourselves of the high hopes expressed in 1939, or shortly afterward, for Steinbeck's future literary career. Reviewing *The Grapes of Wrath* in the *Kenyon Review*, the British novelist Christopher Isherwood felt that Steinbeck "still owes us a great novel." Isherwood went on to declare: "*The Grapes of Wrath* is a milestone in American fiction, but I do not believe it represents the height of its author's powers."[25] In the *Virgina Quarterly* at about the same time, Wilbur L. Schramm gave much the same verdict: "[Steinbeck] is still the most promising novelist in America. ... The only question now is: How high can Steinbeck go?"[26] In his introductory essay to *Contemporary American Authors* (1944), Fred B. Millett predicted that, following the death of Thomas Wolfe, Steinbeck was "the young American novelist whose future seems most exciting and most assured."[27] That same year, J. Donald Adams wrote in his *The Shape of Books to Come*:

> I shall be surprised if Steinbeck does not move on to do even stronger work than *The Grapes of Wrath*, overweighted as it sometimes was by the vehemence of his anger. ... Nobody writing today has a finer descriptive power, not even Hemingway; he has both curiosity and affection in his approach to human conduct, and a strong narrative sense.[28]

The seven years 1939 through 1945 constituted one of the most destructive periods known in the history of mankind. It was also a destructive period in terms of Steinbeck's image as a writer. What, then, brought about this change in Steinbeck's fortunes and the attitude that contemporary reviewers and subsequent critics and scholars have had toward his work? What were the forces, external and personal, that acted upon him during those years, both as a human being and as a creative artist, that resulted in so many critics minimizing his achievements and questioning his skill and his genius as a writer?

Although it is true that Steinbeck's personal life passed through a series of crises and vissicitudes and his health was damaged, possibly even permanently, by his experiences as a war correspondent in 1943, the period 1939—45 was a period of prodigious creativity, in many ways matching and perhaps even exceeding the creativity of the prewar years. There is no denying that Steinbeck produced an impressive (in volume, at least) body of work during the war years, a large portion of which is still unpublished and, for one reason or another, likely to remain so. This body of work, both in its published and unpublished states, has not, to date, been examined in any detail as an organic whole.

Perhaps a close study of this wartime output, including the comparative successes and the frequent failures, together with an examination of his thinking and of the multitude of trials and tribulations that beset him during those seven years, will provide answers to many questions, and will finally give some clue as to whether the so-called "decline" was the result of Steinbeck's deliberate (and arguably disastrous) change of course in mid-career, or, as so many have claimed, the result of an irreversible weakening of his creative powers.

1

The Creation of a Twentieth-Century Masterpiece: *The Grapes of Wrath*

AFTER THE FIASCO OF *L'AFFAIRE LETTUCEBURG*, STEINBECK, THEN AGED thirty-six, commenced writing the new book on 26 May 1938, and completed it in ninety-three working days spread over the next five months. However one approaches it, as layman or scholar, Steinbeck's first draft holograph manuscript of *The Grapes of Wrath* is an astonishing document, not least for the fact that, with the exception of two comparatively short passages of 82 and 228 words, it contains the whole text of the book as it was to be published six months later.[1] Not only that, but a comparison between the texts of the holograph draft and the published book reveals very few major variants, the principal one being, other than the two additional passages already mentioned, the deletion of a passage of approximately 160 words that makes a somewhat tenuous and inappropriate analogy between the invasion of the Roman Empire by the barbarians and the influx of the migrants into California. The minor textual differences are mostly changes in punctuation (there is, in fact, a considerable amount of revision in this respect), paragraphing, and occasional spelling.[2]

Basically, it can be seen that what Steinbeck achieved in those ninety-three days was the complete book, virtually word for word, as we know it. There is no denying the measure of Steinbeck's genius, in that having embarked on the book he was able to begin at Chapter 1 and write the whole text sequentially through to the end of Chapter 30, alternating the general chapters (the "interchapters," or "intercalary chapters," as they are known) with the particular chapters (the chapters dealing specifically with the Joads) as he went along. The degree of artistic control he exercised in writing this epic work, with its overall complexity of theme, structure, and characterization, was truly phenomenal. In this book, no less in the manner in which it was created, Steinbeck demonstrated what a wonderfully instinctive writer he was, able to judge in masterly fashion the natural momentum of the story he was telling.

Steinbeck's first wife, Carol, acted as his stenographer and initial editor, and commenced preparing the typescript at the beginning of September, when her husband was approximately two-thirds of the way through writing the first draft. Until then, the book had no title. It was Carol who suggested *The Grapes of Wrath*, a title Steinbeck enthusiastically endorsed. On the 10th of that month, he wrote to his literary agent and friend, Elizabeth R. Otis of the New York firm McIntosh & Otis, reporting that, although he could not estimate when he would have the first draft finished, he expected Carol would have caught up in preparing the second draft (the typescript). He went on to declare that the typescript was "so clear and good that it, carefully and clearly corrected" would become the final draft for submission to Viking (*SLL* 171). The "clear and careful corrections" were, in fact, mainly carried out by Carol as she proceeded with the typing. In an interview in June 1939, Steinbeck admitted that he had always experienced difficulties with spelling and punctuation, but that since marrying Carol he had relied upon her to copyread all his work. "She's wonderful," he declared, "never misses a thing" (*Conversations* 16).

That Steinbeck owed much to Carol in her role as preliminary editor is patently obvious. The holograph manuscript of *The Grapes of Wrath* is dotted with her red pencil markings, querying certain individual words, or certain phrases or passages, presumably because she found difficulty in deciphering her husband's cramped, minuscule handwriting, despite her long familiarity with it.

Pascal Covici, Steinbeck's editor at the Viking Press, visited the couple at their newly-acquired home, the Biddle Ranch, Los Gatos, in late October 1938, at a time when Steinbeck was within two days of completing the first draft. Covici read the first four hundred pages of the typescript and was so overwhelmed by what he had read that no sooner had he returned to New York than he put into motion plans for a very large edition and for an advance notice of April publication for the book. Covici urged Steinbeck to release all the chapters Carol had typed (something over half the book), but Steinbeck demurred, preferring to send the typescript to his publishers in due course as a completed work. In any case, so he said, he wanted to read through the typescript himself and make whatever small revisions he thought necessary. He told Covici, perhaps somewhat optimistically, that he felt rested enough after the strain of writing the book to begin immediately this work of revision. He confided in Elizabeth Otis that he was disturbed by the way in which Covici had, he felt, gone over the top in his enthusiasm, and, in particular, by the idea of the enormous initial print run Viking was proposing. He warned that in his opinion it would not be a popular book—to most readers even an outrageous one—and that a cautious approach would be more sensible. Viking, he urged, should print a small edition to begin with, and wait to see how the book sold before printing more copies.

Covici's impatience, however, was not to be curbed. Finally, Steinbeck was forced to give way. He sent the first two chapters of the typescript to the editor on 29 November, together with a note, in which he pleaded, "Please don't crowd me any more" (JS/PC 11/29/38). By mid-December, the whole of the typescript was in Covici's hands. On the 22nd, Steinbeck wrote to him, asking anxiously, "I hope you like the rest of the mss [sic] as well as the first. Personally I think it gets better. But I am still sure it won't be a popular book. Anyway it's all I've got so far and maybe always" (JS/PC 12/22/38).

With the book now confirmed for April publication, everything was thrown into top gear. There were, however, problems. To begin with, Steinbeck had arguably not been allowed as much time as he might have wished for revising the typescript, although it is much more likely that when he wrote to Covici in November, indicating he was ready to begin the revision, he had not been expecting any major surgery or rewriting. At any rate, only the minimum of revision was carried out. Indeed, certain very short passages that seem to have been inadvertently omitted by Carol when reading from the holograph manuscript were never reinstated, indicating that Steinbeck never went back to his original text when (or if) he checked the typescript.

There were, on the other hand, some important revisions made during late December and early January. Both his agents and Covici had been dismayed by some of the earthy dialogue in the manuscript, and considered it would have to be toned down to avoid the possibility of the book's being banned. Steinbeck was adamant that the controversial words should remain. Eventually, Elizabeth Otis traveled to Los Gatos to stay at the Biddle Ranch for a few days, and went through the whole manuscript with Steinbeck in the hope of persuading him to see reason. It was not a very propitious time for the visit. Carol was unwell, and Steinbeck himself had been laid low for the first time in twenty years, suffering from neuritis and an exceedingly low metabolic rate. He had been ordered by the doctor to stay in bed for two weeks. Clearly, both he and Carol had worked themselves to and beyond a danger point in getting the book completed and ready for the publishers. Even so, from his sick bed, Steinbeck cooperated with Elizabeth Otis, and on 3 January 1939 he reported to Covici that he had agreed to whatever changes he felt he could make without compromising his integrity as a writer. Even so, there were some changes he would not make.

In the end, commercial reason had prevailed on one side and artistic honor was more or less preserved on the other. We are talking here of no more than twenty or so instances of bowdlerization, including the elimination of three mentions of the word "fuck" or "fuckin'," five mentions of the word "shit," and one mention of the word "screw," and the toning down of several passages of a sexual or scatalogical nature. While the restoration of these deleted words or phrases would probably not cause many raised eyebrows today, such restoration would not really improve the force or authority of the published text to any substantial degree.

Steinbeck was under no illusion that he would be under attack for many of the passages in the book and that these would provide further ammunition for those who already questioned his political loyalties. In his article "A Primer on the 30's," published in *Esquire* in 1960, Steinbeck looked back on the political climate in America during those prewar years, recalling how he had been denounced as a Communist by the Dies Committee (the 1938 House Committee to Investigate Un-American Activities, chaired by Senator Martin Dies) for contributing money toward medical aid for Republican Spain. He had been bitterly amused at the time to discover that the child star Shirley Temple had also been denounced by the committee for the selfsame offense. Steinbeck, however, was never a Communist, simply anti-fascist. But the label stuck and was to cause him a great deal of trouble, both known and unknown to him, in the years to come. It was not only his support for medical aid to the Loyalist cause in Spain but his depiction of communist field workers in his 1936 strike novel *In Dubious Battle* that had been misconstrued in many quarters as clear evidence of his political allegiences. Nothing, of course, could have been further from the truth. While his researches for the book brought him into close contact with many communist fieldworkers, he did more listening than talking when he invited them to visit him at home.[3] Admittedly, his political leanings were to the left of center, but only because he sympathized with the downtrodden. He viewed with undisguised abhorrence all totalitarian philosophies.

Because he feared that the text of *The Grapes of Wrath* would also be open (at least by some) to such convenient misinterpretation, he requested that the score and verses of the "Battle Hymn of the Republic" be reproduced on the book's front and back endpapers as a defense against the anticipated accusations that the book was revolutionary in spirit and communist in outlook.

Some of the passages in the original holograph draft that were, at some stage, either cut or toned down before publication were in fact not sexual or scatalogical in nature, but rather emphasized the depth of Steinbeck's anger and indignation toward those he saw as the evil moneymen who had brought about and perpetuated the desperate plight of the migrant people. For example, in Chapter 5, which deals with the processes that bring about the dispossession of the tenant farmers by the banks, there is an imagined exchange between the farmers and the representatives of the owners. Toward the end of the exchange, two sentences, in which the owner men accuse the farmers of socialism and bolshevism and of wanting to attack the sacred rights of property, have been cut and replaced by a single less emotive sentence: "You'll have to go" (*GOW* 46). Similarly, a direct reference to William Randolph Hearst, identifying him by name and charging him with burning down empty dwelling houses on his land "for fear somebody'd live in 'em," was cut from Chapter 19. These revisions were likely suggested by the Viking editors, but in one place at least, Steinbeck acted as his own censor in this respect, making an extensive deletion in the holograph manuscript during the course of composition. In Chapter 9, the interchapter expressing the impotent anger of the dispossessed farmers forced to sell their farm equipment and personal chattels for a pittance to avaricious dealers in order to raise whatever money they can for the journey to California, one highly charged passage was crossed out by Steinbeck and immediately substituted by a single sentence: "And they'll all walk together and there'll be a dead terror from it" (*GOW* 119).[4]

If in *The Grapes of Wrath* Steinbeck can be accused of advocating radical and possible violent social change, he can also be congratulated for celebrating the indomitability of the human spirit of the "little people" who were doing all the suffering, not only in America but all over the world. As Ma Joad tells her son:

> "[U]s people will go on livin' when all them people is gone. Why, Tom, we're the people that live. They ain't gonna wipe us out. Why, we're the people — we go on." (*GOW* 383)

It was not merely the sexual, scatalogical, and the politically-sensitive passages however that had troubled Steinbeck's publishers when they read the typescript. Covici wrote to Steinbeck on 9 January, and told him that not only he but also Harold Guinzburg, president of the Viking Press, and Marshall Best, the firm's managing editor, had been left emotionally exhausted after reading the typescript. Guinzburg had declared that he would not change a single comma in the whole book, and Best rated it the most important work of fiction on the Viking list. An initial appropriation of ten thousand dollars, had already been allocated for advertising purposes. Having broken the ice by telling Steinbeck all this, Covici then expressed certain misgivings he and his colleagues had about the book's closing episode, indicating that they thought it too abrupt. They considered that the last few pages needed building up, so that the scene in which Rose of Sharon gives her breast to the starving man is seen to be "not so much an accident or chance encounter, but more an integral part of the saga" (*SLL* 177). Steinbeck reacted angrily, and refused to change the ending in any way: "[I]t must be an accident, it must be a stranger, and it must be quick" (*SLL* 178). He must have been dismayed that his intention, as he had recorded in his journal, that the whole narrative and emotional structure of the book should lead to this final scene in the barn (the ultimate expression of the "I to We" concept he had explicated throughout the novel) had not been appreciated.

Steinbeck did concede to his publishers' suggestions to the extent that he wrote an additional 228-word passage describing the two miserable days the remnants of the Joad family spend in the boxcar, while the floodwater rises, then eventually levels off, allowing them to escape.[5] The insertion of these twenty or so lines of printed text serves to rationalize the chronology of the closing sections of the novel, providing Rose of Sharon with acceptable time to recover to some extent from the trauma of giving birth to her stillborn child.

After the stipulated two weeks in bed, the pain in Steinbeck's back had not eased, but grown much worse. In desperation, he made an appointment to see an osteopath on 20 January. Although he went tongue in cheek, to his surprise, after some manipulation, the pain was alleviated. For the first time in six weeks, he was without pain.

He was advised to continue resting in bed, but was increasingly restless to be up and about and living a normal life again. The news that he had been elected to membership of the National Institute of Arts and Letters perhaps helped to revive his spirits a little, but when, toward the end of January, Viking sent him the galley sheets, he found himself faced yet again with the demanding and tedious task of proofreading he had always detested, even when in good health. Carol helped out, double-checking the galleys with him, and by 8 February, to his intense relief, the job was done and the last of the sheets mailed back to New York.

In many ways, it is difficult to imagine so monumental a work being created under more adverse conditions. It was written at white-hot speed immediately following the completion of a discarded full-length work. It was written under a great deal of pressure from both agents and publishers, anxious that Steinbeck should bring out a new novel to follow the success of *Of Mice and Men*, and thus keep himself in the public eye. It was written at a time of domestic upheaval, while the Steinbecks were moving home and often living under difficult conditions in makeshift accommodation. It was written at a time of fairly heavy and unwanted social commitment, as Steinbeck's journal records. It was written, certainly in the later stages, when the author was stretched almost beyond the limits of his nervous endurance. There is little wonder that Steinbeck, exhausted in the aftermath of this period of tremendous, sustained creativity and still pressurized by agents and publishers, did not give the sort of attention he might otherwise have given to the completed text of his book.

The manner in which the novel was written and published does therefore raise one or two questions for consideration. To begin with, masterpiece though it undoubtedly is, we have to ask ourselves if *The Grapes of Wrath* might have been an even better book, an even greater masterpiece, had Steinbeck closely, even substantially, revised that first draft before it was published. It is, of course, unfair to speculate. One can argue with much more conviction that the book was written at exactly the right time, at the precise coming together of all those several elements that go toward producing a masterpiece, chief among them being that it was written at that point in the writer's career when he had reached full creative maturity and had the good fortune to discover the perfect theme to inflame both his imagination and his emotional need. In other words, first draft or not, it probably could not have been bettered.

We should remind ourselves again what Steinbeck achieved. In that first draft there is displayed a unity of purpose, not simply in the narrative structure but also in the emotional and philosophical structures, that is truly phenomenal. It is a unity that is explicit in the treatment of the "I to We" concept, and in the manner in which the narrative and emotional structures complement each other and are additionally supplemented and strengthened by the interchapters. When he had finished that first draft, Steinbeck had produced a manuscript that was, indeed, almost perfect enough to be printed as it stood. As a piece of "spontaneous writing" it invites comparison with and is certainly far more impressive than Jack Kerouac's *On the Road*, which it incidentally predates in composition by some thirteen years.

We must also address the question of the possible long-term effect, if any, the writing of *The Grapes of Wrath* may have had on Steinbeck himself. The process of writing the book nearly killed him. He would not have willingly subjected himself to such an experience again. Yet, although he had released what was, in essence, the first draft for publication, his agents, his publishers, and eventually the vast majority of the critics and the reading public had fallen over themselves in showering praise on him. If, in such manner, it was possible to produce a work proclaimed almost universally as the greatest novel of the decade (and sometimes as the greatest novel ever written by an American), then surely it was possible for the process to be repeated. This is not to suggest that this was a conscious approach adopted by Steinbeck in subsequent work, but it is just possible that the seed may have been implanted in his mind, to be nurtured by the more-or-less general acclaim that was to greet some of the hastily-written work he published during the stressful years 1939 through 1945. Once the wartime interruption to the possible predestined course of his career was at last behind him, Steinbeck's great tragedy could be said to have been that he found it beyond his grasp to achieve again that remarkable synthesis of imaginative spontaneity and high literary quality that is the hallmark of *The Grapes of Wrath*.

In his journal on 5 July 1938, Steinbeck wrote: "When this book is finished a goodly part of my life will be finished with it. A part I will never get back to" (*WD* 38), and on 11 July he added: "[O]nce this book is done I won't care how soon I die, because my major work will be over" (*WD* 41). In retrospect, Steinbeck's prediction seems unfortunately prescient, possibly in more ways than he could have suspected or intended.

2

1939: Into the Public Domain

IF, AS HIS NEW YEAR'S DAY LETTER TO COVICI HAD DEMONSTRATED, Steinbeck fully anticipated the response the book would arouse in many quarters all over the country, it is doubtful if even he was prepared for the torrent of villification it provoked or the intensity of some of the threats to be directed against him.

Indeed, there were sinister rumblings before publication. In a letter to McIntosh & Otis on 4 March 1939, Steinbeck reported that he had been warned by the proprietor of a Monterey bookshop that a group of people, purportedly FBI agents, had been in the shop asking for information about him. They had advised the bookshop owner that J. Edgar Hoover had ordered a thorough investigation into the author's past. Steinbeck had written the letter to ensure that these revelations were on record, in case anything happened. He requested McIntosh & Otis to preserve the letter and the postmarked envelope, and advised them that he had begun keeping a meticulous record of everything he did and everyone he saw, so that he could provide himself with an alibi in the event of being faced with trumped-up charges (*Adventures* 394).

The Grapes of Wrath was published on 14 April with advance sales of forty thousand, and within a fortnight or so was selling steadily at the rate of ten thousand copies a week. The prepublication reviews and those immediately following publication were almost uniformly enthusiastic and frequently ecstatic, although most expressed some aesthetic reservations of one sort or another.

Virtually alone among these early reviewers, Burton Rascoe remained unimpressed. In *Newsweek*, he dismissed the book as being "about tenant farmers in Oklahoma, who got pushed off their land by the wicked landlords and struck out in a jalopy for California, where they thought you didn't have to work but could just live on oranges picked from somebody else's trees." While conceding that the book contained "beautiful and, even magnificent, passages," he went on to complain that it was "not well organized," and that he could not "quite see" what it was about, "except that there are no frontiers left and no place to go."[1] In a follow-up review a fortnight later, Rascoe rounded on the book for its "mess of silly propaganda, superficial observation, careless infidelity to the proper use of idiom, tasteless pornographical and scatalogical talk," and summed it up as "a bad book by a man whose work I have so greatly admired."[2] Another less-than-enthusiastic review came, perhaps surprisingly, from

Philip Rahv in the radical left-wing *Partisan Review*. Rahv criticized the novel for being "far too didactic and long-winded," and for containing "all the familiar faults of the 'proletarian' literary mode" with "the usual idealized portraits and the customary conversions, psychologically false and schematic as ever, to militant principles."[3] The first sustained accusation that the book constituted a statement of Marxist propaganda was made by the Rev. Arthur D. Spearman, S.J., two months after the book's appearance. In a review in the *Albany Times-Union* (NY), Spearman seized on what he saw as the insidious antireligious philosophy pervading the pages of the book. "Mr. Steinbeck," he wrote, "wittingly or unwittingly, has made this book an embodiment of the Marxist Soviet propaganda as the opiate of the people, and which, in seeking to discredit religion, and its moral law of objective distinction and difference between moral right and wrong, does so by setting forth atheistic Communism's other bait, the freedom of carnal indulgence, which is corollary to Marxian Lenin's denial of a supernatural basis of human life and relationship."[4]

This attack, however, lacked the sinister virulence of attacks that commenced from other more expected quarters. The Associated Farmers of California had long been outraged by Steinbeck's writings and activities, in particular the series of articles he had published in October 1936 under the generic title *The Harvest Gypsies* in the *San Francisco News*, exposing the appalling working conditions in the cotton fields and the fruit orchards of the state and the inhuman treatment meted out to the migrants. Aware that *The Grapes of Wrath*, as a highly-publicized work of fiction, would attract a far greater readership on a national scale than the locally-published articles had over the past two or three years, the Associated Farmers redoubled their efforts to trick him by various means into retracting some of the statements made in the book. Steinbeck successfully parried these attempts, feeling safe in the knowledge that the truth of the matters he had aired in the novel had been verified in documents already passed to the Attorney General's office.

The process of vilification nevertheless continued unabated. In July, a rumor began circulating that the Oklahoma migrants hated him and had threatened to kill him because of the way he had misrepresented them in the book. The rumor was, naturally, publicized in the local press. Steinbeck felt himself overwhelmed and intimidated by such reports, however unverified they might be. He made sure he acted very carefully, fearing that the slightest slip would land him in jail on some bogus criminal charge. In August, the Associated Farmers began yet another "hysterical personal attack" on him in the newspapers. He told Elizabeth Otis he had now been accused of being a Jew, a pervert, a drunk, and a dope fiend. His understandable sense of paranoia became so intense that when his agents sent him news about a Frenchman who had been compared to him and had been imprisoned for "defeatist attitudes," his immediate reaction was to make plans to prepare himself against the possible threat of imprisonment if ever the country became actively involved in the war.

There were, on the other hand, certain compensations. During June, at the Third American Writers Congress, a meeting sponsored by the League of American Writers and convened in Carnegie Hall, *The Grapes of Wrath* was voted the best novel of the year, and that same month a favorable notice of the book appeared in Eleanor Roosevelt's nationwide syndicated column, "My Day."

The activities of the Associated Farmers and the bankers and the large landowners of California were not, however, the only unwelcome manifestations spawned by the publication of the book. Steinbeck had always feared the potential destructiveness of success and the possible effect it might have on his subsequent creative abilities. In a rare interview he accorded newspaperman John C. Rice in San Francisco, again in June, he voiced his misgivings:

> I have always wondered why no author has survived a best-seller. Now I know. The publicity and fan-fare are just as bad as they would be for a boxer. One gets self-conscious and that's the end of one's writing. (*Conversations* 15).

In this interview, however, he was only scraping the surface of the problems fame had unloaded on him. Only four days after the book came out, he was complaining to his agents about the incessant telephone calls and telegrams he had been receiving, demanding money for scholarships, memorial prizes, and even for a new liberal newspaper. Not all were begging calls. Hollywood agents were also on the phone, trying to induce him to write movie scripts. He expressed, through Carol, no interest in the money being offered. Two months later, the telephone was still ringing and the unsolicited mail had increased to between fifty and seventy-five letters daily. He received books to be signed, requests to write prefaces for books, pleas for handouts.

Much to his publishers' chagrin, Steinbeck would not involve himself in any personal promotion of the book. He stubbornly refused to make public appearances or speak at luncheons, asserting that the book should stand on its own merits and its author's personality remain as anonymous as possible. Partly for the same reason, he refused to hand over the original holograph manuscript to Covici. He had given it to Carol, for he thought of the book, as its dedication indicates, as "Carol's book." He stressed what was for him the intensely personal nature of the manuscript, and he said he did not want all and sundry poring over his crabbed handwriting.

On the other hand, he was more than happy to sign copies of a small, specially-bound edition of the book for auctioning at a banquet arranged by an organization formed by Hollywood celebrities and calling itself the "John Steinbeck Committee," as this was for the benefit of migrant relief. He also apparently agreed on this occasion to attend the banquet, and to be present at a number of other fund-raising functions, distinguishing between such events and others that were merely designed for publicity purposes.

2

The opportunity to escape from some of the fraught unreality of the initial postpublication period presented itself when, a few days before *The Grapes of Wrath* appeared in the bookstores, Steinbeck received a letter from Miriam Bell, assistant to the documentary filmmaker Pare Lorentz. Lorentz was about to begin shooting a new project in Chicago and invited Steinbeck to join him there.[5]

Steinbeck had met Lorentz in early 1938 at a time when he was carrying out research for *The Grapes of Wrath* in the flooded areas around Visalia in the San Joaquin Valley. The two men seemed to discover an almost instantaneous affinity. Lorentz had been making films under the auspices of Roosevelt's Resettlement Administration on the social and economic situation in the country, and one film, *The Plow That Broke the Plains*, had been concerned with the history of the Dust Bowl. Lorentz indicated to Steinbeck at that time that he would be interested in making movies of *In Dubious Battle* (which he clearly saw as a natural successor to *The Plow That Broke the Plains*) and *Of Mice and Men*. He invited Steinbeck to Hollywood and introduced him to some of the producers, directors, and actors he thought might be sympathetic toward Steinbeck's work. One of these was director Mervyn Le Roy. Le Roy did not impress Steinbeck at all when he put forward a proposal to film *Of Mice and Men*, intimating that he wanted to change Lennie's character and impose a happy ending on the picture. Steinbeck's rejection of Le Roy was swift and complete.

Later in 1938, Lorentz was appointed Director of the US Film Service, established by Roosevelt that August. On a visit to the Steinbecks at the Biddle Ranch, Lorentz spoke of his plans to make a film based on a radio play, *Ecce Homo!*, and suggested that Steinbeck might like to collaborate with him on the project. Steinbeck was, of course, too involved at the time in writing *The Grapes of Wrath* to respond in any way affirmatively to Lorentz's proposal. *Ecce Homo!* was, however, shelved and, in fact, was never made, Lorentz's imagination having been captured the following spring by Dr. Paul de Kruif's book *The Fight for Life*, about the problems of childbirth and infant mortality, and he had chosen it for his next subject.

Miriam Bell's letter of 10 April revealed that Lorentz had been in

Hollywood casting the film, completing the script, and arranging for sets to be constructed. He would be in Chicago on 25 April and wanted Steinbeck to help him find locations for authentic background material and to check over the script he had prepared. Steinbeck anticipated the trip with much enthusiasm, writing to his longtime friend Carlton A. Sheffield that he was learning a great deal about motion pictures through his association with Lorentz, who he considered to be the best filmmaker in the country. The Steinbecks traveled to Chicago on 25 April and stayed there about a month. Steinbeck later confessed to Covici that "Chicago was horrible. ... I never worked such long hours in my life" (JS/PC 5/25/39). All the same, he had been bitten by the filmmaking bug. He told Sheffield that while he had learned a considerable amount in Chicago he had not learned enough, and was planning to join Lorentz again in Hollywood for the shooting of interior scenes.

While in Chicago, Steinbeck had received a telephone call from producer Samuel H. Harris. Harris had been in charge of the 1937 Broadway production of *Of Mice and Men* and owned a stake in the screen rights of the work, together with playwright George S. Kaufman (who had collaborated with Steinbeck in preparing the final text of the play), critic Alexander Woollcott (who owned a ten percent interest in the play), and Steinbeck himself. Harris revealed that film director Lewis Milestone and writer Eugene Solow had written a preliminary script for a movie version of the play and were anxious to secure the screen rights before hawking the idea around the major studios that Milestone should direct the picture. Steinbeck's reaction was favorable. He had met Milestone during his 1938 visit to Hollywood with Lorentz and had been as much impressed with the man as he had been with his movies *All Quiet on the Western Front* and *The Front Page*. He had become even more agreeably disposed toward Milestone when the director expressed his admiration for *Of Mice and Men*. The only reservation Steinbeck made during his telephone conversation with Harris was that he would want to see the script before giving his final blessing.

Milestone and Solow were granted a two-month option on the play. They spent two weeks revising their script and, on Steinbeck's return from Chicago, journeyed north to Los Gatos to confer with him. Steinbeck carefully read through their 170-page script and made a few suggestions, even rewriting some parts of the dialogue. He informed Elizabeth Otis on 22 June that the final script sounded "very good" to him (*SLL* 186).

Milestone and Solow still had to raise the $250,000 they had estimated it would cost to make the picture. Early the previous year, Milestone had been involved in a law suit against independent producer Hal Roach for arrears of salary and damages. Roach was impressed with the idea of the project when Milestone showed him the script he and Solow had prepared, and quickly agreed to put up the money as settlement of Milestone's claim against him — an arrangement that suited both parties.

When word got around that the movie was to be made, James Cagney, Spencer Tracy, and John Garfield were all purportedly eager to get a part in it. Milestone, however, chose Broadway actor Burgess Meredith for the role of George and bit-part player Lon Chaney, Jr., the son of the famous silent screen star, for the role of Lennie. Another newcomer to Hollywood, Betty Field, was cast as Curley's wife. Curley was to be played by the B-class Western actor Bob Steele, and stage actors Charles Bickford, Roman Bohnen, and Leigh Whimper were cast as Slim, Candy, and Crooks.

The original intention was to shoot the picture in the Salinas Valley, in the same location Steinbeck had set his story. Milestone even prevailed upon Steinbeck to identify the actual ranch house he had described in the novel, but it was discovered that the building had fallen into complete disrepair. A replica was erected in the San Fernando Valley on the Agoura Ranch, which was owned, ironically enough, by William Randolph Hearst. The filming was completed within budget in forty-two days.

Milestone, anxious to achieve the perfect sound motifs in the finished production, persuaded Aaron Copland to compose the score. He gave the composer a free hand, willing, if it became necessary, to adapt his direction to Copland's requirements. He was as true as his word. In one scene, Copland had composed a melody to accompany five barley wagons making their way across a field. He needed four extra seconds of screen time for the melody to play itself out, and Milestone obliged by adding the necessary footage to the sequence.

Of Mice and Men was the first film score Copland had written. It proved to be a highly successful piece of work, combining tunes of a folk song nature and eschewing the over-sentimentalized musical clichés prevalent in many film scores. Copland, at this first attempt, thus avoided the pitfalls of the genre, appreciating that overemphasis could be destructive and that it was as important to know what not to do as to know what to do in scoring a movie. In an article he published shortly after the film was released, he summed up the lessons he had learned:

> On the whole, ... the score, as any score, is designed to strengthen and underline the emotional content of the entire picture. The best explanation, I think, of just what is the purpose of music in the films has been given by Virgil Thomson. It is his conception that the score of a motion picture supplies a sort of human warmth to the black-and-white, two-dimensional figures on the screen, giving them a communicable sympathy that they otherwise would not have, bridging the gap between the screen and the audience. The quickest way to a person's brain is through his eyes, but even in the movies the quickest way to his heart and feelings is still through the ear.[6]

If Steinbeck were to recall Copland's words when he came to write the scripts and work as assistant director on such films as *The Forgotten Village* and *The Pearl* during the next few years, he would have appreciated just how superb a job Copland had done on *Of Mice and Men*. Indeed, as a writer, Steinbeck had long been fascinated by the concept of the relationship between literature and music, and a large part of *The Grapes of Wrath* had been written to the phonograph accompaniment of the music of Tchaikovsky and Stravinsky. When, in February 1939, he heard that the composer Edgar Varèse was interested in his work from a musical standpoint, Steinbeck revealed that, from the beginning of his career, he had worked in a musical technique, attempting to use "the forms and mathematics of music rather than those of prose," and that this factor accounted for "the so-called 'different' technique" of each of his books. Using the same terminology, he described *The Grapes of Wrath* as "a symphony and the first," maintaining that "in composition, in movement, in tone, and in scope it is symphonic." He suggested that Varèse might like to see an advance copy of the book, and offered to have one sent to him.[7]

3

Someone else who was interested in *The Grapes of Wrath* at that time, but for different reasons, was the screenwriter Nunnally Johnson. Johnson had been quick to realize from the reports surrounding the book's forthcoming publication that here was great potential for a classic movie. He obtained a copy of the galley proofs, and his belief was confirmed. If *The Grapes of Wrath* were to be made into a film, he was determined to write the script. He began making the rounds of the studios, hoping to promote interest in the still-unpublished book. But, as with *Of Mice and Men*, the studios heads were unduly cautious, fearing insurmountable problems with the Hays Office. Moreover, the moguls understood the book to be extremely political and controversial, even possibly containing blatant Communist propaganda. Darryl F. Zanuck, the head of Twentieth Century-Fox, was however sufficiently intrigued to read the galley proofs Johnson had been hawking around. He obviously agreed with Johnson, for he purchased the movie rights for $75,000, a record for that year.

When the news got around, Zanuck was accused by the extreme left-wing elements in the country of being the agent for the bankers, farm owners, and other vested interests anxious that *The Grapes of Wrath* should never reach the screen, and of being willing to pay an inflated sum for the rights in order to outbid any potential rivals. On the other hand, he was attacked by the California farm owners, who threatened to boycott the film and who began a virulent campaign aimed at preventing the production from ever taking place. Other elements gloomily predicted that the film would be nothing more nor less than a weak, ineffectual shadow of Steinbeck's powerful story, prettied up for the mass movie going public.

Zanuck had no intention of any such watering-down. He hired Johnson to write the script, and told an ever-suspicious Steinbeck he would ensure that the book would be faithfully adapted. He even invited the author to Hollywood to confer with Johnson on the script. On 22 June, Steinbeck reported to Elizabeth Otis that Johnson and the studio had assured him that the movie would be made "straight." Zanuck had, in fact, suspected that the book tended to exaggerate the plight of the Okies, but after having sent out a team of investigators into the valleys he was forced to admit that Steinbeck had, if anything, understated the appalling conditions in the migrant camps. Tom Collins, who had been the director of the Arvin Sanitary Camp ("Weedpatch" Camp in the novel) when Steinbeck was carrying out his research for the book, had been offered the job of technical assistant on the movie, a piece of news that delighted Steinbeck, for he knew that Collins (the "Tom" to whom he had co-dedicated the book with Carol) would raise hell if the studio attempted to manipulate the truth for whatever reason. In a further letter a month later, Steinbeck advised Elizabeth Otis that Johnson had almost completed the script, although the hurdle of the Hays Office still had to be faced.

Zanuck meanwhile had contacted director John Ford and actor Henry Fonda, who were on location in Utah filming *Drums Along the Mohawk*. He asked Ford if he would begin preparatory work on *The Grapes of Wrath* as soon as *Drums Along the Mohawk* was safely in the can, and offered the part of Tom Joad to Fonda. Zanuck had heard that Fonda, who was then a free-lance actor, had admitted he would give his eye teeth for the role. Fonda, Zanuck considered, was exactly right for the role, and he told the actor he had the part, but only on condition that he sign a seven-year contract with Twentieth Century-Fox. Much as he jealously guarded his free-lance status, Fonda was unable to resist accepting these terms.

Steinbeck again visited Hollywood at the beginning of August to look over Johnson's script. "I don't know how that will turn out," he told Covici. "Well, I hope. But I know that if they try any tricks a great howl will go up" (JS/PC summer 1939). He had approved the script by the 8th of the month. "It really is very good," he wrote Elizabeth Otis. "If they shoot it as it is, it will be OK. But," he added darkly, unable to conceal his old distrust of Hollywood, "there is always the cutting room" (*Letters* 19).

He need not have worried. The script was extraordinarily faithful to the book, both in spirit and content. It had been accepted from the outset that the book's final scene, in which Rose of Sharon gives her breast to the starving man, would have to be omitted. Johnson had also dropped all the flood scene in the box car, including the birth of the stillborn child.

He had placed the episode at the Hooper Ranch at an earlier point in the film, and had ended his script with the Joad family in the safety and comparative comfort of the Weedpatch Camp. It is here, after the migrants have foiled the plan of the deputies to break up the peaceful dance and close down the camps, that Tom makes his impassioned farewell speech to Ma and strides off into the darkness.

Ford began shooting the film on 28 September and had completed it by 8 November at a total cost of $750,000. The main filming was carried out on the studio backlot, while a second unit under Otto Brewer filmed location scenes along Highway 66. The whole operation was carried out under conditions of great secrecy for fear of sabotage by hostile interests. The movie was given the working title *Highway 66*, and, contrary to all Hollywood practices, the studio issued no publicity until shooting was safely completed. Ford went off to recuperate on his yacht. He was in need of a rest. *The Grapes of Wrath* was the third picture in a row he had directed for the studio with no break in between. Zanuck, as he always did when working with Ford, began the cutting and assembling of the picture. At that stage, deciding that the ending as it stood was too sad and possibly inconclusive, Zanuck and Johnson devised an additional sequence to make the film end on a more upbeat note, with Ma proclaiming the populist view Steinbeck had her expound earlier in the novel: "We're the people that live. Can't nobody wipe us out. Can't nobody lick us. We'll go on forever, Pa. We're the people."[8]

Further opposition to the film from an unexpected quarter surfaced at almost the last moment, when Twentieth Century-Fox received a letter from Ed Lyman, a lawyer acting for ex-president Herbert Hoover. Hoover, then living in Los Angeles, had apparently been incensed when he heard rumors that references were being made in the movie to "Hoovervilles," the shantytowns built by people made homeless in the Depression. Lyman threatened that if this were true, Hoover would sue for libel and, further-more, would take out injunctions to prevent the movie being shown in any cinema in the country. The studio was able to assure Hoover on 12 December that the movie contained no specific reference by name either to Hoovervilles or to Hoover himself.[9]

4

By mid-October, Steinbeck had still not embarked on any new writing project. As a writer, he had never known such a sterile period. In the past, as soon as one piece of work was completed, he had been ready and eager to begin another. But the spark seemed to have deserted him. In more ways than one, it did seem that *The Grapes of Wrath* could be seen as the end of something, as he had predicted, the closing of a chapter in his life, not only as a writer but also as a human being. The pressures of success were, if anything, having a more detrimental effect on Carol than on him. Matters got so bad that, while they had been on a visit to Hollywood in early August, Carol "went hysterical ... and pulled out" (*Adventures* 412), returning home alone to Los Gatos. Steinbeck felt at a loss what to do as he saw his world disintegrating around him.

After Carol's sudden departure, he had moved from the Garden of Allah Hotel on Sunset Boulevard, where they had been staying, into the rather more down-market Aloha Apartments. An infection in his leg, which had been troubling him more or less continuously since the beginning of the year, had flared up again and, in great pain, he had been confined to bed in his apartment. His boyhood friend, Max Wagner, a movie bit-part player, called regularly at the apartment and generally kept an eye on him. When, after a fortnight, he was fit enough to travel, Steinbeck returned north, not to the ranch but to Monterey, where he stayed with his close friend, the marine biologist Edward F. Ricketts, while he tried to sort matters out in his mind. From Ricketts's laboratory on Ocean View Avenue, he wrote to Elizabeth Otis, spilling out his concern over his marital problems. His agent was already aware that the marriage had been an intermittently tempestuous one and that on one other occasion at least, when the Steinbecks had been in New York, Carol had similarly stormed out on her husband. There was, however, something more disturbing about the current situation. Steinbeck confessed he was becoming obsessed with the notion that Carol no longer liked him, and he told Elizabeth Otis that he suspected it was beyond his powers to rectify matters by making Carol, if not happy, even marginally contented.

He had not been, it must be said, telling the whole story, although possibly he did not himself, in the midst of the situation, fully appreciate the seriousness of the rift and his own vulnerability. The truth was that someone else had entered his life. It is perhaps understandable, the circumstances being what they were, that he should have turned elsewhere for whatever solace was available. Solace in Los Angeles had come in the form of a nineteen-year-old singer and dancer named Gwen (or Gwyn, as she later called herself) Conger, an acquaintance of Max Wagner's. Wagner had told her about his famous friend who was holed up alone in his apartment, in bed with a bad leg, and who was urgently in need of some cheering up. Gwyn was eighteen years younger than Steinbeck, and the combination of her youth, beauty, and vitality obviously supplied exactly the medicine he required.

Steinbeck did not stay long with Ricketts, returning to the ranch, where he sought to make his peace with Carol. They decided to leave California again for a while to escape the pernicious atmosphere of publicity, hate, and unwanted adulation still crowding in on them and poisoning their relationship. They planned a trip across the country to Quebec and down through New England. Most of September was spent traveling, visiting New York and Chicago along the way. They arrived back home on 3 October. Their intention had then been immediately to go on to Mexico for a month, but they were both exhausted and had moreover picked up terrible colds in New York.

For a while, it seemed good to just be home. The furor over *The Grapes of Wrath* was at last dying down somewhat, and the book had been eased from its place at the top of the bestseller list, much to its author's undisguised relief. Perhaps now, Steinbeck hoped, with some sort of order returning to their lives, the way would be clear for him to get back to work again.

But it was not to be. Less than a fortnight after he and Carol had returned home, he observed in his journal:

> Now I am battered with uncertainties. That part of my life that made the *Grapes* is over. I have one little job to do for the government, and then I can be born again. Must be. I have to go to new sources and find new roots. (*WD* 106).

Two days later, he was wondering if he could write what he referred to as "that pipe play." This would be, as he conceived it, a totally lightweight satirical work, aimed at nullifying the unwanted esteem generated by *The Grapes of Wrath*. But he was by no means convinced that he would be able to carry the project through when it came to it.

In retrospect, it seems that the pipe play was doomed before the writing of it even commenced. Around that time, he was assailed by premonitions of death. These were so intense that he felt compelled to destroy all his correspondence going back over many years, as well as several old and uncompleted manuscripts. He explained this radical clearing out and burning of his papers by saying that he did not want anybody nosing about in his past.

It is extremely doubtful if at that time he did much work on the "pipe play", for he was still unable to settle to write anything. His journal entry on 10 November, for example, consisted of two words only: "No comment" (*WD* 109). He was spending a great deal of time in Hollywood, ostensibly giving his approval at every stage in the making of *The Grapes of Wrath* movie. For all that, he continued to have reservations about the final outcome of the picture. Writing to a young Marxist friend, Dan James, in late November, he mentioned that he had just returned from Hollywood and working on the film. "I think the film is pretty good," he admitted, "but of course can't tell until it is all finished and music and words set on the film."[10] He flew down to Hollywood again on 6 December to see the final cut, and was pleased to find that Zanuck had kept his promise to preserve the integrity of the book. He reported to Elizabeth Otis that the movie was more like a documentary than the usual Hollywood production. The following evening, he attended a special showing of *Of Mice and Men*. "Here Milestone has done a curious lyrical thing," he reported in the same letter. "It hangs together and is underplayed. You will like it. It opens the 22nd of December in Hollywood" (*SLL* 195).

Zanuck had decided to postpone the opening of *The Grapes of Wrath* until January, so as not to clash with the opening of *Of Mice and Men*. He also decided not to open the film in Hollywood, but in New York, and then to move west by stages, allowing the film's self-generated publicity to precede it. Consummate showman that he was, he had even gone to the extent of issuing a statement that the film would never be shown in California. This produced, as he had intended, a rash of mail protesting the idea. He hired attorneys to be held ready to combat any local action in California aimed at preventing the showing of the film in the state, and had the notion to engage artist Thomas Hart Benton, who was illustrating a forthcoming two-volume edition of the book, to design the posters.

Steinbeck had every reason to be pleased. He could not deny that he had been well-served by Hollywood. Both movies had been directed by masters in the medium, and each had been superbly interpreted by a cast of mainly unknown or little-known actors. It was understandable, therefore, that he should have been receptive to any further possible projects for adapting his work for the screen. Indeed, during that December visit to Hollywood, he was approached by Spencer Tracy and director Victor Fleming (*Captains Courageous*, *The Wizard of Oz*, and *Gone With the Wind*), who both made it known to him that they were anxious to film *The Red Pony*.

This was not the first time such a project had been broached. Steinbeck had received offers from MGM in July for *The Red Pony*. He had not then been inclined to sell, and told his agents to act accordingly, urging them to stipulate conditions that would assuredly deter any major studio from pursuing movie rights to the work.[11] While not entirely averse to seeing *The Red Pony* brought to the screen, he was anxious that it should be filmed under independent production with, ideally, Milestone or King Vidor directing, Tracy playing the part of Billy Buck, and a completely unknown child actor playing Jody. He had even at that time discussed this sort of setup with Tracy, but nothing came of it.

When Tracy and Fleming brought up the matter again in December, he possibly saw the hand of one of the big studios behind the proposition. This was the last thing he wanted, sensing that he was unlikely to get so honorable a deal from one of the other studio bosses as he had had from Zanuck. He suggested to Tracy and Fleming that, if the film were to be made, no one connected with it should draw any salary, and that the money to finance its making should be raised completely by subscription. Under these terms, he agreed to let them have the story for nothing, but reserved the right to work on the script. The completed film would be distributed only in those towns and cities guaranteeing that the takings from the high admission charges would be utilized to endow beds for children in local hospitals. Tracy and Fleming must have been dismayed when Steinbeck calmly unfolded these plans, but managed to disguise their feelings and told him they thought it possible to obtain at no cost the best actors, technicians, and equipment to make the picture. Fleming even went so far as to predict that such a worthwhile venture was sure to raise something in the region of two million dollars. Not surprisingly, however, Steinbeck heard nothing further from the two men, and formally withdrew his offer in mid-January 1940. He had already decided to contact Milestone and ascertain if he would be interested in making the picture.

5

Although *Of Mice and Men* opened in Hollywood on 22 December 1939, its New York opening was delayed for nearly two months, until after *The Grapes of Wrath* had opened there on 24 January 1940 at the Rivoli Theater. A private preview of John Ford's film took place at the small Normandie Theater on East 53rd Street, and was a socialite occasion, attended by Zanuck himself in the company of Dorothy Lamour. It was an event that typified the unacceptable face of classic Hollywood ballyhoo. Michael Mok, in his satirical piece "Slumming with Zanuck," published a few weeks later in *The Nation*, described how, attired "in bibs and tuckers from the ateliers of Mainbocher and Molineux, the gals from Park Avenue came in gleaming limousines with their men-about-town to take a peek at the raggedy Joads and the miseries of their jalopy migration." Hedy Lamarr was there, "fully clothed for this occasion in pink satin and three or four feet of diamond necklace," and "[m]any of the women, in addition to baubles that would buy sizable farms, wore bunches of orchids the cost of which might have kept the Joads in sidemeat for a year; the plump torso of Miss Jane Darwell, the actress who plays Ma Joad in the picture, was covered with the blooms from chin to waist." The audience sat through the film in utter silence, except for "a smattering of applause from the balcony when the migrant farmers at the government camp foiled the deputies' scheme to break up their dance," and there was a subdued, polite round of applause when the lights went up. As Mok concluded: "[T]he Park Avenue gals and their escorts drove to Fefe's

Monte Carlo for a little champagne supper tossed by Mr. Zanuck. From the Dust Bowl to the flowing one — Glory, glory Hallelujah!"[12]

If comparative silence was the only reaction the film evoked from Zanuck's socialite guests, the critics were almost unanimous in their praise. All the old superlatives, or others like them, voiced when Steinbeck's novel had appeared the previous year, were repeated. Franz Hoellering called it "Hollywood's most distinguished offering,"[13] while Frank Nugent thought the film "just about as good as any picture has a right to be; if it were any better, we just wouldn't believe our eyes."[14] Even *Time* grudgingly admitted that it was probably "the best picture ever made from a so-so book."[15] All the critics were unreserved in their praise of John Ford's direction, Nunnally Johnson's faithful script, Gregg Toland's stunning cinematography, Henry Fonda's Tom, Jane Darwell's Ma, John Carradine's Casy, and the veracity of the acting in the minor roles.

Viewed today, the film's low-key acting seems hardly to have dated, although, now that shooting on location is more the norm than the exception, some of the studio sets do strike a note of artificiality, particularly in the Hooverville and government camp scenes. But this is carping on a superficial level. The film remains today as powerful and as emotionally persuasive a work of art as it was at the time of its release.

New Yorkers had a more subdued introduction to *Of Mice and Men* when it opened in early February. In the *New Republic*, Otis Ferguson regretted that the movie should have been "thrown into inevitable but needless comparison" with Ford's *The Grapes of Wrath*, but predicted that *Of Mice and Men* would be one of the ten best films of 1940, and could lay claim to being "among the good films of any time."[16] *Time* trotted out what had become in its pages the inevitable Steinbeck put-down, congratulating Milestone for making a good film from Steinbeck's somewhat less-than-good material by ensuring that his camera lenses avoided the risk of exaggerating "every flaw that the author had covered with writing craft in the book," and by succeeding "in a succession of swift, spare, terse scenes . . . in making Steinbeck's subhuman characters human."[17]

6

Steinbeck's involvement in the making of *Of Mice and Men* and *The Grapes of Wrath* clearly changed his attitude toward the cinema. For a writer who had for so long and in no uncertain terms declared his aversion toward Hollywood and his deep-rooted suspicion of the undoubted atrocities the moguls in the movie industry would perpetrate on his books if given the opportunity, he had spent an inordinate amount of time in the film capital during 1939, and had mingled with increasing frequency with its actors, writers, agents, directors, and producers. While enjoying the company of people like Charles Chaplin, Lorentz, Milestone, Meredith, and Tracy, he also, by talking with them, became absorbed by the challenge and complexities of movie making.

There is a case for arguing that Steinbeck in fact became far too preoccupied with film technique, and that this, as opposed to his interest in music technique, had a detrimental influence on the books he wrote after *The Grapes of Wrath*. There is, however, no denying, whatever influence for good or bad Hollywood may have had on his work as a creative writer, that the visits he made to the film colony during 1939 (and would continue to make during 1940) provided him with one of the most convenient and effective avenues of escape, not only from his inability to settle down to any sustained program of writing but also from the more evident atmosphere of local publicity surrounding him in Los Gatos. He could to a certain limited, but palpable, extent lose his identity in the sprawling city and suburbs of Los Angeles. Los Angeles, too, was where the young and refreshing Gywn Conger was willing and able to soothe away the accumulated day-by-day cares of a slowly disintegrating marriage. And by no means least, Hollywood, with all its tawdry tinsel and superficial glitter, provided an intangible world of fantasy, which, when he allowed himself to surrender to it, overrode unpalatable reality, and to a measurable degree also helped to dispel for a time thoughts of all his marital troubles and the very real concerns he felt about events in Europe and the war into which he was sure America would eventually be drawn.

7

The fact that the political situation across the Atlantic had been playing an increasing role in Steinbeck's thinking from 1938 onward is evident from his letters and the journal he kept while writing *The Grapes of Wrath*. It is also evident in the novel itself.

The soulless tractors, with their impersonal goggled drivers, crawling across the land and destroying all in their path can be seen as a paradigm for the German tanks that were then lumbering across the war-torn Spanish countryside and would, within the next eighteen months or so, be plowing their paths of destruction through Poland, the Low Countries, and France. Indeed, Steinbeck renders the analogy inescapable. "There is little difference," he writes, "between this tractor and a tank. The people are driven, intimidated, hurt by both. We must think about this" (*GOW* 205—6). The westward-trekking Okies, in the context of 1938, take on the aspect of the pathetic hordes of Spanish refugees, all their worldly goods piled high and precariously on whatever vehicles they possess, taking to the roads in their panic to escape Franco's advancing troops. Perhaps the only immediate difference between the plight of the Spanish refugees and that of the Okies is the absence in the skies above Route 66 of strafing Messerschmitts and Stukas. When Steinbeck writes of bombs falling "out of the black planes on the market place," of prisoners "stuck like pigs," and of bodies bleeding "filthily in the dust," one is inevitably reminded of the press photographs and the newsreels of those days depicting the obliteration of Guernica, Japanese soldiers using Chinese civilians for bayonet practice, and the dust-covered faces of children lying in ordered rows in the streets of Madrid and Nanking. When in Chapter 23, written on 16 September 1938, Steinbeck has one of the migrants describe to his fellows his visit to the local cinema and the newsreel he has seen "with them German soldiers kickin' up their feet—funny as hell" (*GOW* 447), one has the impression that this is Steinbeck's veiled warning to his readers not to make the mistake of treating the German threat lightly, as the migrant had done. By the time *The Grapes of Wrath* was published in April 1939, Hitler had already torn up the Munich agreement, occupied the whole of Czechoslovakia, annexed Memel from Lithuania, and denounced Germany's nonaggression pact with Poland. The German Fuhrer's intentions were plain to see, one would have thought, to even the most committed of isolationists.

Isolationist, Steinbeck was not. He had considered Chamberlain's negotiations with Hitler a "double cross" (*WD* 71). When World War II broke out in Europe following the German invasion of Poland on 1 September, Steinbeck and Carol had embarked on their transcontinental trip. A few weeks after they returned home, Steinbeck, writing to Sheffield, tried to rationalize his thinking in purely biological terms:

> The world is sick now. There are things in the tide pools easier to understand than Stalinist, Hitlerite, Democrat, capitalist confusion, and voodoo. So I am going to those things which are relatively more lasting to find a new basic picture. . . . Communist, Fascist, Democrat may find that the real origin of the future lies on the microscope plates of obscure young men, who, puzzled with order and disorder in quantum and neutron, build gradually a picture which will seep down until it is the fibre of the future. (*SLL* 193−4).

He also saw the biological approach as another possible way out of the creative impasse in which he found himself. As he had written in his journal on 16 October:

> I have written simply for simple stories, but now the conception and the execution become difficult and not simple. And I don't know. I don't quite know what the conception is. But I know it will be found in the tide pools and on a microscope slide rather than in men. (*WD* 106).

He ordered a number of books for study, intending to work in Ed Ricketts's laboratory in Monterey. He was determined to break the stultifying mold in which he felt himself trapped, and escape from the sense of no longer being his own man but someone expected to travel along the paths ordained by others. In his 13 November letter to Sheffield, he told his friend:

> I'm finishing off a complete revolution. It's amazing how every one piled in to regiment me, to make a symbol of me, to regulate my life and work. ... The two most important [things], I suppose — at least they seem so to me — are freedom from respectability and most important — freedom from the necessity of being consistent. ...
> The point of all this is that I must make a new start. I've worked the novel — I know it as far as I can take it. I never did think much of it — a clumsy vehicle at best. And I don't know the form of the new but I know there is a new which will be adequate and shaped by the new thinking. Anyway, there is a picture of my confusion. How is yours? (*SLL* 193—4)

The "confusion" he referred to was mainly manifest in his creative restlessness of those days. Although he had stated in his journal that he felt it essential to work on his own, he was allowing himself to become more and more involved in the intricacies of filmmaking, the ultimate, together with stage productions, in group creative ventures. Not only that, but every project he was considering at that time was a creative partnership of one sort or another. He had a plan, never realized, to write two theses, "Phalanx" and "The Death of the Species," for the composer John Cage to set to percussion music. Another project, and one that although eventually abandoned led directly to the writing and publication in 1941 of *Sea of Cortez*, was to produce in collaboration with Ricketts a handbook of the littoral of the San Francisco Bay area.

Steinbeck had met Ricketts in October 1930, and it is generally accepted that he was considerably influenced in both his thinking and his writing by Ricketts's philosophy of life. Ricketts, who was five years older than Steinbeck, was a prodigious drinker and lover of women, but also a man of impressive intellect. The two of them spent a great amount of time together during the 1930s, sharing their love of music and art and poetry, carousing together and with friends, and talking to all hours of the night on the nature of the universe and the mysteries of existence. Ricketts owned and ran, more or less singlehandedly, the Pacific Biological Laboratory on Ocean View Avenue ("Cannery Row"), Monterey. He made a fair living from the preparation of biological specimens, which he shipped to schools and colleges for exhibition purposes or for experiment and dissection by students. He dealt in all species of marine and animal life — rays, octupi, jellyfish, hagfish, starfish, rats, frogs, turtles, lizards, and

sometimes even cats — and also supplied schools with slides he had prepared
of microorganisms, tissue, sperm, and ova.

In April 1939, the same month *The Grapes of Wrath* appeared, the
Stanford University Press published *Between Pacific Tides*, a study of
marine life on the Pacific Coast. Ricketts had written the book with the
collaboration of Jack Calvin, a writer of children's stories, whose role had
been to convert Ricketts's field notes and scientific text into more readable
prose. When the editor of the Press suggested to Ricketts the possibility
of preparing a booklet, for specific use by schools, dealing with marine
life on the Duxbury Reef, Steinbeck proposed that the two of them might
collaborate on the project in much the same way Ricketts and Calvin had
on the earlier book. The arrangement would have distinct advantages for
both of them. So far as Ricketts was concerned, it would undoubtedly
promote the sale of the book to have Steinbeck's name as co-author on
the cover. As for Steinbeck himself, he would be provided with an
extremely worthwhile piece of work in which he could immerse himself
after the months of virtual creative sterility. Not only that, it would,
perhaps even more to the point, give him some sort of serious recognition
in scientific circles, with all the kudos that would imply.

Certainly, this last factor seems to have been an extremely important
one in Steinbeck's thinking, but from all accounts, and perhaps understandably, Covici was none too pleased when he learned of the proposed
book. He was naturally anxious for his bestselling author to further his
position as a topflight fiction writer by writing a follow-up to *The Grapes
of Wrath* as soon as possible. When Steinbeck made it absolutely clear
that there was no chance of another novel, at least not for the time being,
Covici was forced to go along with the idea of the handbook, even
cooperating to the extent of obtaining at discount through the trade the
books Steinbeck was anxious to have for his biological studies.

Covici was blithely assuming that the handbook, despite its specialized
subject matter, would be published by Viking Press. Steinbeck, however,
had other ideas. He was determined that the book should be published
under the scholarly prestige of the Stanford University Press imprint.
The way he planned it, the university press should print and bind the
book, and Viking simply distribute it. By bearing the imprint of both
publishing houses, the book would then enjoy the best of both worlds.
Moreover, he proposed that if he were then to write a new foreword to
Between Pacific Tides, a new edition of the Ricketts-Calvin volume should
be published concurrently with the handbook, and similarly be distributed
by Viking under the joint imprint. As if that were not enough, Covici was
informed that Steinbeck and Ricketts had already formulated plans for a
more grandiose biological expedition to the Gulf of California. The end
result of this expedition was to be another book (the "Mexican book" or

the "Gulf book," as Steinbeck came variously to refer to it), which although inevitably containing an appreciable amount of specialized material would nevertheless be of interest to a wider audience than the handbook, and would accordingly be published solely by Viking.

Plans and preparations for the two expeditions went swiftly ahead once the decision to embark on them had been taken. A truck was specially equipped with all the instruments and plant they would require to enable them to carry out preliminary work on specimens on site. Writing to Elizabeth Otis on 15 December, Steinbeck reported that Ricketts's laboratory business was picking up. "I can't tell you what all this means to me in happiness and energy," he wrote, "I was washed up and now I'm all alive again, much work to be done and worth doing" (JS/ERO 12/15/39).

On 23 December, the solstice tides being exactly right for the following five days, Steinbeck and Ricketts drove north in their truck to the coastal area beyond San Francisco extending from Tomales Bay to Half Moon Bay. There, sloshing around in rubber boots and slickers, they spent the Christmas period collecting specimens of marine invertebrates in the littoral. Their task completed, they drove back to Monterey to begin the work of identification and classification.

3

1940: The Search for New Beginnings

1

IN THE LABORATORY ON OCEAN VIEW AVENUE, WHILE RICKETTS WROTE UP his field notes, Steinbeck began writing his introduction. He soon discovered it was going to be a much more difficult exercise than he had anticipated. The writing itself seemed to flow enough, but the thinking behind the words he was putting on paper was a different matter entirely. Time and time again, he was slowed by lack of specific knowledge. On 4 January, he roughed out the beginning of the introduction, but when he read it the next day he realized that he had not achieved what he wanted and would have to rewrite it completely.

The difficulty in the writing did not decrease over the next few days, but he was content to have at least fallen into some definite routine of work. This seemed a good sign in itself, and went some way toward attaining the strict and productive self-discipline he so desperately sought. He worked on the text in the laboratory during the week, returning home to the ranch and Carol at weekends. In the latter part of January, he spent a whole week at home, endeavoring to clean up his copy. In a more hopeful state of mind, he reported to Covici on 20 January that he aimed to have the introduction finished by the end of the following week. The discipline of working in this unfamiliar medium was, so he wrote, good for him, mitigating to some degree his sense of dissatisfaction with his own work.

2

During the course of 1940, Steinbeck's relationship with his wife continued to become increasingly distant. His work at Ricketts's laboratory and his unaccompanied visits to Hollywood became more than ever a necessary escape from the uneasy atmosphere pervading the ranch. While he had been away in San Francisco Bay, Carol had spent Christmas alone on the ranch.

They had kept in touch by telephone. In an attempt to take her mind off her confusion and loneliness — and, it is likely, in an attempt to prove to herself as well as to others that her husband was not the only author in the family — Carol had been writing a short book on gardening. She finished typing it in mid-January after she had joined Steinbeck in Monterey for a few days, and sent it off to McIntosh & Otis on the morning of 16

January. Steinbeck fervently hoped that his agents would find it publishable. If he thought that the success of the little book would become a means of salvation for Carol and himself, he was undoubtedly clutching at straws. He must, by then, have already resigned himself to the truth that the situation between them had deteriorated too far for such simple solutions.

Carol returned to the ranch, and their lives resumed the pattern established before Christmas, with Steinbeck at the laboratory during the week and spending the weekends at home. Carol suffered a disappointment when Viking eventually decided against taking her book. She began casting around for something to occupy her time, more urgent when the weather was bad and she was unable to work in her beloved garden. She took music lessons by mail, ceaselessly practicing chords on the piano. Always overcautious where money was concerned and fearful that the recent good times would not last, she took charge of their finances, judiciously investing all the royalty checks that came in.

Sales, both of *The Grapes of Wrath* and *Of Mice and Men*, continued to hold up astonishingly well. *Look* reported on 2 January that the total sales of *Of Mice and Men* had reached 350,000 copies, and of *The Grapes of Wrath* 300,000 copies. Sales were subsequently given an extra boost by the release of the two movies in January. By the middle of February, Viking had printed 430,000 copies of *The Grapes of Wrath*. The book was selected for the Favorite Fiction Award by a cross-country ballot of booksellers.[1] On 3 March, the actor Will Geer organized a "Grapes of Wrath Evening" at the Forest Theater in New York. The show — which featured such artists and singers as Geer himself, Woody Guthrie, Leadbelly, and Aunt Molly Jackson — benefitted the "John Steinbeck Committee for Agricultural Workers." It was a landmark occasion, inasmuch as it was the first-ever important folk music recital to be held before a large, mainstream audience.[2]

Plans for the Gulf expedition were being delayed pending permits from both the United States and Mexican authorities. By the end of February, Steinbeck and Ricketts decided to modify their plans. They abandoned the idea of making the trip by truck, and chartered a boat in Monterey to make the whole journey by sea. The hire of the boat, a purse seiner, and crew would entail considerable addition expense, and Steinbeck suggested to his agents that, to help with the finances, he would write a series of articles based on the log he would be keeping of the day-to-day details of the trip.

By the end of the month, the permits had come through, the boat had been chartered, and all thoughts of finishing the Bay handbook put to one side for the time being.

3

A week or so before the expedition was due to sail, Steinbeck was approached by the young documentary filmmaker Herbert Kline. Kline had recently made four anti-Fascist documentaries and was anxious to make a film concerning his fear of a possible fascist takeover in Mexico. He proposed that Steinbeck write the script, and brought two of his films to Monterey in late February for the author to see. When, after viewing the two films, *Crisis* and *Lights Out In Europe*, Steinbeck agreed to collaborate in making a film in Mexico, he could have had little conception of the many troubles and frustrations he was to pile up for himself over the next twenty-one months or so, troubles and frustrations that would cause him to declare in July 1941 in a fit of exasperation: "There just isn't going to be any more such business arrangements" (JS/ERO 7/9/41).

The two men stayed up half the night discussing the sort of film they should make. Their initial plan was for Steinbeck to write "a strong personal story to take place — like the Joads in the Okie flight to California — during the threatened and expected right-wing attempts of General Almazan to overthrow the progressive Mexican government of President Cardenas," combining "scenes of street-fighting violence and killing with the struggle of ordinary people for a better life."[3] Both men were under no illusion that the whole venture could be fraught with peril if they happened to become involved in on-the-spot filming of street-fighting once the revolution had broken out. The thought of being caught up in such a situation did not, however, deter them. Indeed, Kline has recalled, Steinbeck seemed to act positively to the anticipated frisson of danger.

When the question of financing the project came up, Kline confirmed that he was broke, but undertook to raise sufficient money to make the film on a low-budget, no-salaries, expenses-only basis. Steinbeck would have none of it. He told Kline that he had been offered five thousand dollars a week to write for Zanuck, but while that sort of Hollywood deal did not interest him, the proposed Mexican film did. He not only offered to loan Kline the station wagon he and Ricketts had equipped for the Bay expedition, but said he would himself provide some of the financial backing for the project and would elicit the help of his agents in finding other backers. There was no written contract between the two men. They just shook hands on the deal. Steinbeck sent Kline to New York with a letter of introduction to McIntosh & Otis, while he and Ricketts finalized preparations for the Gulf expedition.

4

Although Steinbeck and Ricketts had endeavored to keep their projected trip a secret, the news inevitably leaked out, and reporters were on the Monterey quayside to witness the departure of the purse seiner *Western Flyer* on 11 March. The event was duly covered in the local newspapers, and a full list given of the people aboard: Steinbeck and Carol, Steinbeck's attorney and longtime friend Webster F. ("Toby") Street, and four crew members. It was, the *Monterey Peninsula Herald* observed, "perhaps the strangest crew ever signed aboard a local work boat."[4] Street was not part of the expedition team, and disembarked at San Diego, before they reached the Mexican coastline.

Toward the end of the month, the *Western Flyer* was well into the Gulf and approaching the town of Loreto. In letters to Elizabeth Otis and Covici, Steinbeck commented with some evident satisfaction that for almost three weeks they had received no news of events in Europe, and that this had allowed them to adopt an entirely different perspective on world affairs.

Much had been happening in Europe during the preceding two months, however. On 1 February, the so-called "phony war" had erupted into action in an unexpected quarter when Soviet troops launched attacks on the Karelian Isthmus and near Lake Kuhmo against neutral Finland. By 12 March, the day after the *Western Flyer* sailed from Monterey, Finland had been forced to sign a peace treaty with Russia, ceding the isthmus and the area around the shores of Lake Ladoga. Steinbeck's thoughts about this latest development in the European-war scene are contained in an unpublished and undated holograph manuscript composed before the expedition left Monterey. In it, he not only expresses his fears for the future, but also makes crystal-clear his nonallegiance to communist philosophy:

The Russian invasion of Finland, horrible as it is, offers a possibility for clarification of the position of such nonpolitical liberals as I, who believe profoundly in democratic processes and the right of peoples to live in freedom and to govern themselves. Such liberals have been too long kicked around among the ideologies. When the Spanish people were overwhelmed by a selfish native minority backed by foreign men, money, and arms, I contributed to and believed in their cause. When China was invaded by a Japanese army of conquest, I believed in and contributed to the cause of the people of China. In the first two cases I was called a communist. Now that Finland is invaded my position has not changed. I believe in and shall contribute to the cause of the Finnish people. It is amusing that I will be called a reactionary for this. But in all three cases I did not understand nor was I very much interested in the politics involved. Politics in all three cases became pale before the hard and undeniable fact that a people through invasion and conquest was being denied the right to live freely, within their own pattern of freedom. I am not wise enough to know all the forces at play in the Finnish invasion as in the others, but I am wise enough to know that when force of arms decides an argument, the conclusion has little chance of being either just or permanent. I am filled with sorrow at the Finnish invasion which following Spain, Austria, Czechoslovakia, and Poland seems to set a direction which, if not stopped, will leave no peace and safety anywhere in the world.[5]

Even had it been published, this statement would probably not have altered the views of Steinbeck's critics and enemies or the activities of the FBI agents who had for some time been monitoring his movements, his pronouncements both in public and in private, and his associates and friends. Significantly, when he and Ricketts were applying to the United States and Mexican authorities for permission to visit the Gulf of California, he was to find that "[o]ur government kicked us in the pants but the Mexican government [gave] us every courtesy" (JS/ERO 2/28/40). He had, of course, been aware that as a suspected radical the FBI had been making discreet inquiries about him. The release in 1984 of FBI files under the Freedom of Information Act has revealed much of the undercover work that was carried out not only in those days but in later years as well, but it is doubtful if Steinbeck fully appreciated just how deep and long-standing the agency's investigations had been, although he clearly had his suspicions from time to time.

5

As was only to be expected, Carol's presence as the only woman aboard the *Western Flyer* did give rise to some problems. She had from the beginning not been terribly happy at the prospect of abandoning the ranch for nearly two months, and after a few weeks at sea she became very homesick for her garden. She resented the assumption that she would naturally take on all the cooking duties, and, to keep the peace, one of the crew members, the mate Horace "Sparky" Enea, volunteered to take charge of the galley. For all that, Carol did her fair share of all the other work on board, helping with the collecting of specimens, and keeping the upper deck and the quarters below clean and tidy. From time to time, however, she indulged in a little light flirting with some of the crew, but this seemed to be more than anything else a defiant gesture aimed at irritating her husband. She wholeheartedly joined in the wild drinking bouts that took place whenever they went ashore.

It is surely inconceivable that either she or Steinbeck could have imagined before they started out on the voyage that being cooped up with five other people on the little boat would do anything to ameliorate the deepening estrangement between them. Steinbeck endeavored to paint a favorable picture in his letters to his agents, telling them how well Carol had adapted herself to life aboard the *Western Flyer*. But when in January the following year he began writing the narrative section of *Sea of Cortez*, he never mentioned Carol's name or indicated in any specific way at all that she had taken part in the expedition. By that time, the break between them was virtually complete.[6]

6

The *Western Flyer* arrived back in Monterey on 20 April, and by the following day Steinbeck and Carol were back at the ranch. Ricketts began work immediately on his specimens and notes. If it had been Steinbeck's intention also to begin work immediately on writing the narrative section of the proposed book, he was deflected off course by other commitments clamoring for his attention: not only the Mexican film but also what had by now become a projected collaboration with Milestone on *The Red Pony*.

Clearly, the Kline film, such being the nature of the subject and the time factor involved, would have to take precedence over both the Gulf book and *The Red Pony*. As Steinbeck wrote to Elizabeth Otis on 21 April: "Do you realize that the thing which seemed to be happening, is happening. I'm so busy being a writer that I have not time to write anything" (JS/ERO 4/21/40). He reinforced his view a week later: "After the Red Pony and the picture let's make no more commitments. I want to do some writing" (JS/ERO 4/28/40).

Carol was particularly thankful to be back home, able once again to enjoy the open-air swimming pool they had installed after moving into the ranch and the greenhouse Steinbeck had bought her for her birthday that year. The garden continued to be her pride and joy. But it was far too large for her to manage on her own, especially with all the absences from home and the entertaining that now had to be done when she was there. They had employed a Japanese houseboy, Joe Higashi, to do the cooking, clean the house, and act as caretaker whenever the two of them were away. He also helped Carol in the garden. In addition, Steinbeck hired a young man from Oklahoma, who came in on a daily basis and helped out generally around the ranch.

The award of the Pulitzer Prize for fiction to Steinbeck for *The Grapes of Wrath* was officially announced on 6 May. The *Saturday Review* welcomed the award as "a foregone conclusion" and as "a happy departure from precedent and an indication of greater flexibility."[7] Possibly to allay any small embarrassment he may have felt at winning the prize when more money than he and Carol had ever seen was already rolling in,

Steinbeck gave the one thousand dollars he received to an old friend, Ritchie Lovejoy. Lovejoy, a Pacific Grove department-store advertising manager, was an aspiring writer, and the gift enabled him to resign from his job and devote himself to a literary career.

7

In New York, Kline had been successful in his financial negotiations and had been able to purchase all the equipment he required. While Steinbeck was still on the *Western Flyer*, Kline and his wife, Rosa, his brother, Mark Marvin, and his Czech codirector and cameraman, Alexander Hackenschmied, who had worked with him on previous films, traveled down to Mexico City by station wagon, and set up a center of operations there, researching the social and political scenes, and seeking locations out in the country. They were assisted in their research by the artist Miguel Covarrubias, who was instrumental in getting them an audience with President Cardenas, as well as introducing them to other Mexican artists and intellectuals. Kline kept Steinbeck fully informed of all that was happening, sending him photographs of the people and places they had come across in their search for potential locations.

Eventually, Steinbeck sent (in Kline's words) "a rough for a screen story based on a family of silver miners caught up in the Right-Left conflicts that would end in civil war exploding in this community."[8] By then, however, it seemed to Kline and his little team that the anticipated right-wing uprising was now unlikely, even though the political climate remained sensitive. A new subject for their film would have to be found.

Carol had no more than five weeks in which to enjoy her swimming pool and garden, for Steinbeck had planned for the two of them to travel to Mexico City on 23 May. He had arranged for Ricketts to drive the expedition truck down from Monterey and meet up with them in Mexico. Before they left the ranch, the news came through that the Germans had invaded the Low Countries and Luxembourg. The impression given by Steinbeck's letters is that ironically, in view of the play-novel *The Moon Is Down* he was to write in the closing months of 1941, the Nazi invasion of Norway, which had occurred while he had been on the *Western Flyer*, had somehow passed him by. But certainly he did not underestimate the gravity of this new turn of events.

No sooner had they arrived in Mexico City than Steinbeck was swept up in preparations for the making of the film, meeting many people and authorizing the purchase of further equipment Kline now deemed essential. Kline had rented a large house in the city, where they could all live and work together. On 26 May, the whole company set out in trucks on a location trip into Michoacán. When Steinbeck saw the conditions in which the peon children were living—and dying for the lack of local hygiene and adequate medical supplies—he immediately agreed with Kline that here was the principal subject of their film. He spent some time traveling around with the film crew, soaking up the ambience of Mexican rural life, seeking out additional locations, and observing some of the preliminary filming.

They were joined for part of the time by the black writer Richard Wright, whose controversial novel, *Native Son*, had been published on 1 March and promptly banned in the libraries of Birmingham, Alabama. Wright and Kline knew each other from several years back when they had been fellow members of the John Reed Club in Chicago. Wright had set up home in Cuernavaca with the wife he had married the previous August and her two-year-old son, but difficulties were already becoming apparent in the relationship, and within a few weeks of meeting up with the film crew Wright returned to the South on his own, despite Steinbeck and Kline's concerned and strenuous efforts to dissuade him.[9]

After they had returned to the base house in Mexico City and he had carried out some further research in the city hospitals, Steinbeck began writing a skeleton script centered on a rural doctor's struggle to combat disease and prejudice and superstition in the remote "forgotten" villages of the country. A series of script conferences were held, during which Steinbeck listened attentively to suggestions put forward by the others and in certain instances proved amenable to making changes to his script.

All the non-Mexican members of Kline's crew were troubled with illness. Hackenschmied went down with amoebic dysentery, and had to seek treatment. Kline had a recurrence of the malaria he had picked up while filming in Spain two or three years before. The two wives, Carol and Rosa, felt out of sorts, and Steinbeck himself suffered from a feeling of enervation, but fortunately nothing more.

About a fortnight after the Steinbecks had arrived in Mexico City, Ricketts turned up in the expedition truck, accompanied by a beautiful girl, a bookstore clerk named Faun. The girl returned to California by train a few days later, having discovered that Ricketts's intentions in asking her along were other than simply for the ride. Although nothing had been arranged for him to work with them on the film, Ricketts nevertheless felt a certain degree of resentment, certainly to begin with, when he found himself excluded from conferences and left on his own to kick his heels while Steinbeck and the others were chasing around the country. Ricketts had not in any case been very happy when Steinbeck had announced his intention of joining Kline in Mexico, thus delaying the writing of the Gulf book, a project Ricketts understandably considered of far greater importance than the film. Nor, when he had the opportunity to read Steinbeck's script, did he approve of the film's theme, which seemed to him to run counter to his concept of nonteleological philosophy, a philosophy he was proposing to explicate with Steinbeck at some length in the Gulf book. As will be noted later, his disapproval of Steinbeck's script took a more concrete form when, on the script's publication in the spring of 1941, Ricketts wrote an "anti-script" titled "Thesis and Materials for a Script on Mexico which shall be motivated oppositely to John's FORGOTTEN VILLAGE."

If, as Jackson J. Benson has suggested, Ricketts tended to overreact to the situation, his resentment did not bring about any serious or lasting breach with Steinbeck, nor did it in any way sully the deep respect and affection the two men had for each other. Indeed, after making good use of his stay in Mexico by carrying out research of his own in the capital's libraries and filling several notebooks with abstracted material about the Gulf of California, Ricketts did eventually assist in the filming of some sequences, and purportedly even contributed some suggestions of his own.

8

From the time of their arrival in Mexico City, Steinbeck had been very aware of all the political rumors that abounded in the capital: that a secret defense agreement had been signed between Mexico and the United States, under which Mexico was pledged to enter the war on the side of America in September; that the country had been infiltrated by United States spies and fifth columnists; and that America itself was in a state of absolute fear and war hysteria. Steinbeck was not at all amused by these rumors, appreciating the effect they must be having on more gullible minds. He felt them to be undermining America's prestige not only in Mexico but also in Central and South America. He was also greatly disturbed by the international situation in general. He wrote Elizabeth Otis in June,

[O]f course there are no certainties anywhere, and perhaps will not be again in our lives. I suppose I'll be carrying a gun before long. And I'll do it. . . . My greatest fear is that the big industrialists will sell out to Germany in the hope of saving something. Our great financial families have little history of loyalty. It's a stomach turning time. (JS/ERO June 1940)

He was so concerned at the way he could see events developing that as soon as he had completed the skeleton script he flew with Carol to Washington, arriving there on 22 June. Ricketts left Mexico City for California at the same time, unable to feel that he had been really accepted by Kline and his crew.

Steinbeck's main purpose in going to Washington was to seek an interview with the president. He was convinced that unless something were done to combat it, the undoubted efficiency of German propaganda, which was completely outclassing that of the Allies, would draw Central and South America away from the United States. In a letter to Roosevelt on 24 June, he expressed his fears of an immediate crisis in the Western Hemisphere, which he suggested could be combatted only "by an immediate, controlled, considered, and directed method and policy." He welcomed the possible opportunity of discussing the problem with the president, considering it to be "one of the most important to be faced by the nation" (*SLL* 206).

The poet Archibald MacLeish, the chief Librarian of the Library of Congress, was among those who advised Roosevelt that Steinbeck be heard, and the president agreed to grant him a twenty-minute interview. The two men seemed to get along well together. Steinbeck made it clear that he was not looking for a government job, to which Roosevelt quipped, "In my experience, you're the only one."[10] In later years, Steinbeck would recount how at that first meeting he had made the president laugh. "To the end of his life," Steinbeck would recall, "when occasionally he felt sad and burdened, he used to ask me to come in. We would talk for half an hour and I remember how he would rock back in his chair behind his littered desk and I can still hear his roars of laughter."[11] But that first interview in 1940 was conducted mainly on a serious level. Steinbeck outlined the sort of rumors he had been hearing in Mexico, and proposed the creation of a propaganda office, whose task would be to coordinate the making of radio broadcasts and movies for the effective dissemination of American policy and the promotion of unity among Western Hemisphere countries on the side of democracy.

Although, according to Elaine Steinbeck and Robert Wallsten (*SLL* 207), Roosevelt apparently took no action after listening to Steinbeck's proposals, it is perhaps significant that only a few weeks later, in August, he created by executive order an organization very much like the one Steinbeck had envisaged, the Office of the Coordinator of Inter-American Affairs (CIAA), and put John D. Rockefeller's grandson, Nelson D. Rockefeller, in charge of it. Film propaganda, organized by the Motion Picture Division of the Office, was to play a crucial role in the CIAA's activities. It is of course possible, as Steinbeck had suspected, that the setting up of such an organization had already been under active governmental consideration before he saw the president, but it is also possible that his fervent representations were at least partly instrumental in supplying the necessary urgency for getting the operation off the ground at an earlier date than had been scheduled.

9

The Steinbecks returned home from Washington at the beginning of July. A constant stream of visitors and house guests at the ranch prevented them from sitting down quietly together in an attempt to sort out their marital problems. This hectic social life also prevented Steinbeck from doing any organized work on *The God in the Pipes*, the work he had briefly contemplated the previous October and that he described as "a little playing novel which is probably lousy but which is fun" (JS/CAS 7/10/40).

Although he did some writing of the play during the latter part of July, it is clear from his journal entries that he was not altogether sure of the direction in which the work was going. He knew that the only way he would do it was by knuckling down to a daily stint of writing and getting back into the kind of routine that had enabled him to surmount the creative effort of writing *The Grapes of Wrath*. There seemed little chance of his doing this in the circumstances, and he consoled himself with the thought that if this new work fizzled out in the middle, nothing of importance would be lost anyway. Such thinking, it would seem, was more an emotional buttress against possible failure than anything else. The truth of the matter was, even though he still did not want to accept it, that the creative drive was not really there.

That August, he began taking flying lessons at Palo Alto airport. Only eighteen months from his fortieth birthday, he feared that if he did not learn to fly now his reflexes would become too slow. He lost a week of instruction while he was in Hollywood negotiating with Milestone over plans for the filming of *The Red Pony*. The visit to Hollywood (including a reunion with Gwyn) and the days spent at Palo Alto made him conscious again that he was not being fair to Carol. In order to assuage his sense of guilt, he bought her a car, so that she could at least drive into town whenever she wanted and not be completely confined to the ranch. The gift of a car was not, however, much of a solution to her loneliness, and not surprisingly did nothing to dispel what he unrealistically dismissed as "a little of the end-of-summer blues" (JS/ERO 9/11/40).

By the end of August, he had achieved a fair proficiency at the airport in taking off and landing. With seven hours flying completed, he needed only three more before he qualified to go solo. He was trying desperately all the time to quell the insistent sense of restlessness, guilt, and approaching doom he had lived with for too long. There was, too, the continuing pressure from his agents, editor, and publishers, all of whom viewed his manifold and, in their eyes, unproductive activities with disapproval.

He expressed something of what he was feeling in a letter to Sheffield:

"Something pretty terrible is about to break on this country. And in it I get to feeling lonelier and lonelier. Remember years ago I wrote in the Cup of Gold that a man got to be alone in his success? I couldn't possibly have known how damnably true that was" (JS/CAS 9/7/40).

Five days later, he was again in Washington. Carol went with him, ostensibly because she did not want to be left alone at home, but it is more likely that she had begun to have serious suspicions of another woman lurking in the wings.

The trip to the capital had been triggered by a second letter Steinbeck had sent the president on 13 August, in which he re-expressed his fears arising from the successes of the German propaganda machine and requested, if possible, another audience to enable him and Dr. Melvyn Knisely, who held the chair of Anatomy at the University of Chicago, to outline a simple and effective plan they had devised for "an easily available weapon more devastating than many battleships" (*SLL* 211). The tone of this letter must have intrigued Roosevelt. At any rate, he made arrangements to see Steinbeck and Knisely on 12 September. Their plan, as they explained it, was to scatter immense quantities of counterfeit German paper money by plane all over Europe, thus destroying the Nazi economy at a stroke. The president was clearly taken by the apparent simplicity and effectiveness of the idea, and passed the two men over to the Secretary of the Treasury, Henry Morganthau, Jr. As soon as Morganthau heard the gist of what they were proposing, he raised his hands in horror, not even hearing them out. "It's against the law," he told them, "and I will have nothing to do with it." When the British ambassador, Lord Halifax, was later advised of the scheme, he, too, firmly rejected it. The idea was shelved and never used, although, ironically enough, the Nazis had themselves conceived a similar plan to destroy the British economy, and after the war bales of counterfeit British banknotes were discovered dumped at the bottom of an Austrian lake.

10

After leaving Washington, Steinbeck and Carol spent a week in New York, indulging themselves in a hectic social whirl in an attempt to exorcise the demons that were driving them further and further apart. It was all in vain. They arrived back home in a washed-out and melancholy mood.

Steinbeck felt physically and emotionally restless, not knowing which way to turn. He was aware of trying to do too many things at once and consequently getting nothing done. In a letter to Wilbur Needham, the staff book critic of the *Los Angeles Times*, he accused the country's politicians of something like the same lack of direction he was experiencing himself, upbraiding them for spouting "nonsense words having no relation to an obvious change and movement of the species" (*Adventures* 467). The biological tenor of his letter continued with a comparison of the way in which he saw mankind (as now) periodically rushing lemming-like toward disaster and mass suicide. On top of all the general depression and restlessness that was bugging him, he still had strong feelings of guilt about his ongoing affair with Gwyn, but in spite of the guilt he continued seeing her as frequently as he could.

He had been receiving letters from Covici, urging him to complete *The God in the Pipes*, but by 5 October, as he recorded in his journal, he had finally decided to abandon it. He simply could not work it out to his satisfaction. As he told Elizabeth Otis: "I am uneasy in it and I don't like it and I'm not going to write it. I have the same uneasiness about it I had about the Salinas book that I burned [*L'Affaire Lettuceburg*]. And I'm sure I would burn this one. It is just a medium that isn't for me. I feel freed from an incubus in kicking it out" (JS/ERO 10/5/40). The medium that he thought was not for him was presumably satire.

He was still committed in various degrees to work on two movies — *The Forgotten Village* and *The Red Pony* — and the narrative section of the Gulf book was awaiting his urgent attention. "I'm trying to clean up everything so I can have a straight run of work this winter," he informed his agents (JS/ERO 10/5/40). Although he had at that time given up all idea of completing *The God in the Pipes*, the project obviously continued to niggle away at the back of his mind. In midsummer the following year — after he had at last finished his part of the work on the Gulf book, *Sea of Cortez* — he decided to have another stab at writing the play from the beginning. He failed yet again, and this time discarded it for good.

11

The God in the Pipes was planned as a work of less than forty thousand words, and, as such, not really within the prescribed length for submission to Viking Press under the prevailing terms of Steinbeck's contract. He envisaged it as "another little story in technique," and "a small novel that can be played" like *Of Mice and Men* (*WD* 171). Significantly, although the actual time he worked on *The God in the Pipes* extended over only a few days at the most, the play engaged his attention on and off over a fifteen-month period, a fact that is indicative not only of the many distractions besetting him at the time, but also of the temporary decline in creative inspiration he was experiencing in the wake of the exhausting trauma of *The Grapes of Wrath*, a decline in inspiration certainly exacerbated by his continuing confusion of mind as to the direction his writing (and his personal life) was to take. What, however, is more to the point is that his persistence with the work was a manifestation of his search for the "form of the new" to which he had referred in his letter to Sheffield on 13 November 1939, as well as the overwhelming need he felt to kill the "damned posterity thing" that had been inhibiting him since April the previous year.

Most of the work Steinbeck completed on *The God in the Pipes* has been either lost or, more likely, destroyed. All that remains is a fragment of approximately six thousand words, which begins part way through the second section of a chapter (or scene) of the work, in the middle of a conversation between two characters, a young man named Cameron and another man named Joe.[12] The setting is a vacant lot in Monterey, on which are set out rows of discarded pipes from the adjacent cannery. These pipes, with cloths draped over their open ends to afford some measure of privacy, provide the homes for the inhabitants of a little community. The pipes are "owned" by, or are under the self-elected supervision of, the eponymous Mr. Boss, who charges his "tenants" rent of sorts, and assumes the role in their eyes of protector and father figure. Cameron is a stranger in town. He has traveled here, so he tells Joe, from "far Salinas," twenty miles away. Joe expresses astonishment that Cameron should have come from so great a distance. Cameron admits to being homesick for the town where he was born and bred. Joe asks him:

"Is it as beautiful as they say?"
"More beautiful than anyone can say. I wonder why when you're homesick, you think so much of evening. In Salinas the sun sets at the end of Central Avenue and it goes at last behind the cypress hedge at Talbot's farm. And there is a bird who lives in a pepper tree near the West End School and that bird sings and helps to draw down the sun toward Talbot's cypress tree. I have never seen this bird, but I know he helps with the evening."
"Here the sun sets in the ocean off Point Pinos," the other said.
"I guess that's a good way too," said Cameron. "But it's going to be hard to get used to a sun that doesn't set at the end of Central Avenue. I suppose the Salinas sun will go right on doing it. I hope so. But some day that bird will die — and what then?" (*Pipes* ms. folio 167)

Cameron goes on to praise the virtues of Salinas, "a city where all greed and ugliness have disappeared," and of its townspeople, who are "so wise naturally that they need never read nor study," and are "confident in their loveliness and virtue" (*Pipes* ms. folio 167). Knowing how wounded Steinbeck had been by the manner in which he had been reviled and rejected by his hometown after the publication of *The Grapes of Wrath*, the satire here becomes painfully obvious.

When Joe asks him how he could bring himself to leave so beautiful a place, Cameron reveals that he left Salinas to follow a dream. That dream is a grail. He has heard that in Monterey there is a champagne bottle, and he has come to find it. He tells Joe that he does not want to own the bottle, only to see it, and he expresses the belief that such objects should not be owned privately.

Joe, who has lapsed into silence while Cameron has been telling him this, then volunteers the information that the champagne bottle does indeed exist and is, in fact, very close to where they are. It is owned by Mr. Boss, who, as benefits his high status in the community, lives with his wife in an iron boiler. Joe tells Cameron that Mr. Boss allows only a few people to see the champagne bottle, but that sometimes, when he is feeling merry, he would bring it out and show it to everyone. Cameron realizes that his only likely opportunity of seeing the champagne bottle would be by becoming one of Mr. Boss's tenants. Joe warns him not to knock on the boiler door at this time of day, but to wait until Mr. Boss emerges.

The tiny community comes to life. Scuffling sounds come from within the pipes, the cloths over the ends are pushed aside, and heads poke out:

> ... It would be hard to say exactly how many people lived in the Pipes, for if you watched one end of the pipes, some were bound to come out of the other ends. But the people did begin to come out of the pipes. Mothers herded groups of little girls up behind the cypress trees. Men came out and sat on the pipes and their eyes were still rusty with sleep. And those people who moved about seemed half asleep. Then a ray of sunlight fell across the pipes and as it did, the cannery whistle, low and fierce and insistent, blared out the news of day. At the sound, the men stood up and faced the cannery and removed their hats and the women turned toward the cannery and bowed and even the children made their duty. Joe stood up and took off his cap and when he saw that Cameron remained seated, he tugged at his arm until he stood, and snatched off his cap for him and put it in his hand. Then the whistle stopped and the men put on their hats and women went about their business. (*Pipes* ms. folio 168)

Just then, Mr. Boss opens the boiler door and crawls out. He is "a man of middle age, kind and restrained," with "a sternness in his face, a token of authority" (*Pipes* ms. folio 168), so that no one would need to inquire who was Mr. Boss. He walks down the path, and when he reaches the two men remarks that Cameron is a stranger in these parts. Joe tells him that Cameron wants to find a place to live, but Mr. Boss demurs, saying they are all going through hard times, and that already he sits up at night wondering what he can do to look after his own people. Cameron makes it clear that he is not indigent, is not seeking charity, that he has funds, and all he wants to do is to rent a small pipe where he could live very modestly. The news brings an immediate change to Mr. Boss's attitude.

He offers Cameron "a forty inch section of smoke stack" (*Pipes* ms. folio 169), recently vacated by a family who, against his advice, had been trading in abalone shells instead of scrap iron. But when he sees it, Cameron decides it would be far too big for him. Mr. Boss offers a short piece of heavy-gauge casing, which Cameron finds more to his liking, but then wonders if perhaps his feet might protrude when he is inside. A little crowd has gathered, curious to know what Mr. Boss and this stranger are discussing, and watches while Cameron lies on top of the pipe to measure his body against it. When he has satisfied himself it is long enough, Cameron says he will rent the pipe, if the price is right.

He and Mr. Boss squat down together and, watched by a semicircle of onlookers, the young prospective tenant reveals the contents of his gunny sack, bringing out the objects one by one for Mr. Boss's inspection. He places on the ground first the leg of a cow, then, when Mr. Boss pronounces the bone of little value, a brown beer bottle, a gear ring with only two teeth missing, two big carriage bolts, a big book weighing four-and-a-half pounds with all its pages intact, sundry small pieces of iron, and a half a mirror. All these so-called "funds" are dismissed offhandedly by Mr. Boss, who asks if there is anything else in the sack. Although Cameron says there is not, Mr. Boss observes that there does, in fact, appear to be something there. Cameron tells him: "These other things are mine to do with as I choose. I can spend them or lend them or throw them away. But what is left is — something else" (*Pipes* ms. folio 170). When Mr. Boss insists on seeing what it is, Cameron reluctantly draws a large package wrapped in cloth from the sack and announces that it was his father's dying gift to him. He recalls how on his deathbed his father put it into his hands a moment before expiring. Mr. Boss regrets that Cameron has brought his dying father into the bargaining process, pointing out that the young man has broken the first rule of business by doing so. Nevertheless, he expresses the wish to see "in all reverence" the bequest, if Cameron is willing to show it to him (*Pipes* ms. folio 171).

Cameron unwraps the package with great care and reveals at last "polished and clean a connecting rod and cylinder, complete with rings and riding free on the wrist pins" (*Pipes* ms. folio 171). He announces that it is a "Chalmers 1917," and, for proof, indicates the raised lettering on the rod, the size of the cylinder, the displacement, and the size and thickness of the casting. "Yes," he says. "it is genuine. A true antique" (*Pipes* ms. folio 171). He hands it to Mr. Boss, who inspects the letters on the rod, confirming that it is what Cameron has claimed. He tells Cameron that he is jeopardizing his safety by carrying so priceless an object around with him, and, after persuading the onlookers to disperse, admits to the young man that the other property on the ground is sufficient to cover the rent on the home he has decided upon, and suggests that he himself should take over the care of the rod and cylinder. He tells Cameron it will be safe from thieves in the boiler, and that Cameron can come in at any time he wishes to see it. Cameron asks him if he has a champagne bottle. Startled, Mr. Boss asks him how he knew. Cameron explains that he heard about the bottle "in far Salinas," and that he has "followed the story as children follow will-o-the-wisps" (*Pipes* ms. folio 171). Mr. Boss admits the story is true, and promises Cameron that he can see the bottle as well as the cylinder any time he wishes. Moreover, Mr. Boss undertakes to return the cylinder if Cameron decides to leave Monterey. "That I swear by the Constable," Mr. Boss tells him, and they solemnly shake hands on the deal. "May his great night stick smite me down if I lie." "I trust you without oath," says Cameron (*Pipes* ms. folio 171).

The sky clouds over, and there is a faraway roll of thunder. Heads appear at the entrances of the pipes and men stand around apprehensively. Then:

> From behind the cypress trees emerged the ancient Chinaman, his flat straw hat firmly down over his eyes. He walked falling from step to step down the path in front of the Pipes and a little thunder sounded in the sky. His basket hung from his loose arm. He looked neither left nor right. The people of the pipes watched him, frozen where they were, watched while he passed the front of the pipes and disappeared in the direction of the small wharf. When he had gone the sun returned. An old woman whimpered in her pipe. (*Pipes* ms. folio 171)

The second section of the work concludes at this point. The third section opens as Mr. Boss returns to the boiler with the Chalmers 1917 connecting rod and cylinder. He shows his latest acquisition to his wife, but she displays little interest in it. Failing to obtain any response from her, he asks her if anything is wrong:

> Mrs. B. raised her head and she said angrily, "I wonder if you actually ever *think* of me, if you ever really *see* me."
> "Why — dear — " he began.
> "I know," she went on sharply, "I am your wife. You are conscious that you have a wife — a stick, a doll, something to dress and undress. Someone to keep the boiler and be a credit to it. And you bring me presents, I agree. That black aluminium little handle — very pretty, very valuable and fine. But did you bring it to me or to *your* wife. ... You're too easy going, shiftless it would be called if we were poor. You have a great position and you do nothing but moon around your collection, polishing your Champagne bottle, handling your gun barrel. Wasting your position."
> "But what would you have me do?"
> "Do?" she cried angrily. "Do something, anything."
> "But I do. I collect the rents and see to my tenants."
> "I know. That's just what I'm talking about. You muddle through your life,

fixing leaks in pipes, collecting pieces of art." And then she changed her tack. "Look at the walls of your home," she cried. And obediently he looked. "Well — what do you see?"

"Why — I see the walls curving and beautiful. What should I see?"

"You don't for instance see any curtains do you — or do you?"

"There aren't any curtains," he said. "Of course there aren't. Why should there be."

"Why should I be, why should anything be. That's what I'm talking about. Your Champagne bottle, your gun barrel, your wife. Why should there be a Champagne bottle or curtains?"

"But, dear," he said, bewildered. "There aren't any curtains because there aren't any windows for them to go over."

"There," she cried. "There you have put your finger on it. You apply some obtuse logic and it seems all right to you that our home should not have curtains. How do you think I feel when Mrs. Bean comes to call. Mrs. Bean of the big[?] upper pipe and there aren't any curtains. Have you any idea how that would feel."

"But the Beans haven't any curtains either," he said mildly.

"The Beans do not live in this Boiler." Her tone was icy. "I felt quite sure you didn't understand. ... ." (*Pipes* ms. folios 172—3)

She tells him how the previous day she had gone for a walk out past the city dump in the sandhills. She discovered a large number of people were living there, in houses built of wood, with curtains *and* windows, and chairs rather than the boxes that are all they have to sit on in the boiler. Mr. Boss supposes that these possessions have been obtained from the Dump. His wife points out to him that, whereas their own people have to work for every single item they acquire, the people who live by the Dump have everything literally dropped on their doorsteps. She tells him how she had observed the items deposited from just one truckload: "two stove lids, eighteen bottles, assorted, a part roll of chicken wire, a bed springs [sic], three five gallon cans, a half bushel of green paint, the entire but unarticulated skeleton of a horse, six gunny bags and enough tin cans to fill this room" (*Pipes* ms. folio 173). He can hardly believe what she is telling him. But she continues to rail against his sloth and against the "la de dah" attitude of the Dump people, who would not think twice of throwing away an empty can if it happened to have a hole in it. She again stresses that nearly all of their dwellings have curtains. It wasn't right. Also, they are "foreigners" and "their culture is degenerate" (*Pipes* ms. folio 173). On top of all that, she warns him, the Dump people intend to come at them and take over the Pipe community.

"Did they say that?" Mr. B. demanded.

"They will. They're preparing. They're getting ready for it. Then you can report to them once a week. You can go and knock at the door of a wooden house and maybe you'll only be kept waiting a little while. You can see the curtains hanging there, perhaps blue curtains. But are you asked in? No — you wait, your hat in your two hands. And in good time, his Lordship of the Dump comes out. 'Well, my man," he says. 'Speak up. What have you to say for yourself. Don't waste my time.'"

"He wouldn't dare."

"Who wouldn't."

"This man."

"Are you so sure? Have you been out there. Have you seen them, taking their ease, sitting among their splendid things. You have a champagne bottle — why to them a champagne bottle is dirt. (*Pipes* ms. folios 173–4)

At that point, six lines down the last page of the manuscript, in the middle of Mrs. Boss's reply to her husband, the fragment abruptly ends, where Steinbeck abandoned it in 1940.

Tantalizing though they are in their brevity and incompleteness, these surviving pages can be seen as the precursor of the novel Steinbeck was to write four years later, and which was to become one of his most popular and enduring works, *Cannery Row*. The pipes in the 1940 fragment are the pipes of the vacant lot (to the left of Lee Chong's) in which Mack and the boys would shelter when it was damp, before they took up residence in the Palace Flophouse Grill. The mysterious Chinaman is the same mysterious Chinaman who first appears in Chapter 4 of *Cannery Row*. Mr. and Mrs. Boss's boiler is the same one occupied by Mr. and Mrs. Malloy in the book, and Mrs. Malloy displays the same fixation about curtains as Mrs. Boss. Moreover, Mr. Malloy, like Mr. Boss, is in the business of renting pipes as homes to the less fortunate members of the Cannery Row community. The Chalmers 1917 connecting rod and cylinder reappears as one of the finest pieces in Mr. Malloy's antiques collection — the connecting rod and piston from a 1916 Chalmers that is presented to Doc at the fabulous second (and this time successful party with which the book ends (*CR* 178, 195).

In all its comment on the absurdity of comparative so-called "riches," the preoccupation with class and the obsessive desire to be seen to be superior to one's neighbors, the envy for other people's possessions, the need for everyone to have some sort of personal Grail objective to give purpose to life, the fragment has considerable power in its satire and in the wisdom of its humor. Its true significance, however, lies not only in its Arthurian overtones,[13] but more importantly in what it perhaps reveals of Steinbeck's state of mind during the period he was writing it.

Just as Cameron was seeking his Grail, so Steinbeck was seeking his: in his private life by way of his quest for personal happiness, and in his work by way of his quest for a new form of literary expression to replace what he saw as the exhausted novel genre. Like Cameron, he had shaken the dust of Salinas from his feet. Although he had been living in Los Gatos, less than fifty miles as the crows flies from the city of his birth, Salinas had become "far Salinas" in his mind and heart. For all that, there is no denying the deep strain on nostalgia he felt for the past and for his roots. This is clearly demonstrated through Cameron's recollection of the way the evening sun goes down at the end of Central Avenue, where the Steinbeck family house stood and where he spent his childhood and early manhood. As he had written in his journal, he was conscious of one whole part of his life coming to an end, with his marriage approaching its inevitable breakup. The dialogue between Mr. and Mrs. Boss may indeed be viewed as containing rather more elements of truth regarding his own relationship with Carol than he would have been prepared to admit to the world at large. Certainly, Mrs. Boss's obvious sense of neglect and loneliness; her need for the security and comforts of a stable home; her anger at the manner in which her husband, having secured a "position" in the world, seemed to be frittering his life away on a string of irrelevancies; all seem to mirror Carol's current emotions. Perhaps, too, there is a comment of sorts on the state of their marriage implicit in the Freudian symbol of the detached and no-longer-effective Chalmers 1917 connecting rod and cylinder Cameron cherishes so much but is willing to abandon in his search for the Grail.

There is no way of knowing how Steinbeck might have developed the work, particularly as it was apparently designed for ultimate stage presentation, with all the rather rigid structures and conventions the genre demands. One gets the impression of a vagueness of approach and purpose, of a desperate reaching forth for that "new form" that still eluded him. Not even the introduction of Arthurian artifacts and legend, one suspects, would have sufficed to provide the necessary disciplines for imposing a controlled shape and rationale on a work for the theater. There is no denying that here Steinbeck was writing himself into a dead end out of sheer desperation and emotional confusion, and that he eventually came to realize not only this but also the fact that the work itself was too personally revealing to be comfortably committed to paper.

12

Shortly after he and Carol returned from New York toward the end of September, Steinbeck was back in Hollywood for a private showing of the completed cut of Chaplin's new film *The Great Dictator*. He had first met Chaplin in August 1938, at the time he was writing *The Grapes of Wrath*, when Dan James brought the actor-director to his house in Los Gatos. As had happened with Lorentz, the two men seemed to reach a swift rapport. They became very friendly, visited each other's homes, sometimes staying overnight and discussing politics, filmmaking, and social issues to all hours of the morning. At the time of their first meeting, Chaplin was making his preliminary plans for *The Great Dictator*, and Steinbeck closely followed the progress of the movie during most of its stages, even, so it has been implied, offering Chaplin occasional advice. The showing of the completed cut took place on 3 October and Steinbeck's verdict was that it was "a very strange picture and very effective" (JS/ERO 10/5/40).

The probability is that Steinbeck did not see much of Gwyn during this visit, for, although he traveled to Los Angeles alone, Carol joined him for the viewing of the Chaplin film, and they returned together to the ranch the following day. A fortnight later, he flew alone to Mexico to finish up work on *The Forgotten Village*.

Since late June, when Steinbeck had left Mexico City, Kline had been hunting out locations and had gathered around him a cast of amateur actors — the Pueblos themselves, who were to act out their normal lives — to follow the story Steinbeck had sketched out in his skeleton script. Filming commenced on 1 September. The arrangement was that Steinbeck should return to Mexico once the filming had been completed, view the rushes, and then finalize the commentary for the finished movie. Steinbeck had become worried when he did not hear from Kline for several weeks, the director being busy on location. Eventually, word came through that Kline would finish shooting by the end of October and would expect Steinbeck sometime during the first week of November. This, however, was not good enough for Steinbeck, who had become impatient at Kline's apparent slow rate of progress and had decided that the project had dragged on long enough. He wanted to be free of it, so that he could concentrate on writing the Gulf book. Fueling his own agitation was the increasing pressure from Ricketts, who had been remarkably patient over the past several months. Feeling that his presence in the field would spur everyone to greater effort, he advised Kline that he would be joining him in mid-October, with the idea of working on the commentary for the completed sections of the movie, while Kline finished the shooting of the later scenes.

What Steinbeck had not appreciated were the difficulties under which Kline had been working since June. When Steinbeck had left, the ideal location for the film had not yet been discovered, and it was not until two months later that Kline and his crew decided they had at last found what they had been looking for. They were then faced with the problem of assembling a viable cast to bring Steinbeck's script to life on the screen. When he handed over the skeleton script, Steinbeck had told Kline: "You must try to direct this, Herb, as I try to write — on one top level for our peers, those who know as much as we like to think we know, and on another level to keep it simple and true for people with little or no education so they can understand and be moved by our story."[14]

Even when Kline had created a suitable "family" from various sources, he was dismayed to find that the villagers chosen tended to regard him and his crew with as much suspicion and fear as were the doctors in Steinbeck's script. For a while, the villagers refused to cooperate, convinced that the make-believe situations in which they were being asked to perform and in which children were pretending to fall sick and die would surely lead to real illnesses and deaths. On one occasion, during the filming of a religious procession, the crew was actually stoned, fortunately without any injury, and with only superficial damage to some of the equipment.

Steinbeck flew down from Los Angeles on 18 October, and joined Kline and the crew on location in a maguey field. They were shooting the sequence in which Juan Diego, the enlightened eldest child of the family, steals his sick sister from the house to take her to the doctor for a life-saving injection.

During Steinbeck's absence from the country, there had been rioting and street fighting in Mexico City during the summer elections, and a great deal of this had been captured on film by Kline at considerable danger to himself and the crew. They did briefly contemplate reverting to the original idea of making this another anti-fascist film by dovetailing this footage into Steinbeck's script. Indeed, when Steinbeck was shown these sequences, he was so impressed by them that he, too, for a time seriously considered altering the film's storyline by devising a new ending in which Juan Diego and the teacher would become involved in the fighting to defeat the attempted fascist coup. But on second thought, following the effective suppression of the uprising, he argued that these scenes should not be used, that the film should confine itself to the single subject of the fight against ignorance and suspicion and not lose itself in trying to contain too many themes.

A rough cut of the film was ready for showing to the Mexican authorities at the Teatra Principal in Mexico City on 15 December. Steinbeck was not present at the screening, having returned home two or three weeks earlier. According to Kline, Steinbeck's contribution to the making of the film had been crucial, extending far beyond simply writing the original skeleton script and the final commentary. "He contributed valuable ideas even if he never once interfered in the direction," Kline recalled in 1971.[15] On the other hand, once the storyline had been decided upon, he would brook no interference in the writing of the script, which he regarded jealously as his sole province. On more than one occasion, he told Kline, "Herb, you and Sasha [Hackenschmied] stick to directing and photography—just don't tell me *how* to write any changes you want that I agree with."[16]

13

When he arrived back at the ranch, Steinbeck immediately became caught up again in all the old uncertainties and the increasingly manifest antagonism. Although on 29 September he had in his journal covertly referred to his ongoing affair with Gwyn as a "bad thing," he had been unable to deny his true feelings, which deepened day by day and which he expressed in a suite of twenty-five love poems written in a small pocket-size notebook. Robert DeMott adjudges that Steinbeck wrote the poems at the Biddle Ranch under, as it were, the nose of his wife during the period from late September through late November between his trips back and forth to Mexico and Hollywood.[17] In a letter dated 23 November to Max Wagner, Steinbeck asked his friend and confidant to tell Gwyn that he was "making a song for her and I have never made a song for anyone before" (*SLL* 217). It is not known when he eventually gave Gwyn the little notebook, but it was presumably soon afterward. It was found among her possessions at the time of her death.

Throughout that fall and winter, Steinbeck remained worried about the worsening news from Europe: the heavy air raids on London, the intensification of the U-boat campaign, the seizure of the Romanian oil fields by the Germans. He also found the political situation in America additional cause for concern. In a letter to his agents on 14 October, he commented on the forthcoming presidential election, observing that "the Republicans are rapidly putting themselves in the position of traitors against the country," and went on:

They don't seem to realize it but there is a growing feeling against Willkie as an obstructionist. This is probably part of the Democratic tactics but it is getting more effective all the time. I rather think that Willkie will go the way of Landon. Maybe not quite so badly but pretty much all right. (JS/ERO 10/14/40)

His prediction, of course, proved to be correct when Roosevelt was reelected for a third term on 5 November, carrying thirty-eight states, but with a reduced majority in the popular vote.

The Steinbecks visited Hollywood again in December. It is clear that on this occasion Steinbeck did contrive to arrange a meeting with Gwyn. On the day before they were due to drive home, Carol was taken ill, ostensibly with a hangover. But she was no better the next day, and then Steinbeck himself became ill.

The journey back to Los Gatos, starting out in pouring rain, was a nightmare. Neither of them was fit enough to make the journey, and Steinbeck was certainly in no state to drive all the way, as he did. They were both so ill by the time they reached the ranch that Joe Higashi immediately called the doctor.

Influenza was diagnosed. Carol's temperature was 103, and Steinbeck's 104. Within a few days, Steinbeck had developed pneumonia and had to be dosed up with sulfanilamides. He was still in bed on 29 December, although by then both he and Carol were on the mend. They were left feeling terribly weak and washed out. Christmas had passed them by, and they had no plans for New Year celebrations. Not that there was anything to celebrate.

"I for one don't resent it a bit," Steinbeck told Elizabeth Otis in a New Year's Eve letter. "Usually have a lousy time anyway. These parties never do work out." He ended the letter: "Happy New Year. Whatever that means" (JS/ERO 12/31/40).

4

1941: Conflict and Creativity

1

FOR THE FIRST WEEK OR SO OF THE NEW YEAR, STEINBECK AND CAROL WERE confined to the ranch, recovering in the aftermath of the influenza and pneumonia. Steinbeck's depressed state of mind was again evident in the letter he wrote Covici on New Year's Day:

> And speaking of the happy new year. I wonder if any year ever had less chance of being happy. It's as though the whole race were indulging in a kind of species introversion — as though as a species we look inward on our neuroses. And the thing we see isn't very pretty. (JS/PC 1/1/41)

Early in the second week of January, Kline brought the completed rough cut of *The Forgotten Village* to Hollywood. Steinbeck, although still feeling a little groggy, joined him there in the hope of getting the film into final shape and to supervise the narration. The original intention had been for Max Wagner to speak the commentary and he had been more or less promised the job. But while in Mexico in November, Steinbeck had learned that the film's backers wanted someone with a well-known name as narrator. Spencer Tracy's name had come up, and when approached he had agreed to do it. Steinbeck had been both angry and dismayed at this turn of events, feeling that he had let his old friend down, but he reluctantly accepted that the backers were probably right.

As it turned out, however, shortly after Steinbeck arrived in Hollywood, Tracy fell victim to the influenza epidemic, was admitted into the hospital, and was expected to be out of action for at least a week. This delay was the final straw for Steinbeck. "I've done my part — I'm all through," he complained to Elizabeth Otis. "I don't wait any more" (JS/ERO 1/21/41). If he was deliberately turning his back on some unresolved problem, he was at least content that the picture would be assured a good distribution. Zanuck had wanted to release it, and had offered all the facilities at Twentieth Century-Fox for them to work in. Walter Wanger had also expressed interest on behalf of United Artists. Steinbeck, however, felt beholden to MGM, who was, after all, loaning Tracy for the narration, and he decided that when it came time to consider bids MGM should be given preference.

He returned to the ranch on 19 January. By now, bored with the whole protracted and wearisome process of filmmaking, he was literally straining at the leash to begin work on the Gulf book. The day after he returned home, he confided to his journal that he thought the film would not be anything he would be proud of (*WD* 124). He appreciated all too well the mistakes that had been made. Neither he nor Kline and his crew had ever made a film with actors before, Kline's previous films having been edited compilations of newsreels with added commentary. He himself had not exercised any overall supervision, leaving too much, so he now thought, to Kline and the others. Even the script, for which he bore main responsibility, had suffered because everyone wanted to contribute their own ideas. "The final tragedy," he told Elizabeth Otis,

> was the music which was written separately so that this last time I had to *pad* the story to fill in between music. And I have never padded in my life. Altogether I came away with a fine sick feeling in the stomach and a resolve never to do it again. Milestone says that democracy is not successful in making a film, and I believe him. And no one was final boss.

However, contradicting his journal entry, he added defiantly: "And still the film is good" (JS/ERO 1/21/41).[1]

2

His feelings of guilt over cheating on Carol weighed more heavily on him day by day, as indeed did his feelings of frustration at not being able to continue more vigorously his affair with Gwyn. It was clear that matters were rapidly reaching a point of no return. A decision would soon have to be made. Yet he still procrastinated. On returning from Hollywood, he almost believed the decision had been made, as it were, by default, and that his relationship with Gywn was burning itself out naturally. It was only a feeling he had, but he hoped it was true, persuading himself there was no future in it for either for them.

Carol had suffered a recurrence of her flu symptoms and was in a very low physical and emotional state. When Steinbeck urged her to go off to the desert for a fortnight's vacation in the sun and escape the wet weather that was depressing her so, she would not go without him. By then, he felt too much committed to the long-delayed Gulf book to take any more time off. "What a time of waiting this is!" he wrote Elizabeth Otis. "Everyone poised between two breaths" (*SLL* 222). He seemed to sense disintegration all around him. In his journal, he wrote how the familiar world was slowly crumbling and melting away, and how "the powerful voices of hysteria and terror" were in the air (*WD* 125). In another letter to his agent, he told her how confused he was about the war, and declared that he found himself horrified by the mood of the country, "the nastiness growing" and "the patriots rushing to the trough" (JS/ERO 1/21/41). He even briefly toyed with the idea of becoming a war correspondent in either London or China. Such a course of action would allow him to escape from, but certainly not solve, his current problems. But no sooner was the thought there than he had to dismiss it. His overwhelming preoccupations were still Carol and Gwyn and the Gulf book, and they, unfortunately, were irreconcilables. Carol needed comfort and warmth. He ached for Gwyn. The book was demanding to be written. In order to write it, he had to distance himself from Carol and the disruptive atmosphere of the ranch. He decided to return to the former routine of simply spending weekends at home, working on the book from Mondays to Fridays in Pacific Grove, in a cabin owned by his sister Esther.

He arrived at the cabin on Monday, 28 January and prepared to begin work immediately. His plan, prior to the expedition setting out the previous March, to write an ongoing series of articles during the voyage to help finance the project had not been carried through. He had neither produced such articles nor even kept a journal of any description. In writing his narrative, he would have to rely on the extensive notes Ricketts had kept, which had subsequently been typed up into a forty-six-page, single-spaced manuscript.

As with every new work, when the moment came to begin the first page, he delayed picking up his pen as long as possible, finding every little excuse for not starting. When he did at last begin, the opening paragraphs went well, and the following day he felt satisfied when he read over the first day's work. Ed Ricketts, too, expressed his approval. "I hope," Steinbeck confided to his journal, "this can be a relaxed book. There are so few of them now and the world really needs them for the world is tight and knotted now" (*WD* 126).

But he was not relaxed, of course. His phrase "tight and knotted" exactly described his own state. Concern about Carol was not giving him the peace of mind he required to work well, although he did halfheartedly attempt to blame his mood on the possible recurrence of influenza. By the third day, he was telling himself that the book was not going too well, and was beginning to be troubled once more by all the old doubts he always felt when working on a major project.

On Friday, he returned to the ranch, and there found all his worst fears about Carol justified. She was in a desperate state. The continual rainy weather had completely dispirited her. He felt impelled to act without delay, and made arrangements for her to go on vacation to Honolulu for six weeks, booking passage for her on the liner *Lurline*, sailing from San Francisco the following Thursday. This time she made no protest about going without him. Indeed, the prospect of the voyage and the island sunshine seemed to perk her up immediately.

As soon as he had seen her off on the liner on 7 February, he flew down to Los Angeles. A few days earlier, he had received an urgent telephone call from Tracy, asking him to return to Hollywood to supervise the recording to *The Forgotten Village* narration. Tracy was not happy working under Kline's direction, accusing the director of not having a real ear for rhythm or tone, with the result that his reading of the lines was not all it should be. When Steinbeck reached the studio, however, he discovered the true reason for Tracy's call. Kline was, in fact, in hospital, another victim of the influenza epidemic. The real problem was with MGM. The studio was effectively preventing Tracy from continuing with the recording.

Steinbeck was infuriated at this unexpected turn of events, especially when he was told the circumstances in which the studio had manipulated the situation. The studio heads had wanted Tracy to star in a new version of *Dr. Jekyll and Mr. Hyde*, but the actor was against playing the role. On the other hand, it was widely known that he very much wanted to do the commentary for *The Forgotten Village*. The studio bosses agreed to his working on the Steinbeck-Kline film, but only on the understanding that Tracy, in his turn, would agree to appear in the Jekyll and Hyde movie. No sooner had the movie gone into production and Tracy was committed to it than the studio reneged on the agreement. Steinbeck was so incensed by this duplicity that, in a letter to Elizabeth Otis, he vowed, at every opportunity and in every way he could, to sabotage MGM's projected film version of *Tortilla Flat*, as well as the movie the studio was proposing to make based on Marjorie Kinnan Rawlings's 1938 Pulitzer Prize novel *The Yearling*.

The Yearling was about a boy named Jody (the same as the name of the boy in *The Red Pony*) who has affection for a baby deer. There was no question of plagiarism. The letter was written in the heat of the moment. He was, as he well knew, clutching at straws. He had no real control over the filming of *Tortilla Flat*, and as for *The Yearling*, as he admitted in a subsequent letter to his agents, he would be satisfied if he could simply create "just a little mess" for the studio. He had no ax to grind so far as Miss Rawlings was concerned (JS/ERO 2/17/41).

He was in Hollywood for one day only, but during the few hours he was there he arranged for Burgess Meredith to record the commentary.

Confident now that this element of the film was in safe hands, Steinbeck returned north to the cabin in Pacific Grove and to the more important business of writing the Gulf book.

The dubbing of the commentary and music was completed by 28 February. But there were further troubles ahead. Kline wrote in mid-March, asking for three hundred dollars to pay some Mexican technicians who had money owed them. The request angered Steinbeck, who considered that Kline and his little team had been enjoying a very good life for several months on the thirty-five thousand dollars originally raised, some of which he had contributed himself. He maintained that if they had run out of money it was their fault and their problem. He did not see why he should be expected to bail them out, and tersely suggested they borrow from a bank. "The quicker this relationship is terminated, the happier I'll be about it," he told Elizabeth Otis. "I just don't want to be mixed up any more" (JS/ERO 3/16/41).

Difficulties had also arisen over the film's distribution. Steinbeck suspected that Kline's general attitude was not being helpful, for the big studios, having now viewed the completed film, no longer seemed interested in taking over its release. Kline, on his part, probably felt that Steinbeck's own recent attitude might have been sending the wrong signals to the studios. Certainly, he too was most disappointed at the course events had taken, having been sure, as Steinbeck himself had been, that with the advantage of first-class distribution and buttressed by the name of one of the major studios, *The Forgotten Village* would be a money-maker.

3

By 17 February, Steinbeck was able to report to New York that he was making good progress on the Gulf book. "I am enjoying it," he wrote. "It has everything in it. Kind of like a letter containing everything that happened and was discussed and thought about. Formless it would be if there weren't the physical form of the trip to hold it in bounds" (JS/ERO 2/17/41).

Gwyn had by then joined him at the cabin. She would sleep late in the mornings, while he got up, built a big fire, and then worked steadily until midday. Once she was awake, all thoughts of work had to go out of the window. They walked among the sand dunes and feasted on doughnuts and coffee. In those idyllic surroundings and circumstances, his work went well and their relationship, which only a few weeks before he had half-believed to be over, blossomed.

Not all the book, however, was written in the cabin. During this period, he had his portrait painted by a local Monterey artist, Ellwood Graham. Graham has recalled how Steinbeck used to work from Ricketts's typescript while sitting for the portrait in Graham's studio. Steinbeck and Ricketts had devised their own system for cooperating on the narrative. Sections would be passed to Ricketts as they were written, and he would pass them back to Steinbeck, having made any necessary comments, corrections, and verifications of or expansions to technical material embodied in the text. Ricketts was delighted with Steinbeck's work, and enthused to Toni Jackson — then living with him as his common-law wife, acting as secretary to both men and doing all their typing: "It's so damned beautiful I can hardly stand it. He takes my words and gives them a little twist, and puts in some of his own beauty of concept and expression and the whole thing is so lovely you can't stand it."[2]

By mid-March, Carol having extended her vacation in Hawaii by a further fortnight, Steinbeck was able to report to his agents that the book was going "merrily along" and that he had completed thirty thousand words. He described it as "a monster job" (JS/ERO 3/16/41). He was by now exceeding his target quota of two thousand words a day. By the following week, he had notched up forty-five thousand words. "It's a very rambling affair," he warned Elizabeth Otis, "which considers almost everything but very good humoredly. It will be fun to read but not by the take-a-book-to-bed public. I think there is some fine work in it. ... By far the hardest work I've done. ... I have a good feeling about it" (JS/ERO 3/23/41).

Ricketts had written a discourse, "Essay on Non-teleological Thinking," which, after it had been typed by Toni Jackson, he sent to Steinbeck sometime during March. The essay appears, virtually verbatim, in the book as the "Easter Sunday" chapter (SC 131-51). Steinbeck advised Covici on 29 March that he had now written fifty-five thousand words, but was by no means near finished. He wrote:

> It may go as much as eighty or ninety thousand words and I don't care. It is a timeless job—one of the few being done in the world today—a world that is concerned with immediacies. ... It seems to me a better and more important book than I had thought. But in some places it is thoroughly disreputable. But if it is part of the book, it goes in. And it is fun. (Fensch 23-24)

Covici could not have been reassured by these comments. He was naturally still anxious that his author should write a worthy successor to *The Grapes of Wrath* at an early date, and the Gulf book was patently not going to be that book. Furthermore, with all the scientific photographs, some in color, and line illustrations that would be required, it was going to be an expensive book to produce. The most Covici could hope for was for his author to get this particular book out of his system, the sooner to start work on another novel. But when he encouraged Steinbeck to release the manuscript as quickly as possible, he received an impassioned response on 18 April. Steinbeck told him:

> The main answer is to keep your shirt on. You know I won't send out second draft mss ever [and] this less than any. Don't rush us. We're trying to do a good job and hurry [won't] help us at all. So don't sell this book until you have it. It is a huge undertaking. (Fensch 24-25)

As much as anything, Steinbeck was anxious that Viking should not misrepresent the book in any forthcoming announcements as any sort of adventure story. He stressed that, above all else, it was a scientific book aimed at a fairly specialized readership.

Apparently Covici still seemed not to have grasped the extent to which the Steinbeck-Ricketts collaboration was an inseparable concept, for in May he wrote the biologist and suggested that the title page of the book should show Steinbeck as sole author, with Ricketts being merely credited as the compiler of the scientific appendix. When Steinbeck heard of this, he again reacted angrily: "This book is the product of the work and thinking of both of us and the setting down of the words is of no importance. I not only disapprove of your plan—but forbid it."[3]

4

By the time Carol arrived home on 2 April, Steinbeck had decided, after experiencing the uninterrupted idyllic weeks in the Pacific Grove cabin, that his passion for Gwyn and the prospect of a future life with her overruled his failing sense of loyalty to a wife from whom he felt increasingly estranged. The idea of continuing to live at the ranch had become extremely distasteful to him. He began formulating plans to sell the property, and purchased a small house in Eardley Street, Monterey, where he proposed to set up home with Gwyn.

Shortly after Carol's return, he summoned up sufficient courage to make a clean breast of his relationship with Gwyn, making it clear just how deeply he had become involved and how little of himself remained for their marriage. Carol told him in no uncertain terms that she still wanted whatever did remain and that she would fight for him tooth and nail.

He contrived for the two women to meet face to face at the Eardley Street house. In a desperate attempt to save her marriage, Carol claimed she was going to have a baby. Gwyn, too, announced that she was pregnant, declaring she was prepared to fight for her man and would have his baby, come what may. In fact, Carol was not with child, and Gwyn, despite what she said, subsequently had an abortion. Having engineered the meeting, Steinbeck was at a loss how to handle the explosive situation. He did not come out of the encounter well, at one stage leaving the two women to fight over him while he retreated into another room. Following this extraordinary episode, Steinbeck reluctantly agreed to stay with Carol on a temporary basis, but when some days later she admitted there was no baby she lost her last hold over him. They separated officially on 27 April.

In acute distress, Carol fled to New York, while the two lovers established themselves in the Eardley Street house. Steinbeck wrote to Mavis McIntosh, urging her to be kind and patient with Carol when she turned up in New York, and to believe everything she said except when it was obviously nonsense. On the other hand, he warned Mavis McIntosh that Carol would surely talk a lot of nonsense and asked her to "kind of knock some of it out of her" (JS/MM c. April 1941). He also asked his agent to arrange for Carol to receive one thousand dollars each month for the time being. A few days later, in another letter to Mavis McIntosh, he began, for the first time, to explain and justify the inevitable disintegration of the marriage:

> Whatever Carol may believe now, we have never been easy together. There has been tension from the first, from the first moment. It was nobody's fault but it was just so. I thought that was the way everyone was. It was a very shocking thing to find that it was not part of living with a woman to be in a state of constant hostility with her. ... My shortcomings may have had a great deal to do with it. But just as my shortcomings were applicable to her and hers to me, and since those same shortcomings do not seem to apply to other people, perhaps she can find or meet someone who will not have them. ... I really think and believe that she will suddenly [be] having a better time than she ever had in her life. Certainly thirteen years proved that I couldn't give it to her. (JS/MM c. May 1941)

All this time, and despite all the emotional and physical upset he had been experiencing, he continued to make progress on the Gulf book. Gwyn was cushioning him within a cocoon of domesticity that helped to facilitate his recovery. Within a few weeks, he was able to report to his agents that he was calm and that the stomach bleeding from which he had been suffering had almost ceased. He was drinking plenty of milk and looking forward to being in good physical shape once more before very long.

In time, the question of legal financial settlement would have to be resolved. While he was certain that the separation was permanent, he suspected that Carol secretly banked on his tiring of Gwyn and wanted her back with him. He asked Toby Street to tie up all the necessary financial arrangements and work toward an eventual divorce. He was adamant that the settlement should, if anything, err on the side of over-generosity. By such means, he perhaps hoped to go some way toward salving his inescapable sense of guilt.

His letters to his agents during this period are a curious and sometimes erratic blend of praise for the way Carol was behaving and suspicion of her possible motives. This suspicion he justified with long complaints about her past failings and her obsession for confusing security with money. It would seem that he was conditioning himself to overlook the fact that Carol had shared with him the years when they had been indigent, when she had to be ultracareful with whatever little cash came their way from his writing. He chose to reduce comparisons into terms of black and white, implying that, whereas life now with Gwyn was all sweetness and honey, life with Carol had always been a great deal less than perfect. As in all situations, the truth of the matter undoubtedly was that both sides were to lesser or greater degree at fault, and both sides were deserving of a large measure of sympathy.

Steinbeck had instructed Street to calculate the current value of the estate, in order that Carol's share could be determined with all possible speed. Although he had given no indication to Carol by the end of May that from his point of view the separation was permanent, he asked Street to act as Carol's attorney in the coming divorce proceedings. For her part, Carol was still obviously clinging to the hope that the regular monthly one thousand dollar payments she was receiving constituted no more than a temporary arrangement to tide her over until such time as her husband came to his senses, rejected this other woman, and turned again to her for haven and solace. This undoubtedly is why her letters to him tended to be so "full of goodness and sweetness" (*SLL* 231) during this period of uncertainty. Only when the inevitable truth dawned on her did she begin to show her claws. Indeed, although she became extremely agitated upon hearing that the separation had become common knowledge in Monterey, it is quite possible that she herself had leaked the story to the press in a perverse bid for public sympathy. Steinbeck maintained it was none of his doing. He had, as always, been careful to keep a tight lip in the company of reporters.

5

The distribution of *The Forgotten Village* had eventually been taken over by a small independent firm run by Arthur Mayer and Joseph Burstyn. It had been originally intended that the film be premiered in New York in May, but the distributors decided against this. To begin with, they wanted to exhibit the film on a roadshow or two-a-day policy, and that sort of scheduling would not be advantageous with the hot weather coming. Then, more importantly, Covici, still impatient to have a new Steinbeck work in the bookstores, had suggested that Viking should publish Steinbeck's script with accompanying stills from the film. Steinbeck and his agents accepted the proposal and publication date was fixed for 26 May. Mayer and Burstyn approved the idea, anticipating that the publicity created by the book could be utilized for the film's benefit during the coming months.

Steinbeck was never greatly enthusiastic about the publication of the script, but he consented to write a short preface, in which he recounted some of the difficulties encountered in making the movie, and that ended: "A curious and true and dramatic film has been the result" (*FV* [6]). Privately, he dismissed the book as "a phony," for he considered it nothing more nor less than a trailer for a film, and an exorbitantly expensive one at that at two-and-a-half dollars.

The reviews of the book, if not overwhelmingly favorable, were on the whole uniformly respectful. The *New Yorker* called it "one of the better picture books,"[4] and Margaret Marshall referred to the writing as "typical Steinbeck — eloquent and sentimental but suited to the subject."[5] Several of the reviewers anticipated the forthcoming film, and by so doing justified the distributors' decision to delay its showing. "The film is to be released this Autumn," Ralph Thompson noted in the *New York Times*, "and if it is half as effective on the screen as *The Forgotten Village* is in print, it will be the finest thing of its kind since Eisenstein's *Thunder Over Mexico*."[6]

Steinbeck's script is a work of approximately four thousand words only. The theme and the setting are firmly established in the opening lines of the commentary:

> Among the tall mountains of Mexico the ancient life goes on, sometimes little changing in a thousand years. But now from the cities of the valley, from the schools and laboratories, new thinking and new techniques reach out to the remote villages. The old and the new meet and sometimes clash, but from the meetings a gradual change is taking place in the villages.
>
> This is the story of the little pueblo of Santiago on the skirts of a hill in the mountains of Mexico. And this is the story of the boy Juan Diego and of his family and of his people, who live in the long moment when the past slips reluctantly into the future. (*FV* [7] & 9)

Although Ricketts had been aware all along of the theme of the film, it was not until he read the final, published script that he expressed the force of his disagreement with it. While his antagonism against the script may have partly stemmed from a feeling of resentment that Steinbeck had concentrated on this work at the expense of the Gulf book, the main thrust of his objection was against the film's theme and the philosophy of the benefits to be derived from man-imposed change and progress that ran completely counter to the nonteleological theories to be expounded in the Gulf book, especially in the "Easter Sunday" chapter. As Richard Astro has pointed out in his important study *John Steinbeck and Edward F. Ricketts: The Shaping of a Novelist* (1973), while Steinbeck's many primitives may well conform to Ricketts's nonteleological worldview, such primitives are not Steinbeck's real heroes or his personae:

> In viewing Steinbeck's work in perspective, it becomes increasingly evident that the novelist carefully and analytically forged his own conception of the human

ideal; the vigorously energetic and creative individual who "walks up the stairs of his concepts" and "emerges ahead of his accomplishments," that rare man among men to whom the novelist accords his highest praise and in whom he places his greatest trust. Indeed, along with his unique ability to portray nature and the natural world, the manner in which Steinbeck deals with the choice between escape and commitment is his supreme attribute as a writer: few novelists have ever dealt so completely and so eloquently with what they regard as the fundamental basis of human character.[7]

Ricketts's vision of "the noble savage" enjoying "the true civilization," which, in a phrase taken from one of Diego Rivera's murals, "will be the harmony of the men with the land and of the men among themselves," was an attitude that Kline, for one, found distasteful. Kline recalled how, during the filming on location in Mexico, Ricketts was absorbed "with Rousseau and the joys of the primitive man while [that man's] children and wife were dying unnecessarily from the inadequate treatment of witch doctors."[8] Ricketts's antiscript, "Thesis and Materials for a Script on Mexico," proposes a more appropriate subject than the story of how medical science was introduced to the forgotten villages:

A new road [is] being forced through an unwilling country ... by a non-resident socialist government which believes in good roads and rapid communication, whether the district wants it or not. A wise old man, seeing this, would realize that the sudden change would destroy a lovely old way of life, and that the school teacher or government official who was the instrument of the change would be all the more dangerous if he were a good man who himself had the fire of zeal for the new thing. The old harmony between the people and the land would be upset by the new high speed road with its strange people passing by, with its trespassers and picnickers, and by the changed economy incident to a high speed road. The good relations between parent and child would be upset by the boys hitch-hiking into Ensenada to the movies and pool halls, and by the gals getting themselves screwed by flashy strangers in shiny cars.[9]

Such a work based on Ricketts's outline might possibly have been also attractive to Steinbeck, but one he would probably have treated in an ironic or even satiric vein. There would have been, in his view, a vast difference between, first, cutting a new, high-speed road with all the doubtful benefits it would bring to those living alongside it, and, second, the establishment of a pure water supply with the very real benefits of ensuring a general improvement in the health of the village and a spectacular decline in the incidence of infant mortality. So far as Steinbeck was concerned, the second achievement was the more imperative and the more important.

Ricketts's criticism of *The Forgotten Village* was not, it should again be stressed, in any way damaging to his relationship with Steinbeck. Their friendship and respect for each other was too firmly bonded for that to happen. They were able to continue their collaboration on the Gulf book without the slightest hint of the sort of friction Steinbeck had experienced with Kline. Although Steinbeck had made his peace with Kline by July, he had not forgotten the previous difficulties arising from their partnership. In a letter to Elizabeth Otis on 9 July, he mentioned having seen Kline recently and of liking him "all over again now that I have no more business association with him." He felt that although they had lost their "jitteriness" with each other he could not visualize the two of them ever collaborating again. "With Ed it is different entirely," he wrote (JS/ERO 7/9/41).

6

In a possible attempt to mollify to some degree his agents, if not his publishers, for his not having written any new work of fiction, Steinbeck had sent them that February the manuscript of a short story, "How Edith McGillcuddy Met R. L Stevenson." This, however, was not a new work, but dated from 1934, the year in which he had written many of the stories collected in *The Long Valley*. "How Edith McGillcuddy Met R. L. Stevenson" was based on a true incident that happened to Mrs. Edith Wagner, Max Wagner's mother. She had told Steinbeck how, when she was a twelve-year-old girl in Salinas, way back in the summer of 1879, she had been persuaded by a little waif to cut Sunday school and join her on a free funeral ride to Monterey, and how, after a series of adventures and before catching the train back to Salinas, she had, unknowingly at the time, encountered the Scottish writer Robert Louis Stevenson. After Steinbeck had written the story and sent it to his agents, he discovered that Mrs. Wagner had written her own version of the incident and had, moreover, already submitted it for publication. Steinbeck immediately instructed his agents to withdraw his story. Edith Wagner's version was never accepted for publication, but Steinbeck did nothing with his own manuscript until he heard, early in 1941, that Mrs. Wagner was in poor health and short of funds. He resurrected his manuscript and sent it again to Elizabeth Otis, asking her if she could sell it to some leading magazine for a good price and then pay the money over to Mrs. Wagner. Early in June, Elizabeth Otis succeeded in selling the story to *Harper's Magazine*, the same magazine that had published two of *The Long Valley* stories. "Edith McGillcuddy" was published in the magazine's August 1941 issue. Steinbeck sent the $225 he received to Mrs. Wagner, apologizing that it was all he could get for the story. Even if it does not possess the power and depth of most of the other stories he wrote during 1934, "Edith McGillcuddy" is a delightful vignette and belongs in *The Long Valley*, more so than does the earlier-written "Saint Katy the Virgin," which has no relation whatsoever to the other stories in the volume.

7

In early June 1941, Steinbeck was approached by Kenneth McKenna, story editor at MGM, to work on the script for a proposed film version of *Tortilla Flat*. MGM had acquired the screen rights from Benjamin Glazer, a former story editor at Paramount. Glazer had been instrumental in Paramount originally purchasing the screen rights for four thousand dollars in 1935, and had subsequently purchased the rights from Paramount when he left the studio's employ some years later. Glazer should be credited with commendable business acumen and foresight or with just plain old-fashioned luck, for, following the runaway success of *The Grapes of Wrath*, the *Tortilla Flat* rights became hot property, and he sold them to MGM for a sum variously quoted at sixty thousand and ninety thousand dollars.[10] Whatever the true figure may have been, Glazer made a very handsome profit.

Steinbeck had no intention of accepting McKenna's proposal. Not only was he somewhat miffed when he discovered the extent to which Glazer had lined his pockets, but he was still smarting from the way in which the studio had doublecrossed him over the Tracy affair. However, he decided to play along for a while. Learning that MGM had no usable script, he replied to McKenna, laying down terms similar to those he had stipulated to the studio in 1939 with regard to *The Red Pony*: that he should work at home and not at the studio, that he should have full control over the script, and that he should be paid a great deal of money for his services. Before the month was out, MGM had written him an "insulting letter," which he countered with an insulting letter of his own, and, as he put it, "that was that" (JS/ERO 6/24/41). Or so he thought.

A few weeks later, the MGM producer Sam Zimbalist contacted him and and fixed a meeting one evening in a Monterey bar. Zimbalist brought along the screenwriter John Lee Mahin, who, together with Glazer, had prepared a working script. It did not take much putting two and two together for Steinbeck to latch on to the truth that the studio was in real difficulty in creating a suitable script. The two MGM men turned on all their powers of persuasion, and, although he had no intention of changing his mind, Steinbeck led them on, eventually intimating he might be willing to cooperate.

Not long afterward, Spencer Tracy got in touch with him. Tracy was most anxious to appear in the film, but was concerned, as was everyone else at the studio, by the inadequacy of the script. He asked Steinbeck if he would work on it, but this time Steinbeck made it clear that he would take on the job only if he could be guaranteed full control over the final script. Tracy suggested that Steinbeck might take a different view if some arrangement could be reached whereby Milestone would direct the picture. Steinbeck agreed that this, in his eyes, would be tantamount to his having control over the script.

Tracy reported back to Zimbalist, and the script was sent to Steinbeck, who read it and pronounced it not very good. When he telephoned Zimbalist to tell him what was wrong with it, the producer urged Steinbeck to work for him. The author reiterated that he was perfectly willing to do so, but only if Milestone were to direct the picture, if he could work on the script at home, and if he was paid a lot of money. Zimbalist then revealed there was bad blood between Milestone and Mayer, dating back to the time when the director had refused to sign for MGM. Zimbalist nevertheless offered to try, with Tracy's help, to sway the balance in Milestone's favor. Steinbeck, who was vastly enjoying all this, loftily indicated that when they had sorted out all their little squabbles they should let him know. He made it clear that he wanted nothing to do with their internal machinations, and reported delightedly to Annie Laurie Williams, the agent associated with McIntosh & Otis, who dealt with film and stage negotiations: "I've planted all the seeds of uncertainty I could and then got out. They must hate Milestone because they offered me John Ford and they hate him too" (JS/ALW c. 8/5/41).

There was apparently no further communication between Steinbeck and MGM on the subject, and when the film was finally released in May 1942 the screenplay was credited to Mahin and Glazer.

8

Toward the end of May, Steinbeck had sent some pages of the typescript of the Gulf book to Covici so that a salesmen's dummy could be made up. By mid-June, he had reached the beginning of Chapter 24, having just completed the dissertation on cannibalism that appears on pages 230—3 of *Sea of Cortez*. When Ricketts read this section, he told Steinbeck: "Well, you have outraged every other kind of people in the world, now I think this closes the circle and everybody will be outraged at you" (Fensch 27).

On 19 June, Steinbeck advised Covici that, provided he could keep up his present pace and barring accidents, he estimated the first draft of the book would be completed in two to three weeks — that is, by the first or second week of July. The second draft would be ready a month after that. He had been working on the book for something like four-and-a-half months, and the indications are that he may have been running out of steam. Not only had the work taken rather more out of him than he cared to admit, particularly in conjunction with his domestic travails, but he was beginning to experience the inevitable sense of boredom that so often assailed him after he had been concentrating too long on one project. Noticeably, the chapters from that point on become shorter in length and contain somewhat less philosophical discourse. Indeed, the last five chapters of the book — Chapters 25 through 29 — represent only one-eighth of the total text of the narrative, and contain approximately twelve thousand words, no more than six days' work at his normal rate until then.[11]

Despite what he had said to Covici in April, he now offered, in order to save time, to submit the second draft typescript "very carefully corrected ... rather than clear and perfect copy in a final [draft]" (Fensch 27). What he was proposing, in effect, was to repeat the precedent established in 1938 with the submission of Carol's corrected typescript of *The Grapes of Wrath*. If Covici agreed to this procedure, Steinbeck indicated it might be possible to submit the complete narrative section to Viking sometime toward the end of August, leaving Ricketts to submit his second half of the book in the early days of September.

As was to be expected, Covici welcomed Steinbeck's offer, but suggested, in order to minimize loss of time in getting the book to the printers, that the chapters be mailed to him as they became ready. Steinbeck's manuscript draft had been completed by the first week of July and the typing of the second draft was well under way. The typing was in fact completed by the end of July, but the task of correcting the whole of of the second draft took another month. In the meantime, as they were corrected, Steinbeck mailed sections of the draft to his agents for forwarding to Viking. The process was not without its accompanying traumas. Steinbeck complained to his agents about the manner in which the book was being marketted. He even considered for a time that there had been bad faith on Covici's part in going back on certain undertakings regarding color illustrations and other matters. He did not approve of the proposed dust jacket, which he dismissed as the weakest one he had seen for a long time. But, more than anything else, he was worried that Covici's advance publicity campaign continued to be misleading, plugging the book as if it were certain to be a potential best-seller on the lines of Margaret Mitchell's *Gone With the Wind*. Elizabeth Otis passed on Steinbeck's misgivings to Viking, making it abundantly clear that the two authors were more concerned to have a well-produced book, with all the features they had been promised, than to have a wide sale. She was able to convey to Steinbeck the reassurances she subsequently received from Harold Guinzburg.

On 22 August, Steinbeck mailed the final section of his narrative to Elizabeth Otis, together with a large section of Ricketts's work, and followed these the next day with a statement, addressed to Viking from the two authors, designed to clarify for once and for all the nature and purpose of the book, and, of equal importance, the extent of the closely knit collaboration that had gone into its creation. On this second matter, the statement read, in part:

> Originally a journal of the trip was to have been kept by both of us, but this record was found to be a natural expression of only one of us. This journal was subsequently used by the other chiefly as a reminder of what actually had taken place, but in several cases parts of the original field notes were incorporated into the final narrative, and in one case a large section was lifted verbatim from other unpublished work. This was then passed back to the other for comment, completion of certain chiefly technical details, and corrections. And then the correction was passed back again. (*Adventures* 481)

Ricketts completed his work for the book by the end of August, so the deadline agreed with Viking for the submission of all the material was met. "I don't know whether you like it or not now you have seen it all in one piece," Steinbeck wrote his agents. "I think shivers went through Viking when they found the book was what we said it would be. Maybe they will give up their ideas of [a] hundred thousand copies now" (JS/MM c. Aug−Sept 1941).

Covici, however, was ecstatic about the book, and told Steinbeck:

> It is four o'clock in the morning. I just finished your book, and I say it is a great book. I feel as if I were among some distant stars, bewildered, amazed with the mystery of it all. Why am I here, and where am I floating? Yours is gigantic thinking and it takes gigantic reading. I don't claim that it is all clear to me but I want to read it again and again till it becomes part of me. I don't remember another reading experience like this.[12]

9

It was not until the pioneering studies of Richard Astro and Betty Perez began appearing in the early to mid-1970s that the question of the true extent and division of the Steinbeck-Ricketts collaboration was at last made clear. Then, with the publication of Joel W. Hedgpeth's *The Outer Shores, Parts I & II* in 1978, Ricketts's previously unpublished essays, including "Notes from the Sea of Cortez" and "Essay on Non-teleological Thinking," became available. These published findings and interpretations have completely transformed many long-cherished but erroneous concepts of Steinbeckian philosophy, as well as eradicating some of the confusion that had arisen from the apparent dichotomies both in Steinbeck's avowed aims as a writer and in his stated philosophies, particularly with regard to the fiction that followed *The Grapes of Wrath*.[13]

An examination of Ricketts's "Notes from the Sea of Cortez" reveals that, while Steinbeck relied to a large extent on the log Ricketts kept during the trip, a great deal of the narrative section of *Sea of Cortez* covers factual matters not recorded by Ricketts, and elaborates on others, omits several incidents, and, in one or two instances, even repositions events to obtain a more logical or pleasing effect within the flow of the narrative. The whole structure of the published text displays a literary skill that Ricketts's log, for obvious reasons, does not. As Steinbeck told his agents while he was still sending the corrected second draft to them piecemeal, "The architecture of the journal will gradually become apparent. It was built with enormous care but albeit it sounds easy and spontaneous" (JS/ERO 8/23/41). He further stressed this in the opening words of his introduction: "The design of a book is the pattern of a reality controlled and shaped by the mind of a writer" (*SC* 1). As Peter Lisca has observed, whereas Ricketts's log begins as the *Western Flyer* leaves Monterey, Steinbeck's narrative contains a four-chapter preamble detailing the preparations for the voyage. Contrariwise, at the end of the book, Steinbeck omits several pages of Ricketts's account in which he records the voyage back from the Gulf to San Diego and his adventures in Hollywood while Steinbeck and the other members of the expedition were sailing back through rough seas to Monterey. As previously noted, this truncation of the narrative may have been occasioned by Steinbeck's running out of steam, but, having regard to the aesthetic and symmetrical structure he imposed on the work, making the important "Easter Sunday" chapter both the philosophical and textual center of the narrative, it was arguably a conscious decision on his part, after all.[14] Ricketts recognized what Steinbeck had achieved. He told mythologist Joseph Campbell:

> I was very charmed with the book. [John] certainly built it carefully. The increasing hints towards purity of thinking, then building up toward the center of the book, on Easter Sunday, with the non-tel essay. The little waves at the start and the little waves at the finish, and the working out of the microcosm-macrocosm thing towards the end.[15]

Steinbeck fully deserved Ricketts's approbation for making the long nonteleological essay the central point of the narrative, particularly as, after all their disagreements over the philosophy motivating Steinbeck's storyline for *The Forgotten Village*, Ricketts may understandably have feared that his essay, or even a précis thereof, would be afforded comparative minor attention in the book. Although Steinbeck used the concept of nonteleological thinking in *Of Mice and Men*, even to the extent of originally giving the play-novel the title *Something That Happened*, it is obvious that he had modified his approach to nonteleology, if indeed he had ever completely embraced it, finding it to be essentially at variance with the gathering sense of commitment that governed his worldview, no matter what he may subsequently have chosen to claim.

On the other hand, the concept of "group man," also explicated in *Sea of Cortez*, was one Steinbeck had long accepted and used to immense effect in such works as "The Vigilante" and *In Dubious Battle*, as well as in *The Grapes of Wrath*. The most extended treatment of the group man concept in *Sea of Cortez* occurs in Chapter 25, when, after anchoring in Puerto San Carlos, the expedition members observe that the waters of the harbor are teeming with tiny fish:

> We had never been in water so heavily populated. The light, piercing the surface, showed the water almost solid with fish—swarming, hungry, frantic fish, incredible in their voraciousness. The schools swam, marshaled and patrolled. They turned as a unit and dived as a unit. In their millions they followed a pattern minute as to direction and depth and speed. There must be some fallacy in our thinking of these fish as individuals. Their functions in the school are in some as yet unknown way as controlled as though the school were one unit. We cannot conceive of this intricacy until we are able to think of the school as an animal itself, reacting with all its cells to stimuli which perhaps might not influence one fish at all. And this larger animal, the school, seems to have a nature and drive and ends of its own. It is more than and different from the sum of its units. (*SC* 240)

It is perhaps not all that long a step from the theory of group man to the holistic view of existence Steinbeck and Ricketts also shared and Steinbeck expressed most vividly in fictive form in *To a God Unknown* and by way of Jim Casy's musings in *The Grapes of Wrath*: "Maybe all men got one big soul ever'body's a part of" (*GOW* 33). In *Sea of Cortez*, Steinbeck declares: "Ecology has a synonym which is ALL" (*SC* 85). The statement is developed later in the narrative:

> And it is a strange thing that most of the feeling we call religious, most of the mystical outcrying which is one of the most prized and used and desired reactions of our species, is really the understanding and the attempt to say that man is related to the whole thing, related inextricably to all reality, known and unknowable. ... [A]ll things are one thing and that one thing is all things— plankton, a shimmering phosphorescence on the sea and the spinning planets and an expanding universe, all bound together by the elastic string of time. It is advisable to look from the tide pool to the stars and then back to the tide pool again. (*SC* 216—7)

The concern that is expressed in *Sea of Cortez* for the misuse, the rape, of the environment is most potently manifested in Chapter 27, following the visit to the Japanese dredge boats and the observation of the senseless waste ensuing from the process of bulk, indiscriminate fishing for shrimp. The warning is spelled out unequivocally:

> We in the United States have done so much to destroy our own resources, our timber, our land, our fishes, that we should be taken as a horrible example and our methods avoided by any government and people enlightened enough to envision a continuing economy. With our own resources we have been prodigal, and our country will not soon lose the scars of our grasping stupidity. (*SC* 250)

It is salutary to remind ourselves that this was written a half-century ago, and to ponder on the fact that it is only in comparatively recent years that the warning has begun to be heeded, and not everywhere even now. The subject of the ecological disaster humanity was piling up for itself was a concern Steinbeck returned to, for example, thirteen years later on the first page of his novel *Sweet Thursday*, a book all too often summarily dismissed by many Steinbeck scholars, but which, amid all the knockabout and occasionally bawdy comedy, contains a great deal of sober good sense and is a much more serious work than appears on the surface. In that book, reflecting on the greed and thoughtlessness of the Monterey fishermen and cannery owners during the war years, Steinbeck comments:

> The canneries themselves fought the war by getting the limit taken off fish and catching them all. It was done for patriotic reasons, but that didn't bring the fish back. ... It was the same noble impulse that stripped the forests of the West and right now is pumping water out of California's earth faster than it can rain back in.[16]

Awareness of the war in Europe looms ominously throughout *Sea of Cortez*. On the voyage, the expedition members are, to an extent, divorced from the war for most of the time, not merely because their distance from it seemed even more remote once they were at sea, but also because the boat's radio was continually troubled by static. The end of the phony war and the invasions of Denmark and Norway occurred without those on the *Western Flyer* knowing until later. But it is clear that the war was frequently discussed, and, as with so many other topics, inevitably became the subject of purely biological interpretation:

> We have looked into the tide pools and seen the little animals feeding and reproducing and killing for food. ... If we used the same smug observation on ourselves that we do on hermit crabs we would be forced to say, with the information at hand, "It is one diagnostic trait of *Homo sapiens* that groups of individuals are periodically infected with a feverish nervousness which causes the individual to turn on and destroy, not only his own kind, but the works of his own kind. It is not known whether this be caused by a virus, some airborne

spoor, or whether it be a species reaction to some metereorological stimulus as yet undetermined." ... And perhaps our species is not likely to forego war without some physic mutation which at present, at least, does not seem imminent. And if one places the blame for killing and destroying on economic insecurity, on inequality, on injustice, he is simply stating the proposition in another way. (*SC* 16—17)

And later in the book Steinbeck, the sociopolitical biologist, takes over:

Conscious thought seems to have little effect on the action or direction of our species. There is a war now that no one wants to fight, in which no one can see a gain — a zombie war of sleepwalkers which nevertheless goes on out of all control of intelligence. Some time ago a Congress of honest men refused an appropriation of several hundreds of millions of dollars to feed our people. They said, and meant it, that the economic structure of the country would collapse under the pressure of such expenditure. And now the same men, just as honestly, are devoting many billions to the manufacture, transportation, and detonation of explosives to protect the people they would not feed. And it must go on. Perhaps it is all a part of the process of mutation and perhaps the mutation will see us done for. (*SC* 88)

There is little doubt that passages like this last one, taken in conjunction with the seemingly radical attitudes promulgated in *In Dubious Battle* and *The Grapes of Wrath*, were to upset the susceptibilities of the Washington hierarchy, and possibly were later instrumental in hardening the doubts and suspicious of the establishment, both civil and military, concerning Steinbeck's commitment to the prosecution of the war. What those in authority did not appreciate (and it is perhaps understandable) was that Steinbeck's fervent patriotism was based — and had always been based — on the twin concepts of truth and free speech, and that these required him to criticize wrongs whenever and wherever he came across them, and to support, if he thought it necessary, what in some contexts would seem like extreme revolutionary views. All this, of course, could never go down at all well with the establishment. Ricketts, it would transpire, was not far off the mark when he had suggested that, here and there, whole sections of society would be outraged by some of the views expressed in the book.

By definition, Ricketts, as the other official half of the authorial "we," was aware that he too would have to accept equal responsibility for those views. There is no reason to suspect that he was unwilling to assume such responsibility. In any case, he fully shared or had even originated many of these opinions and theses discussed during the voyage. While much of his thinking can be identified in the text, the exact line of demarcation between his thinking and Steinbeck's own thinking is often blurred — but that, after all, was the way it was designed to be.

If, prior to the researches and findings of Astro and Perez, too many critics had been willing to accept that the first part of *Sea of Cortez* was the sole work of Steinbeck and so provided a convenient key to the rationale of his fiction, it would be as incorrect to underestimate Steinbeck's contribution, for this went far beyond merely taking the texts of Ricketts's log and his biological and philosophical essays and fashioning them into a readable narrative. Even had that been all he did, it would have been enough. Steinbeck's skill and artistry in transforming the basic facts Ricketts recorded into a work of literature can best be illustrated by taking two short passages from, as it were, the raw material, and then look at what Steinbeck did with that material.

The first of these extracts taken from Ricketts's log is dated "24 Mch Easter Sunday":

> From about 10 or 10:30 until 11:30 or 12, Tiny and I walked along the ridge between Amortajada Bay and the lagoon beyond. On the lagoon side of the ridge, there were thousands of burrows, presumably of a big land crab (since we saw what I took to be one, which, however, scuttled into his burrow in a hurry). Hopeless to dig out, lacking time, shovel and man power. The shore of the lagoon were teeming with fiddler crabs and estuarine snails, of which we took representatives. Mangroves (the flowers may have caused the fine, fragrant tropical hay-ey smell we noticed while coming into Cape San Lucas that midnight). A Salicornia-like shore plant. From where we were wading around in the lagoon, there was fine picture of still water, with the green fringing leaves against the burnt red-brown of the distant mountains, like something out of Conrad, or like some fantastic Doré engraving of heaven.[17]

Steinbeck, appropriately enough, utilizes Ricketts's description of the lagoon as part of his preamble to the Easter Sunday essay, but, by taking Ricketts's words and giving them, as Ricketts himself had noted, "a little twist" and putting in "some of his own beauty of concept and expression," he converts it into a piece of pure, clear prose, possessing that external stylistic rhythm and that inner emotional rhythm that are the hallmarks of the best of his writing:

> The beach was hot and yellow. We swam, and then walked along on the sand and went inland along the ridge between the beach and a large mangrove-edged lagoon beyond. On the lagoon side of the ridge there were thousands of burrows, presumably of large land-crabs, but it was hopeless to dig them out. The shores of the lagoon teemed with the little clicking bubbling fiddler crabs and estuarian snails. Here we could smell the mangrove flowers without the foul root smell, and the odor was fresh and sweet, like that of new-cut grass. From where we waded there was a fine picture, still reflecting water and the fringing green mangroves against the burnt red-brown of the distant mountains, all like some fantastic Doré drawing of a pressed and embattled heaven. (*SC* 131)

The second extract from Ricketts's log is dated "13 Apr Saturday." On the morning of that day, the collecting phase of the voyage over, the *Western Flyer* sailed out of the Gulf of California into the open sea. As its bow was pointed to a northwesterly course for home, there was a sudden loud clap of thunder overhead. Ricketts describes the moment thus:

> 11AM, back on Pacific Standard time, and back into the open Pacific, there was a tremendous clap of thunder. In an immediately menacing sky, I was above making things shipshape against the coming storm; picking up a couple of boxes of matches before the rain should soak them—we were short anyway. When the perfectly tremendous clap of thunder came, it sounded as though we had been shot; I nearly fell overboard. Below, Sparky had been taking a leak. That stopped that. But Tiny was best. He was sleeping and awoke suddenly to say, "What are they shooting at us for?" (I guess Navy training; there had been another boat on the horizon before he went to sleep.)[18]

Steinbeck ditches all the somewhat prosaic recollections of the incident and of the various reactions it stimulated, and conceives a simple and almost mystical passage that conveys perfectly not only the moment of confrontation with the threatening vastness of the ocean after the enclosed and comparatively sheltered waters of the Gulf, but also the realization that, for all of them, the scientific exploration, which had become so much an integral and dominating part of their lives for the past four weeks, was finally over.

> ... In the morning the tip of the Peninsula was on our right. Behind us the Gulf was sunny and calm, but out in the Pacific a heavy threatening line of clouds lay.
> Then a crazy literary thing happened. As we came opposite the Point there was one great clap of thunder, and immediately we hit the great swells of the Pacific and the wind freshened against us. The water took on a gray tone. (*SC* 268)

As can be seen from the two examples, Steinbeck considerably edited and refined the text of Ricketts's log. One can estimate the true measure of Steinbeck's own work, other than the first four chapters, that went into the narrative when one recalls that Ricketts's account of the trip was, after all, only forty-three pages long (admittedly closely-typed pages), that the last tenth of Ricketts's log, covering the period 13—26 April, plays no part in Steinbeck's text, and that additionally there are some matters recorded in Ricketts's account that Steinbeck chose to omit altogether. Against all that must, of course, be set the long nonteleological essay and other of Ricketts's set pieces weaved so impeccably by Steinbeck into the fabric of his narrative.

Some of Steinbeck's omissions are worthy of mention. For instance, the amount of heavy drinking that went on during the trip is delicately passed over, with only an occasional, humorous comment indicating, contrary to what he maintains at the end of Chapter 1, that a suitably adequate supply of liquor (or "medicine," as he prefers to call it) had formed an important part of the provisions taken on board before they left Monterey. But possibly the most significant omission of all is his failure to acknowledge Carol's presence on the *Western Flyer* during the whole of the trip. He did not, it is true, by implication entirely ignore her, for the careful and perceptive reader can detect her shadow here and there. In his account of the provisioning of the vessel, Steinbeck notes: "It is amazing how much food seven people need to exist for six weeks" (*SC* 10). He had by then established that there were only four crew members on the trip: the captain, Tony Berry; the engineer, Tex Travis; and two seamen, Sparky Enea and Tiny Colletto. Clearly then, the editorial "we" should consist of not just two persons, Steinbeck and Ricketts, as the book's title page was to imply, but three. Carol played a useful part in the collecting of specimens, and, as Ricketts's log makes clear, several of the happenings attributed to the editorial "we" were properly attributable to her. She, for instance, caught the horned shark (and, moreover, she caught it on a hook and line), whereas in the book Steinbeck relates how the shark was pulled on board after becoming ensnared in a baited bottom net (*SC* 212). Steinbeck's motives for deciding not to mention Carol are in many ways understandable. By the time he was ready to write the book, their relationship had become extremely fraught. Even so, it is just possible that when he began the actual writing (before the final break with her had occurred) he did intend including her in the narrative, and the reference to the "seven people" ostensibly bears out this assumption.[19] However, the deeper he got into the writing the deeper in actual life he was becoming emotionally involved with Gwyn and distancing himself from Carol. If he did include Carol in the early pages, there must have come a time when he went back over all he had written, and deleted every specific reference to her. It would not have proved a difficult task. Certainly, Carol was not the only one of his wives to be given such treatment. His third wife, Elaine, is never mentioned at any time as his traveling companion while he was undertaking the tour of the country he recounts in *Travels With Charley* (1962), although she did accompany him on various stages of the journey. The mystery is not so much why Carol is left out of the narrative, but why Steinbeck did not make that simple alteration from "seven people" to "six people." All said and done and all personal and emotional considerations aside, he was arguably justified on aesthetic grounds (and any possible charge of sexism has nothing to do with this) in eliminating her, for strictly she was an "intruder" in what was essentially a male environment, just as Elaine was an "intruder" in what was essentially a lone journey of rediscovery.

In 1963, five years before his death, on his way home from a cultural exchange visit to the Soviet Union as a guest of that country's Writers' Union, Steinbeck was asked by a student at the University of Helsinki which of his books afforded him the most pride. Unhesitatingly, Steinbeck replied: "*Sea of Cortez*."[20]

Steinbeck's choice, on first consideration, may seem somewhat curious.[21] Having regard to the circumstances of the book's genesis and its status as a full-scale collaboration with Ricketts — and also incidentally having regard to his statement in one of the authorial asides in *East of Eden* to the effect that no collaboration was ever responsible for creating a single true work of art[22] — one might be forgiven for assuming that *The Grapes of Wrath* or *East of Eden* would have been the book he would have chosen.

On the other hand, and for several obvious reasons, the book had special significance for him. To begin with, as his letters at the time attest, he wanted to write a book that would show the critics he was not merely a writer of fiction, a writer who could find his most rewarding material only in depicting the "little people" — simple paisanos, impoverished farmers, mental defectives, or unemployed workers who had become mere pawns in the hands of big business and prone to easy manipulation by radical agitators. He wanted to write a book that would demonstrate that he was not just another exponent of the current "hard-boiled" school of writing, but that he did have an intellectual mind possessing a theory of life explicated in all his fiction. Furthermore, *Sea of Cortez* was the first book since *Cup of Gold* he had written completely detached from Carol's influence. He had been irritated by her contention in one of the increasingly acerbic letters she had written during the summer that she had found him "a bad Donn Byrne" and had left him "a good writer" (JS/MM n.d.), and he had come to regard the successful completion of *Sea of Cortez* as the first published repudiation of Carol's claim. Certainly, the narrative ranks among the best sustained pieces of prose he ever wrote, its technical and biological aspects presented in a simple expository language easily assimilated by the layman, and the whole shot through with typical dry Steinbeck humor.

10

At the beginning of August, Steinbeck at last heard from Milestone, who was able to outline the terms of a possible contract he was negotiating with RKO for the projected movie of *The Red Pony*. These negotiations continued throughout August, and by the end of the month, when Steinbeck was all but free from his commitment on *Sea of Cortez*, a satisfactory deal with the studio had been tentatively agreed. It was arranged that Steinbeck would prepare a synopsis, and as soon as Annie Laurie Williams had studied and approved the contract, Milestone would come up to Monterey to work with him on the script.

By the time Milestone arrived early in September, Steinbeck had "mapped the whole thing out" and found "a way to make it carry the dramatic load and one which might work" (*Adventures* 483). The two men immediately set about devising the narrative treatment for the movie, and, despite the fact that Steinbeck felt the inevitable impatience in going back over old material, they worked well together and made excellent progress. By 11 September, they had decided upon the overall design of the script, leaving Steinbeck to begin the treatment from which the final version would emerge.

Some hitch had arisen in the meantime concerning the terms of the RKO contract, the studio seemingly having gone back in part on the original terms, offering the excuse that there had been an internal reorganization in the company. While Steinbeck and Milestone were content with the new financial terms proposed, they nevertheless required firmer clarification of the film's potential front-office treatment. As Steinbeck pointed out to Elizabeth Otis on 20 September, when the original negotiations had been in progress all they had had were four short stories. Now they had almost achieved a script that would give them additional bargaining power, particularly as Twentieth Century-Fox now seemed very anxious to make the film. Steinbeck was concerned that *The Red Pony* should have better promotion than that accorded *Of Mice and Men* and that any contract with the studio should stipulate the theater in which it was to open in New York and details of the proposed advertising campaign. Neither he nor Milestone, he informed Elizabeth Otis, would be willing to sign unless these points were established and agreed.

Although *The Red Pony* was yet another collaboration, one can speculate — and evidence seems irrefutably to point this way — that the text was solely Steinbeck's work, and that Milestone's role in its creation extended to little more than his giving approval to Steinbeck's vision and contributing ideas as to how the action and specific scenes might be handled to obtain maximum emotional impact on the screen. Apart from a number of peripheral revisions to the basic story line suggested in the preliminary notes Steinbeck had drawn up before Milestone joined him in Monterey, Steinbeck's original concept had been carried forward into the narrative script, which itself bears a remarkable similarity to the final movie version released in 1949, after a few of the linking episodes had been trimmed, both for cutting the film's running time and tightening up the action.[23]

In his preliminary notes, Steinbeck had already devised the dawn opening sequence and the rather ill-conceived Jody "dream sequences," the latter, although carried over in much watered-down versions from the original short stories, proving to be the weakest episodes in the film. He had also hit on the method by which he could convert the somewhat loosely-connected narratives of the four-story cycle into an integrated entity. This integration had however been achieved at some cost by sacrificing completely the second of the stories in the cycle, "The Great Mountains," and some of the material in the third story, "The Promise." Balancing these omissions, Steinbeck introduced some new material, and bound it all together by bringing in the final story in the cycle, "The Leader of the People," as an essential element extending throughout the whole chronology of the script narrative. Grandfather — who never appears and, indeed, is never mentioned in the first three stories of the cycle — becomes one of the leading characters at a comparatively early stage in this and subsequent versions of the script, playing the role of Billy Buck's occasional mentor and father-confessor figure. What Steinbeck achieved in this initial narrative version of the script was not simply a straight translation into the movie medium of the first, third, and fourth stories of the cycle, but something that was essentially an entirely new work: in fact, a complete short novel that, with a modicum of revision and elaboration, is publishable in its own right.

11

The opening paragraph of the narrative script, vividly setting the physical scene and the emotional climate of the action to follow, is, in its insistent cadences and exact descriptions of animal life, vintage Steinbeck:

> In central California many small ranches sit in the hollows of the skirts of the Coast Range Mountains. Some of them are the remains of Spanish grants, some the last remnants of old and gradually disintegrating homesteads. On one of them, in the foothills to the west of the Salinas Valley, the dawn came as it came to a thousand others. As the light edged the rim of the Gabilan Mountains it brought no actual light into the valley, but the rooster, who for an hour and a half had flapped his wings and entertained the dreams of the ranch, crowed and flapped and crowed again. In the bottom of the bowl of the little ranch, along the brush line and in the stubble of cut hay, the field mice were activated by the ending night, as they always are. In the lower limbs of a cypress tree beside the bunkhouse the roosting turkeys shuffled their feathers, talked clickingly for a time and then, dropping to the ground, stretched their wings and settled their feathers for the day. (*RP* script 1)

In the course of the initial evolution of the script, certain changes were made by Steinbeck to the names of the characters from those by which they are known in the story cycle, and also between those they are given in the preliminary notes and in the narrative script. "Grandfather" and "Billy Buck" remain unchanged throughout. The mare, "Nellie," which belongs to Carl Tiflin in "The Promise," is renamed "Rosie" and is owned by Billy Buck in both the preliminary notes and the narrative script. The "Jody" of the stories becomes "Joady" in the preliminary notes — a possible misspelling on Steinbeck's part, or perhaps a conscious throwback to the Joads of *The Grapes of Wrath* — but reverts to "Jody" in the narrative script. "Carl Tiflin" is initially called "Gus" in the preliminary notes, and then later "Frederick" or "Fred," the name he retains in the narrative script. Mrs. Tiflin, who has the name "Ruth" in the story cycle, is referred to, on one occasion only, in the preliminary notes as "Amy." In the narrative script, she becomes "Alice."[24]

The rather vague and disjointed, but extended, chronology of the three short stories from the cycle is considerably telescoped in the narrative script. Not only is the character of Grandfather introduced early in the story line, but it is established that he, rather than just visiting the ranch, as in "The Leader of the People," actually lives with the Tiflin family. His absence in the first quarter of the script is explained by the fact that he is on a visit to Pacific Grove, staying at the Rogue Club, where he can reminisce to his heart's content and swap stories with the other old, westering pioneers he meets there. It is also established at the very beginning of the script that the mare — Billy Buck's Rosie — has already been to stud and is, in fact, nearing the end of her gestation period. Jody, who is longing for a colt of his own, pesters Billy, asking him what he intends to do with the colt when it is born. Mr. Tiflin tells his son that the colt, reared from good prize-winning stock, will be worth a hundred and fifty dollars and thus far too valuable for Billy to give it to him. Jody, however, chooses to go on half-believing that Billy will give him the colt, and he boasts as much to the other children at school.

While Fred Tiflin and Billy are in town buying stock, they attend an auction. Fred buys Jody a little ex-circus pony for $25. The story line then follows fairly closely the action in the first story in the cycle, "The Gift," except that it is liberally interspersed with dialogue from "The Leader of the People," Grandfather having returned home a few hours before Fred and Billy arrive back at the ranch with the pony.

One day, while Jody is at school, the pony, Gabilan, left as usual in Billy Buck's care, escapes from the barn and catches a chill by being out in the rain for several hours. Jody blames Billy for what has happened, although the fault is partly his own for having taught the pony how to butt open the barn door. When the pony becomes very sick, Billy seeks Grandfather's advice and reassurance. Jody, having lost faith in Billy's infallibility, also consults Grandfather, and persuades him to come to the barn with him to check that Billy is doing the right thing in performing a tracheotomy on the sick animal. Billy realizes that Jody no longer trusts him. He is hurt, aware that a distance has been created between himself and the boy. After Billy has performed the operation, Jody stays in the barn to watch over the pony, but he falls asleep, and once again the pony escapes. When Jody awakes in the morning, he frantically follows Gabilan's tracks, finding the pony just as it dies and is attacked by the buzzards.

Billy promises Jody he can have Rosie's colt, but the boy continues to blame him for Gabilan's death. Nothing that Billy can do, or that the rest of the family can do, will alter Jody's attitude of unforgiving mistrust. When Billy has to go to the San Francisco stockyards for more new stock, Grandfather, in an attempt to bring the boy and Billy together, suggests that Jody should go as well. Normally, Jody would have jumped at the chance, but now he demurs, saying he has examinations at school he cannot miss. Billy asks Fred to look after Rosie while he is away.

Jody and Rosie grow very close during Billy's absence, and Jody quickly assumes responsibility for looking after the mare, feeding her, cleaning out her stall, and keeping her well-curried. When Billy returns, he thanks Fred for the fine job he has done in looking after Rosie, but then realizes and acknowledges that it was Jody who had looked after the mare. Jody is both pleased and embarrassed to hear Billy's praise, and shortly afterwards, while they are discussing Rosie's progress, man and boy slip easily back into their old relationship.

When the birth seems to be going wrong and the point is reached when it seems Billy has to choose between saving either the colt or the mare, he decides, come what may, he will not fail Jody a second time. Jody, however, is determined that Billy should not sacrifice Rosie. Jody's love for the mare far outweighs the prospect of his having a colt of his own. When the crisis is imminent, he steals Billy's knife to save the mare, but while he and Billy are quarreling, the mare delivers the colt safely without help from anyone. All ends in true Hollywood tradition, in tears of happiness. The final shot is of Jody furiously riding the colt, now a full-grown horse named Black Demon, up the hill road to the valley, and of Billy Buck riding up alongside, admonishing Jody "not to run a horse up a hill."

Told in such bare outline, the story seems, in this script version, in some ways hackneyed and sentimental.[25] Certainly, with its unlikely happy resolution, it lacks the power and the uncompromising realism of the short-story cycle. This failing is surely due in part to the change in perspective Steinbeck was obliged to impose on the telling of the story when creating the new work. Jody's subjective view of adults and of the world around him, as presented in the short-story cycle, is replaced by the cinematic objective viewpoint. On the other hand, it has to be admitted that the objective viewpoint, being essentially less restrictive in its scope and in its conclusions, does provide Steinbeck with the opportunity to portray his characters in more depth — if possibly not Jody, then undoubtedly the adults.

For instance, Billy Buck as seen through Jody's eyes in the story cycle is a quasi-heroic figure who apparently can do no wrong. He is also inevitably a completely sexless character. In the film script, on the other hand, he is revealed as being very unsure of himself in several matters, and of having his hang-ups, the same as everybody else. In the film script, too, we learn that Billy does have a sex life of sorts, an activity he keeps quite separate from his generally-held idealized concept of women:

> On the walls [of his room in the bunkhouse] hung pictures of women, but not nudes or Police Gazette darlings, but rather the heads of women with dear melting eyes, with soft curling hair; calendar pictures of sweet, smiling or sad women, unvoluptuous. For Billy was very sentimental and not at all sexually obsessed. His sexual pressures he released in a whore house in Salinas once a month, but calmly and coolly, as he would take a physic to relieve abdominal pressure. This had little to do with women. The women Billy had pictured in his room were mothers and wives and brides and fiancees, women seen through a romantic and idealistic haze — women, in a word, whom Billy had never known. For, reared in a motherless shack by a father who was a Government packer, suckled sometimes on mare's milk, Billy had never known any woman well. The whores he patronized were not women to him at all, but necessary treatments for a condition which occasionally made him nervous. There was a strong asceticism in Billy. He adored Alice Tiflin as some unreachable goddess who was part Mother and part Deity. And the lovely passionless women on his walls were like the religious pictures in a chapel — to be looked at and loved, but not desired. (RP script 22—23)

And Alice Tiflin herself, a shadowy figure in the stories, becomes a more fully-rounded character in the film script:

> She was a tall woman, not middle-aged and yet not far from middle age and there was about her a feeling of motherhood, of deftness, of tact and a curious womanly understanding of things she did not think about. She wore a gingham dress of faded blue sprinkled with small white flowers and a brown apron tied at the waist, along the hem of which were three broad pale yellow stripes. At her bosom there was a small cameo broach pinned neatly in. Her hair, not gray and not black but an intermixture of the two was parted in the middle and drawn back and rolled behind her head, and rolled neatly with no stray hairs escaping. (RP script 6)

Fred Tiflin also becomes a far more substantial character in the film script:

> He was a tall neat man, Frederick Tiflin, one of those men whom no dirt can soil, whose hands, emerging from a manure pile, are clean, and whose trousers after years retain some vestige of their natal crease. Dressed although he was like Billy Buck, the farm hand, in denim and shirt and jacket identical in style and age, his clothes looked new and just a little out of place on him. As awkward indeed as evening clothes would have looked on Billy Buck. And oddly enough, he too wore a leather band to protect a fancied hurt on his right wrist. He smiled slightly, touching his hair slightly to verify what he knew perfectly—that his hair was neatly combed. (*RP* script 10)

In the story cycle, Tiflin, as seen through Jody's eyes, is a rather remote and authoritarian figure. Here and there, however, he is seen through eyes that cannot be Jody's, and we are given brief glimpses of the sense of insecurity that makes him act the way he does. For example, after he has given Jody the red pony, we are told that he "went out of the barn and walked up a side-hill to be by himself, for he was embarrassed" (*LV* 211). He simply does not know how to cope with his son's gratitude, and escapes before that gratitude can be expressed. Elsewhere we are told that he "hated weakness and sickness, and he held a violent contempt for helplessness" (*LV* 225), that he "was angry and hurt" (*LV* 230), that his feelings "were badly hurt" (*LV* 235), and that he "didn't like to be cruel, but he felt he must" (*LV* 246). Jody would not have been aware of his father's embarrassment and hurt, or the motivation behind his little calculated cruelties; he would only have seen the stern face and heard the anger in his father's voice. Even at the end of "The Leader of the People," the last story of the cycle, Carl Tiflin has not changed, has not consciously mellowed in his attitude toward his son. He still resents Jody's lack of ease with him, and his son's preference for the company of Billy Buck or Grandfather.

In the narrative script, Fred Tiflin is comprehensively revealed in all his inadequacies as a man starved of the sense of brotherhood with his peers he so desperately desires. He is a man who has not found his place in the world. His sense of inferiority, his need to belong, is exemplified in the brief exchange of dialogue that takes place as he and Billy walk along the street of the town before they attend the auction:

> A couple of farm men passed them walking fast.
> They said, "How do, Billy," "Hiyah, Billy!" And they said formally, "How are you, Mr. Tiflin[?]"
> Billy and Mr. Tiflin walked on down the street and they passed another man and he said, "Hello, Billy. How do you do, Mr. Tiflin [?]"
> Frederick Tiflin turned to Billy and he said, "Do you suppose in this whole county anybody knows my first name?"
> And Billy said, "Oh sure, Mr. Tiflin. It's Fred."

And Tiflin knew that Billy didn't get his point and he agreed quietly, "Yes, it's Fred." (*RP* script 37–38)

Fred Tiflin's sense of isolation probably reaches its most painful manifestation two-thirds of the way through the script, when, having stopped Jody from going to the barn to help Billy tend the sick pony, his wife challenges and upsurps his authority by telling Jody to run along and take care of the ailing Gabilan. After that incident, Tiflin feels himself to be "surrounded by enemies" (*RP* script 114). His authority is usurped on two further occasions. When Billy, watched by Jody, performs the tracheotomy on the pony, Tiflin enters the barn and rather peremptorily tries to order his son outside. Billy turns on Tiflin angrily: "Let him alone. It's his pony, isn't it?" (*RP* script 134). Later, as has been noted, when Billy is to go to San Francisco for new stock, it is Grandfather who suggests that Jody should accompany Billy, even though it will mean his missing school, something Tiflin would not ordinarily condone for a moment. By then, however, Tiflin has become concerned over his son's unhealthy and prolonged mourning for his dead pony and the manner in which he has antagonistically distanced himself from Billy. Astonishingly, Tiflin agrees to Grandfather's suggestion: "Yes, I think Jody would be all right for the job. Another week away from school wouldn't hurt him any" (*RP* script 147).

It is only to be expected in the process of tidying up all the loose ends for the traditional happy ending that Tiflin at last receives universal acceptance and makes his peace with all and sundry, including Grandfather. When Billy is about to go to the barn to tend Rosie, the birth of the colt now imminent, Tiflin tells him to wait a moment, since he wants to come with him. Billy stops, somewhat startled, looks at his employer closely, and then says, "O.K., Fred." In the short-story cycle, Billy would never have the temerity to call Tiflin by his given name. That would have hinted at a possible relationship between employer and employee that would have been completely out of character. But in the movie it is perhaps the first step in the presumed establishment of the sort of relationship a movie audience would expect. After the two men have left for the barn, Grandfather turns to Alice and, so that there shall be no ambiguity as to the significance of the brief exchange, tells her: "I knew he'd be all right. It was just a question of time. You see, Fred was a stranger. It takes a long time to get used to something. You just ought to be patient" (*RP* script 172).

It follows that Grandfather, his role much extended, is also given a fuller characterization in the narrative script. In "The Leader of the People," he is, like all the adults, seen entirely through Jody's eyes, and is therefore understandably a somewhat idealized figure. We, as readers of the short story, can sympathize with Tiflin, however, when he grumbles about having to listen to Grandfather's word-for-word, oft-repeated stories about westering. In the script, Steinbeck's initial description of Grandfather pulls few punches and portrays him as he really is:

> Jody's grandfather sat in his cart — a mean, stringy, humorous old man, half patriarch and half vagrant, and incorrigible, a chronic complainer and a fairly large understander. His cheeks were weather-beaten and his stringy neck strong and wrinkled. His white eyebrows were quarrelsome and below his lower lip he wore a small white "zitz" — a violation of every rule of dignified whisker-wearing. His eyes were sharp and sparkling and there was just a little jauntiness about his bearing. He was dressed in a black, broadcloth suit and he wore congress gaiters and a black string tie around his short, hard collar. His black, slouch hat he carried in his hand. There was about him a good deal of dignity, although he could break out of his dignity with outrageousness. A shot gun rested between his knees and there were two dead brush rabbits on the seat beside him. (*RP* script 45)

12

While it is not intended here to discuss the 1949 movie in any detail, it has to be mentioned that there were several differences between Steinbeck's narrative script and the final shooting script, and that many of Steinbeck's telling nuances of character and dialogue fell by the wayside during the transition.[26] Indeed, to make it more acceptable for the younger audience at which it obviously became aimed, the whole story, although retaining its essential outline, was somewhat sanitized for presentation on the screen. In the process, what could have been a memorable cinematic experience became a run-of-the-mill movie, which gained neither popularity at the box office nor general critical acclaim.

There is a strong likelihood that these changes, if not supervised by Steinbeck himself, were at the very least approved by him, for he always had the greatest confidence in Milestone's taste and skill as a director. In the final analysis, however, it has to be said that Steinbeck's narrative script — in spite of tending to trivialize the great theme of Jody's progress toward maturation, and in spite of all its voluntary concession to cinematic (and more especially Hollywood) requirements — is a greater work of art than its realization on film. From a number of aspects, as a reworking of six- or seven-year-old material, it was a brief return for Steinbeck to the themes and the style of the past, a pausing for breath, as it were, before he embarked on the next stage of his literary career — not exactly, so it was to prove, in the way in which he had vaguely planned he would do, but in the way in which the imminent war was to dictate he should do.

13

Steinbeck hoped that he had at last found some stability in both his private and professional lives. The atmosphere of love and domesticity Gwyn had been weaving around him was beginning to work wonders for his emotional and artistic well-being. The two of them were happy in the Eardley Street house, but they were soon to discover that the Eden they had made there was only transitory. Carol had begun to realize more and more that the battle for her husband was lost and that perhaps the war against Gwyn could never be won. She reacted sharply, stepping up her attempts to consolidate public opinion on her side as the innocent and wronged party, and in this she had no small measure of success. Steinbeck and Gwyn felt the situation was rapidly becoming intolerable, and they decided that if Carol (as they had heard) was returning west they would escape to the East Coast.

In fact, the move east was not altogether self-motivated. Steinbeck had received what he described as "a request which amounts to a command to go to Washington for a conference" (JS/ERO 9/20/41). This call was a direct consequence of the suggestions he had made to Roosevelt the previous year for a coordinating body to rationalize and direct American propaganda. Beginning in early 1941, and following upon the success of the pilot Office of the Coordinator of Inter-American Affairs (CIAA) with its limited hemispheric brief, a series of new government agencies and departments had been created, all of which were designed to bring a comprehensive American propaganda machine onto a projected wartime footing as quickly as possible. The Division of Information, headed by Robert Horton, a former Scripps-Howard editor, had been instituted in March 1941 within the Office of Emergency Management (OEM) for the purpose of operating a central press room for the dissemination of news releases to Washington correspondents. In May 1941, Fiorella La Guardia, New York's charismatic mayor, was appointed head of the Office of Civilian Defense (OCD). In July, the Office of the Coordinator of Information (COI), with William "Wild Bill" Donovan in charge, was set up to gather intelligence and engage in "covert actions" in foreign parts. The following month, and under the umbrella of the COI, a further department, the Foreign Information Service (FIS), was created under the playwright Robert Sherwood to promote a strategy of inspirational propaganda, which eventually was to establish its most famous outlet in the "Voice of America" broadcasts beamed overseas. In the fall of 1941, the Office of Facts and Figures (OFF), a propaganda agency run by the poet Archibald MacLeish, was formed to carry out the task of boosting the morale of the American people, as well as feeding them accurate information.[27]

Steinbeck had been requested to present himself in Washington on 7 and 8 October to discuss the possibility of his taking a position within the FIS. Before he left for the east, he had little idea what such a job would entail, nor had he any way of knowing, of course, whether, following his meeting with Sherwood and his team, his services would be wanted or, indeed, if he would want to join them. Once the Washington meeting was concluded, he intended that Gwyn and he would travel on to New York. There, they would make whatever plans might then seem most desirable, always assuming they knew at that stage what Carol was intending to do. He found himself again beset by the old uncertainties, and it was probably more a case of wishful thinking on his part than anything else that prompted him to suggest to Elizabeth Otis that he might at last be able to work on and finish *The God in the Pipes* while he was in New York.

He was, at least, able to leave California, content in the knowledge that he had successfully discharged his obligations in respect to *Sea of Cortez* and *The Red Pony* script. Viking was determined to have *Sea of Cortez* published as soon as possible, and even before Steinbeck and Gwyn set out for Washington, the first galleys were arriving for his and Ricketts's attention. His collaboration with Milestone on the script was completed only a few days prior to his departure from Monterey. The two men had worked hard and well, and even though negotiations with RKO seemed to be still at a crucial stage, they were both satisfied they had produced an extremely saleable and aesthetically pleasing piece of work.

Steinbeck and Gwyn arrived in Washington on 6 October in an exhausted state, having encountered storms throughout the journey, only then to find that the capital was sweltering in a heat wave, with temperatures in the mid-90s and the atmosphere insufferably humid. Burgess Meredith had offered them the use of his farm near Suffern, New York, and they had made up their minds they would escape there as soon as they could after the two days of meetings at the FIS were completed.

According to Benson, the purpose of the meetings was to obtain ideas from people within the whole spectrum of arts and communications for possible propaganda use by the department. It is not clear whether Steinbeck was at this stage offered a paid post with the organization and turned it down, or volunteered (or was induced) to take on a series of assignments in an unpaid consultative capacity (*Adventures* 487). The likelihood is that the latter was the case, now that the history of his covert crucifixion by government and army officials obsessively suspicious of his allegiances and his motives has finally been revealed.[28] However, no decision had apparently been made in this respect when he wrote to Street on 24 October. "The organization I'll probably join up with for the war is just being drafted," he reported, "but that is not to be mentioned because it is not complete and it will probably never be very public" (JS/WFS 10/24/41).

Shortly after he arrived on the eastern seaboard, he heard from Milestone that new difficulties had already arisen with RKO over financial matters. The studio now proposed a short budget of only $275,000 for *The Red Pony*. Neither Steinbeck nor Milestone considered this anywhere near sufficient for the standard of production they had been led to anticipate and that they felt their script deserved. Steinbeck sent a telegram to the studio on 27 October, expressing in forceful terms his disappointment and disillusionment, and advising RKO that unless a deal were closed within a week, guaranteeing the production and exploitation conditions they expected, he and Milestone would withdraw from the negotiations and seek arrangements with another studio. There was no satisfactory response by the deadline, and negotiations with RKO ceased forthwith. Milestone came to New York toward the end of November to discuss with Steinbeck and his agents the details of an offer from other prospective backers willing to put up money for the film, but it appears that this proposed deal, for one reason or another, was unsatisfactory. It was not until 1948 that a contract was eventually signed with the Republic studio.

14

Steinbeck was learning the hard way that little in the film world is cut and dried. On top of all the difficulties he and Milestone were having in finding a home for *The Red Pony* script, the long-drawn-out saga of *The Forgotten Village* was still lumbering on. The film, which had been scheduled to open in New York on 16 September, was banned following a decision on 21 August by the censors of the Motion Picture Division of the State Department of Education, on the grounds that the scenes of a childbirth and of the mother nursing her baby were "indecent" and "inhuman." The film could not be shown, the censors ruled, until these offending scenes had been eliminated. The distributors protested against the ban, alleging that the sequences were the crux of the film and that to remove them would destroy the whole rationale of the picture. Steinbeck issued a statement in early September in which he stressed the damage that would be caused to international relations if the ban were enforced:

> The Mexican government has felt that this film is an honest and friendly picture not only of its people but of its efforts toward health and education. The government cooperated in every way to help in the making of the film. It is interesting that a little group of New York censors should forbid a state of many millions of people to see what one of our neighbors is like — and this on moral grounds. ... It is not good manners for us to find an honest account of Mexico "unfit to be shown." It is even a little smug.[29]

There were protests against the banning by various groups, including the Women's City Club, the National Board of Review of Motion Pictures, and the American Civil Liberties Union. Mrs. Roosevelt endorsed the film after seeing it in October. The newspapers printed letters in its support from other leading figures privileged to see it at a private screening. For all that, when the censor's ruling was reviewed by a subcommittee of the State Board of Regents, the recommendation was for the ban to be upheld. However, a subsequent meeting of the Board on 14 November overturned the subcommittee's recommendation in a very close vote, and the film was finally approved for public showing. Steinbeck wryly commented that censorship had ensured that the film "should have a little success because of the advertising it has had ... if for no other reason" (JS/WFS 10/24/41).

The film opened at the Belmont Theatre in New York on 18 November, and was greeted with excellent reviews. *The Forgotten Village* was subsequently to attain the status of a film classic after winning first prize as the best Feature Documentary at the Brussels World Film Festival in 1947. It is also included in the Brandon list of the "Ten Best" American documentaries. Despite such accolades, it has never been seen widely by the public. Denied the block booking available to the major studios, its distribution was restricted to small, independent art theaters.

15

Steinbeck returned to Washington on 16 November to confer again with the FIS people, saw a number of officials, and considered several possible projects suggested to him. It was arranged that he would write broadcasts, and early in December he paid another short visit to Washington. There was even some talk of his setting up home with Gwyn in the capital, but he was anxious to avoid this, particularly because of the acute housing shortage in the city. Instead, returning to New York, they rented a tiny apartment in the residential Bedford Hotel on East 40th Street in Manhattan.

They looked upon the "funny, small hotel" with its "pleasant room" as a haven, for they wished to maintain the pretense that they were still living out of town and to keep their whereabouts a secret except to a small circle of intimate friends. This subterfuge had become necessary partly because Steinbeck had been bombarded with a constant stream of letters addressed to him in care of his publishers, asking him to appear at various functions, including one for the benefit of Russian war relief. He refused, as he had almost invariably in the past, to have anything to do with such events, especially those of a political nature.

If he had intended to resume work on *The God in the Pipes* once he had established himself in the East, he soon abandoned the idea, for shortly after his meetings with the FIS people he became interested in the information that had been filtering through to the organization about conditions in the occupied countries of Europe. He set aside the *Pipes* play—this time it would be for good—and concentrated his energies on the more urgent subject of the war overseas and the New Order being imposed by the victorious Nazis on the conquered peoples of Norway, Denmark, Holland, Belgium, France, and now Russia. He had begun writing a new play-novel in late October, while he and Gwyn had been staying at Meredith's farm, but, as he told Covici, "it went wrong and I had to tear it down and start again" (JS/PC 10/27/41). He had set the work in an American town that had been invaded, and it had been conceived by him as a "blueprint" to the people of America, "setting forth what might be expected and what could be done about it."[30] The work had "gone wrong" because when he submitted it for approval to his superiors at the FIS they had been horrified and had rejected it out of hand. By the beginning of November, he had completed the first draft of a new version, this time set in a quasi-Norwegian town, but, on hearing it read, realized that the third act would have to be rewritten.

The play had been given the working title *The New Order*, and still bore this title when initially offered to two of Broadway's leading producers, Herman Shumlin and Oscar Serlin. Steinbeck revealed to Street that the play was about the invasion of a typical, little town, situated anywhere, which is invaded by enemy troops. The play would chronicle the reactions of ordinary men and women in the town to the invasion, as well as the feelings of the invaders themselves. "It's one of the first sensible things to be written about these things," he told Street, "and I don't know whether it is any good or not" (*SLL* 237). Whatever his formal or informal arrangements were with the FIS at that time, he was granted an extension of "leave" from his duties so that he could finish the play.

The second—and, as he imagined, final—draft of the play-novel was completed on 7 December, the day the Japanese attacked Pearl Harbor. He had found a satisfactory title for it, *The Moon Is Down*, and hoped that the play version would go into some sort of production during the coming week, the novel version having been immediately accepted by Viking for spring publication. It was not until the new year, however, that final arrangements were made for a Broadway production of the play.

16

The Moon Is Down is a concise, tightly-structured thirty-thousand-word novella that can be comfortably read at a single sitting. As Steinbeck himself observed, choosing apparently to overlook the aborted *The God in the Pipes*, the work was "a second attempt at a hybrid form of prose writing," *Of Mice and Men* being the first and, in the event, the only wholly successful attempt he was ever to achieve in the genre. In an unpublished statement, he went on to elaborate:

> It is designed to be a novel that can be played from the dialogue with description used as stage direction, or a play that is easy for the layman to read. For some reason, possibly academic, this hybridness irritates some critics. It is not a novel and not a play. For myself, I don't care what it is. The argument as to what constitutes a novel or a short story seems to me to be the province of certain critics with columns to fill. However, this short piece of fiction does set itself a job to do and does impose upon itself certain disciplines not simply as disciplines but for the purpose of letting it cut through to a larger group than read novels. It was my desire to reach as many people as possible, even those people who do not read novels.[31]

To this extent, he had even gone beyond the play-novel concept of *Of Mice and Men* by designing the work also "as a shooting script for a moving picture," with camera angles defined and close-ups indicated. "Perhaps," he admitted, "it will fail in all three through trying to be all three."[32] The cinematic qualities of the novel version are inherent in the passages with which the majority of the chapters open, for these encompass descriptions of scenes and events taking place beyond the confines of the drawing room of the Mayor's palace and Molly Morden's living room, the two stage settings in the play. Indeed, in the final analysis, *The Moon Is Down* was always potentially a more impressive movie than either a novel or a play.

In this unpublished statement can be detected the germ of the "form of the new" Steinbeck had been seeking, first mentioned in his letter to Sheffield in November 1939, and first experimented with in *The God in the Pipes*. The form, basically an adaptation and extension of the original experiment conducted in *Of Mice and Men*, proved to lead to a dead end, culminating after *The Pearl* in the unmitigated disaster of *Burning Bright*.

In its bald outline, the first draft (*The New Order*) of *The Moon Is Down* closely follows the plot of the published novel. The little coastal mining town is invaded by enemy troops. The colonel in charge of the invasion force, together with his officers, makes his headquarters in the mayor's palace. Mindful of his experiences in occupied Belgium during the last war, when the ruthless execution of hostages failed to prevent the continual militant resistance of the inhabitants, the colonel appeals to the mayor for his cooperation in encouraging the acquiescence of the townspeople to the situation. The mayor replies that he has been elected by the people, has no control over them, and will know when and how they wish him to act. A young miner kills one of the officers, is summarily tried, and executed by firing squad. Immediately, the townspeople react, passively by withdrawing into themselves, and actively by sabotaging the mine and the little railway that transports the coal to the ships in the harbor. The soldiers find themselves prisoners in the town they have conquered, oppressed by the unspoken hatred that surrounds them. Nerves begin to crack. One of the young lieutenants goes to the house of a woman in town, seeking the warmth of companionship, of love, without realizing she is the widow of the executed miner. Some of the young men of the town escape to England to carry on the fight from there, conveying with them a message from the mayor that British planes should drop small packages of dynamite to fuel active resistance. The mayor is arrested and duly executed by the invaders in a desperate attempt to end the unceasing and ever-intensifying acts of sabotage. The mayor goes to his death quoting the "Apology" of Socrates. A second or so after he is shot, another explosion is heard from the direction of the mine, a defiant proclamation that the people's collective will remains unbroken.

Despite their many similarities, there are a number of extensive and important differences between the original draft and the published book. One of the most striking aspects of the work, indeed, is the number of revisions and additions Steinbeck made before arriving at his final text. Whereas, when writing *The Grapes of Wrath*, he had been able to produce an initial text almost perfect enough to serve as the final text, he clearly encountered many more difficulties in creating this later work. One can speculate on one of the reasons why this should have been so. In writing *The Grapes of Wrath*, he had the luxury of being able to build organically on the work's predetermined narrative and emotional structures. In writing *The Moon Is Down*, on the other hand, he had imposed upon himself not only the restrictive structure of a play designed to be viewed through the proscenium arch (for all his forward-looking toward the cinematic form), but also the conventions of dramatic art, neither of which allowed him sufficient opportunity to develop character, because of the large cast he introduced.

Although the holograph manuscript of *The New Order* is in the narrative form of a novel, it is described as "A Play in 3 Acts." It is divided into seven scenes, or chapters, the first two of which comprise the first act, the next three the second act, and the last two the third act. The staged play, as subsequently published, was divided into two acts (or parts) only, the first-act curtain falling at the end of the third chapter of the manuscript (the execution of Alex Morden and the wounding of Lieutenant Prackle). Each act of the published play version is constructed of four scenes, the last two scenes of the first act covering the action contained in the third chapter of the manuscript. The eight chapters of the published novel coincide with the eight scenes of the published play.[33]

The play origin of the work seeps through occasionally into the text of the published novel in some of the descriptions of the rooms in the mayor's palace and of Molly's living room. These descriptions are of rooms as they would be seen by an audience through the proscenium arch, and contain such phrases as "the doorway to the right" (*MID* 73), "the left-hand door" (*MID* 77), and "the back wall" (*MID* 121). The artificiality of these stage directions, which have no place in a novel, was originally compounded on page 19 of the holograph manuscript by a blatant authorial interpolation omitted from the published text. Toward the end of the passage on page 44 of the novel, describing Captain Loft (named Lunt in the manuscript), Steinbeck had originally written:

> Captain Lunt believed that all women fall in love with a uniform and he didn't see how it could be otherwise. If this story had not been written he would have been a brigadier general at forty-five and had his picture in many illustrated papers, flanked by tall, pale, masculine women in lacy picture hats. But we kill him in the second act with a very unmilitary weapon and bury him without bugles. (*NO* 19)[34]

It is, of course, not Loft but Captain Bentick, the lover of the English way of life, who, later in the same chapter and not in the second "act," is killed by Alex Morden's pick. On page 36 of the holograph manuscript, Steinbeck does, in fact, initially have Lunt/Loft as the victim of Alex's attack, and Bentick as the officer who supervises the return of the body to the palace and reports the details of the incident to the colonel. The passage, as originally written, was scored out by Steinbeck and substituted by a new passage on the reverse of the previous page, with Bentick as the murdered officer.

The holograph text of *The New Order* displays many of the hallmarks of Steinbeck's work. It is, for example, a remarkably clean manuscript, like that of *The Grapes of Wrath*, with a minimum of additions or minor emendations. The revision mentioned in the preceding paragraph is one of only two revisions comprising more than just a few words. Perhaps most significant in the context of this particular manuscript, there is a gradual quickening of narrative pace and thinning of content in the latter part of the work. This can be seen as indicative not only of Steinbeck's apparent growing impatience to bring the work to conclusion, but also of the undoubted external pressures exerted on him to do so. Whereas the first three chapters of the draft are 17, 20, and 18 pages respectively in length, the last four chapters are only 12, 24, 11, and 8 pages long. In a novel this disparity in narrative pace may not be of excessive importance, but within the intended structure of a play it becomes a fairly crucial factor. It was one Steinbeck soon realized, and, although he revised and expanded his original text quite extensively throughout, the later chapters were much more heavily revised than the earlier ones. By the time he had arrived at a satisfactory first typescript (although this time it was by no means a final text), he had already thrown out large sections of the fifth and seventh chapters of the holograph draft (Chapters 6 and 8 in the published book) and substituted new extended texts, with certain plot changes, to balance the overall structure of the work and to build up to and strengthen its final, emotional scene.

There are many instances in which Steinbeck filled out the narrative following the completion of the first draft. Some of the revisions and additions, as noted, were incorporated into the first typescript, but many more were introduced at a later date. For example, the preliminary inspection of the palace rooms by Captain Bentick in the first chapter of *The Moon Is Down*, and his conversation with Dr. Winter, during which he makes known to the doctor the extent of Mr. Corell's treachery, does not appear in the first draft. The colonel simply presents himself without any preliminary action being taken by his officers to ensure that the necessary protocol be observed and precautionary measures taken for his safety. This would not have happened in real life, as Steinbeck obviously realized, or was advised. Also, Corell does not appear in the first chapter of *The New Order*. In fact, the Corell role in the narrative was greatly expanded by Steinbeck during the course of his subsequent revisions. In the first draft, Corell's one and only appearance is in the second chapter, as in Chapter 2 of *The Moon Is Down*. He makes no appearance in the penultimate chapter (Chapter 7 of *The Moon Is Down*), where, in the published text, he asserts his newfound authority over the colonel. In *The New Order*, Corell apparently perishes at the hands of the Anders boys, and the colonel receives his instructions to take the mayor hostage directly from the capital.

In *The Moon Is Down*, it is Lieutenant Prackle who is in charge of the firing squad that executes Mayor Orden. In *The New Order* this duty is carried out by Lieutenant Tonder, who, prior to the radical changes Steinbeck made to the nocturnal events in Molly Morden's house two chapters earlier, has not fallen victim to her scissors. In *The Moon Is Down* the sequence of events in Chapter 6 has become rather complicated. Tonder arrives at the house first and endeavors to make love to her. To get rid of him, she reveals who she is—the widow of the man executed for killing Captain Bentick—and Tonder, unable for the moment to deal with the situation, quietly leaves, but not before asking her if he may return. Then Annie arrives, preparing the entry of Mayor Orden and Dr. Winter, together with the two Anders boys, who are planning to escape that night by fishing boat to England. Tonder returns while they are still in the house, and hurriedly and in some confusion they depart by the back way. Molly opens the front door, a pair of scissors behind her back, and lets Tonder in.

In *The New Order*, however, there is no preliminary visit by Tonder. He calls while the little clandestine gathering is still in progress, and Orden, Winter, Annie, and the two Anders boys hide in the kitchen, while Molly opens the front door to the lieutenant, hoping to get rid of him quickly. There then follows between Molly and Tonder more or less the same dialogue they exchanged during his first visit in the book, but the outcome is entirely different. Molly does not reveal her identity, and Tonder is persistent in his advances. All the time, Molly is conscious of the need not only to protect her friends hiding in the kitchen but also of the necessity of the Anders brothers not to delay their departure by sea. She therefore accepts Tonder into her bedroom, allowing the others to make good their escape through the front door.

Molly and Tonder meet once again in the final chapter of *The New Order*. Molly has come to the mayor's palace to be with Madame during her ordeal. Tonder comes into the room while she is sitting at the big table, trying to comfort Madame.

> Suddenly Tonder's eyes fell on Molly and he was startled. "What are you doing here?" he demanded.
> She said, "I came to be with Madame." And she said fiercely, "She stayed with me when you killed *my* husband."
> "How could you———?"
> She smiled and caught him up. "I told you we humans were versatile," she said. "Your people have never known it and so they have always lost their wars."
> Madame said, "What is he saying, Molly dear?"
> "Nothing, Madame, nothing," and she put her arms around Madame's shoulders. Tonder went back to the door and he stayed inside the room and his eyes were full of young terror. (*NO* 96)

Not only does Tonder survive (at least, for the time being) in *The New Order*, but some of the dialogue attributed to him in the manuscript is transferred to Prackle in the published version, most extensively during the discussion between the officers on pages 110—19 of *The Moon Is Down*. In *The New Order*, it is Prackle who becomes hysterical and originates the vivid analogy of the flies conquering the flypaper. Whereas in *The Moon Is Down* Tonder appears as a romantic virgin, the manuscript presents a somewhat different picture of him, for Tonder, it seems, "had wooed and won a beautiful if smelly waif and was still taking injections of salvarsan" (*NO* 20). In the published version, we are told that Tonder is in the habit of imagining for himself a glorious death in battle, and that, in his mind, had even rehearsed the words he would utter as he expired. But we are not told what these are. In the manuscript, the outcome of his fantasies are recorded in full:

"Leader," he would gasp. "Tell the Leader, I have given — my promised gift to him." And then Tonder's beautiful young head fell sideways and he was gone and the scene shifted to the Leader, stern but inwardly shaken with sobs. (*NO* 20–21)

It is clear from a comparison of the texts of the novel and of the play just how extensive were the revisions Steinbeck carried out after the novel version of *The Moon Is Down* had been rushed into print. In the course of this revision, he made Colonel Lanser a marginally harsher character, as, for example, the final exchange between him and Orden and Winter demonstrates. In the novel, following Orden's observation that, while herd men win battles, free men win wars, Lanser replies: "My orders are clear. Eleven o'clock was the deadline. I have taken hostages. If there is violence, the hostages will be executed." Winter then asks him: "Will you carry out the orders, knowing they will fail?" Lanser tells him: "I will carry out my orders no matter what they are," and concludes by making one last plea to Orden to cooperate so that further bloodshed may be avoided: "I do think, sir, a proclamation from you might save many lives" (*MID* 186).

In the play version, the tone of the exchange has been subtly altered. "My orders are clear," Lanser says. "Eleven o'clock is the deadline. I have taken *my* hostages. If there is violence *I will* execute them" [italics added]. Winter's reply too has a different emphasis. It is no longer a question, however rhetorical by implication, seeking response from a man who might be persuaded to see reason, but a statement that recognizes that reason has been jettisoned in the cause of military expediency. Winter says: "And you will carry out the orders, knowing they will fail." Lanser answers: "I will carry out my orders" (*MID* play. 99).

If the novel version of *The Moon Is Down* is artistically an improvement over *The New Order*, the play version is, to some extent, aesthetically also an improvement over the novel. Steinbeck himself was to recognize and admit the problem eight years later while he was working on the third of the play-novels, *Burning Bright*. "There is one disadvantage to the play-novel form," he told Covici. "The novel has to go to press and stay that way but little changes take place in the play right up to opening night" (*SLL* 404–5).

While there is no way of knowing for sure, one can speculate that Steinbeck may retrospectively have regretted releasing the novel text so readily to his agents and publishers before tackling the task of preparing the work for stage production. Not only might much of the dialogue in the novel been more convincing, but he might also have avoided some of the criticism that was to be directed against his portrayal of Lanser.

On the other hand, had there not been a stage version to prepare, it is doubtful if he would have taken time to revise the text of the novel. The rewriting for the stage was a process he obviously found something of a chore, imposed on him by unavoidable circumstance and influenced by the requirements of the play's director and its actors. However, the revisons he did introduce during the gestation of the play, while making the dialogue more convincing and his thesis more persuasive, did not unfortunately make the work more dramatically viable overall to any appreciable degree. Had these revisions been introduced into the novel, it is just possible that they might have improved the novel's effectiveness; but the intrinsic failure of the work in its two versions can be seen to have been inherent in its fundamental concept. It fails as a novel in its insistence in observing the requirements of drama, and it fails as a play because it is too literary.

The failure, however, goes even beyond that. To begin with, it should be recalled that many of the most successful of Steinbeck's previous novels — *Tortilla Flat*, *In Dubious Battle*, and *The Grapes of Wrath* — had been well-researched books and had been building up in his mind over a long period before he even put pen to paper. *The Moon Is Down*, on the other hand, was obviously written almost on impulse, a burning need to make some solid contribution to the allied war effort, and after the briefest of contacts with materials he had examined at the FIS offices. Also, as the dust jacket of the book noted, *The Moon Is Down* was the first of Steinbeck's novels since *Cup of Gold* in which he wrote about people and locations outside his own experience. It shows. As a 1947 critic observed:

> [T]he essential quality is so indigenously American, in characterization, physical setting, and mind and emotion, that anything of his which strives to deal with other lands suffers from the absence of the soil that nourishes his writing and gives it its spirit.[35]

Not even the trick of studiously omitting to specify the actual setting or nationalities involved could save the work, for it was patently obvious from the beginning that Steinbeck was writing about the Nazi invasion of Norway — even though the timings of the fictive and actual events do not correspond — and the deliberate conversion of the work into a sort of allegory did not make its basic artificiality any more acceptable.[36]

Not only is there the failure to create believable flesh-and-blood characters, but there is also an intermittent failure of language, a fault that had been present, but to a far-less-apparent degree, in Steinbeck's previous work. Here, in this more formalized work, it becomes uncomfortably intrusive. There is, for example, an increasing use of the unspecific noun "thing," that swift and convenient substitute in conversation that should be avoided so far as possible in prose, if it is not to suggest a lack of vocabulary. There is, too, an abundance of such words as "quiet," "quietly," "softly," "wearily," and, with the coming of snow, "muffled" — words that, while emphasizing the undercurrent of violence implicit throughout the novel, become overrepetitive and in the end hardly meaningful. In the same way, there is an emphasis on the adjective "little" in all manner of contexts (descriptions of objects, degrees of emotion, etc.) that seems to overelaborate the subliminal analogy of David pitted against Goliath.

There is, furthermore, as John Timmerman has observed, a failure of stylistic technique, in which "repetitively short sentences seem more like a recording from someone bored with his own work." Timmerman's quantitative rhetorical analysis of Chapter 5 of the book illustrates that the rhetorical structures "are virtually the same in length and pattern."[37] Timmerman's choice in selecting Chapter 5 for this analysis is possibly unfortunate, for the opening paragraphs (describing the first winter of the occupation) are admirably suited to this stylistic treatment. Here, if not always elsewhere in the work, Steinbeck's touch is sure. The slow, inevitable pace of the prose transmits the sense of dragging time, and with its measured consistency of tempo builds toward the scene in which the approaching final breakdown of morale among the occupying troops is made manifest in Lieutenant Tonder's hysterical outburst that the flies have conquered the flypaper.[38] Nevertheless, for the most part Timmerman's criticism holds good in a consideration of the work as a whole. The rhetorical prose style tends to become ultimately monotonous and would be unacceptable in a longer work.

Pursuing his general criticism of Steinbeck's stylistic technique, Timmerman notes the frequency with which sentences begin with the conjunction "And." This psuedo-Biblical mode is a recurring feature of all Steinbeck's original holograph drafts. Employed sparingly, it can be effective in maintaining prose rhythms, but used promiscuously, as here, it becomes merely an irritating mannerism.[39] Significantly perhaps, *The Moon Is Down* was the first of Steinbeck's novels subsequent to *Cup of Gold* not to have been initially edited by Carol. On previous evidence, it is possible that with Carol's judicious weeding of the text, few of those "Ands" would have survived into the first typescript.

Richard Astro has proposed that one of the reasons for the comparative failure of *The Moon Is Down* is that at the time he wrote the book Steinbeck was "still immersed in the Ricketts material he used in shaping the narrative portion of *Sea of Cortez*," and that it was not until his next books that he "deliberately decided to detach himself from Ricketts's person and ideas."[40] To what extent this is true is debatable. Although Dr. Winter is patently a Ricketts figure, the thematic content of *The Moon Is Down* suggests that in many respects, rather than being swamped by Ricketts's thinking, Steinbeck was already beginning in this book to distance himself from, even reject, certain major areas of Ricketts's philosophy, having probably concluded that in the context of war they could no longer be morally sustained.

It is doubtful if Steinbeck ever was a wholehearted subscriber to non-teleological thinking. The disagreement he had with Ricketts over the thematic and philosophical content of *The Forgotten Village* confirms this view. In *The Moon Is Down*, neither the invaders nor the townspeople can be said to represent humans governed by nonteleological concepts. If they did, then the invaders would never have planned the invasion, and the townspeople, certainly after awakening from their brief initial period of confusion, would never have acquired their dedicated determination to free themselves from the bonds of their oppressors. The townspeople's campaign to throw off the yoke of the invader has an analogy with the battle waged by the doctors in *The Forgotten Village* to change the status quo and eradicate disease in the Mexican villages. In prosecuting a war, as in conducting medical research, there is no place for nonteleological thinking.

Phalanx behavior, on the other hand, does have a relevance in the context of war. War madness affects whole communities, whole nations, as Steinbeck was to demonstrate in Chapter 46 of *East of Eden*, written out of his recollections of boyhood in Salinas during World War I. In exactly the same way, blood lust infects the lynch mobs in "The Vigilante" and the unpublished short story "Case History."[41] The phalanx theory was not a new concept to which Steinbeck had been exclusively introduced by Ricketts. It exists, admittedly in a rudimentary form, in *Cup of Gold*, written some years before he met Ricketts. In that novel, there is a description of Henry Morgan's expeditionary force thrusting its way through the jungle toward the prize of Panama: "At a command, the head of the wriggling column swung to the left and began to gnaw its way through thicker underbrush."[42] The image was to be repeated in "The Leader of the People," written after Steinbeck met Ricketts. Grandfather is telling Jody about the pioneers who crossed the continent during the previous century:

> It was a whole bunch of people made into one big crawling beast. And I was the head. It was westering and westering. Every man wanted something for himself, but the big beast that was all of them wanted only westering.[43]

This unstoppable urge to discover and take over new territory has its parallel of sorts in Dr. Winter's description of the "time-minded people" (the invaders) who "hurry toward their destiny as though it would not wait. They push the rolling world along with their shoulders" (*MID* 15).

This latter image immediately and inevitably conjures up, as Steinbeck clearly intended, the idea of lemmings on their self-destructive and seemingly purposeless headlong rush to the sea. Indeed, Grandfather's nineteenth-century trailblazers end their lives in a sort of death when they reach the Pacific and become reduced from heroic figures to "a line of old men along the shore hating the ocean because it stopped them."[44] In the same way, Steinbeck implies in *The Moon Is Down*, the invaders will ultimately suffer the death of defeat. As Winter observes toward the end of the book, the time of the invaders

> is nearly up. They think that just because they have only one leader and one head, we are all like that. They know that ten heads lopped off will destroy them, but we are a free people; we have as many heads as we have people, and in time of need leaders pop up among us like mushrooms. (*MID* 175)

Orden himself, on the brink of violent death, carries the thesis one step further when he addresses himself for the last time to Colonel Lanser:

> The people don't like to be conquered, sir, and so they will not be. Free men cannot start a war, but once it is started, they can fight on in defeat. Herd men, followers of a leader, cannot do that, and so it is always the herd men who win battles and the free men who win wars. (*MID* 185–86)

While reading *The Moon Is Down*, one gets the impression that Steinbeck is attempting to preserve some vestiges of the "group man" philosophy in the war context by introducing this additional idea of "herd man." The distinction between the two concepts is, it must be said, in many respects tenuous. There is, of course, a relationship of sorts between group man and herd man and nonteleological thinking, in that group man and herd man are both controlling collective organisms created from myriad units, each of which has relinguished control over his individual destiny by allowing his individual psyche to assume the character of the collective group or herd psyche. However, what Steinbeck seems to be implying through his mouthpieces, Winter and Orden, is that, while admittedly losing his identity when he becomes part of group man (as distinct from herd man), the human unit nevertheless retains the ultimate choice and ability to opt out of the collective psyche and regain his own individuality, as Mike does in "The Vigilante." Herd man, on the other hand, is completely dominated by the leader, who alone represents the collective psyche, and because of this the human unit possesses neither the freedom nor the initiative to opt out before the herd perpetuates its own destruction. This, as Steinbeck knew, is a convenient, if rather simplistic and not altogether convincing, propaganda message; but it was a message he felt bound to convey and perhaps at the time wanted to believe in himself. At any rate, Orden's farewell warning to Lanser provided a comforting line of thought to be pondered over by all those who were waging war from the shadows against a ruthless, single-minded, and seemingly invincible enemy.

17

In an obvious attempt to drum up a more universal interest in *Sea of Cortez*, on 12 November Viking had made a prepublication release to book reviewers of Steinbeck's narrative, on the basis that "this advance section contains the material which will be most interesting to the general public and which the literary reviewer (as opposed to the scientific) will undoubtedly give most attention." In anticipation of the principal question that would arise in the minds of most reviewers, the accompanying Viking handout explained that Steinbeck and Ricketts had "worked in close cooperation," and that "all sections of the book bear the imprint of both." The handout concluded: "Steinbeck, however, is a writer and Ricketts is a scientist, so each man was in turn the dominant partner in the section corresponding to his special talents."[45]

Publication day had been fixed for 5 December to catch the Christmas trade, but no worse timing could have been imagined, for when the first reviews — in Steinbeck's opinion, "extremely good and lively" (*SLL* 238) — appeared on Sunday, 7 December, the reading public had other, more momentous, matters to occupy its mind.

One of the other factors against its success was surely its price: a hefty (for those days) five dollars. Ricketts, in fact, suggested the following year that a new edition containing only the narrative should be issued, at a more attractive price. For one reason or another, the idea never got off the ground, and it was not until 1951, three years after Ricketts's death, that the narrative was published separately under the title *The Log from the Sea of Cortez* with Steinbeck's sixty-seven-page memoir of Ricketts as an introduction to the book.

As had been expected, the question of the authorship of the various parts of the book exercised the minds of most reviewers. "You aren't allowed to know who wrote which line," Charles Poore complained in the *New York Times*, but he concluded:

Mr. Steinbeck and Mr. Ricketts have written one of the most unusual books of the year, and their publishers deserve some praise for having given it such an effective embodiment. Putting all this material together coherently must have seemed, in the early stages, only slightly less difficult than building Boulder Dam.[46]

In a long *New Republic* review, Stanley Edgar Hyman noted that Edmund Wilson's observation that Steinbeck presented life in animal terms seemed to find confirmation in the pages of *Sea of Cortez*,[47] but then went on to suggest that while the animal symbols and images had a definite function in Steinbeck's fiction, they were "just the simplest examples, not of man, but of the problem that concerns the author most, the problem of ecology, in which man is only a more complex example." He recognized Steinbeck as being primarily an ecologist, and maintained that all Steinbeck's books were ecological studies.[48] R. L. Duffus in the *New York Times Book Review* asked, "Was this project of a literary and scientific consolidation a success?" His verdict was that he did not think it entirely was, and he summed up his overall feelings thus: "If the book is in any sense a failure it is an admirable one. Mr. Steinbeck's novels will be better for the experience."[49]

It was a great tragedy for both Steinbeck and Ricketts that, appearing at the time it did, *Sea of Cortez* failed to attract the attention it deserved. In the shadow of momentous national and international events, the book simply did not capture the imagination of the general reader, who wanted not a "leisurely journal of travel and research" but exactly what Steinbeck's agents and publishers had been desperately waiting for — another novel. As it transpired, the new novel was already in Viking's hands and the general reader had only three more months to wait for it. Although *The Moon Is Down* was a pale successor to *The Grapes of Wrath*, it inevitably succeeded, as *Sea of Cortez* had not, in catching the mood of the times, and while, like *The Grapes of Wrath*, it was to attract a great deal of opposition from some quarters, it proved to be in many ways an even greater popular success than had been the saga of the Joads.

18

What Steinbeck and so many others had, for years, seen as inevitable had at last come about. The nation was at war. He possibly felt, and in America he was not alone in this, a certain sense of relief that the long period of waiting was over, that now there could be no more doubt or prevarication. He saw his patriotic commitment clearly, and was ready to devote himself unequivocally to the service of his country by direct action as a member of the armed forces, or by carrying out whatever job the government saw fit to give him that would employ his talents to the best possible advantage in the prosecution of the coming conflict.

Back in Monterey, Carol was stirring up as much trouble as she could and threatening, among other things, to take over the Eardley Street house so as to deprive her rival of the home she had made there. Carol was in fact acting so erratically and vindictively that even Ed Ricketts, who had always attempted to assume a neutral stance, felt bound to write to Steinbeck and warn him it was obvious that Carol was set on hurting him and Gwyn by fair means or foul.

Steinbeck and Gwyn traveled by train to New Orleans for the Christmas and New Year holiday period. He took the first proofs of *The Moon Is Down* with him to work on during the journey. It was a bumpy and jerky ride and, when he sent the proofs back to Covici on Christmas Eve, he apologized for the "shaky" corrections. They stayed initially at the Roosevelt Hotel on Baronne Street, and then, having to give up their room owing to a prior booking, became the house guests of the writer Roark Bradford, author of *Ol' Man Adam an' His Chillun*.

On New Year's Eve, relaxing in Bradford's French Quarter home, Steinbeck must have reflected on the past year with very mixed feelings. But whatever he felt about the mess of his private life and his ultimate failure to complete *The God in the Pipes*, he must also have felt a sense of deep satisfaction at the thought of all the work he had accomplished during the year: the·final realization of the film *The Forgotten Village*, the composition of the narrative section of *Sea of Cortez*, the creation of *The Red Pony* film script, and last, but not least, the writing of the new play-novel *The Moon Is Down*. Yes, it had been an exhausting year, but after the comparative artistic sterility of 1940 it had also been an exceedingly rich one. He could surely now feel himself on course again, his objectives, with Gwyn at his side, clear and inviting.

5

1942: In Limbo

1

Steinbeck and Gwyn returned by train from New Orleans to New York on 7 January. Roark Bradford and his wife had made them most welcome, and the two weeks of rest had recharged Steinbeck's batteries. It was only then that he realized how exhausted the events of the past twelve months or so had left him before the Christmas holiday.

As a temporary measure, they again took a room at the Bedford Hotel while he waited to discover what assignment, if any, the FIS had planned for him. He had heard nothing from Washington for several weeks. He was, however, thankful for the breathing space, for, on arriving back in New York, he had immediately become embroiled in matters relating to the possible production of the new play. Herman Shumlin, who had rejected *Of Mice and Men* in 1937, proved to be also unimpressed by *The Moon Is Down* in the form Steinbeck had written it, and had indicated he would have preferred an entirely different sort of play. Oscar Serlin, on the other hand, expressed his eagerness to produce it. The intention was that the play be presented on Broadway within the next six to eight weeks. In the meantime, Viking was pressing ahead with its plans to publish the novel version by the end of February or the beginning of March.

Steinbeck did not have, as he had had five years earlier with *Of Mice and Men*, the expertise of George S. Kaufman to help him prepare the work for stage presentation. Instead, he acquired the professional assistance of his contemporary Lee Strasberg, the actor, director, and teacher who in 1931 had been one of the cofounders of the influential Group Theatre and who in 1948 was to become director of the equally influential Actors Studio. Strasberg called daily at the Bedford, and he and Steinbeck went carefully over the script, scene by scene, testing lines and even individual words, to ensure not only that the maximum dramatic effect was achieved but that the dialogue was as perfect as possible for the actors who had to deliver it. This was not the sort of work Steinbeck could ever be happy with. Not only was it another form of collaboration, but he soon found the going over and over of the same material extremely tedious. This time, however, he could not, as he had been able to do with Kaufman, opt out and leave Strasberg to finish the job for him. Casting began early in February, and the first rehearsals had commenced by the middle of the month.

He was becoming increasingly irked by the apparent lack of interest the FIS was showing toward his offered services, and it was not long before the welcome breathing space became transformed into a delay that caused him intense irritation and frustration. Washington's failure to assign him to a specific appointment, while at the same time refusing to release him to take up other work, meant that he was having to turn down some interesting and possibly lucrative jobs that had been offered him. He complained to Street that the past year had in many ways been wasted, although he conceded that nevertheless he had managed to complete a great deal of work.

It was contemplation of his future financial situation that was causing him most disquiet. He had convinced himself that his days as a big money-earning author were probably over. *Sea of Cortez* was selling very slowly. The projected movie of *The Red Pony* had, it seemed, been shelved, perhaps indefinitely. Whatever income he might earn from the novel and the play versions of *The Moon Is Down* would, he predicted, be more or less swallowed up in meeting his income tax bill for the coming year. He knew that even if he were eventually given a worthwhile assignment by the FIS, it was unlikely he would receive any salary, and much would therefore depend on the free time he had available to pursue his professional career.

While his immediate monetary prospects seemed by no means rosy, he was still determined to honor his financial commitment to Carol. To this end, he asked Street, who knew more about his finances than anyone else, himself not excepted, to act as Carol's attorney in the impending divorce proceedings in California. Uncomfortably aware now of the hatred Carol obviously felt toward him, he kept closely in touch with Street, monitoring the direction of Carol's sometimes irrational demands and accusations. He accepted that he had been cruel to her, both physically and mentally, and she had reciprocated in like manner, neither of them apparently being able to prevent the hurt they were causing each other. There was on his part a deep sadness that their marriage, which had been fruitful in so many ways and which represented "a good big slice" of his life (*SLL* 243), had gone bad and was soon to be legally terminated. His emotional restlessness and insistent feelings of guilt rubbed off on Gwyn, who feared he was beginning to regret his decision to divorce Carol. Gwyn was very conscious of her own uncertain status as the third side of the triangle. The continuing instability of living constantly out of suitcases, of not being settled in a home of her own, did not make the situation any easier for her. Perhaps it was because of this that she felt it necessary to write to Street on 24 February, reaffirming her feelings for Steinbeck.

In spite of his gloomy predictions, it soon became evident that Steinbeck's big-earning days were by no means behind him. Covici reported that prepublication sales of the new novel were double those of *The Grapes of Wrath*. A prepublication sale of eighty-five thousand copies in the trade edition was forecast, and on top of that the Book of the Month Club had ordered two hundred thousand copies. "It is kind of crazy," Steinbeck commented (*SLL* 242).

2

The Moon Is Down was published on 6 March. The blurb on the back of the dust jacket noted:

'The scene of the book is any conquered country in any time. The author has purposely refrained from making it literally true to actual events. Although the weapons and ideologies may be of the present, they are only vehicles for the theme that a free brave people is unconquerable.'[1]

Nobody, of course, was fooled by the deliberate vagueness: the conquered country depicted in the book was patently Norway and the invaders patently soldiers of Hitler's Third Reich. In the main, the reviews were favorable, often glowingly so, but certain nonliterary aspects of the book became the subject of violent controversy.

The first inkling of the storm to come surfaced the day after the book was published. In his review in the *New Yorker*, Clifton Fadiman declared that the message of the book was "inadequate" and represented "a melodramatic simplification of the issues involved."[2] The real attack, however, came in the 16 March issue of the *New Republic*. In a dismissive review, James Thurber asserted that the book needed "more guts and less moon." He carried his argument further:

The point upon which Mr. Steinbeck in these pages has so lovingly and gently brooded is that there are no machines and no armies mighty enough to conquer the people. "The people don't like to be conquered, sir," says Mayor Orden to Colonel Lanser, "and so they will not be." This shining theme is restated a great many times. ...

At one point in *The Moon Is Down* the little people of the little town are aided by the falling of a curious manna from Heaven: small blue parachutes come drifting to earth, carrying dynamite and chocolate. The little children of the conquered town go hunting for the candy with as much excitement as if they were searching for Easter eggs. The Steinbeck story will make a very pretty movie.

I keep wondering what the people of Poland would make of it all.[3]

Thurber's review initiated a flood of correspondence to the editors of the *New Republic*, most of the published letters either questioning or condemning Steinbeck's portrayal of the Nazis and the basic premise the book advanced. A letter from Marshall A. Best, Viking's senior editor, suggesting that the review had been "a slap in the face for all the decent people who had been moved by the book's shining sincerity" and that "Thurber's is the sort of softy cynicism that might yet lose us the war,"[4] drew an instant response from Thurber. He predicted that Best would most likely live "to see more letters protesting against Mr. Steinbeck's gentle fable of War in Wonderland, not only from Poles who have endured German conquest, but from Jugoslavs, Greeks, French, Dutch and all the rest." He added: "Mr. Best is quite right when he says we might yet lose the war. Nothing would help more toward that end than for Americans to believe Steinbeck's version of Nazi conquest instead of its true story of hell, horror and hopelessness."[5]

On 4 April, Fadiman launched a further attack in the *New Yorker*, recording that, following several objections to his March 7 review, he had, "in a mood of acute self-distrust," reread the book and, having done so, had not changed his opinion that it was nothing more than "brilliantly manipulated melodrama, the effect of whose propaganda is at least debatable."[6]

In a letter to Street, written the same day that Fadiman's second review appeared, Steinbeck gave his immediate and forthright reaction:

Isn't Fadiman's stuff in the New Yorker nonsense. I would like to answer it except that I do not believe in answering a reviewer. But his theory of a stock nazi is absurd and the Hitler stock Jew and he should be told that and in print. Why, if all Germans are alike, do so many Generals die of pneumonia and if the General officers do not see eye to eye with the new order there must be their counterparts in the arm[y] other places and among the people. I am sick of the frightened fuzzy thinking of the Fadimans and the Thurbers. They act hysterically afraid. (JS/WFS 4/4/42)

While the *New Republic* did publish some letters, in addition to Marshall Best's, in support of the book, the general drift of comment in the magazine's columns (including the editorials) continued to be mostly unfavorable. Of three letters that appeared on 4 May, one expressed the fear that the campaign being waged against *The Moon Is Down* smacked of an attempt to control the ideas explicated through literature in the United States. The two other letters, one by a Frenchman and the other by a Norwegian, were again fiercely critical of Steinbeck's portrayal of the Nazis. The Frenchman referred to "Mr. Steinbeck's sugar candy" and to his "moonshine," and offered an explanation for the book's undoubted success in that it answered "a demand — the public's desire to be told by a famous writer that things are, after all, as they would like them to be."

The Norwegian correspondent insisted that those of his fellow-countrymen with whom he had discussed the book felt that Steinbeck's characterization of the Germans *per se* was "wide of the mark," and that they were in reality tough, brutal, cynical, and ignorant men with a fine flair for perversion and sadism." On the other hand, the writer did consider that Steinbeck had portrayed the heroic resistance of the Norwegian people "with great understanding," believing that "the kind of opposition rendered by the people of Norway against the powers of occupation is a concrete contribution to the winning of the war."[7]

Steinbeck's wish that Fadiman should be reprimanded in print was soon to be granted, when John Chamberlain, in the *New York Times*, discussed Fadiman's introduction to a new edition of Tolstoy's *War and Peace*. Chamberlain pointed out that Fadiman wrote that Tolstoy brought out the eternally normal in human beings, and quoted from Fadiman's introduction: "[Tolstoy] would say that human nature is a constant, that it will rise to the surface despite all the deformation, the drill, the conditioning, the dehumanizing, to which it may be subjected." That, Chamberlain insisted, "is exactly what Steinbeck is trying to say in *The Moon Is Down*. ... In rapping Steinbeck over the knuckles for treating the Germans in the ranks as human beings who have been led astray by the Berlin popinjay, Mr. Fadiman is setting up a double standard for criticism."[8]

If Steinbeck was understandably somewhat irked, if not angered, by the derisive and misguided slurs directed at *The Moon Is Down*, he would have been immensely delighted, and to a degree mollified, to know how seriously the ideas expressed in the book were being taken by those responsible for the overall prosecution of the war. No less a personage than the British Prime Minister, Winston S. Churchill, had read *The Moon Is Down*, considered it "a well-written story," and, in a memorandum dated 27 May 1942 to his Minister of Economic Warfare, pointed out how the book stressed the importance of smuggling arms and explosives to the resistance fighters in the occupied countries.[9]

As a work of literature, as opposed to propaganda, *The Moon Is Down* was roundly praised by the majority of contemporary reviewers, one of whom regarded it as "much the best thing Steinbeck has done so far, and written with a restraint he seemed incapable of in his earlier books."[10] John Gunther summed up his review in the *New York Herald Tribune Books* with the declaration: "It is one of the best short novels I ever read,"[11] and Norman Cousins, in the *Saturday Review*, called the book "a unique reading experience," observing that Steinbeck "tells his story with simplicity, force, dignity, and even beauty," with images that "are strong and closely knit."[12] In the other camp, Margaret Marshall, writing in *The Nation*, felt that the method Steinbeck had adopted for the telling of his story — "studied understatement, simple, unaccentuated language, matter-of-fact tone" — failed to match the "important, timely, universal" theme of the book.[13]

In a long essay in the *Antioch Review*, during which he surveyed Steinbeck's career to date, Stanley Edgar Hyman regretted Steinbeck's apparent reversal in *The Moon Is Down* from the objective scientific viewpoint to which he had advanced in *Sea of Cortez*, returning to the sociality and sentimentality of his earlier books. Hyman, it would seem, had fallen marginally into the trap he had previously warned others against in his review of the earlier book of not blindly assuming that the ideas and theses explicated in that book were necessarily Steinbeck's alone. Hyman concluded his essay by expressing the hope, even though he considered "the noticeable commercialism" of *The Moon Is Down* made it highly unlikely, that Steinbeck might go on "to greater and more directed writing than he has ever achieved."[14]

3

Today, a half-century later, with wartime passions long since spent, we can regard *The Moon Is Down* with a more objective eye and accord the work its true place in the Steinbeck canon. Time, it seems, has for the most part exonerated Steinbeck from the charges made against him by Thurber and Fadiman and others for his imagined account of life under the Nazi New Order. Donald V. Coers's *John Steinbeck as Propagandist: THE MOON IS DOWN Goes to War* (1991) tells the whole story of how the novel boosted the morale of the peoples of the occupied countries when copies of the book began circulating and they realized that they had not been forgotten by the free world, that a great American writer had written so passionately about their plight and their courage in facing their ordeal. In Scandinavia, the novel was first published in Sweden and several thousand copies in Norwegian translation were smuggled across the frontier in the fall of 1942. These copies were widely circulated in Norway, and more often than not ended up "completely tattered by constant use."[15] A further edition, in a new translation, again smuggled out of Sweden, became available in 1945, and went through two editions of ten thousand copies. Additionally, the text was copied and mimeographed or printed on small hand presses in Denmark, Holland, and France. "The Germans did not consider [the book] unrealistic optimism," Steinbeck observed in 1963. "They made it a capital crime to possess it, and sadly to my knowledge this sentence was carried out a number of times. It seemed that the closer it got to action, the less romantic it seemed."[16]

Virtually every occupied country had its own translation circulating by the time of the Allied landings in Normandy in June 1944. In November 1946, Steinbeck was invited to Oslo, where he was awarded the Haakon VII Cross for the account he had given of Norwegian resistance during the war. Although Steinbeck maintained that the awarding of medals and decorations had always seemed to him "a kind of vanity that doesn't touch me," he confessed in 1963 that the Haakon VII Cross, the Norwegian king's personal medal and normally only conferred on patriots in the resistance movement, had "meant very much" to him (*SLL* 767). Soviet reaction, however, tended to side with that of Steinbeck's American detractors, in considering he had been too compassionate toward the Germans, not only failing, as one critic charged in 1948, to show the Nazi officers "in all their inhumanity and monstrosity" but also sentimentalizing the Norwegian patriots.[17]

Whatever its ultimate reputation as a work of literature, it will never be entirely possible to disregard the tremendous popular success *The Moon Is Down* enjoyed and the powerful influence it exerted both at home and abroad at the time of its publication during those dark days of war. In America, by arousing well-meaning controversy, it likely helped the nation, recovering from the immediate trauma of Pearl Harbor, to rationalize its attitudes toward the war in Europe. In the subjugated countries of Europe, it gave real hope at a period when hope was at a premium, its doubtful verisimilitude and formalized dialogue paling into insignificance before the power of its message. In 1951, the Swiss scholar Heinrich Straumann opined that "to the European reader" *The Moon Is Down* "appears as the most powerful piece of propaganda ever written to help a small democratic country to resist totalitarian aggression and occupation."[18] Although at the time Straumann wrote those words the war was still very much an open wound in the minds of those who had experienced its horrors, it is, at this further distance in time and on the evidence available, difficult to argue against the conclusion he reached, overstated though it may seem. Literary considerations aside, the novel remains a brilliant piece of propaganda, beaming its message of hope to all oppressed peoples in the world today, while acknowledging the predicament of troops, far from home and their loved ones, who find themselves policing territory inhabited by a resentful and actively antagonistic population. To that extent, even if it is a work inescapably of its own time, it can arguably also be claimed to be timeless.

4

Although the controversy over *The Moon Is Down* rumbled on for several weeks after its publication, sales were not damaged in the least, and the book went through a number of printings. According to *Time*, sales had reached 450,000 by the end of June.[19] In May, it was announced that the movie rights had been sold to Twentieth Century-Fox for an all-time record sum of $300,000, double the current record price Hemingway had received the previous year for his Spanish Civil War novel *For Whom the Bell Tolls*. While this latter fact undoubtedly pleased Steinbeck, he was not altogether pleased by the attendant publicity surrounding the news of the sale of the book, for the released details were somewhat misleading. Steinbeck, of course, never received anything like the $300,000 quoted. To begin with, Oscar Serlin, as part-owner of the rights to the play, was entitled to 40 percent. Steinbeck was thus entitled to only the balance of $180,000, which, after deducting his agents' 10 percent, left him with $162,000 from the deal. This sum was to be paid to him in equal annual instalments of $54,000, the first due in 1942 and the balance over the next two years. So far as the general public was concerned, however, he had the full $300,000 in his pocket just as soon as the contract with the studio had been signed, and before long, as had happened after the success of *The Grapes of Wrath*, hundreds of begging letters began flooding in.

There were matters other than the controversy over the book that were to occupy Steinbeck's mind that spring. On 12 March, Carol was granted an interlocutory decree in Salinas, within six minutes of filing her complaint that her husband had left her too frequently on her own at home, thus causing her "great mental anguish and physical pain." She blamed his absences on "too many women — one in Hollywood particularly." The judge approved a settlement under which it was agreed Steinbeck would pay Carol $111,922.10 in cash and something in excess of $100,000 in various bonds and shares.[20] It would be another full year before the divorce became final and Steinbeck and Gwyn were free to marry.

Frustrated by the reluctance or the inability of the FIS to find him an active assignment — even though he had been called on several occasions to meetings with officials in Washington — Steinbeck decided to escape from New York to the country. In mid-March, he rented a house, "The Palisades," at Snedens Landing, Rockland County, New York, about twelve miles from the George Washington Bridge and a mere forty-five-minute drive along the Hudson Parkway into the center of town. The house was old and comfortable and overlooked the river. The sense of peace was wonderful after life in hotels. For the first time in a long while, he was able to sleep soundly at night.

As neighbors, they had the playwright Maxwell Anderson and his wife, the painter Henry Varnum Poor, the composer Kurt Weill, Burgess Meredith and his current lady friend Paulette Goddard, the Paul de Kruifs, and Max Wagner and his wife. To make the country life complete, Moss Hart gave them an English sheepdog puppy named Willie, who was swiftly house-trained and became an inseparable companion.

Pending his being given a permanent assignment, Steinbeck had been allocated a temporary job on the planning board of the FIS, "designing both the intent and form of the propaganda directed at Europe" (JS/WFS 3/17/42). He was attached to an office in New York, and drove in occasionally in his 1937 Plymouth to report and to obtain new instructions. Mostly, he worked at home, writing the talks that were to be beamed overseas, driving into Nyack in the late afternoon to the telegraph office to mail his day's work. It was suggested he should make the broadcasts himself, but when his voice was tested it was found not suitable. His enunciation was not clear enough and there was a boom in his voice that was accentuated through the microphone. To his intense relief, the idea was dropped.

On those occasions when he motored into New York, he quite often attended rehearsals of the forthcoming play. Inevitably, he became involved in a certain amount of rewriting. He had agreed to go to the out-of-town opening of the play, scheduled for 23 March in Baltimore, but had determined that nothing on this earth would induce him to be present at the first night on Broadway.

He had been content with the way rehearsals had been going, but the opening in Baltimore was clearly something of a disaster. Everything that could go wrong did go wrong: cues, lights, everything. He had to carry out hurriedly further work on the text, cutting some of the long speeches that were holding up the action. By the end of the run, he was satisfied that most of the problems had been ironed out and that he had done all he possibly could to have the play ready for its New York opening at the Martin Beck Theater on 7 April. Even so, it was not until three days prior to the opening, following further cuts and rewriting of dialogue, that he was able finally to announce that he thought the play was in good shape. By the day of the opening, however, his confidence was already beginning to wane. He became convinced that all the advance publicity would kill the play, certainly so far as the critics were concerned.

5

Steinbeck and Gwyn stayed at Snedens Landing on opening night. They sat up, fortifying themselves with stingers, awaiting the promised telephone calls from New York after the final curtain and later, at three o'clock, when the first reviews came out in the papers. Steinbeck's worst fears were realized. He considered the reviews to be "uniformly bad" and "uniformly right" (*SLL* 244). The play seemed dull and did not capture the imagination of the critics or the first night audience. "I don't know why the words don't come through" he wrote to Street (*SLL* 244).

The play notices appeared while the public controversy stirred up by the book was still in progress, and the drama critics reiterated and developed all the old arguments and counterarguments over the portrayal of the Nazis. In his initial review in the *New York Times* on 8 April, Brook Atkinson wrote: "Without raising his voice or playing tricks on a plot, [Steinbeck] has put down some of the fundamental truths about man's unconquerable will to live without a master. It is a remarkably convincing play because it is honest in its heart." In his follow-up review five days later in the Sunday edition of the paper, Atkinson declared that for him *The Moon Is Down* was "an impressive and heartening play," and suggested to those who disagreed:

> Take Mr. Steinbeck on his own terms. Although he is no virtuoso dramatist, he knows what he is doing. Under the casual surface of *The Moon Is Down* there is firm tension. It represents the inner serenity of a man whose mind is clear about basic things. He believes in human beings.[21]

Atkinson, as it transpired, was one of the few who felt able to praise the play almost unreservedly. *Newsweek* regarded the play as "one of the major disappointments of a disappointing theater season," and complained that the heroism of the inhabitants of the little invaded town was "largely an off-stage phenomenon."[22] *Time* made the same point, noting that the play "lacks sustained action and commits the dramatic crime of having almost everything exciting take place offstage." *Time* also criticized Steinbeck's writing: "The dialogue, more like subdued rhetoric than human talk, often seems stilted and formal when spoken aloud."[23]

The casting of the play also came in for a goodly share of general and specific criticism. The *Commonweal* reviewer considered Otto Kruger's Colonel Lanser "military in dress only," and failed to find a better comment on Ralph Morgan's Mayor Orden "than the remark of a young lady sitting behind me when at the end he was led off to be executed: 'Isn't he *cute?*'"[24] The *Newsweek* reviewer thought Morgan, "miscast and misguided as Mayor Orden," projected "the white-haired hero of the people as a bewildered, sentimental old dodderer."[25]

One critic may have been very near the truth in suggesting that Steinbeck had given the actors very little to do or say, while expecting them to create convincing roles of their own from the dramatic ambience he had failed to supply. In an interview he gave to Milton Bracker of the *New York Times* just over a week after the play opened, Kruger revealed that while he had found the original character of Colonel Lanser, as Steinbeck had conceived him, "interesting and sympathetic," he was not attempting to play him as the part had been written. He added significantly: "We agreed on that." He also revealed that "endless lines" had been eliminated from the original text in order to make the colonel a less-sympathetic character than appeared in the novel.[26] Obviously, so far as the *Commonweal* reviewer for one was concerned, all these changes had been in vain.

The blame for the play's generally unfavorable critical reception in New York cannot, it would seem, be laid wholly at Steinbeck's door. Even so, if the casting was uninspired, as it undoubtedly was, if Chester Erskin's direction was possibly "heavy-handed," if the acting left much to be desired, particularly in the way of character interpretation, it has to be accepted that the principal defect lay in Steinbeck's text. As he himself admitted: "It is not a dramatically interesting play" (*SLL* 244). Without the guiding hand of a George F. Kaufman to steer him through the theatrical minefield, Steinbeck's third attempt (and second completed attempt) at the play-novel form was unhappily an artistic and critical disaster on the stage — and he knew it.[27]

6

The reason for the delay by the FIS in giving Steinbeck the permanent assignment he hankered after was the direct result of the continuing FBI investigation into his credentials and political background. He had been aware, of course, for some time that an investigation of sorts was proceeding and that this was holding up matters. While he and Gwyn were still staying at the Bedford, he had written rather irritatedly to Attorney-General Francis Biddle, requesting Biddle to use his influence to stop Hoover's men "stepping on my heels." He went on: "They think I'm an enemy alien. It's getting tiresome."[28]

It is doubtful if, at the time, he suspected that the investigation was anything more serious than "tiresome," and that it was simply the general screening to be expected of anyone seeking an appointment with a government agency and being allowed access to restricted information. By the following year, however, he had good reason to suspect that there was indeed something more sinister behind all the checking up that was being done on him. The opening of FBI files in 1984 under the Freedom of Information Act certainly reveals the true extent and depth of the investigation conducted into his background — particularly by Army intelligence agents during the spring and early summer of 1943 — and of the ludicrous and spitefully antagonistic conclusions drawn from the information gathered from a multitude of often unreliable sources.

The FBI files make it clear that Steinbeck had been under scrutiny even as far back as the mid-1930s. Shortly after the publication of *In Dubious Battle*, it had not escaped the notice of the authorities that he had been one of the sponsors of the Western Writers Congress, held in San Francisco on 13–16 November 1936. This congress had been organized by the circle of writers connected with the left-wing *Pacific Weekly*, which, until his death on 9 August that year, had been edited by the muckraker Lincoln Steffens. Steffens had close affiliations with the Communist Party, particularly in his later years. Steinbeck and many other writers — including Kenneth Rexroth, William Saroyan, Irwin Shaw, Upton Sinclair, Tess

Slesinger, and Nathanael West—who had been contributors to the *Pacific Weekly* and who had actively supported the congress were labeled by the House Un-American Activities Committee as a "communist front." Additionally, as has already been noted, Steinbeck's contribution to the League of American Writers pamphlet, *Writers Take Sides*, and his lending of his name and his giving of financial support to the Republican cause in the Spanish Civil War all helped to build up a case against him as a dangerous radical. In many respects, *The Grapes of Wrath* was the last straw, seen by those who chose to regard it in the narrowest sense as advocating the sort of popular revolution the Communist Party preached. There is a sad irony in the fact that Steinbeck's innate sense of patriotism sowed many of the seeds of his destruction in the eyes of the governmental and military establishments, for his particular brand of patriotism was based on the concepts of truth and free speech—of criticizing wrongs and supporting, when necessary, unpopular beliefs and political views. No shred of evidence exists however to show that he was at any time a member of the Communist Party, or even a sympathizer. But the unconfirmed suspicion that he was, or had been, was to cost him dearly in the months to come.

If, while he continued to send his radio scripts to New York each day from Snedens Landing, he obtained a certain satisfaction from the work he was doing for the FIS, he nevertheless felt, and understandably so, that his full potential was not being used. To the extent that he was doing something tangible toward the war effort, he was content to give his services gratis. He was not alone in doing this. As he told Street: "There are people in our office who haven't had a day off in months and they haven't been paid either. It's a crazy mess but we're doing a good job" (JS/WFS 4/30/42). It sounds suspiciously like a man trying to convince himself.

He took a week off in mid-April, when, after having been approached with an offer to take over the running of a radio station in New Orleans, he and Gwyn traveled south to explore the possibility of his accepting the job. He decided against it. As he explained to Street: "I wouldn't spend a summer in New Orleans for anything" (JS/WFS 4/30/42). Heat and humidity had always been anathema to him. The week-long trip was not entirely wasted, for the two of them spent an enjoyable time renewing old acquaintances and visiting friends they had made in the Crescent City over the Christmas and New Year holiday period.

Back once more in harness on the East Coast, he soon began to groan under the weight of work being put on him. "They give me more and more work to do," he wrote to Street, "and I'm going to reach a saturation point. There are only a certain number of words that can come out of one man in a day and they have me about ten percent past that point now.

But it is what I want to do and I am doing a pretty good job. Better than anyone else could do anyway." He was troubled by the speed at which he was being forced to work, fearing this was resulting in prose that, in normal circumstances, he would not want to put his name to. In the same letter to Street, he observed:

> The typewriter may get you enthusiastic but I sit over this one so many hours a day that I am not enthusiastic at all. I compose on it because there just isn't time to do it by hand and get it into type. The writing suffers from that but the stuff has to be on the air too soon after it is written. There isn't time. (JS/WFS 4/30/42)

He was also concerned, of course, that this burden of official work was allowing him no time to pursue his literary career. The idea that he had probably abrogated his freedom as a writer for the duration of the war, however long that might prove to be, undoubtedly disturbed him. Already, the fear was growing at the back of his mind that he might even lose the ability to write fiction once he was released from his commitment to the war effort. To counteract this possibility, he instituted a schedule for writing a five-hundred-word story each day.

During that April, he again collaborated with Ricketts, this time in sending a letter to the Navy Department, drawing the attention of Navy intelligence to the wealth of invaluable information about certain islands in the Pacific mandated to Japan by the League of Nations after World War I and declared out-of-bounds to the rest of the world ever since. This information was contained in the zoological and ecological reports and scientific papers of Japanese biologists who had investigated the area and promulgated their findings on a worldwide basis. Steinbeck and Ricketts suggested that these documents, widely and freely available in universities throughout America, would provide the Navy with crucial data in the event of any United States attacks being launched against the islands. As they pointed out, the reports contained detailed maps that specified soundings, reefs, harbors, buoys, and lights, as well as providing some photographs. The Navy Department responded by way of a formal, mimeographed acknowledgment, simply thanking them for their patriotism. Although Ricketts was amused by the Navy's reaction, Steinbeck was angered by it, to the extent of sending a further letter addressed personally to Frank Knox, the Secretary of the Navy, repeating the information contained in the earlier letter.

After a two-month interval, Ricketts was visited by a plainclothed naval intelligence officer, who asked a number of searching but basically irrelevant questions, many of which seem, in retrospect, to have been aimed principally at undermining Ricketts and Steinbeck's expertise and credentials. Nothing further was heard subsequent to this interview, and they never did discover whether or not the Navy Department checked on the Japanese scientific reports. Clearly, by writing direct to Knox, Steinbeck had not only flouted protocol but had most probably stepped badly on someone's toes. His temerity undoubtedly gained him new enemies, and very likely triggered a further full-scale character investigation, this time by the Navy. The incident provides yet another example of his patriotic zeal rebounding on him in an adverse way.[29]

By then, the security question had reached some sort of a crossroads at the FIS. Steinbeck warned Street to expect a visit from the FBI in the near future:

> I gave your name as reference when I signed civil service papers the other day. I was a clay pigeon on that. We have been losing so many good men from our office just because they happened to contribute some money to Spain that I was requested to fight the thing out. The FBI and Dies Committee has completely forgotten whom we are fighting. If they clip me off there will be a fight and that is why I signed the papers. Our whole office will walk out for one thing. But they will probably ask you a lot of very funny questions and they may attack me on my morals, which God knows are just as bad as I can make them, which isn't enough. (JS/WFS 5/13/42)

By whom Steinbeck had been requested "to fight the thing out" is not entirely clear, but the situation had been brought to a head by a general reorganization and rationalization of the United States information and propaganda programs. A new agency, the Office of War Information (OWI), was to be formed by the coordination of the FIS and other information and propaganda sections from several government departments and agencies. Steinbeck was offered a permanent, paid post in the OWI, but was warned that if he accepted and signed the necessary papers he would automatically be agreeing to a security check being run on him

While all this was going on, he was appointed special consultant to the Secretary of War and assigned to the headquarters of the Army Air Force. In this new capacity, so he was advised, he was not required to take orders from any officer below the rank of lieutenant general. He was called to Washington for an interview with General Henry A. ("Hap") Arnold, who suggested that he might consider writing a book detailing the training of a bomber crew from the time of induction to the time when its separate members coalesce into an efficient flying team. The assignment would entail his flying from one training camp to another, living with the trainees and their instructors, and making himself fully conversant with all aspects of Air Force life and operations. He was told that if the book were successful he might get the job of writing a sequel, following the crew into combat. It was not a job that particularly appealed to him and he decided to turn it down, but was persuaded otherwise by the personal intervention of the president himself. He anticipated being about a month in the field and then spending a further month, or six weeks, actually writing the book.

His last reservations about the project were swept away when it was revealed to him that the eventual intention was for him to move back to the West Coast for three months to assist in making a film based on the book. Indeed, even before he set off gathering the necessary material for the book, a movie deal had been concluded with Twentieth Century-Fox, who had agreed to pay $250,000 plus a percentage of the takings for the rights and had moreover undertaken to make the picture in style. When reporting all this to Gwyn, who was visiting her mother in Los Angeles, he told her he hoped to be in California by mid-June. He had no illusions that the assignment would be other than "a tough job—a very tough job" (JS/GC 5/20/42), estimating that he would probably cover about two hundred thousand miles in completing the itinerary mapped out for him and John Swope, the photographer who was to accompany him. He met Swope for the first time on 20 May and looked foward to working with him.

7

Although *The Moon Is Down* had been running to good houses at the Martin Beck Theater for the first three or four weeks, by mid-May audiences had begun dropping off appreciably. Serlin decided to close the play on 23 May, store the sets, and perhaps open again at a later date, but the play did not, in fact, close until 6 June. A road company was subsequently organized, with a change of cast and emphasis, and attracted a succession of enthusiastic audiences while on tour.

MGM's movie of *Tortilla Flat* opened at the Radio City Music Hall in New York toward the end of May. Steinbeck went to see it on the 22nd. Putting aside for the moment his past differences with the studio, he charitably pronounced it as being not bad. For all that, as he had antici- pated, it was a travesty of his book, and in later years he had some unkind comments to make about it. John Lee Mahin and Benjamin Glazer's screenplay provided a typical happy Hollywood ending, with Danny marrying Sweets Ramirez and everybody else returning contentedly to the old way of life they had been leading before Danny had become contaminated by the acquisition of his grandfather's properties.

The New York critics were, on the whole, generous rather than, one suspects, entirely honest in their reviews. *Commonweal*'s Philip T. Hartung allowed that "in spite of its sentimentality and touch of condescension about things religious, *Tortilla Flat* is an intelligent, charming movie."[30]

Manny Farber of the *New Republic* took the diametrically opposite view, berating MGM and its scriptwriters for "extracting the philosophy out of Steinbeck's *paisanos* by conforming with the episodes [of sex and drinking in the novel] but garbling them into something of astounding bad taste."[31] In the *New Yorker*, John Mosher adroitly referred to recent controversy when he ended his review with the observation: "There is clearly a charm about the whole affair, and surely Mr. Steinbeck understands his shiftless *paisanos* far better than he does his Nazis."[32] Joseph Millichap, writing in 1983, had arguably penned the best overall verdict on the film: "From today's perspective it seems a rather unreasonable sepia-toned sham that could only have been made in Hollywood."[33]

8

Two days before he and Swope set out on their tour of the air bases, Steinbeck was given final details of their proposed itinerary. From Washington, they would fly down to Randolph Field, San Antonio, Texas, and then on to New Orleans, Albuquerque, Phoenix, Las Vegas, Los Angeles, San Diego, Sacramento, Illinois, Florida, and then back to New York.

They flew down to Randolph Field in a heavy bomber on 24 May. Wearing a bulky parachute and in some discomfort because his jug ears were tightly imprisoned in his flying helmet, Steinbeck spent most of the flight in the observation nose of the aircraft. He seemed to find the experience exhilarating, although it was quite rough for a couple of periods when they ran into storms. By the time they landed, he was dog-tired, but at eleven o'clock that night, alone for the first time, he wrote to Gwyn, telling her about the trip.

He wrote to her almost every day, sometimes only a postcard, but mainly he jotted down his thoughts and impressions on pages torn from the notebook he carried around with him, even when flying. It was the first occasion for many, many months that they had been separated for any length of time, and he was missing her dreadfully. The letters he wrote, or partly wrote, while he was flying were full of the wonder at seeing the world from above:

> We're very high now. Can see most of Texas. San Antonio right below. Texas *is* very green and *fruit*ful. (JS/GC 5/24/42)

> We're up 8000 feet. It's a quarter of eight and the sun isn't even down. We're flying right into it. Like those Astounding Stories. ... It's nice up here. The lights are coming on below and we're still in the sun. (JS/GC 5/27/42)

The pace did not let up at all. He was sometimes out of bed at five in the morning and boarding a plane at six. In addition to all the flying, he attended psychology tests, navigation classes, and demonstrations of one sort or another. On the third day, they flew from Randolph Field to Ellington Field, then to Kelly Field, and finally back to Randolph to accompany trainee navigators on night-flying instruction. He did not finish work until eleven o'clock that night, but still found time, in bed, to write a short note to Gwyn before turning out the light. He admitted that he was feeling "really pooped" (JS/GC 5/27/42). All the time, Swope was taking his photographs. The two of them usually roomed together, and on the occasions they did, Swope seized the opportunity to take some candid shots of his roommate in bed, seated on the toilet, or wandering naked around the room.

There were few diversions from the long working hours, the physical and mental strain of keeping up with the young airmen as they carried out their training. Steinbeck sat the tests they sat, used the equipment they used. As he recorded later: "I've had practically to learn the training of the whole air force. And I don't learn very easily — not the memorizing kind of learning anyway. I never was any good at it" (JS/WFS 7/31/42). So as to get a fully rounded picture of the trainees' lives, he and Swope went with the cadets to local night spots, and the drink flowed. He paid physically for such outings, for he found that if they flew the next day the high altitude would bring on a massive hangover. There was, too, a certain inevitable repetitiveness about the whole training process, and this he found wearisome. Nor was the southern weather at the height of summer to his liking. He complained about the weather being "god awful hot," and reported to Gwyn that he was suffering from "a lovely fever blister from sunburn" (JS/GC 5/27/42). Even when they arrived at their last base in Florida, he discovered that there, too, were other environmental disadvantages to be endured, and reported to Street on 18 June that his body was covered with mosquito bites.

By the time he wrote that letter to Street he was back home at Snedens Landing with Gwyn, luxuriating in the coolness and peace of "The Palisades" and intent on avoiding the heat and bustle of New York as much as he could. Immediately on arriving home, he set his mind to the writing of the book. He had been given a deadline for its completion: 1 August. In the recent, comparatively brief period he had seen so much and been expected to assimilate so much that he was now finding it difficult to unravel it in his mind before setting it down on paper. To facilitate the process, he began dictating into an ediphone, a new experience, but one forced upon him by expediency. There was again no time for the first holograph draft he preferred, not even for direct composition on the typewriter. So he dictated from his notes, choosing to use the ediphone rather than a stenographer. He felt he might be inhibited to a certain extent by the thought that, if he worked late, he was possibly preventing the stenographer from going home and doing what she wanted to do. The machine, on the other hand, was simply a slave to his bidding, with no rights nor any home to escape to. The new way of working proved surprisingly successful within its limitations. Steinbeck had always striven for a prose that read as easily as speech is spoken and had long been in the habit of reading over his written texts aloud to ensure that their texture and rhythms were exactly right. Here, however, he was experimenting with that practice in its most basic form—but it was not going to produce great prose.

The writing, the dictating, went well, and within a week or so he was averaging four thousand words a day, double his normal output. In a letter to Street, he gave some indication of his current state of mind: "I get farther and farther away from the old realities," he wrote, "and more and more immersed in this dreamlike war. When it is over I'm not going to be able to remember what it was like" (JS/WFS 6/24/42). The good progress on the book was not sustained for long. He became irritated when he was not given the material he had been promised by the Army and was accordingly obliged to mark time. He knew all too well that no matter how tardy the Army might be in sending him the material, he would still be expected to honor the deadlines that had been set. The only way he could see of retaining his sanity was to acquire the Washington attitude of doing nothing and passing the buck, even though he hated the very thought of the idea.

The Office of War Information had been established while he had been away on his trip. All the previously created propaganda and information agencies, except the CIAA (which was still Rockefeller's baby) and all sections of the COI other than the FIS, were now under the unifying umbrella of the OWI, with the radio commentator Elmer Davis at its head. Steinbeck was notified he had been accepted for the Civil Service, and he once more warned Street to expect a visit from the FBI. He was now holding down two jobs, one as foreign news editor in the OWI at a salary of three thousand dollars a year, and the other in the unpaid capacity of special consultant to the Secretary of War on assignment to the Army Air Force.

What did continue to concern him, for one reason or another, was that his draft status had never been determined. He had never been called before Draft Board 119 in Monterey, although he had never requested deferment and did not propose to claim exemption if he were called. His feelings about being drafted were somewhat ambivalent. It probably hurt his pride to think he might not be considered suitable, on whatever grounds, for induction in the normal way. He also possibly suspected that some members of the draft board felt personal animosity toward him—

either on account of *The Grapes of Wrath*, or even because of the recent publicity of the divorce proceedings—and that they had something unpleasant lined up for him. Furthermore, he was certain that were he to be called up, the Air Force would strongly object. Arnold had told him that the Air Force considered it essential he remain a civilian, since he would be more useful to the service as such.

The reason for this soon became clear. He told Street that he had received "the damndest set of orders you ever saw" (JS/WFS 7/8/42). The War Department, through the Air Force, wanted to put him in charge of a newly-authorized Air Force intelligence subsection, a job that, retaining his civilian status, would occupy him for the next two years. He indicated to the Air Force that he would accept the assignment on the proviso that were he to be drafted he would not be required to request a deferment, and that one would not be applied for on his behalf. His attitude clearly puzzled the Air Force command, and put them into some sort of predicament. If, in order to preempt the draft board's authority, they offered him a commission, it would remain desirable, if not essential, such being the nature of the work he would be doing, that even as an officer in the Air Force he should be allowed what would virtually amount to the same sort of free hand in running the show as he would have had taking over the post as a civilian. If he were not given a commission and then was drafted after having taken over the job, his services would be lost altogether before the new subsection had been fully established.

The commanding general of the Air Force took the initiative by writing to the Monterey draft board, requesting that Steinbeck not be called, and, at the same time, apparently accepting the possible military hierarchal difficulties that might ensue, indicated to Steinbeck that, just as soon as he had completed his work on the book and subsequent film, he would be inducted into the Air Force at an appropriate rank to enable him to assume charge of the proposed new subsection.

Nothing further transpired until the end of July, when, presumably as a preliminary to his anticipated commissioning, he was asked to undergo a tough Army physical. He passed with flying colors. A couple of weeks later, he received a draft questionnaire from Draft Board 119. He completed and returned it. From then on, there was only deafening silence, both from the Army and from the draft board.

There is little doubt that a great deal was going on behind the scenes, including some intense soul-searching. With hindsight, it seems completely incongruous that the Air Force command should have ever entertained the idea of offering work in Army intelligence to someone already labeled a security risk. The whole history of the affair points to a lamentable lack of communication between the various government and military establishments. The real possibility exists that the Army was totally unaware of the existing FBI reports at the time the proposed intelligence job was first broached, and that everything subsequently ground to a halt when the OWI passed on the reports. While the FBI findings were not sufficiently damaging to prevent Steinbeck having access to the restricted material he needed for his work at the OWI, it was an entirely different kettle of fish when it came to his having access to top-secret Army material. From then on, the whole sorry story seems to have been one of incredible delay on the part of Army intelligence in setting up yet another investigation into Steinbeck's background.

This continuing uncertainty inevitably had an unsettling effect on Steinbeck. His feeling of homesickness for the Monterey peninsula, his need to return to his roots, was very great indeed. "I'm in a period of wishing I was in P.G. [Pacific Grove] sitting on a rock [f]ishing," he told Street. "Never get over that tendency" (JS/WFS 7/31/42). The knowledge that he would be going to Hollywood once he had finished the book gave him at least something to hold on to, even though, by now, he had come around to the way of thinking that nothing whatsoever could be taken as certain.

Toward the end of June, he had sent Covici some introductory pages of the Air Force book, enjoining him to return them without making copies, since they had not yet been cleared by the censor. Would Covici have a look at them and let him know if he liked them? Covici's verdict was very favorable, and it was agreed that Viking should publish the book in November. The editor also had the idea of publishing an anthology of Steinbeck's work in the newly-conceived Viking Portable Library series. With this is mind, Covici asked Gwyn to suggest material for inclusion in such a volume.

By mid-August, Steinbeck was writing the last section of the Air Force book and estimated he would finish it by the end of the month. "It isn't very good," he admitted to Street, "but it is the only thing of its kind and with the time they gave me it was the best I could do" (JS/WFS 8/17/42). He was already making preparations to leave the East Coast for California. He sent Street twelve small boxes of books he and Gwyn had acquired since their arrival in the east and asked Street to unpack them and put them on the shelves in the Eardley Street house.

At the end of the month, he finished off his corrections to his typescript. Life was becoming increasingly hectic. Not only was he helping Gwyn to close down the Snedens Landing house and being swept up in the urgency of completing the book, but in view of his imminent departure to the West Coast he was also having to report every other day to the OWI office in New York. "You know," he confided to Street, "I often wonder whether, given leisure again, I could write slowly and with the old joy. If it is ever peacetime again I am certainly going to try" (JS/WFS late August 1942). His intimate contact and dealings with the establishment had not improved its image in his eyes, for he saw the way in which the up and coming men were scrambling for place and position in the halls of government by every conceivable method. These were the people who would become the new generals and make the new fortunes, while he was keeping his head down at work and trying to ignore what was going on around him.

As soon as the final pages of the book had been dispatched to Covici, his current work at the OWI wrapped up, and the house cleared of their possessions, he and Gwyn set off for California. He drove all the way in their 1941 Cadillac convertible, packed with clothes, papers, files, journals, and a large record collection. The dog Willie accompanied them, perched high on the piled-up back seat with a rug under him, so that he could look ahead through the windshield. Steinbeck sat behind the wheel for ten hours or so each day. They paused briefly at Wake Robin, Michigan, to visit the Paul de Kruifs, and then proceeded by way of Albuquerque, where they took a two- or three-day diversion to Santa Fe and Taos, and then on to Los Angeles. The total journey, including the side trips, took something over a week, and Steinbeck completely exhausted not only himself but Gwyn and Willie in the process.

Arriving in California, they negotiated a three-month lease on a small and pleasant house with a large garden in Sherman Oaks in the San Fernando Valley, and while it was being made ready for them stayed with Max Wagner in Hollywood.

9

The new book was given the title *Bombs Away*. John Ditsky has referred to it as "arguably [Steinbeck's] weakest book," describing it as "for the most part [a] simply hurriedly written hack work with a patently propagandistic purpose: to reassure the folks back home of the integrity of the training program then in the process of turning their sons and those of their neighbors into bomber crews."[34]

Nothing more nor less than the equivalent of a recruiting poster, specifically designed to overcome the insistent, widespread suspicion and fear aroused by the idea of flying still prevalent among many young men and their parents, it seems an anachronism today when flying is regarded by the majority of people — sons, daughters, parents, grandparents, and even great-grandparents — as being nothing more than a swift, safe, and moderately convenient way of traveling from A to B. The establishment's opinion of the success of *Bombs Away* as a recruiting tool can be gauged by the fact that, until the 1990 Paragon House paperback edition, the only other American edition of the book after the Viking first edition in all its reprintings was one issued by Harper & Brothers in 1942 for specific use in schools. It was obviously seen as being desirable for future recruitment to be initiated well ahead in the classrooms of the nation.[35]

In these more-sophisticated times, Steinbeck's text might seem to most of us overly obvious and simplistic in its call to arms. There is, however, little doubt that Steinbeck was sincere in most of what he was writing and that he had convinced himself he was disseminating truth and serving the nation well. If occasionally his tongue was in his cheek, it does not show. He told potential recruits and their families exactly what they wanted to hear: that to get into the Air Force the potential recruit had to be "a very special kind of young [man] ... far above the average in intelligence and physique" (BA 32). The glowing future prospects for the potential airman are also not overlooked, it being noted that it was certain in the postwar world that the country's development, and that of the hemisphere and the whole world, would be "very closely tied to the use of the airplane" (BA 32—33). These desirable prospects are inevitably linked to a desirable patriotic attitude. The ideal recruit is described as one who, as well as being "very healthy," must have "great faith in his country, in its future and its future greatness ... for he will emerge.from the war in a position of leadership and in the postwar peaceful world he will have a strong hand" (BA 33). There is much more in the same vein, all aimed to appeal to the need for self-aggrandizement of youthful egos. The typical cadet will be "above the average mentally and physically;" will, because he is healthy, "like girls very much indeed;" will, through an exceptional sense of coordination, timing, and rhythm, "generally be [a] good [dancer] and will like to dance;" will, because of his aural high awareness and precision, "like music;" and will, because of all these attributes, "be good-looking without necessarily being handsome." Moreover, while neither braver nor less brave than young men generally, he will possess "the ability for self-discipline which passes for fearlessness because fear is controlled." To sum up, Air Force cadets "are drawn from a cross-section background of America but they are the top part of the cross section. They represent the best we have" (BA 44—45).

It all reads uncomfortably like a riposte to the concept of the Nazi master race, though admittedly without the essential element of controlled breeding. But, at the time, its propagandist message was exactly what was required. What young man who read these words would not be tempted to prove to himself that he satisfied to perfection all the desired qualifications that would enable him to join the ranks of the elite in the Army Air Force?

War, however, is about fighting, about man pitted against man, machine pitted against machine, and all that results therefrom: death, physical mutilation, psychological wounding. *Bombs Away*, naturally, is coy about such matters. They are not within the parameters of its purpose. The potential recruit — the healthy, good-looking, heterosexual, wellcoordinated, music-loving, unpanicky leader of men — is assured that he will be flying planes that "are as good or better than anything in the world" (*BA* 182), and that he will be part of a crew that will "function like a fine watch" (*BA* 155). Certain myths, stories, and misconceptions are swiftly swept under the carpet, and reassurance is additionally provided by the statement that the trainees had "found in the papers that when forces were equal, our force won" (*BA* 182). All this, of course, skates neatly over the fact that in wartime, more so than in peacetime, truth is manipulated and that the public is told only those truths or half-truths or even lies the establishment wants it to hear. Propaganda begins in the newspapers, and the first casualty of war, as Senator Hiram Johnson observed in 1917, is truth.

Bombs Away fulfilled its four main purposes to perfection: first, to tell recruits in advance what would happen to them on induction and what the process of their training would be like; second, to demonstrate how the raw components of a bomber crew are welded into an integrated team; third, to proclaim that American airmen, planes, weapons, and equipment are second to none; fourth, to reaffirm that America and her allies would win the war against the Axis powers.

The book has a straightforward structure. Following a short preface and a slightly longer introduction, Steinbeck begins with a general chapter in which he outlines the history and development of the heavy bomber, notes how the men who are to fly these planes are drawn from every walk of life and from every corner of the nation, and recounts how, before they commence their specialized training, they undergo manual and mental aptitude tests to ensure they are assigned to the jobs that suit their individual talents best. Then follow six chapters detailing the specialized training of the separate members who will make up the bomber crew: the bombardier, aerial gunner, navigator, pilot, aerial engineer, and radio engineer. Each chapter stresses the overriding importance of the individual crew member to all the other members of the crew, each ultimately having an essential role to play. Although the fully-complemented bomber crew consists of nine members — for there has to be a copilot, and two other gunners are necessary to protect the ship — it would have been pointless to repeat the details of the training of more than one pilot and one gunner. The penultimate chapter follows the group training of the crew after each member has completed his own specialized training, and demonstrates the marrying of all their individual skills into the desired flawless team. The final chapter considers in rather more detail some of the training missions the crew completes before flying off to war.

In his preface, Steinbeck writes that while a book "should have a dedication," this whole book should be regarded as such, "a dedication to the men who have gone through the hard and rigid training of members of a bomber crew and who have gone away to defend the nation" (*BA* 5), and he explains, presumably for those very few who may not be aware of the significance of the words, that the book's title is derived from the call given by the bombardier when the bombs have been released and are falling toward their target. "That means that the mission is completed, that means it is time to go home. Someday the call will ring above a broken enemy and then it will be time to go home for good" (*BA* 6).

The introduction traces America's reluctant path to the war it never wanted, did everything to avoid, but deep down knew was inevitable, and observes how war when it came gave direction and purpose to the whole country, providing an effective antidote for the poisons and aimlessness of the Depression, uniting a disunited nation as nothing else could have done. Moreover, as Steinbeck points out, the war proved to be exactly the kind of war that America was "peculiarly capable of fighting — a war without established technique or method, a kind of war rooted in production in which we surpass." He goes on to observe: "If we ourselves had chosen the kind·of war to be fought, we could not have found one more suitable to our national genius" (*BA* 14).

Steinbeck's six members of the future bomber crew are clearly composite characters, but to endow them with some semblance of individuality they are each identified by name and by a brief pen picture of background and pre-induction history. Each is dedicated in his own field, the whole of his training directed toward the moment of ultimate action and accomplishment.

The further each man progresses into his training program the more detached he becomes, not only physically but mentally too, from the day-to-day concerns of the old life he had so recently left back home. Bill, the bombardier, for instance, does not invite his father to the army graduation ceremony, feeling there is too much work to be done for mere socializing and that his father would not be able to understand his surgeonlike attitude to the job he had become qualified to do: "There is only time for hatred among civilians," Bill decides. "Hatred does not operate a bombsight" (*BA* 66). When he goes home on leave, he does not "out of some kind of diffidence," warn his parents he is coming. When his mother asks him how many days leave he has, the distance he has already put between himself and his parents and his eagerness to get on with winning the war is manifest in his brief reply: "A week" (*BA* 66). To Al, the aerial gunner, it seems "very long ago" (*BA* 91) since he had been jerking sodas in the candy store, even though that had been only two months before. He realizes he is no longer the same person he had been in civilian life. Now he is "the hunter of the air, the stinger in the tail of the long-range bomber, and he wanted to join his group" (*BA* 91). At the end of his leave, Joe, the pilot, has a sense of elation: "He wasn't leaving home — he was going home" (*BA* 139). When Abner, the aerial engineer, has completed his study, training, and practice, he is "ready for his permanent post in a bomber crew" (*BA* 147).

The human components of the bomber crew are brought together in the final two chapters of the book. They meet for the first time at the assembly field in Florida: pilots from a four-motor school in Texas, bombardiers from New Mexico, gunners from Nevada, navigators from Kelly Field, radio operators from South Dakota, crew chiefs from Illinois or Mississippi. Here, they are allocated to their particular crew units, and, once a crew has been finally established, the men know they will remain together. They will come to "know each other as few men ever get acquainted, for they will be under fire together ... will play together after a victory ... will plan together and eat and sleep together on missions ... [a]nd finally there is a chance that they may die together" (*BA* 154–55). The crew becomes "a tight unit, a jealous unit" (*BA* 155), its members maintaining unbreakable bonds with each other and with their own ship, whether it be a Flying Fortress B-17E or a Consolidated B-24. Not for the first time, Steinbeck is careful to point out that, whether B-17E or B-24, the ships "are about equal in performance," although each has its own "passionate adherents" (*BA* 155). Moreover, individual ships are recognized to have personalities of their own, and become in time part of their crews as well. This sort of mystique is not unknown in many other walks of life, but here Steinbeck endeavors to elevate the concept of the bomber crew into a projection of group man — presumably, and the distinction needs to be made, consisting of free men and not herd men. Not only that, but the group that is the crew is shown to be part of the group that is the squadron, the group that is the Squadron is part of the group that is the Wing, the group that is the Wing is part of the group that is the Air Force, and so on until we logically arrive at the ultimate group, which is the nation at war, singleminded in its direction and purpose. It is an extreme thesis of almost holistic proportions that perhaps does not bear too close a scrutiny.

For a moment, following all the detailed factual material he has until then spilled out on paper, Steinbeck patently lets his imagination run away with him in an improbable sequence in which, during a training mission over the Gulf of Mexico, the bomber crew fortuitously sight an enemy submarine cruising just below the surface. After first obtaining confirmation from base that there are no friendly submarines in the vicinity and after reporting back that they are conveniently carrying live bombs, they are exhorted to attack the submarine. Bill directs Joe on the bombing run, releases all his bombs, and destroys the submarine. The unexpected action welds the crew as one: "Very strange ties had been established. These men would not be apart again" (*BA* 163). The whole purpose of their individual training and their subsequent training together as a crew has at last been achieved:

> This cross section, these men from all over the country, from all the background of the country, had become one thing—a bomber crew. They had changed but they had not lost what they were, they were still individuals. Perhaps that is what makes our crews superior. (*BA* 184)

As John Ditsky has observed:

> Seen close up, the freedom of the bomber crew and its individuals must have started to seem to exist by definition merely, its distinction from the herd a patriotic wish-dream. ... Perhaps I err in ascribing self-doubts to Steinbeck largely on the premise of his celebrated humaneness, but *Bombs Away* is such a house of cards that one wants to believe its maker had begun to question its assumptions in his heart of hearts.[36]

There is, indeed, evidence that shortly after he had completed the book Steinbeck *was* assailed by doubts, recognizing the work for the "straight recruiting job" that it was, and expressing concern "about playing the role of the goat who leads the sheep in, only to step aside himself."[37] It may be that, on reflection, he accepted there had been some possible confusion in his thinking as to the true nature of the cadets. Could it be that he had portrayed them, after all, not as free men, but herd men, just like the Nazis he had portrayed in *The Moon Is Down*? As Ditsky proposes, we need to believe that the truth of the matter is that Steinbeck did not at the time, for all his initial unwillingness to embark on the project, question the validity and the logic of the words he was dictating into his ediphone, for to suspect otherwise is to attribute to him a moral duplicity that is, knowing the man, unthinkable.

We may, then, with some justification, regard the blatant propaganda of *Bombs Away* as naive today. But however much we may choose to pour scorn on the book it is undeniable that, in any war situation we find ourselves in, most of us are all too ready to embrace wholeheartedly much of the philosophy behind the sentiments Steinbeck expressed in the book. For the message broadcast, or the modern equivalent of that message, contains the basic and seemingly unassailable facts we wish to hear and believe, particularly if we have a loved one engaged in the conflict. It is surely a truism that sophistication closely follows truth as the second casualty of war.

10

As seemed almost predestined, the film version of *Bombs Away*, which Twentieth Century-Fox was to produce in partnership with the Air Force, never got off the ground. When he arrived in Hollywood, Steinbeck discovered that the Air Force liaison officer he had been advised to contact, Colonel Adamson, was in England and nobody seemed able to get in touch with him or to know when he would be back. Steinbeck sarcastically observed that for all he knew Adamson might have been shot down. What was certain was that Adamson had left no delegated instructions with the officers in charge of the local Air Force photographic department, and so they had no free hand to cooperate with Steinbeck when he put in an appearance. What is more, Steinbeck discovered that everything he had been sent out to do had already been done, and in true Army fashion was being done over and over again. Far from overseeing the making of a film, he had no apparent role to play at all. From his point of view, the whole situation was a complete waste of his time — an unholy mess that left him twiddling his thumbs while the slow wheels of bureaucracy lurched to a halt.

During the long drive across the continent, he had been turning over in his mind an idea that had surfaced while he had been lunching with Elizabeth Otis and an editor from *Collier's* magazine shortly before he left New York. Now, with work on the Air Force film failing to materialize, he looked again at the idea, which was for a film about the invasion of a small American town, rather like the one in *The Moon Is Down*. The original concept discussed at the lunchtime meeting had been about an attack on the East Coast by a German invasion force, but on the trip across the continent he had become dismayed by evidence of what seemed to him the greed and apathy displayed by the people inhabiting the central areas of the country. He saw them as deluding themselves that, protected by the coastal mountain ranges, they would be safe whatever happened. It occurred to him that insufficient attention had been given to the possibility of an attack in the west by the Japanese, and that, if it came, the attack would not be on the coast itself, but would be carried out "using the usual Japanese tactics by cutting through and attacking where there is no protection, inland by parachute or something like that. Such places are also the most apathetic. ... I would sketch the small town and then invade it with Japanese and show what would happen to our system if we happened to lose the west to the Japanese. It would be a brutal and awakening picture and story and might do some good in waking the people who don't know there is a war" (JS/ERO 9/13/42).

He discussed the idea with Nunnally Johnson and Darryl Zanuck. Both were intrigued by the idea, more so than they had been for the Air Force film. The movie would be made on the same basis as had been agreed for the other, with a payment and a percentage of takings to be handed over to the Air Forces Aid Society Trust Fund. Steinbeck would write the original story and leave Johnson and the studio to do the rest. They were under no illusions that they would encounter considerable opposition from some quarters if such a picture went into production, and it was decided that, if necessary, they would resort to the old ploy used at the time the film *The Grapes of Wrath* was in production. The movie would be shot under the title *Bombs Away*, or whatever, not being given its proper title until it was safely in the can. Steinbeck wrote to Elizabeth Otis, asking her to sound out *Collier's* about his writing and the magazine publishing such a forty- to sixty-thousand-word story in which Twentieth Century-Fox had already expressed keen interest, making it clear to the editors that whatever they paid for the story was to be passed on to Air Force Aid.

Steinbeck was apparently confident that Adamson, when he eventually returned from overseas, would approve the project and recommend to Washington that the author be allowed to use his three-month official stay in California in overseeing the new movie rather than the original *Bombs Away* project. So far as the Air Force itself was concerned, Steinbeck was also confident of being able to demonstrate he would still be using his time in pursuit of the principal purpose of his mission to Hollywood: that is, raising funds for Air Force Aid. Before Adamson returned, however, the Bureau of Motion Pictures officials of the OWI intervened. The Bureau, which possessed a number of unwritten draconian powers, let it be known that it did not approve of the proposed movie, since the subject would not be in the public interest. The studio had no alternative but to pull out of the project. Zanuck decided it was simply not common sense to expend a great deal of money on a picture, only later to be involved in an inevitable fight with the government and faced with the very real possibility that the film would never reach the screen. One can even speculate that the mere fact of suggesting the theme of the movie was yet another strike against Steinbeck, for to some governmental eyes that theme could be interpreted as thoroughly subversive, an attempt to undermine civilian morale.

With the evaporation of the excitement raised by the prospect of new and worthwhile work, Steinbeck once again found himself at a loose end. He was angry and unhappy and restless, and gave vent to his feelings in a letter to Elizabeth Otis:

> There are so many frightened men in the government who are so afraid of being blamed that they do nothing because nobody can blame that. They just want to hold on. You see, nobody can tell the picture companies what they

shall not make but the penalties come in lack of cooperation in material and personnel later so that it works the same way. Meanwhile I don't know where I stand. I have written to Washington telling them either to use me or to get off the pot and let me go back to OWI but of course that means nothing. There are just as many frightened little men in the army holding onto their jobs as there are any place else. ... I am itchy. It seems impossible for me to rest. I don't take to vacation very well. I guess it is just generally the war itch that every one has. ... It seems that for the duration of the war at least, an awful lot of people have their hands on my work as wasn't true before. (JS/ERO 9/24/42)

Preparations for the publication of *Bombs Away* were well under way at Viking Press. Covici, however, felt that the book, ending with the bomber crew, its training completed, flying off to war, needed a further chapter taking the crew into actual combat. At first, Steinbeck was tempted to try creating such a chapter from the stories he had heard from airmen who had been in action, but almost immediately he realized that to write such an account would be a betrayal of his probity and his self-respect as a writer.[38] He had told the Army on several occasions that he refused to do shoddy work, and had been assured that the only reason he had been chosen to write the book was because it was known that he had never lowered his standards. Now, it seemed, the Army wanted him to do just that, for he suspected that the idea of the additional chapter had been initiated by someone in Washington and not in the Viking office at all. He sent Covici a telegram, telling him that he could not do what had been asked. Covici had half-expected what the reply would be and wrote to Steinbeck noting that while the chapter did cry out to be written from the sales point of view he fully understood and applauded the stand Steinbeck was taking on the matter.

The galleys, Covici advised him, would be on their way shortly. He requested that they be returned by air mail. He also informed Steinbeck that the Army had found it necessary to make only about sixty corrections to the manuscript. He reminded Gwyn that he was still awaiting her suggested list of contents for the Portable Library anthology, and proposed to Steinbeck that he might like to write some "helpful notes" of his own that could be incorporated into the introduction Covici would be writing for the volume.

By now, after all that had transpired, Steinbeck had lost interest in *Bombs Away*. He hurriedly wrote to Covici, suggesting that the proof-reading be carried out at the Viking office if the galleys had not already been dispatched. "They do it better than I do anyway," he commented, adding: "Very troubled dreams lately. The confusion of my work I guess. And it is confused. Will be until the war is over. Anyway I'll take a crack at your introduction" (JS/PC 9/30/42).

Instead of the "notes" Covici had asked for, Steinbeck produced a full-blown "introduction" of his own, with Covici's name appended. Surviving only in part and in the vaguest of terms in Covici's own fine introduction, Steinbeck's unpublished text is an important document, for in it Steinbeck spells out his faith in himself as a writer, his aims and his commitments, and the almost mystical and close relationship he strove always to attain with his readers. It provides supreme evidence, if any were needed, of the fact that in late September 1942, despite all his railings against his lot and his fears of possible creative sterility, the driving necessity within him to write, to communicate, remained undiminished, as the following extracts illustrate:

> There are some books, some stories, some poems which one reads over and over again without knowing why one is drawn to them. And such stories need not have been critically appreciated—in fact many of them have not been. The critic's approach is and perhaps should be one of appraisal and of evaluation. The reader if he likes a story feels largely a participation. The stories we go back to are those in which we have taken part. A man need not have a likeness of exact experience to love a story but he must have in him an emotional or intellectual tone which has keyed into the story and made him a part of it.
>
> *   *   *
>
> A writer if he is to tap the reservoir of potential stories of the reader must write commonly of the common need in the common mind.
>
> *   *
>
> The work of an honest writer does not grow out of knowledge. It is the record of a man's mind trying to understand his world, groping his way, inventing the symbols of his investigation as he goes on. No one can understand his world from a single event. The writer sets down a story, saying in effect—"This happened—does it point toward anything—does it indicate anything?" And if your writer is convinced of some principle or some direction he will warp his story to prove his conviction. If he is not certain of things his story will sound realer and truer to the reader and together they will continue the search—the constant searching which is the mental and emotional pattern of every human being.
>
> When reader and writer go together into a story, a warm pleasure is the result. ...[39]

11

Steinbeck and Gwyn moved into the rented house on Delgardo Drive, Sherman Oaks, on 18 September. There, they were joined by the Haitian housekeeper, Ivon, who had looked after them at Snedens Landing. The house was small, but had a large yard that was completely surrounded by a fence—ideal for Willie, who could be left to roam out there at his leisure and pleasure. It was by no means the sort of house Gwyn would have cared to own, but she seemed content to stay there for the time being, for she had become reconciled to the transient way of life that had been imposed upon them and said that she was prepared to put up with it for as long as it was necessary.

At least in one sense she felt at home here, near her mother and in touch with her old friends in the movie business. Steinbeck, on the other hand, hated the idea of being abandoned, as he felt, in the film colony. There was a touch of irony in that he had avoided employment in Hollywood like the plague in the past, only now to be sent here, completely at his own expense as it happened, because of the war, and to find that nothing had changed, that Hollywood was still Hollywood, with all that implied, except that these days some of the studio executives were parading around town in uniform. Jack Warner, now Colonel Warner, ran his studio as if he were conducting a private war. "It would be very strange," as Steinbeck commented bitterly, "if a warner changed his spots when he covered them up with a uniform" (JS/ERO & ALW 9/23/42).

Through his publisher, Harold Guinzberg, he heard that the Army wanted him now for a "quick job" to write about the American defenses in Alaska. Someone in Washington had obviously got the wires crossed. He told Guinzberg he could not accept such assignment without clearance from his present masters, and advised his publisher to draw the matter to General Arnold's attention. Following the recent reports he had been making to Washington, complaining about the pointlessness of his situation in the movie capital, he had been informed that he should consider himself on twelve-hours notice again. He treated that piece of advice with the contempt he thought it deserved. If past experience was anything to go by, he was willing to bet he would be left to stew in limbo, probably for the next three months or so, and that it would only be until, in desperation, he made up his mind to plan some work of his own that he would be called to undertake a new assignment. The Air Force had, in fact, warned him he would very likely be sent on a new mission around 15 October, but again he had no faith in such vague possibilities, much as he would have welcomed anything rather than the present inertia.

Early in October, he heard that Ed Ricketts, then in his forty-sixth year, had been drafted, a piece of news that once more set him to wondering what the Monterey draft board might be storing up for him. He was fully aware that, although General Arnold had advised the draft board that his services were required by the Army, the board need not necessarily be influenced by such considerations. His position was still vulnerable and uncomfortably uncertain. With Ed, he told himself, they had really started reaching down, and there was no reason to suppose that he, five years younger than his friend, might not soon be called.

A week or so later, his other great friend, Max Wagner, was also drafted. Steinbeck became even more restless. "I still don't know what I am going to do — when I am going in the army or anything," he wrote to Annie Laurie Williams on 15 October, the very day on which the Army had indicated he might be given a new mission. "I'm a little dispirited and my morale is a little low at the mess I seem to be in." He declared he would welcome it if he too were now drafted. "The messing around has me worn out. Why do we have to fight war so obliquely?" (JS/ALW 10/15/42).

Nunnally Johnson had been engaged to write the film script of *The Moon Is Down*, and before he started work on it he asked the author "if he wanted him to take any particular line or if the novelist had any ideas about how the story should be developed for the screen." Steinbeck's reply had simply been, "Tamper with it" (*Adventures* 410). When the job was finished and Steinbeck read the script, he thought it "very fine," and declared it would "make a wonderful picture" (JS/ALW 10/15/42). He reported to Elizabeth Otis that Johnson had "changed nothing," but had "added a number of external scenes to accentuate the cold and the hatred" (JS/ERO October 1942).

Sometime during October, Steinbeck obviously turned over in his mind the possibility of writing a book with a Mexican theme. This could have been the work that eventually became the novella *The Pearl* he was to write in the winter of 1944—45. But in 1942 he never seemed to have a clear week to start work on it, and, in any case, such was his agitated state of mind that he could never have settled to doing it. As he told Elizabeth Otis:

> Haven't had much heart for it mainly because there was no indication that I could finish it. So I haven't been doing much of anything and it is the hardest kind of work. I rather imagine that if and when I am assigned, it will be in the east but when that will be I have no idea. (JS/ERO October '42)

The call came, perhaps sooner than he expected. Toward the end of October, he received orders to report immediately to Washington. He managed to get a seat on a scheduled Transcontinental & Western flight, and arrived in the capital on the 27th or 28th. Inevitably, having got him there, the Army were not ready for him. Arnold briefed him on his new assignment, but then broke the news that it had been found necessary to re-form the whole operation and to appoint a newly-promoted colonel to take charge of it. Military protocol being what it was, there would understandably be some delay. Steinbeck still had very much on his mind the likelihood that the Monterey draft board would call him any day now, and he was fully aware how quickly he could find himself a private in the Army if the board did decide to act. Ed Ricketts was already in uniform and Max Wagner had received his orders to report to the Army on 12 November. He must have mentioned all this to Arnold, for he was instructed to apply to the draft board forthwith for a sixty-days' deferment. He wired Street on the 29th to attend to this for him.

Pending the setting-up of the new operation in Washington, Steinbeck flew back to Los Angeles on 4 November. He had not been at all happy about applying for the deferment. His doing so had, of course, gone against the spirit of what he had insisted upon three months earlier. As he told Street: "These Washington sons of bitches are putting me in the position of a draft dodger and I don't like it" (JS/WFS 11/6/42).

The sequence of events at this point is not entirely clear, but it would seem that the draft board either would not accept the deferment application by proxy, or, having accepted it, then refused it. General Arnold himself wrote to the board again, requesting that Steinbeck be given a thirty-day deferment. This the draft board also denied. Street attended the hearing of Arnold's petition, and advised Steinbeck that "the members of the board couldn't figure how you who had always written trash could write anything that could be of any benefit to the army" (*Adventures* 509). Steinbeck was, however, placed in Category "P" for the next thirty days, which gave Arnold the grace he had requested, but which could apparently be revoked by the board, if they so wished, at a mere two-hours' notice.

Steinbeck received Street's special delivery letter informing him of the board's decision on 7 December. He replied at once:

> I love the draft board as literary critics. I love also their taking it upon themselves to know better than the commander of the air force to know what he needs and who can supply it. ... I am writing to Col. Starry, General Arnold's aide, telling him that the headquarter's request has been turned down. The draft board may get a firework or two out of that. Arnold likes to think that he knows what he wants and he will not be pleased with the literary critics of Monterey County. If you care to tell the draft board, the job I have just done and the one I am just undertaking is recruiting on a large scale and with 19,000 mechanics a week needed for the air force every week, recruiting seems necessary to the air force if it doesn't to the draft board. (JS/WFS 11/7/42)

That same day, Steinbeck received a letter from Air Force Headquarters advising him that Arnold had at last set up the mission with its new commander and had ordered that Steinbeck should be processed and commissioned without further ado. Steinbeck, however, had no illusions that it would take other than some considerable time. For one thing, the validity period of the physical he had taken in July had expired and he would have to take another. From his point of view everything seemed to have degenerated now into an undignified race to the finish between the

Army and the draft board. He had already determined that if he were to be called by the draft board before his commission came through he would allow matters to take their course as he had originally intended, enlist in the Air Force as a private, apply for officer training, and then, after obtaining his commission, get transferred to the operation Arnold wanted him for. His contempt for the draft board knew no bounds. He unburdened himself on Street:

> The sense of power some of these hounds feel is unpleasant. I don't want them to succeed in it with me. Being unable to reach me in any other way they take this method. . . . These bastards think I am trying to stay out of active service I guess. In the mission I'm to have, I'll see ten times as much active service as nearly any one in the army. . . . I don't want these malicious men to have their little triumph. (JS/WFS 11/8/42)

Unbelievably, a week or so later, he received a letter from General Arnold informing him that, as there had been a change in regulations, it was now impossible to arrange his direct commissioning from civilian status. This astonishing *volte face* was particularly annoying as only a few days before he had been offered a job by the Navy, and had turned it down, feeling that his first loyalty should be with Arnold and the Army Air Force. A day or two after receiving Arnold's letter, another path out of the morass presented itself, when Colonel Higgs of the Air Force in Santa Ana asked him to enlist under his command, since he had "some interesting work" for him to do. This sounded like an attractive alternative proposition, so he wired Washington, advising them he intended to enlist with Higgs. A telegram was shot back at him the next day, forbidding him to do any such thing, reiterating the story that Arnold had ordered him to be commissioned and that this would be accomplished within the next four weeks.

By now, only two weeks remained before his "P" Category status expired, at which point — after all that had happened — he imagined the draft board would lose no time in calling him. His best option, it still seemed to him, was to take the post Higgs had offered, and he again advised Washington he proposed to act accordingly, pointing out that, were he to be drafted, there would surely be some difficulty in Washington securing his release, whereas Higgs could see no problem in releasing him from the Santa Ana enlistment should the occasion arise. Would it not be better, he argued, for him to enlist with Higgs, where he could carry out some valuable work, rather than get lost passing through the selection process in some induction center?

Yet another player in the grim comedy appeared on the scene: General Yount, the officer in charge of the Flying Training Command. Yount had written to Arnold complaining that Adamson had succeeded in totally mismanaging every aspect of the *Bombs Away* project, accusing him of incompetence and of treating Steinbeck badly. Yount asked Steinbeck if he would make a film for the Flying Training Command, using the resources of the RKO studio. The only drawback to such a plan was that it would again require Steinbeck to enlist—and his orders not to do so had still not been rescinded by Washington.

Steinbeck began to be seriously worried about the possible terrible damage all this turmoil and uncertainty was doing to his creativity. "I'm grown rusty and fusty—it is actually hard for me to write," he told Covici (JS/PC 11/19/42). He was not alone in his concern. Elizabeth Otis expressed her own fear that his "prose style may go to pieces," to which Steinbeck commented to Mildred Lyman, one of the McIntosh & Otis staff members: "I should think that any prose style I ever had has already gone to pieces. What a mess" (JS/ML November '42).

A mess it certainly was—and continued to be. On 26 October, the War Department had sent him a letter with instructions that he should present the letter to the draft board. The letter stated that he was to be accepted into the Air Force under the aegis of the Secretary of War, that the necessary processing would take two more weeks, and that no action should be taken by the board in the meantime. He was instructed to make a formal request for a further thirty-days' deferment when he presented the letter. Since the Army had addressed the letter to the Eardley Street address, however, he did not receive it, and learned of its existence only after he had telephoned Washington on 2 December immediately after having received a frantic call from his agents informing him that another letter from the War Department, this time addressed to him in New York, had been passed to them. This second letter ordered him to appear that very day in New York for an interview and physical. Over the telephone, Washington advised him to phone the procurement office in New York, explain what had happened, and request that his papers be sent to Los Angeles. He eventually received a notice to attend the Federal Building in Los Angeles for an interview on 9 December. The outcome of this was apparently again inconclusive.

It is a remarkable fact that, despite the sense of ever-mounting frustration he was experiencing and despite what he had told Covici to the contrary, he was still able to apply himself to creative work of some sort or other. Even though he was unable to commit himself fully to Yount's outfit, he nevertheless agreed to go to the RKO studio and prepare a script for the Flying Training Command. The work, he anticipated, would last only a few days, and he had taken it on merely "to keep from going nuts" (JS/ERO 12/8/42).

12

Bombs Away was published on 27 November and received a thumbs-up verdict from most reviewers. Even Clifton Fadiman, while conceding that Steinbeck had written better books, had only good things to say about the work.[40] As perhaps was to be expected, however, the *New Republic* did not follow Fadiman's example of making peace with Steinbeck after the attacks on *The Moon Is Down* earlier in the year. In fact, the *New Republic* did not publish a review until almost two months after the book appeared. Acknowledging that it would make an enormous amount of money for the Air Forces Aid Society Trust Fund, the reviewer dismissed it as a "patriotic hack job," bearing "about the same relationship to literature that a recruiting poster does to art."[41]

The movie version of *The Moon Is Down* had by now gone into production. Steinbeck was invited to the Twentieth Century-Fox studio during the latter part of November to inspect the sets. These had originally been designed to represent a Welsh mining village for the recently-completed *How Green Was My Valley*, the movie, directed by John Ford, based on Richard Llewellyn's best-selling novel. Steinbeck was delighted with the sets, and rated them "Very fine! Beautiful job!" (JS/ERO November 1942). On the first anniversary of Pearl Harbor, he was again invited to the studio, this time to see the rushes of the few scenes that had been shot. After the viewing, he wrote to Nunnally Johnson: "There is no question that pictures are a better medium for this story than the stage ever was. It was impossible to bring the whole countryside and the feeling of it onto the stage, with the result that the audience saw only one side of the picture."[42] To Elizabeth Otis he enthused: "It is a really beautiful job and there is a curious three dimensional quality in it. It is something like the best English and before the war German pictures, you know a sustained mood" (JS/ERO 12/8/42).

Soon after seeing the rushes, he collaborated with Max Wagner's brother, Jack, then working in Hollywood, on writing an original story for the movies, a comedy titled *A Medal for Benny*. They wrote the synopsis in one night and a day. When Steinbeck told Johnson about it, the screenwriter made a bid for it, sight unseen. Another screenwriter, Dudley Nichols, who had scripted John Ford's *The Informer*, *Stagecoach*, and *The Long Voyage Home*, and the exiled French director Jean Renoir, whose *La Grande Illusion*, *La Bête Humaine*, and *Le Règle de Jeu* were universally regarded as cinematic masterpieces, both read the synopsis and, according to Steinbeck, "went quite crazy about it" (JS/ALW 12/24/42). Both Nichols and Renoir made it clear that they did not want to turn the synopsis into the conventional Hollywood story, but to make it exactly as Steinbeck and Wagner had written it. Steinbeck sent a copy of the synopsis to Annie Laurie Williams and asked her to negotiate its sale on the basis that he and Wagner should share everything (ideally, a down payment and a percentage of the gross) on a fifty-fifty basis. "Jack knows these people," Steinbeck noted, "and would watchdog the story through production. ... I think it could be a warm, humorous picture and still topical. And such things are very badly needed now" (JS/ALW 12/24/42).

The synopsis, or "sample script," of A Medal for Benny is a mere twenty pages in length, and the story is simplicity itself.[43] The entire action takes place in Chilinas, "one of those little California towns which is active, ambitious, and a little absurd,"[44] a town that is bisected by a slough. In the superior quarter of the town, this slough has been turned into the central feature of a park, but in the poorer part of town the slough is polluted and used as an ofttime rubbish dump by the paisanos whose little houses back on to it. The Chilinas Chamber of Commerce, anxious to have their town put on the map, realize they have all the publicity they could ever desire when the news comes through that the President of the United States has announced the posthumous award of the Congressional Medal of Honor to a soldier from Chilinas. The members of the Chamber are, however, somewhat in a quandary when they discover that the town hero was Benny Fado, an aggressive ne'er-do-well, who had been run out of town and ordered by the Justice of the Peace to stay away for a year. Telephone calls and telegrams come in from all over the country, and newspaper and magazine editors clamor for details about Benny and his family. The medal is to be presented personally by a general to Charlie Fado, Benny's father, and the state governor has made it known that he intends to attend the ceremony.

The town officials move the Fado family from their tiny, rundown house by the side of the stinking slough and into a house in a much-more-salubrious neighborhood, but when Charlie realizes that the move has been made not in recognition of his dead son's heroism but merely for the honor of the town and for all the money and publicity it will attract, he is incensed and moves his family back to their real home. When the day of the ceremony comes, the general and the governor arrive, but Charlie makes no appearance. He is persuaded by his friends to participate only after it has been suggested to him that there might be a big fight during the presentation, for it is well-known that Charlie can never resist a good fight. The Fado family takes its rightful place on the reviewing stand while the parade goes by. After the general has read the citation and pinned the medal on his jacket, Charlie makes his own little speech, with which it is intended the film should end:

I didn't want to come. When honor came to Benny and his family, it was good. But then there were people who did not think that honor could live by the slough. I didn't know about that. So we moved to a new house — away from our friends and away from our people. And you know, I thought maybe we were wrong. And I was mad because I thought we were wrong. And then I was studying last night. Benny came from the house beside the slough and Benny is a hero. I know there can be heroes from other kind of houses, too — but a man is only what he grows out of — his family and his friends and his home. Maybe it was kind of people to want to change us. But Benny came from us and we will not change. Maybe that is a good thing for the whole country. I think I am glad for the whole country that Benny came from the slough, and that the medal came to Benny. Maybe it is good that the country has to depend for its life on all kinds of people — even Benny.

The little speech survives almost intact in the final script of the movie, one of the few elements to remain unchanged.[45] While the basic storyline was retained, it was obviously too slight to meet the requirements of a full-length Hollywood production. Steinbeck himself clearly had no hand in the subsequent rewriting and expansion of the story or in the actual making of the picture, but Jack Wagner is credited as having written some additional dialogue for the ultimate script by Frank Butler. There is no way of knowing to what extent Wagner may have introduced into the final script ideas and even dialogue he and Steinbeck possibly discussed and recorded at the time they wrote the synopsis, so it is simpler and safer to assume that Steinbeck's interest in the movie effectively ended with the writing of the synopsis.

There are a number of typical Steinbeckian touches in the synopsis. Charlie's final speech (the longest piece of dialogue in an otherwise mostly dialogue-free text) is an example. Sentimental, even simplistically obvious though it may be, the speech is undoubtedly the *raison d'être* of the whole work. Benny, had he survived the war, would surely have become the post-World War II counterpart of the post-World War I Danny of *Tortilla Flat*, although returning as a war hero would have posed several problems for the old devil-may-care Benny. While it is clear that Benny could never have been portrayed as one of the elite recruits Steinbeck had been extolling in *Bombs Away*, the same sort of patriotic message delivered in that book still comes through loud and strong in Charlie's speech. There is, however, a false note in that final" — even Benny." Charlie, we feel, would never have said that.[46]

One of the most delightful episodes in the synopsis is that in which the town dignitaries discover "That there are only two photographs of Benny in existence and both of them are in the police station — one full face and one profile." In decorating the town, "these pictures are blown up and the numbers taken off — and on one street lamp there is a full face, and on the next a profile." These doctored mug shots are unfortunately not used in the movie, for, unlike the synopsis, which provides for the acting out in flashback of some of Benny's escapades and misdemeanors (engaging in a barroom brawl, battling with five policemen), Benny's face is never shown on the screen.

If Benny as an identifiable character was dropped from the movie, Butler's script introduces a number of new characters who played no part in the Steinbeck-Wagner original, including two of the movie's three leading characters. Charlie is still there, although he now goes under the name of Charlie Martin, but love interest, patently lacking in the synopsis, is provided for by the characters of Lolita Sierra, Benny's fiancée, and Joe Morales, Benny's friend and rival for Lolita's hand. Most of the movie is taken up with their on-off romance. Even if Joe is not allowed to win her in the final reel, it is made clear that she will eventually agree to marry him. This is the same brand of stereotyped Hollywood relationship typified by Sweets Ramirez and Danny in the forgettable MGM version of *Tortilla Flat*. Among other new characters, are Chito, Lolita's cheeky much younger brother, and Toodles Castro, who provides a necessary plot foil for Joe in making Lolita jealous.

There is not a great deal that needs be said about the original Steinbeck-Wagner synopsis, except that it must have been Steinbeck's name alone that made it so attractive to the studio. It is not, and was never intended to be, a work of significant literary value, and, apart from providing a basic plot and structure, it plays only a small part in the detailed plotting of the movie. While there is no way of assessing to any useful degree the extent to which it does actually represent Steinbeck's own work, this really seems a matter of little account. It is, on the other hand, tempting to speculate on the extent, as coauthor, Steinbeck was taking the opportunity to pay off some old scores in his satirical portraits of the devious and incompetent Chilinas town officials, so reminiscent of many of those on the West Coast who had, one way or another, been making his life uncomfortable since the publication of *The Grapes of Wrath* — and even more particularly in recent months through the agency of the Monterey draft board.

13

Steinbeck and Gwyn were due to give up the Sherman Oaks house in mid-December when the lease expired, but in view of the continuing uncertainty of the situation, they obtained an extension. For obvious reasons, they had never really felt happy and settled there, but although the house was in many ways too far out of town there did not seem much sense in moving again and searching for other accommodations to tide them over while matters were in such a fluid state. Indeed, mainly owing to the continuing uncertainty, they had decided not to celebrate Christmas that year and not to exchange presents.

In the closing days of the year, Steinbeck wrote to Covici, advising him that nothing had changed, that he was still left dangling and waiting for someone somewhere to decree what was to become of him:

> The red tape has tied me up for four months now. My patience is completely exhausted. If I am not assigned by the 15th of January [the date on which the extension to the lease was due to expire], I am withdrawing my application and going into something else. My desire to help in this war does not include sitting in Hollywood for the duration. If the thing goes past the fifteenth I shall go east and get into something else. There's so goddamned much to do, that's why I am wild at doing nothing. This is the longest period of non-work in my life and at this time it seems criminal to me. (JS/PC 12/29/42)

He mentioned, however, that, apart from the minor work he had been doing, he had been shaping in his head a major work on which he planned to embark after the war.[47]

A further irritant was caused that month by the public revival of the *The Moon Is Down* controversy in an article by the theater critic George Jean Nathan in the December 1942 issue of the *American Mercury*. Under a subheading, "Drama at War," Nathan pointed out that dramatists who wrote war plays during time of war were obliged to recognize the public's attitude toward the war, and warned that they would ignore it at their peril. Nathan noted:

> John Steinbeck, for example, found that out all too soon. His *The Moon Is Down* which pictured the Nazis in a fairly human light, was spurned by the public until, for its road engagement following the New York debacle, the enemy was presented in a more villainous manner and hence was more publicly acceptable. ... At this moment, Steinbeck, I hear, has a new play that he refrains from offering for production simply because its theme and treatment differ from the necessarily conventional dramatic war philosophy.[48]

Annie Laurie Williams, clearly anxious to protect her client's interests against such insinuations, wrote to Nathan, deploring the tone of his article, and advised Steinbeck what she had done. Gwyn wrote to her on 24 December, applauding her action, pointing out that she and Steinbeck had had a laugh at Nathan's article, for the play he referred to was the abandoned *Pipes* play, which by no stretch of the imagination could be called a profascist work. "If John isn't being called a Red, it's a Fascist," she wrote, "and he works so hard at being a democrat, and has for twenty years" (GC/ALW 12/23/42).

The following day, Steinbeck added his own comments:

> In the first place Nathan is confused. You remember the Pipes play of which I wrote one act before the war? That is what he is talking about and he is a little

mixed up. I wouldn't argue with the little old spinster of '21.' He has made a living out of these little literary quarrels for years. They are his living. I'm glad you simply said he was a liar. He isn't of course, he is just confused. (JS/ALW 12/24/42)

Earlier in the month, the two of them had taken a trip north to Monterey. They had seen Ed Ricketts, who was then serving as a medic in the Presidio, and Toni Jackson, Webster Street, and Steinbeck's sisters, Esther Rodgers and Mary Dekker. Mary's husband, Bill, was serving with the Army in Africa, and Mary was worried about him and proud of him at the same time. Her state of mind could not have helped her brother in the feelings of guilt he was experiencing over his current abject inactivity.

While they were in Monterey, they went to Eardley Street and made arrangements to close up the house for the duration of the war. They could not know when, if ever, they would return to live there. The garden had already begun to grow wild again. They sprayed all the books with insect repellent, and locked away all the bottles of wine they had abandoned more than a year ago. Before they finally left, they cleared the house of whatever linen and bedding was still there, as well as all the small, sentimental articles that had gone to make it a home.

They both felt a sense of regret at leaving, recalling the happy times they had spent in the house during the spring and summer of the previous year. "Wish we could have stayed," Steinbeck wrote to Covici. "It was so pleasant and quiet. I would have liked just to sink into it. The garden was so quiet and nice and the ocean just the same as always. Of course the town was different but that won't matter when the war is over, for the town will go back to what it was" (JS/PC 12/29/42). But he did not realize, or refused to accept, that nothing returns to what it once was. In closing down the house, he and Gwyn, although they had no way of knowing it at the time, were closing down a part of their lives they would never be able to recapture.

6

1943: European War Correspondent

1

IT HAD BEEN NO IDLE THREAT OF STEINBECK'S WHEN HE DECLARED THAT IF his situation vis-à-vis the Army and the Monterey draft board had not been resolved by 15 January he would pack his bags, shake the dust of Hollywood from his feet, and return to New York, there to concentrate on whatever work the OWI and the War Department saw fit to give him. A week before his deadline, he wrote to Annie Laurie Williams and told her he had heard nothing further from the Army. It appeared that yet another investigation into his background was being carried out. Moreover, he had heard that the replacement colonel who had been put in charge of the mission he was supposed to be joining had been removed and that no successor had yet been appointed. The whole business seemed to be spiraling completely out of control. He began to wonder if the mission would ever materialize, or even if it had always existed only in the Army's imagination. Inevitably, his suspicions grew that someone in Washington with a great deal of undercover influence had chosen, despite the work he had turned in on *Bombs Away*, to brand him a communist, thus, for the immediate future blocking the commission General Arnold had planned for him, and for the foreseeable future blackballing him entirely from the Army.

He went ahead and booked reservations for Gwyn and himself on the Super Chief for the 19th, and arranged that between the 15th and their departure they would stay with Jack Wagner in Hollywood.

In the letter Steinbeck wrote to Annie Laurie Williams on 8 January, he advised her that RKO had opened the bidding for *A Medal for Benny* by indicating that they considered twenty-five thousand dollars (a figure the studio itself had apparently suggested) plus a percentage was too much. He told Miss Williams to use her own judgment, not necessarily confining her negotiations to RKO, as there was a lot of interest in the script being shown by several studios. The script was finally sold to Paramount for twenty thousand dollars and eventually released in May 1945.

Contrary to his intentions, he discovered that he had not yet finished with Hollywood. The same day he wrote to Annie Laurie Williams, he was contacted by Kenneth MacGowan, the Twentieth Century-Fox producer, inviting him to the studio to discuss a new project. The Maritime

Commission had asked Zanuck to make a propaganda film about the North Atlantic convoys menaced by the German U-boats. The British director Alfred Hitchcock, who had been on loan to Fox from Selznick since November, had agreed to direct the picture, and someone had suggested Steinbeck as possible scriptwriter. The idea must have seemed extremely attractive, particularly with the opportunity of working with another top-flight director like Hitchcock. Not wanting to commit himself too deeply, however, he suggested to MacGowan that he would work for a week on the script and then decide whether or not he wanted to continue. If he did not, the studio should compensate him for a week's work and call it a day. Alternatively, if he liked what he had done and the studio approved, he would go ahead and complete the script, for which he would require a fat fee. MacGowan was very happy to go along with these proposals. There was even talk of Hitchcock going east with Steinbeck to talk to some of the seamen who had survived torpedoings. The plan was that Steinbeck would write the script in the form of a novella, which he would be free to publish if he wanted to.

If he was pleased with his dealings with the studio heads, Steinbeck soon became disenchanted with his relationship with Hitchcock. The two did not take to each other from the word go. For his part, Hitchcock was perhaps oversensitive and wary because of the rumors he had heard about Steinbeck's radical political leanings. They obviously had one or two script conferences before Steinbeck began writing, and it seems more than possible that the basic concept of the movie originated from Hitchcock. He had been anxious for some time to make a sea story and also to face the technical challenge of devising a film shot entirely within a confined space — the perfect setting in his mind being a telephone booth. A movie concerned with the adventures and misadventures of a group of survivors in a lifeboat seemed an excellent subject.

Within four days, work on the script was going well, so well in fact that Steinbeck was even hoping to have the job done before leaving for the East Coast. He was beginning to find the old excitement in work again, and hoped that he would be able to recapture the sort of intense creative stimulation he had experienced so often in the past. For the moment, he felt at last his own master, even though having premonitions that his story might be doctored before reaching the public. He also had misgivings about the sort of work he might find himself doing again once he was back on the East Coast. He told Street:

'I'm beginning to have a few doubts about letting brass hats tell me what to write. ... So much crap is coming out of public relations offices and the treasury department that I wonder if I wouldn't do better to judge my own material. That's what I'm doing in the story I'm writing now anyway — good or bad. (JS/WFS 1/11/43)

He had, as it turned out, been optimistic in estimating that he could finish the script before leaving Hollywood, for he still had much work to do on it when he and Gwyn, with the dog Willie in tow, arrived in New York on 22 January. They again booked into the Bedford while they hunted around for more permanent accommodations. Before the month was out, they had found an apartment at 330 East 51st Street. It was on a quiet thoroughfare and was exactly what they had been looking for. The large, pine-paneled living room had two fireplaces, and French doors that led out onto a garden at the rear. Gwyn set about finding furniture—not an easy task in those days—while Steinbeck concentrated on his script, which he had given the simple title *Lifeboat*. He was also involved in a number of small assignments allocated to him after reporting back to the OWI office. In his spare time, he was writing "some little things" for himself. "Kind of keeps some sanity," he wrote Ritch Lovejoy. "There isn't much sanity going around" (JS/RL Feb/Mar. 1943). Now that he was back in New York, he began aching for the West Coast again. His ideal was to live in the Carmel Valley, preferably by the river, but he knew he would have to wait until the war was over for that. In the meantime, he and Gwyn had this very pleasant apartment, which was not like being in New York at all, being in some respects even more quiet than the country.

On 1 February, he reported to Street that he hoped to have *Lifeboat* completed in a week to ten days. Again, he was being optimistic. Possibly he had hit some snag with it—the extant typescript suggests this might have been so—but it is more likely that his work for the OWI and the War Department was increasingly encroaching on his time. At one stage, he was working for no less than a half-dozen different agencies on war-related projects. Despite all these pressures, he comforted himself with the thought that what he was doing now was preferable to the possibility of being commissioned and incarcerated in some Washington office, "bracketted by rank and the old slow methods of protocol." As a specialist consultant to the Secretary of War, he at least had a fair amount of freedom, and was able to talk "to anyone from the Secretary and generals to privates" (JS/WFS 3/11/43).

It was not until 11 March that he was at last able to complete the script and mail it off to Twentieth Century-Fox. He anticipated that he would, in a month or so's time, have to fly out to Hollywood to work on additional dialogue. But the call from Hollywood never did come.

2

Although when he had written *Bombs Away* Steinbeck had refused to compromise his art by faking an account of a bomber crew in action over

Germany, maintaining he would never write about anything outside his own experience, he had, in *The Moon Is Down*, done just that — and he was to do it again in *Lifeboat*. Admittedly, *Bombs Away* had been a factual work, whereas both *The Moon Is Down* and *Lifeboat* were works of the imagination. To some extent, he did also justify himself in *The Moon Is Down* by setting the story in an unnamed country and by making its characters people of unspecified nationalities. *Lifeboat*, on the other hand, as Steinbeck conceived it and wrote it, is here and there almost like a documentary. The scenes on board ship before and after the torpedo strikes and subsequently in the lifeboat do have an authentic and authoritative ring about them, so that the characters become on occasion almost secondary to the detailed accounts describing the intricacies and mechanics of seamanship and navigation. Clearly, in addition to interviewing sailors who had survived similar ordeals, Steinbeck was able to draw on his own experiences during the Gulf of California trip, and, to a lesser degree, while sitting in classes with Air Force trainee navigators at Kelly Field.

In many respects, *Lifeboat* anticipates the work Steinbeck was to do during the coming summer and early fall while he was overseas: the skillful blending of factual war reporting with the accounts of what may, on reflection, seem to many readers suspiciously like fictionalized or semifictionalized characters who were to appear in the war dispatches but who were mostly real people, faithfully reported. Steinbeck was nothing if not faithful to his medium at that time.

The original typescript of *Lifeboat* ran to 244 pages, but before submitting it to Hitchcock and the studio, Steinbeck revised the first 196 pages, reducing them in the process by 44 percent to 110 pages and cutting the length of the work overall by 36 percent to 158 pages.[1] While it is possible that he decided the finished work was not, after all, up to standard for publication as a novella in its own right, as he had once contemplated, it is more likely that events simply took the matter out of his hands: he just did not have the time nor, ultimately, the inclination to revise the work for publication.

As several commentators have pointed out, Steinbeck's lifeboat and its motley occupants can be viewed as a miniature ship of fools, a metaphor for the American nation of war. The seven survivors from the torpodoed freighter represent a fair spectrum of American society: the twenty-two-year-old helmsman, Bud Abbott, an ex-High School student with a definite left-wing turn of mind, a child of the Depression; Albert Shienkowitz, a Pole from Chicago, a first-generation American still ultraconscious and proud of his European roots; the Army nurse, Second Lieutenant Alice Both, the eternal girl-next-door who, because of the war, has become an angel of mercy; the ex-actress congresswoman, Mrs. Constance Porter, a ruthless socialite snob; the ex-racing driver, Brennan, a self-made millionaire, president of an aircraft factory manufacturing planes for the government; the Negro steward, Joe, dignified in his quiet acceptance of his subordinate status; and the unnamed Englishwoman nursing her dead baby, a confused refugee from the London Blitz and among the most recent of the "huddled masses" — all these characters initially being given a degree of added unity by the presence of the German sailor, the apparent sole survivor from the U-boat sunk by the freighter's gun crew in a last desperate exchange of fire.

The story is narrated by Bud. Not by any standard intellectually brilliant, he is nevertheless able to express commonsense opinions on most matters and to act responsibly in an emergency. Running to not more than forty-five thousand words in length and containing two storms, a suicide, and a killing, the narrative clearly has not been given the final polish Steinbeck would assuredly have given it before releasing it for publication. The actual dialogue content, as in *A Medal for Benny*, has been kept to a minimum, the drift of most conversations and the views expressed by the others being summarized and filtered through Bud as he writes down his account of what happened, while later recovering in a seaman's rest home.

Bud recalls how after the torpedo strikes it quickly becomes clear that the freighter has received a mortal blow. No rescue is at hand. The freighter, bound for England, is not in convoy and has therefore been avoiding the recognized shipping lanes. When the order is given to abandon ship, Bud is wounded in the leg by a shell splinter as he makes his way down to his lifeboat station. He is forced to jump into the oil-covered water, and swims to a waterlogged lifeboat a short distance away, the sole occupant being Albert. The two of them pull the other survivors one by one from the water, and finally the German sailor. Albert is all for throwing the German back into the sea, but Brennan, who has automatically assumed command, argues that the man is a prisoner of war and should be so treated. As the German's arm is broken, he is no physical threat to them. Indeed, after Albert's outburst, the gist of which the German could not have misinterpreted, he is understandably more frightened of them than they are of him. They suspect that he is an officer, even the captain, of the U-boat, but he has had the foresight to rip all insignia from his uniform and maintains he was only a junior member of the crew. By now, they have managed to bail out the boat. Alice Both sets the German's arm, and pours iodine over the gaping wound in Bud's leg. Brennan takes the dead baby away from the English-woman while she is asleep and hands it to Bud, but the woman wakes and becomes hysterical on finding her baby gone. Brennan yells to Bud to get rid of the tiny corpse, and, almost as a reflex action, Bud throws it into the sea.

Owing to Brennan's incompetence in forgetting to fasten the locker where the food is stored, all their supplies are lost that night during a terrible storm. The boat has become waterlogged again, but the bailing boxes have also been washed overboard. They use their shoes to scoop out the water. The boat is just drifting. With Mrs. Porter as his interpreter, the German suggests they should steer a south-easterly course in the direction where he insists are some islands. Bud, however, is not so sure that this is so, and moreover becomes suspicious of the German's motives. He organizes the erection of a makeshift mast and sail, and then steers a westerly course, arguing that this must inevitably bring them to landfall. The Englishwoman goes suddenly berserk and attacks the German. She is restrained and her movement curtailed by a length of rope tied around her waist. During the night, when Brennan falls asleep on watch, the demented woman slips over the side into the sea. In the morning, Bud silently cuts the body free.

Days pass and no land appears. They are in a desperate state, hungry and sunburned. They encounter a school of porpoises and sail through a shoal of tiny crablike creatures that they scoop out of the water by the handful and devour alive. Brennan steals a diamond ring from Mrs. Porter's vanity case to use as fishing bait, and sparks off a vicious quarrel between the two of them. He does eventually get a bite, which is immediately seized by a shark, and both fish and ring are lost. Brennan does not try his hand at fishing again.

Bud mans the tiller most of the time. When the German indicates that he will relieve him for a spell so that he can get some sleep, Bud agrees, but keeps an eye on the man and notices that almost as soon as he has control of the tiller the German changes course to the east. When Bud alerts the others to what is going on, they all, except Joe, attack the German. Albert reaches him first and hits him on the jaw, sending him reeling overboard. The German sinks from sight, although Joe dives into the sea after him in a vain attempt to save him. Burdened by recriminations and guilt, they argue and quarrel among themselves. Another storm hits them, and once more the boat becomes waterlogged.

By this time, they are all at the end of their tether. It seems as if a miracle has happened when Albert sights a merchantman flying the American flag steaming in their direction, but as it draws near their elation turns to dismay when they see that the men on deck are in uniforms: German uniforms. Fortuitously, two United States destroyers appear on the scene and begin firing on the enemy ship. Within seconds, the ship transforms itself from an innocent-looking freighter into a fighting ship, bristling with guns. A shell from one of the destroyers explodes in the sea near the lifeboat, blowing the survivors into the water. They all manage to swim back to the overturned boat, Alice Both helping Albert, who is unconscious after hitting his head, and Joe helping Mrs. Porter. They cling to the sides of the boat until eventually, after the raider has surrendered, they are picked up by the Navy.

The principal disadvantage of the book's first-person narrative mode is that much of the verbal interplay between the characters has been necessarily sacrificed, together with many of the fine shadings of character Steinbeck can convey so brilliantly through nuances of speech. On the other hand, he has triumphantly assumed the persona of his young narrator, who, for all his rough-edged and intermittent simple wisdom, has had only a limited experience of life. By the end of the story, we feel we know him as well as if we had met him and heard his story from his own lips. We appreciate his uncertainties, his fears, his views on life and politics, and his hopes for the future, all of which have been comprehensively conveyed to us through the rather free-ranging and unsophisticated style Steinbeck has chosen to employ. Bud speaks and thinks the thoughts of the ordinary man in the street, expressing opinions that although not, one suspects, always ones with which Steinbeck himself would wholly agree, they are opinions he understands and sympathizes with.

Bud Abbott is one of Steinbeck's most successful fictive characters. One of life's natural survivors, it is undoubtedly this instinct for survival that, despite his occasional and understandable brief moments of doubt, brings him and the others through their collective ordeal. He is the only one of them, other than the German, who is injured, yet at no time does he complain about his wound or use it as an excuse to avoid pulling his weight, even though it is a considerable time before Alice Both — because of other more compelling distractions, such as trying to revive the English-woman's baby and setting the German's arm — can give her undivided attention to his gashed leg. Indeed, Bud does more than his fair share of the work, caulking the leaks in the bow of the boat, helping to bail, taking turns at rowing whenever it becomes necessary to do so, and maintaining his post at the helm throughout the second storm. He accepts it all as part of the job that has to be done, and shows a flair for making do with the tools and materials available. When, for example, he snaps off the blade of the only knife they possess while caulking the holes in the bow, he carries on and completes the job with Mrs. Porter's nail file. The possibility does of course exist that this impressive display of stoicism and aptitude has been assumed retrospectively in order to present himself in a good light, but one senses that this reading cannot be valid. He gives the impression of being almost totally without guile. The account he gives is surely genuine, for he also admits his lapses from grace as well as revealing his virtues.

Accepting as a fact of life that he is one of those born to obey orders while there is some superior to issue the commands, Bud is perfectly willing to acknowledge the nonseafaring Brennan as captain, and is initially willing to find excuses for Brennan's disastrous inadequacies. But he later becomes increasingly impatient with the tycoon's failure to make decisions or to accept commonsense advice or warnings. Bud, however, never once challenges Brennan's authority outright. The nearest he gets to telling Brennan what a fool he is occurs when they come upon the school of porpoises. Brennan gets extremely excited, and starts yelling: "Isn't there some way we can kill one of them?" To which Bud drily replies: "Well, I might go after one with a nail file" (*Lifeboat* ts. 198). Bud's respect for authority, even Brennan's brand of authority, is exemplified toward the end of the story when, yet again, the argument arises as to the correct course they should be sailing. He tells Brennan: "We elected you Captain, and if you tell me to go East, I'll go East, but I won't on my own judgment. I just simply won't do it" (*Lifeboat* ts. 220). Typically, Brennan avoids committing himself, instructing Bud to do whatever he thinks fit.[2] For all Brennan's inadequacies as captain and despite most of the right-wing views he postulates, Bud still retains a grudging admiration for the tycoon for the way in which he has worked his way up in life from race driver to industrialist.

Connie Porter carries around the fruits of her success as actress, politician, and professional socialite in the alligator-skin box upon which she lavishes such extreme care. Immediately upon being pulled on board, she places the box under the thwart, where it will be safe, and at the earliest opportunity secures it with a line attached to its handle. Bud is intrigued by the box as soon as he sees it. "I figured that Congresswoman's got a lot of guts to hang on to that little box," he muses, "not forgetting it or dropping it no matter how scared she was, but of course, that's before I knew what she's got in that box" (*Lifeboat* ts. 20). He does not take to Mrs. Porter from the start, describing her as "blonde, probably a natural blonde, too, 'cause it had that sort of grayish tinge that a blonde gets when she's along thirty-five or nearly forty." He continues: "You could see she'd been a hell of a pretty woman at one time; you could see she was beginning to get a little crepey around the throat. So far she hadn't really said much; she's just made a few remarks, and she talked with her mouth pinched, she sort of bit words out of her like she knew what she was talking about" (*Lifeboat* ts. 30).

Hauled from a lingering death in the oil-covered sea, Mrs. Porter's first concern, once she has stowed her alligator-skin case safely away, is to do something about her appearance. She tears off a piece of her underskirt and starts to clean the oil off her arms and hands. A day or so later, after the boat has survived the first storm, she opens her case and takes out a comb and lipstick. With female solicitude, she shares these with Alice Both. The sight of the two women fixing their faces provokes some disbelieving comments between Bud and Albert, until Mrs. Porter in "a level kind of voice — with iron filings in it," tells them: "You know you'll be begging me for some of this lipstick before we're through" (*Lifeboat* ts. 63). She is right. After several days of exposure in the open boat, their lips begin cracking from the salt in the air and from the sun, and they realize that the lipstick will give them some measure of relief and protection. Bud swallows his pride and asks Mrs. Porter if he may use her lipstick. "She gave it to me," Bud records, "and then everybody put on lipstick, even Joe. Albert and Brennan and the German and I had beards. It looked kind of terrible to see those red lips. Terrible, and funny and a little sickening" (*Lifeboat* ts. 215).

Although she shares her lipstick for the good of all, Connie Porter remains a bitch to the very end. It is not possible to conclude whether or not she has indeed salvaged anything from the whole experience she has gone through. Even the fate of her alligator-skin box after the capsizing of the lifeboat is not revealed.[3]

Of all the people in the boat, apart from Bud who discovers reserves within himself he had not known existed, only Albert and Alice gain something good and permanent from the ordeal, for they fall in love. Neither are very vividly drawn characters, although they play important roles in the narrative. Alice Both rarely expresses an opinion about anything, going quietly about her work, tending wounds, trying to comfort the distraught Englishwoman, and finally saving Albert when he is knocked unconscious into the water. She reveals the passions that lie beneath her calm exterior on only two occasions, the second being when she is trying to save Albert from drowning. "She was just as fierce as an animal," Bud recalls, "she was like a wolf bitch" (*Lifeboat* ts. 243). Earlier, shortly after the death of the German, there is a heated discussion following Bud's suggestion that perhaps, after all, they should have taken the German's advice and headed east. Bud asks her what she thinks.

> She said, "What have I got to say about any of this? I don't understand any of it." She said, "I don't understand about the war. I don't understand about people hurting each other and killing each other. I don't understand any of that. It doesn't make any sense to me at all. I'm doing the only thing I can, trying to put them together again when they get hurt." She said, "That's the only way I can keep from going crazy, because the whole thing is crazy to me. ... When you've helped take the arms and legs off young men, when you've heard them raving in the night, then maybe it wouldn't make any sense to you either." (*Lifeboat* ts. 231–32)

There is no denying the forlorn wisdom and rationality of Alice Both's attitude. The deaths of the Englishwoman and her baby are pointless. The killing of the German is pointless: as matters turn out, it does not even contribute one iota toward the winning of the war. We never learn the German's name. It is never revealed whether or not he is the U-Boat commander. We remain unaware if he understands English, although the distinct possibility is that he does. What, however, is certain is that as soon as he is hauled aboard the lifeboat he suspects in his heart of hearts that he is doomed. He cannot know what the reaction of these people, his enemies, will be, or how he will be treated. Because of his broken arm, he cannot defend himself when he is attacked, first by the Englishwoman and later by Albert. If he knows there is a German raider in the area and that his only salvation lies in somehow effecting a rendezvous with her, he cannot even be sure, after all the days the lifeboat has been aimlessly drifting, exactly what easterly compass bearing he should try to persuade the Americans to steer. Everything has to be in the hands of providence.

Despite his hatred for the enemy and his instinctive suspicions about the man's true identity and motives, Bud cannot help feeling a certain "brotherhood of the seas" attitude toward the German, and indeed a strange, tentative relationship does grow between them. After they have come through the first storm and all are endeavoring to recover not only from the terrifying experience but also from the realization that their food has been lost, Bud is the only one who seems to have any thought for the German:

> He looked like an awfully sick man, and he was blue. I could see half the side of his face and it seemed to me his chin was quivering like, maybe he was crying, but I'm sure he wasn't because he wasn't a crying sort of guy at all. But he must have felt terrible with that broken arm under his wet clothes. He couldn't even have got them off himself. I guess he was too weak by that time. I wanted to offer to get his coat and sweater off because you don't like to see a guy suffer that way, even if he is a German-son-of-a-bitch. (*Lifeboat* ts. 64)

Eventually, when the sun comes out, Bud does help the German out of his coat and sweater. The two of them engage in a curious one-sided conversation, with Bud saying "Ja" every now and then, and it is this conversation that galvanizes the Englishwoman into her frenzied attack on the German. In the end, of course, the German does become for Bud "that Son of a Bitch." It is Bud who is directly responsible for the assault that ends with the death of the defenseless man. Afterwards, he has a bad conscience about the way he handled the situation and his own part in the assault:

> 'I kept thinking about that German's face when he knew we were going to kill him. I guess he knew it from the way we looked and he was scared. He was scared so bad you could smell him almost. ... I couldn't get the look of his face out of my mind. ... In a fight sometimes you feel good about even getting hurt, but not this German, not the way he went overboard. (*Lifeboat* ts. 227)

Bud is not the only one with a conscience about what has happened. Albert, being the one who actually landed the blow that sent the German reeling back into the sea, feels an overwhelming sense of guilt, which he endeavors to expiate by assuming the whole collective guilt on his shoulders and by publicly confessing to all his past sins. Brennan, too, feels a certain guilt in failing to exert his authority and take the initiative in damping down the explosive situation and preventing the death of his prisoner of war. While it is possible that Mrs Porter experiences no twinge of guilt, Alice Both is overcome with revulsion, and Joe is burdened by his inability and his fear as a black man to assert himself and defend the German. Joe is the only one to hold back when the assault takes place and speaks with the voice of reason, pleading with the others: "Don't you do nothing to him — don't you do nothing to him" (*Lifeboat* ts. 224). After Joe has been picked up after his abortive rescue attempt, Brennan demands to know why he had jumped in after the German. Joe replies: "Hell you fellows were a mob and I'm scared of mobs, I don't like mobs. . . . I seen mobs before and I know what they look like" (*Lifeboat* ts. 225). As Bud expresses it earlier in the narrative: "For quite a while I thought how hard it must be for [Joe] to be in this boat, even harder than it was for the German. Nobody had anything against Joe except his color. We hated the German because he was an enemy" (*Lifeboat* ts. 203).

Joe's most precious possession is the flute that hangs permanently from a length of fishline around his neck. He plays it beautifully, conjuring tunes out of his head. The first time Bud hears it, while he is half-asleep, the music seems to him unlike any playing he has ever heard:

> I thought I was dreaming it. Then I remembered how some people say when you're going to die you hear music, and I wondered if that was it. It was kind of thin, low, sweet music, and I thought it was all in my own mind. . . . It was a strange kind of music he was playing; it kind of went with the water, and it kind of matched the wind. It was a nice kind of music, I thought. It seemed like it came from inside your head — not from outside at all. (*Lifeboat* ts. 50—51)

The music works its magic on all of them, so that in time the flute and Joe's music become a tenuous bridge that closes the distance between him and the others. Just how tenuous a bridge is demonstrated on the morning the German is killed. When Joe is pulled back into the boat, he discovers that his flute is gone. As Bud recollects: "The flute was a loss to all of us. Everyone of us missed it when it was gone. We had come to depend on Joe playing in the evening. It soothed us. Some kind of life went out of that boat when Joe lost his flute. It was like a person being lost, like someone we knew, and it was gone" (*Lifeboat* ts. 226).

From then on, Joe isolates himself from the others. "He just didn't trust us any more. He couldn't trust what we'd do when we got out of hand" (*Lifeboat* ts. 228). By the time they are rescued by the Navy, the loss of the flute no longer matters and the renewal of the distance between Joe and the others can be viewed as simply part of the re-establishment of the norm. Joe will return to serving at table, resigned to be at everyone's beck and call; Alice and Albert will get married, before war sweeps them on their separate ways and possibly separate destinies; Brennan will continue to rule his industrial empire, increasing his fortune, forgetting the job offer he had made to Bud, and boasting all the while about his experiences and how his leadership ensured that they had lived through the ordeal; Connie Porter will continue to be, as she has always been, Connie Porter, and will regale her socialite friends and acquaintances and hangers-on with accounts of how ghastly it had all been, but fun in a perverse sort of way; the Englishwoman and her baby are dead, pathetic victims of the war they tried to escape; and the German, the enemy, is also dead — satisfactorily and deservedly dead — after trying to kill them all, the precise circumstances of his death conveniently pushed to the back of everyone's mind.

Only Bud will want to remember it all in every detail, exactly as it happened. His simple honesty shines through the whole narrative. In assuming the Bud persona, Steinbeck has told the story straight, without any heightened drama. In some respects, this accounts for the narrative seeming ultimately disappointing. *Lifeboat* does in fact display all the signs Elizabeth Otis had feared: the apparent disintegration of Steinbeck's prose style. Bud's mainly uninspired prose, with its constant use of the phrase "kind of" and the excessive repetition of the all-purpose dead noun "thing," is singularly appropriate to the narrator's persona, but by eschewing the distinctive rhythms that play their part in making the best of his work so memorable, Steinbeck is here too successful in reproducing the manner in which someone like Bud would write. Consequently, the whole work has been reduced to a strange monotony of tone and pace. There are, it is true, occasional glimpses of the old Steinbeck magic, particularly in the descriptions of natural phenomena — the fog through which the freighter is steaming in the opening paragraphs, the various seascapes, the storms, the play of porpoises, the sky in all its different moods — that do relieve, but all too briefly, the overall monotony. It is a measure of Steinbeck's masterful grasp of his material that these passages do not seem in the least incongruous as expressions of Bud's thoughts and observations, but it is perhaps a measure of Steinbeck's failure, if such passages are perfectly acceptable, that he did not use a degree of artistic license and compose the whole work in like manner.

To be fair to Steinbeck, it should not be overlooked that *Lifeboat* is merely the narrative outline for another work in another medium, and that the extant typescript is the rough first draft for a possible finer work, a work that he might have indeed embarked upon were it not for his preoccupation with other, more pressing matters.

For all its many defects, *Lifeboat* is a work of considerable interest, not the least in the way in which, through the Bud persona, Steinbeck was able to express some of his own strongly held views and sentiments about the war, the Washington establishment, and the literary critics who had been so acerbic in their columns about his recent work. In apparent defense of his portrait of Colonel Lanser in *The Moon Is Down* and in anticipation of the possible reaction to his portrait of the German in *Lifeboat*, Steinbeck has Bud ruminating:

> It seemed to me that most people were kind of comfortable with war, because they didn't have to think any more. We were all good and the enemy was all bad ... [B]ut I'd like to take a small bet that everything we say, they say, only it's the other way around. I bet it's that way and I bet they believe it just as much as we do. (*Lifeboat* ts. 75)

Bud also has some very strong opinions about the "chiselers in the Government," maintaining that "we know there's crookedness, but now it's unpatriotic to say it. Now you can't·say it because you're interfering with the war effort. Those chiselers are absolutely protected for the duration of the war" (*Lifeboat* ts. 78). Bud/Steinbeck, the radical patriot, goes on, in a passage partly reminiscent of a similar passage in Chapter 10 of *Sea of Cortez* (*SC* 88), to issue his stern warning to those he sees as having seized their opportunity and effectively taken over power in the country:

> Well, sir, in the Depression it was kind of slow. People went into it so slow they didn't know what was happening to them until finally they were so weak they couldn't do anything about it. But this time they're going to come back and they're going to be all full of vitamins and vinegar and they're going to be tough guys, and they'd better come back to something besides relief because they're not going to like that. I don't think anybody in the Army or out of it is so dumb to think that there is nothing wrong — with this country. But it seems to me the reason they're all fighting is because the good thing, the one thing that's best of all is that in this country if enough of you don't like a thing — you can go about and change it. Well, all those fellows are going to come back from the Army, and they're going to find a lot of people elected to office, that were elected by people who weren't in the Army, and they're not going to be the kind of people who'd — well — see that the Army didn't go back on relief. You see I remember the time when a bunch of Congressmen got up and said if they voted two billion dollars to feed starving people in this country it would bankrupt the nation and then a little later those same Congressmen they voted a hundred million dollars for the war. Maybe they weren't scared then. But when we were hungry that

two billion dollars looked awful big to us. Maybe we were as scared as those Congressmen are now. Maybe all this kind of thing isn't a good thing to think about and talk about in a time of war, but I never could get the idea the best thing to do wasn't to tell people the truth. I think that most people got sense enough to take the truth — most of them have. And I think most of them got sense to know when they're being lied to, too. (*Lifeboat* ts. 81–82)

Lifeboat undoubtedly carries a considerable political punch in presenting its microcosm of America at war and by filtering the varying philosophies of its ill-assorted cast of characters through the recollections of its twenty-two-year-old narrator. Bud's own simple philosophizings are certainly not "the kind of thing ... to think about and talk about in a time of war," and in using the fictive Bud to work off his bile and his frustration over the way he was being treated by the establishment, Steinbeck was being rather idealistic and optimistic in assuming his script would be accepted in the quasidocumentary format he had adopted, with all its political content left intact. No Hollywood studio in those days would have attempted to make such a movie.

3

Two days after he had sent the script to Hollywood, Steinbeck heard via the grapevine that his application for a commission had been finally rejected, ostensibly by reason of the recent War Department edict that no further commissions were to be granted to civilians on direct entry into the service. His reaction to this piece of news was mixed. On one hand, he was relieved that some decision had at last been made, so that, released from one uncertainty, he no longer need postpone any other plans he might have. On the other hand, the withdrawal of the Army's interest meant he was now completely at the disposal of the Monterey draft board, whose members, he felt sure, were out for his blood in whatever way possible.

There was at one time talk of his being sent to England to make a film, presumably under OWI auspices, but this project, or his part in it, was, like so many others, canceled. In mid-March, in an attempt to break out of the impasse, he elected to take decisive action of his own. One evening over dinner, he asked a longtime friend, the *New York Herald Tribune* literary critic Lewis Gannett, if he could use his influence to secure him a job with the newspaper as a war correspondent. Such work would not only give him the opportunity to taste the action that he now craved, but would also free him finally from all the petty jealousies and all the red tape that had been throttling his work for the government. Washington, he pronounced, was "very much like the fraternity system at Stanford" (JS/WFS 3/15/43).

But even this idea was fraught with further bureaucratic difficulties. When Gannett mentioned the matter to the *NYHT*'s assistant editor, Wilbur Forrest, the newspaper did not hesitate in agreeing to hire Steinbeck, but advised him that clearance would first be needed from the War and State Departments. It was a complicated process. Not only was there more form-filling to be carried out, but, even after accreditation was approved in the United States, the whole matter had to be referred to the commander of the North European Theatre, to which it was intended he should be sent. Only when that commander approved was the accreditation considered complete (JS/WFS 4/9/43).

The plan was that he be sent initially to England to cover the training of troops in preparation for the opening of the long-awaited Second Front, and to accompany the troops during the invasion, whenever it was launched. He undertook to submit five hundred to one thousand words of copy per day. There would be no restriction on his subject matter, and he would be able to move around at will. His reports would be syndicated nationwide. The whole setup seemed to be flexible enough for him to feel he had at last found the sort of job he wanted and to which he was best suited. He was soon to discover, however, that the Monterey draft board did not intend to let him off the hook without a struggle, and still had a card or two up its sleeve.

March 1943 was an eventful month in many ways. On the 18th, Carol, now working as a mechanic in the Army's Fort Ord motor pool, obtained her final divorce, under the terms of which she was awarded a $220,000 property settlement by the Salinas judge. The way was now clear for Steinbeck and Gwyn to legalize their relationship. They traveled down to New Orleans, and on 29 March were married in the French Quarter home of writer Lyle Saxon. Gwyn was 23, Steinbeck 41.

4

On 14 March, before an audience of approximately three hundred young Norwegian trainees, the world premiere of the Twentieth Century-Fox movie version of *The Moon Is Down*, directed by Irving Pichel, took place in a flimsy pine building in "Little Norway," Toronto, the training center for the Royal Norwegian Air Force. The movie was publicly premiered at the Rivoli Theater in New York later in the month.

Inevitably, some of the old controversies were rekindled by the critics, although the majority seemed to take the view that Nunnally Johnson's adaptation, even though the script closely followed Steinbeck's text in essence, showed the Nazis in an appropriately harsher light, and the movie never had to withstand the sort of extreme critical venom directed the previous year against the novel and the play. *Time*, for example, thought that Sir Cedric Hardwicke, in the role of Colonel Lanser, looked "more like a cold-blooded Junker than the unmilitary officer described by Steinbeck."[4] Johnson had opened up the action by introducing, at the very beginning, a scene on board a German cruiser with Lanser receiving his briefing from a naval staff officer, and, later, the mowing down of the young Norwegian soldiers as they hurry back to town after spotting the enemy paratroopers. These initial scenes served to establish the cold ruthlessness of the invaders, which was in course of time accentuated by the subsequent on-screen executions. In this manner, while retaining the main elements of Steinbeck's story, the movie manages to center more on the plight and courage of the mayor and his people, and the way in which, as well as carrying out effective acts of sabotage, the townspeople undermine the morale of the German troops by refusing to talk to them or even to recognize their existence unless forced to do so. There was widespread recognition at last among the critics that Steinbeck's view of the nature and potential vulnerability of the invaders was perhaps not all that farfetched. As Hermine Rick Isaacs observed in *Theatre Arts*, almost echoing Steinbeck's own words about the film, the portraits of the invaders had "a three-dimensional quality that stands out in bold relief against the usual run of Nazi villain, Hollywood style."[5]

The movie did not, however, do well at the box office, the public clearly preferring two other movies about invaded Norway released about the same time: *The Commandos Strike at Dawn*, screenplay by Irwin Shaw from a story by C. S. Forester, featuring Paul Muni and Sir Cedric Hardwicke (on this occasion playing the role of a British officer), and directed by John Farrow; and *The Edge of Darkness*, screenplay by Robert Rossen from William Wood's novel of the same name, featuring Errol Flynn and Ann Sheridan, and directed by Lewis Milestone. So far as audiences were concerned, Nazis were more acceptable if portrayed as dyed-in-the-wool Hollywood villains, and plots were more acceptable if they conveyed their propagandist didacticism by way of typical Hollywood melodrama and full-blooded action.

It is just possible that reports that had been coming in from Sweden may have influenced some critics when they reviewed *The Moon Is Down*. The play had opened the previous month in Sweden to rave notices. *Time* noted that the production had been so successful that it had been moved to a larger theater. "Swedish critics," *Time* reported, "speaking of ever-growing Norwegian resistance, praised Steinbeck for prophetic insight, remarked that *The Moon Is Down* is truer today than when it was written. Judging by reports which have sifted through, the widespread US criticism that the Nazis in the play are too weak has not been voiced in Sweden."[6]

Steinbeck must have felt himself completely vindicated. Certainly, the reports instilled in him the idea that once he had arrived in England, he would explore the possibility of visiting Sweden to report on the situation there. The Nazis had been badgering Sweden for some time and he anticipated that an invasion was not improbable, even though he felt that Sweden, with its considerable army and air force, would put up a good fight. He had heard that two planes a week flew from London to Stockholm, and he determined that as soon as he reached London he would seek an appointment with the United States ambassador, John Winant, in an attempt to get a seat on one of the planes.

5

All this time the process of accreditation had been proceeding. Anxious to have everything sewn up and be on his way by the middle of April, he had, toward the end of March, arranged for Street to make his intentions known to the Monterey draft board, who would have to release him before he could make application to the State Department for a passport. In normal circumstances, there should have been no difficulty — he was not applying for a deferment, for his current draft classification was 4F, itself a deferred classification. The draft board, however, chose to drag its heels, refusing to issue the required clearance until he had been accredited by the War Department.

By the end of the month, no progress had been made, although he had submitted his application for a passport to the State Department on 26 April, without waiting for the draft board's release. By 4 May, however, he had been accredited by the War Department and released by the draft board. He had still not received his passport. He was itching to get away, and had elected to make the journey across the Atlantic by troopship rather than plane, for he knew that some ships were getting ready to sail and he did not want to miss getting a passage on one.

His passport was eventually issued on 14 May, nearly two months after he had secured the job with the *New York Herald Tribune*. But there were to be still more delays. "Psychically," he confessed to Street, "I think I am falling to pieces" (JS/WFS 5/12/43). While waiting for passage, he underwent two courses of innoculations. He survived the first course without too much discomfort. The second one, on 17 May, for typhoid, paratyphoid, tetanus, and cholera made him really suffer. According to Gwyn, he had a highly allergic reaction to the tetanus shot, and his arm swelled up so badly it was as large as his thigh. He was delirious and in a semicoma at times, and was still shaky when, on the penultimate day of the month, he embarked on the troopship. At least, by then he could get his arm into a jacket sleeve. "I'm taking a minimum of equipment with me," he told Street, but included are four quarts of scotch which has already been around the world and now I'm going to give it another short trip. They say the snake situation at sea is pretty bad and I would hate to be snake bitten and to have no remedy. That and a lot of sulphur dyazine are about the only things I am taking for health purposes except for a hundred multicebrins which were a gift from Paul de Kruif. They are very good stuff. I'm also taking a couple of pounds of pipe tobacco. Good tobacco is getting rare. (JS/WFS 5/30/43)

If he went off almost gaily to war, he was leaving behind a very unhappy wife, who was feeling, not unnaturally, somewhat abandoned, and resentful that he should be leaving her after only two months of marriage. She had tried to dissuade him as far as she knew how, and, without his knowing, had endeavored to get others to dissuade him too. She has maintained that when the time came for him to leave, very early one morning, she woke up to find him completing his last-minute packing. He said he did not even have time to sit down and have a last cup of coffee with her. Indeed, by her account, she barely had time to get out of bed before he was out the front door, without even saying goodbye. After all the frustrations he had gone through during the past several months, it seemed that he simply could not wait to be off. If Gwyn's account is true, he was guilty of inexcusable callousness, but it may have been that in his own strange way he did not want to upset her (and perhaps, when it came to it, even himself) with a long goodbye, feeling that the quick break, brutal though it would seem at the time, was best in the long run.

A little over a week later, Gwyn received a telegram from London: "ARRIVED SAFELY I LOVE YOU JOHN STEINBECK."

6

When Steinbeck arrived in London on 8 June, apart from a few sporadic "nuisance raids" carried out by one or two enemy bombers that had managed to evade the defenses, the capital had suffered no major aerial bombardment for two years. The evidence of the Blitz, however, was everywhere to be seen: the unsightly gaps in the elegant Nash terraces and in the rows of shops in the main thoroughfares, the burnt-out Wren churches, the emergency water tanks on the cleared bomb sites, the pock-marked masonry, the sandbagged government buildings in Whitehall, the windows crisscross taped against the effects of blast. "The story of the War is right here," Steinbeck was to observe, "it's in the people's faces, and in those fireplaces hanging on a broken wall three stories up."[7]

The voyage across the Atlantic had been uneventful, and, once in London, he initially took up residence in the luxurious Savoy Hotel overlooking the Thames. Interviewed by a bevy of British reporters in his room on the day he arrived, he expressed an apparent lack of interest when reminded that his play, *The Moon Is Down*, was opening that very evening at the Whitehall Theatre. "Is it?" he commented. "I don't know. I heard it was in production over here, but that's all."[8] Although his lack of interest may have stemmed from weariness after the long journey, it may just as likely have been that he was still very conscious of the play's failure on Broadway fourteen months before. Possibly, he suspected the play would fare no better in London, perhaps even worse.

The 620-seater Whitehall Theatre, one of London's smaller and newer theaters (it had opened in 1930), stands at the Trafalgar Square end of the famous street of British government. Somewhat detached from the center of London's theaterland, it had been home to a succession of short-run productions during the preceding months. When the forthcoming production of the Steinbeck play was announced in September 1942, the revelation that one of the principal backers was the vaudeville performer Wee Georgie Wood, a popular diminutive child impersonator, gave cause for some raised eyebrows. The play opened in the northern seaside resort of Blackpool on 6 April 1943, and then went on provincial tour prior to its West End presentation.

By the time the curtain rose in the Whitehall Theatre, it was common knowledge that the author was in town, and there was a buzz of speculation in the bar during the intermission as to whether or not he was in the theater and might make a curtain speech. Although invited by the management and moreover informed by them that the exiled King Haakon of Norway would be in the audience, Steinbeck declined to attend, and thus missed the enthusiastic applause and cheers at the play's conclusion. The curtain speech was in fact made by Lewis Casson, the actor playing the part of Mayor Orden. Casson suggested that the play would help to remind everyone of the continuing heroism of people in the occupied countries, and that this, of course, had been the author's intention.

On the whole, the Whitehall production was received more favorably by the London critics than their American counterparts had received the Martin Beck Theater production the previous year. The two main objections leveled by the New York critics against Steinbeck's text (on both moral and dramatic grounds) and the casting of the principal roles proved not to be matters for contention in London. While the critics did tend to find the pace of the play sometimes rather slow and monotonous (although this was not always necessarily considered a disadvantage), the dialogue was almost universally praised. The performances of the actors playing the two leading roles — Casson as Mayor Orden and Karel Stepanek as Colonel Lanser — were also generally praised. Certainly, Casson gave a moving and dignified portrayal of the condemned mayor, a portrayal that contrasted favorably with that of Ralph Morgan in the Broadway production. Casson's Orden was described by W. A. Darlington, one of

London's foremost drama critics, as "a man whose simple clarity of vision gives him the right to go to his death with the last words of Socrates on his lips."[9]

Whereas Otto Kruger had been not at all happy in his role as Lanser, as had been revealed in his interview with Milton Bracker, Stepanek had no such doubts. Stepanek, a Czech who had acted for many years in Berlin before coming to England after Hitler came to power, entertained no illusions about the man he was portraying. "The Colonel Lanser type, I know from observation, is very prevalent in the German Army," he told an interviewer, "and to my mind is far more dangerous than the typical fanatical Nazi."[10] With his clipped and slightly rasping voice, Stepanek conformed more to the general public's concept of Lanser than did Kruger's rather suave "English gentleman" interpretation.

The play really succeeds or fails on the acting in the two leading roles, but the Australian actor W. E. Holloway (Dr. Winter) and the Canadian actress and film star Carla Lehmann (Molly Morden) both received honorable mentions from most critics, even though, as Darlington pointed out, Miss Lehmann should not have looked "quite so well-nourished in the scene where she says she is starving."[11] The minor but important role of Molly's husband, Alex, was played by Paul Scofield, who, at the age of twenty-one, was at the beginning of his distinguished international career.

In an article appearing in the *New York Times* of 11 July, Darlington reported that *The Moon Is Down* was playing in London to appreciative audiences, who were more prepared than those in New York to accept plays about the war. He also noted, as had *Time* two months or so earlier, that news infiltrating through from the occupied countries indicated that Steinbeck's thesis in the play was not so farfetched as it may have seemed in 1942. "There are," Darlington wrote, "stories on all sides of Nazi officers whose hopes have faded, whose spirits have failed and whose nerves have cracked under the strain of living on top of a volcano of hatred."[12] He prophesied good fortune for the play in London, and considered it altogether likely that the Whitehall run would be longer than had been that at the Martin Beck.[13]

7

Steinbeck wasted no time in getting down to work, even if he had come with no fixed program in mind. He was not at all pleased at having to wear an Army uniform, which was the war correspondent's official garb. As he rather disparagingly told a reporter: "You see, the army has charge now, and it seems to like uniform; it's part of their stock-in-trade, just as the undertaker likes long black coats and chimney-pot hats."[14] There were other conventions and procedures he was obliged to accept.

He had to visit the Vine Street police station, near Piccadilly Circus, where the Aliens' Passport Office was situated and where all persons not possessing a British passport, even the most distinguished and fully accredited war correspondents, were required to report on entering the country. The sergeant at the desk looked askance at the identity photograph in Steinbeck's war correspondent's pass. Steinbeck explained that owing to his aversion to being photographed the photo had been taken eight years before and happened to be the only full-face one he had available at the time. He was apparently able to allay the sergeant's doubts.

Two days after his arrival in London, there occurred one of the occasional briefings American correspondents attended with Brenden Bracken, the British Minister of Information, at his Westminster office. Steinbeck duly presented himself at the meeting to "get the atmosphere" and pay his respects to the minister. Only two of his compatriots recognized him and troubled to speak to him, and he was able to make his escape long before the meeting broke up. Probably it was at this gathering that he first became aware of the sense of unspoken resentment some of the other correspondents felt toward him. He was, after all, an amateur in the field, one whose arrival in the war zone had been accorded a blaze of publicity (however unwanted it had been by him personally) in the British press, and whose dispatches were guaranteed to attract far greater attention and praise and to earn far larger sums than most of the professional correspondents could aspire to. It had never been his intention to poach on the territory of the professionals: he simply wanted to write the sort of stories they had neither the opportunity nor the inclination to cover. As the London *Daily Express* of 25 June, announcing the forthcoming publication of Steinbeck's dispatches in the paper, put it:

> He has come here to see the war through the eyes of the Common Man. He is going to tell the story of the Common Man first from the base of operations in Britain, and then wherever the news takes him. Steinbeck's commission for the *Daily Express* supplements the brilliant corps of war correspondents whose spot-news dispatches appear daily. He will be looking at the war not with the object of giving you the latest news and giving it to you quickly, but from the point of view of the man in the ranks.[15]

The first six articles Steinbeck sent to the *NYHT* collectively covered the account of the Atlantic crossing on the troopship: the crowded conditions on board, the humdrum existence, the boredom of the men, the various ways in which they endeavor to combat the boredom, and the welcome they receive when they at last reach landfall. The first of these articles, "The Americans Embark for War," appeared in the *Herald Tribune* on 21 June, and the sixth, "Steinbeck Tells How Bagpipes Greet

US Troops in Britain," on 26 June.[16] In a private memorandum, the *Herald Tribune*'s editor declared: "[Steinbeck's articles] are even better than we had hoped. In fact, I haven't read anything better about the war — anything to equal them in graphic description or in beauty of writing."[17] The editor of *Reader's Digest* was similarly impressed, offering twenty-five hundred dollars for the rights to reprint in his magazine an edited version of four of the articles.[18]

One of the first callers at Steinbeck's hotel room was American journalist C. Patrick Thompson. Thompson was also working for the *Herald Tribune* and had obviously been requested by the editor to look out for Steinbeck, show him the ropes, and, if and when necessary, introduce him to useful contacts. Thompson had recently visited United States Fighter Command Headquarters to obtain material for an article he had been commissioned to write for the *NYHT*'s Sunday magazine. He had mentioned Steinbeck's imminent arrival in England to Captain Arthur Gordon, the acting liaison officer, and had suggested that Steinbeck might welcome having some project lined up and ready for him. Gordon agreed to see what he could do. In the hotel room, Thompson asked Steinbeck if he was perhaps interested in beginning his work in England by visiting a bomber station. Steinbeck jumped at the opportunity. Without more ado, Thompson phoned Gordon, and within two hours Gordon joined them at the Savoy. Within three minutes the proposed visit to the bomber station was arranged, Steinbeck insisting that he should receive no VIP treatment, saying he wanted to bunk down and eat with the airmen.

One of the reasons for Steinbeck's immediate enthusiasm for visiting the bomber station was that it would enable him to meet up with Annie Laurie Williams's husband, Maurice Crain, a sergeant air-gunner who manned the ball turret of the Flying Fortress *Mary Ruth*. Maurice had been credited two days before Steinbeck's arrival on the station with the shooting down of his first enemy plane, a Focke-Wulf 190. The two men spent the evening in the barracks together, catching up on each other's news, and the following day Steinbeck had to sweat it out on the ground while the *Mary Ruth* flew another mission over Wilhelmshaven. On his return from the mission, Maurice was given a forty-eight-hour pass, and went to London with Steinbeck, sharing his hotel room until his leave was up. In the 27th of his dispatches, Steinbeck recalled the time they spent together in the capital:

The next day we walked in London to the places we knew from books — Fleet Street where newspapers were born and the house where Dr. Johnson fulminated and the apartment where Macauley wrote his history. We went to the temple where law was made and to the round church the Norman Knights built nearly a thousand years ago and left to go to the Crusades. Crain loved the city with

its continuing ghosts. You talk of old things intimately where they happened —
as though they were still happening.

The temple was blasted and fire-blackened. The city was destroyed as all
cities are again and again. But he could see the rising new city here, just as he
could at home. He was as certain that the better thing would come as he was
that the old thing had been. And above all he was clear. He knew what he was
and what he wanted and he knew how to go about it. There was nothing
confused in him.

Sunday night he went back to his station, to his ball turret, to his two fifty-
caliber machine guns, his implements into the future.[19]

There had been a note from Max Wagner waiting for Steinbeck at the
Savoy when he had returned to London with Maurice. Max, too, had
been in England for several months, and, reading that Steinbeck was in
London, had come up to town on a forty-eight-hour pass on the off-
chance that he might meet his old friend, arriving while Steinbeck was at
the bomber station. Max had been forced to return to camp when his
leave expired. The note gave the news that Max was half expecting to be
shipped back to the States on medical grounds. Steinbeck called him
immediately, but Max did not feel free to give him any information over
the phone. The following day, however, he contrived to get another pass,
and joined Steinbeck and Maurice in London. The hotel room at the
Savoy was becoming rather crowded.

Wagner was far from happy at the prospect of being sent home. He had
a good record as a soldier, and Steinbeck subsequently spent one whole
afternoon at army headquarters in an attempt to get Wagner transferred
to another unit that would enable him to stay on in England. It was a long
shot, and one that did not ultimately pay off. Wagner's current medical
problem had been officially diagnosed as a "nervous stomach," the consequences of his heavy drinking over many years before his enlistment.
While not by any stretch of the imagination on the wagon, he had
managed to cut down radically his consumption of alcohol since he had
been in the Army, and Steinbeck was encouraged to see that he had lost a
lot of weight and looked fitter than he had for years. Steinbeck feared for
his friend if he were to be sent home. He knew Max's pride would be
badly hurt and that this was exactly the sort of situation to send him
quickly back to the bottle. He took Max along to see film director
William Wyler, then in England working on the documentary *Memphis
Belle*, the story of a bomber crew, in the hope that he could persuade
Wyler to give Max a job in his unit. Wyler, however, was on the point of
returning home himself, his assignment completed. Although he explored
other avenues, Steinbeck was unsuccessful in pulling any strings for his
friend, and by the beginning of July Max was on his way back to the
States.

One of Steinbeck's most consistent and increasing gripes was that he had not received one letter or cablegram from Gwyn since arriving in England, although he had faithfully written to her every day he could. The lack of contact with her was beginning to drive him crazy. His appreciation that mails were subject to severe delay and that everyone was in the same boat did nothing to mitigate his distress. Maurice had told him that when he first came to England it had been six to eight weeks before he heard from Annie Laurie.

Steinbeck immersed himself in his work to keep his mind off Gwyn's silence, going in search of promising stories whenever the opportunity presented itself. He found it impossible to write his dispatches out in the field. Too much was happening then, so he averred, to get the material rationalized in his mind. He waited until he returned to London before doing anything with his notes, and wrote his reports in the mornings, sitting at his typewriter in his dressing gown, producing four thousand to five thousand words a day. This high output enabled him to send a six hundred- or one thousand-word dispatch each day to New York, while ensuring he had always something in reserve against the time he might temporarily run short of material. He had put himself on a writing treadmill no one could possibly have kept up for very long, but he was happy doing it for the time being, for it prevented his mind from dwelling on other matters. In any case, he was relieved to discover that after a long spell of doing little or no writing he was able now to turn out more than his required daily quota.

After a week or so, he moved out of the Savoy, which he had come to regard as a madhouse where everybody talked and drank too much, and rented a small, top-floor, one-room apartment in Athenaeum Court in Piccadilly, overlooking Green Park. The bed made up into a couch during the day. Sitting at the desk in front of the expansive windows, he could look out over the park and the London skyline: St. Paul's, Tower Bridge, St. James's Palace, Whitehall, Big Ben, and the Houses of Parliament. Buckingham Palace was only a quarter of a mile away and if the wind was in the right direction he could hear the music and drumming that accompanied the Changing of the Guard ceremony. If it were not for the barrage balloons overhead, it would have been difficult to imagine, looking from his window, that London was a city at war.

He continued to avoid whenever possible any invitations or engagements of a social or professional nature that would keep him from his work. He met Burgess Meredith and became briefly acquainted with some of the other war correspondents then in London — Robert Capa, Richard Watts, Richard Tregaskis, William Shirer, and Larry Rue — but he firmly refused to give talks on BBC radio and to have lunch or dinner with various peers, politicians, and businessmen who sought his company at table. He even declined the opportunities to meet Bernard Shaw and H. G. Wells. His ability at shrugging off these unwanted social commitments was not always successful. On one occasion, the Ministry of Information invited him to dine with Brenden Bracken. He made his excuses, saying that he could not go owing to another (fictitious) engagement he could not possibly break. He was advised that Churchill would be there, and that he should not miss this opportunity of meeting the great man, and so eventually he allowed himself to be persuaded, even though it meant, as he complained to the very last, that he would have to wear his one remaining clean white shirt. As it turned out, Churchill did not turn up, and the clean white shirt was sacrificed to no purpose. Another time, he attended a luncheon at a London hotel given by the correspondents' association in honor of General Wavell, who had been appointed Viceroy of India, and contracted a nasty bout of food poisoning, which he blamed on the chicken that had been served. "It serves me right for going to a luncheon," he told Gwyn. "I will never make that mistake again" (JS/GS 7/5/43).

Thompson, still eager to act in a liaison capacity, asked Steinbeck next if he would like to visit the Royal Navy. Steinbeck said he would, expressing a wish to go to Scotland, where he had first landed on British soil. But the river Clyde was, unfortunately, closed to journalists. Thompson suggested as an alternative that he might like to consider a trip to Dover, the focal point of many operations by minesweepers, motor torpedo boats, and air-sea rescue patrols. There, so Thompson informed him, he could, if he so wanted, also visit an antiaircraft mixed battery and a nearby train-busting RAF station. The idea appealed to Steinbeck and he was called to the Admiralty for an interview. Arrangements there were made for him to stay with a Commander Eykyn in Dover.

On Saturday, 19 June, he visited the headquarters of General Ira C. Eaker, the commander of the United States expeditionary Bomber Command in the United Kingdom. The visit had been initiated at the general's request. Steinbeck found Eaker pleasant, and he was given more or less *carte blanche* to do whatever he wanted. He enjoyed his stay at the headquarters complex, especially as it was sited in "beautiful country of little forests and little fields with a light over it like that on Monterey Peninsula in September, a clear blue light" (JS/GS 6/22/43). He stayed overnight, getting into a poker game, a game he had never cared for very much, and won "rather heavily."

Four days later, he was picked up by an Admiralty car and driven to Dover. While waiting for the car to arrive, he dashed off a letter to Gwyn. In a rush of understatement, he admitted to "a feeling of disappointment" that he had not heard from her, and pointedly mentioned that he had received letters from his sisters, Esther and Mary, both of whom had mailed their letters some time after he had embarked on the troopship. He wondered if Gwyn's letters had perhaps been lost at sea on the way over, and urged her to use air mail in future. In spite of his dispirited mood, he could still indulge in a touch of whimsical humor:

> I want to look for these blue birds waiting to fly over Dover. If there are none I will have finally destroyed the filthy lies American song writers have put over. Have you ever noticed their overwhelming interest in ornithology? I went to Berkeley Square the other evening and if there is a nightingale there, she is wearing a ten shilling summer dress and soliciting. (JS/GS 6/24/43)

When he returned to London a week later, there were still no letters from Gwyn. By now, he was becoming really frantic. He was realizing from his own bitter experience how the absence of letters from loved ones at home could wreak absolute havoc on the morale of troops.

While in Dover, he had sailed on a routine minesweeping operation.[20] What was more important was that he had, at long last, seen some real action, and he wrote to Gwyn, telling her that one of the big questions he had always asked about himself had now been answered: how would he react under fire and, more specifically, how scared would he be when it came to the crunch? He discovered that he was no different from most men — scared beforehand, but all right once the action had started. He assured her that he had not been hurt in any way, other than suffering a bad case of sunburn, even though they had got "knocked about a bit, which is British for they shot the hell out of us" (JS/GS early July 1943).

Steinbeck's dispatch describing this particular operation obviously did not meet with the approval of the censor, for only a watered-down and truncated account appeared in the *Herald Tribune*, with all details of the action eliminated.[21] Twelve years later, he was able to publish a fuller story of his experiences:

> One night, one sloppy, dirty night, we crossed the Channel with the purpose of prematurely detonating some German ammunition ships. By an unhappy piece of miscalculation, hereinafter called an Act of God, we found ourselves inshore of a group of German flak barges, and they laid it down on us. I still have the scars on my chest from trying to tunnel through the deck grating. We had seven craft and we lost four.[22]

The first letters from Gwyn arrived on 2 July: three letters in two envelopes, the last being dated 21 June. He wrote her a long letter the following morning before he started work on his dispatches. The strain of the schedule he had been setting himself was, he confessed, beginning to tell:

You know I took on a terrible job. That is a frightful lot of work. It wouldn't be if only I did it every day but having to double up so that I can get away makes it very difficult. However, it was my own idea and I'm stuck with it and it is amazingly good discipline. I'm getting some writing done whether it is good or bad and the thing does go easier in execution but not a bit in the planning. (JS/GS 7/3/43)

The previous evening, he had had dinner with Alexander Korda, the film magnate, and had discussed with him the possibility of getting Gwyn over to England on some professional pretext or other. The whole business, he told Gwyn, appeared to be so hedged around with regulations that it was possibly best to abandon the idea. If she wanted to come over, he would explore other avenues.

He spent the Fourth of July in London. Feeling particularly homesick and restless on this special day, he roamed the streets for hours and struck up conversation with several groups of soldiers. All the men, he found, were similarly plagued by debilitating homesickness and filled with resentment at what they saw as the mishandling of affairs in Washington. His own sense of despondency had been deepened by the news that the *Mary Ruth* had been lost over enemy territory. The *Mary Ruth* had been on three missions in rapid succession since he had said goodbye to Maurice, and the loss of the bomber had occurred before the end of June. He endeavored to find out all that he could of the circumstances in which the bomber had been downed, but, despite all his contacts, he was unable to learn little more than that the other planes in the formation had observed several parachutes opening as the *Mary Ruth* was plunging earthward. Even then, nothing was certain. None of those witnessing the scene could be sure from which parts of the doomed plane the parachutists had jumped, and not all the witnesses reported seeing the same number of parachutes anyway.

His daily output of words, on those days reserved for writing, had fallen somewhat. He had found it impossible to sustain the original five thousand words a day he had set himself: four thousand was the absolute maximum he could hope for. Moreover, he felt he could achieve better results if he spread his efforts and attempted only three stories per week, rather than attempting to write two or three stories in a day. But he was only too aware that the gulf between what might be desirable and what was necessary was too wide for him to relax his present program. The schedule of work he had undertaken and had promised his editor to maintain forced him to continue producing at full speed just to keep up the expected flow of dispatches. If ever he took a day's break, he had to work twice as hard the following day.

On 10 July the news came through that the Allies had invaded Sicily. Sometime earlier, he had applied to be sent to Africa, but permission had not yet materialized. Having tasted action and come through the experience physically and mentally unscathed, he was eager for more. This waiting resurrected the old sense of frustration. "Everything is by permission," he complained to Gwyn.

> The most things an army does is wait, too. That is much more deadly than the fighting. I haven't seen any fighting yet, at least where I could see an enemy. All long range stuff ... I'm filled with apathy. Must get out of here. I'm going sour. Flubbed my work yesterday. I did three thousand words and had to throw them away. That never makes for good feelings. (JS/GS 7/10/43)

Over a week had passed since he had last received a letter from Gwyn, or indeed anyone else. His sense of isolation is demonstrably apparent in the letter he wrote two days later.

> I'm lonesome for you beyond words. When I think that I came of my own will without being dragged, I wonder how I could have in spite of the fact that I knew I had to. There wasn't any help for it. You would never have liked me and I would never have liked myself if I hadn't come to this war. And the separation can be good though I hate it. It can solidify things beyond what they were even. (JS/GS 7/12/43)

8

The movie *The Moon Is Down* opened in London the same day he wrote that letter to Gwyn, and was presented concurrently at two West End cinemas. On the whole, the reviews were favorable, sometimes laudatory. "A gallant tragedy to make your blood boil," wrote one critic. Another referred to Steinbeck's "immaculate story," which epitomized "the essential drama of this particular war."[23] In the *Spectator*, Edgar Anstey was even more profuse in his praise. In a thoughtful review, he wrote:

> 'John Steinbeck's *The Moon Is Down*, a story of Norway, is the latest, the quietest and one of the best films about occupation. It may well remain the most memorable. Perhaps the profounder tragedies of Europe are matters, not of blood and high-explosive, but of feelings and thoughts and of the attempt to articulate these intangibles.'[24]

Steinbeck must once again have derived a considerable amount of satisfaction and pleasure in realizing the extent to which his work was being appreciated outside his own country. Not only was the book still on sale in London bookshops, but the play and film were attracting audiences to the Whitehall Theatre and to two of the capital's most prestigious cinemas. Soon, too, his war dispatches were to appear in the *Daily Express*, one of

Fleet Street's most popular daily newspapers. Certainly, at this moment in time, Britain could be said to be experiencing a glorious surfeit of Steinbeck.

In these circumstances, it was perhaps only to be expected that the resentment some of the other American war correspondents felt toward him should eventually manifest itself in public. One evening, he was taken out to dinner and then to the Embassy Club, where a party of his compatriots were already making merry, including a group of very drunk, young American correspondents who made it known in no uncertain terms what they thought of him as a newspaper man and how his dispatches stank. The ferocity of their attack left him considerably saddened and shaken. He tried to rationalize their attitude. "This island was sucked dry of material or so it was supposed," he wrote Gwyn, "and then I came over and found more stories than I could write, most of which had been lying under their noses all the time. That may be some of the trouble. Anyway, they were filled with hatred" (JS/GS 7/22/43). There is little doubt, although he ostensibly shrugged off the whole incident, that he had been shocked and hurt by the virulence of the hostility he had encountered, especially as it had happened in a public place and when he was in the company of his British hosts of the evening.

Despite his earlier aversion to socializing, he decided he needed to develop semiprofessional relationships at least, not only for the purposes of making contacts that were essential to the work he was doing, but also for ameliorating some of the sense of loneliness and regret that had been gradually overwhelming him once the initial euphoria of coming to the war had dispersed and he realized what he had let himself in for. He did not find this self-imposed gregariousness entirely unenjoyable, and he met many people who were destined to become close friends. In addition to meeting other American correspondents, like Shirer and Ed Murrow, who were secure enough in their field not to feel compromised by his success as an outsider, he also met Hector Bolitho, the unofficial court biographer and historian to the royal family, several British journalists including Frank Owen, the historian Dennis Brogan, politicians such as Lord Beaverbrook and Aueurin Bevan, notables from the world of film and theatre like Sam Spewak and Noel Coward, and old friends like Burgess Meredith and Eugene Solow. There were also meetings with various United States and British military bigwigs, and these could on occasion become something of an ordeal for him. No matter what resolution he had made after the Wavell luncheon fiasco, he accepted an invitation one evening to dinner in the company of nine generals and twenty-eight colonels, unappreciative of the fact that he had been invited as the guest of honor and was, to his dismay, expected to make a speech. The horror of that evening remained with him for a long time afterward.

A couple of days or so after this disastrous function, returning very late to his apartment, having spent five days in the field, he called his office and was told there was some mail for him. He asked for it to be sent over immediately, and it arrived at one o'clock in the morning. As well as letters from Covici and Elizabeth Otis, there were four from Gwyn, the last dated 8 July. He sat reading his wife's letters over and over, savoring all her news and the renewed contact established with her through them. The following morning he wrote to her and told her she would be unable to imagine what a difference getting her letters had made to him. He reported that he had had "a super G.I. haircut," which meant he had all his hair cut off except for a small top-knot. It was in this letter that he first told her about his driver, known to all and sundry as Big Train Mulligan. "[H]e is wonderful and a kind of goldbrick Casanova. I must do a piece about him" (JS/GS 7/21/43). In the weeks ahead, he did, in fact, write several pieces about Mulligan. He also did a day's work on a film Meredith was making for the Army, and then was persuaded to write some dialogue for it.

He was beginning to feel seriously exhausted, both physically and mentally, from the effort of turning out six stories a week. He desperately wanted to get to Africa. His application to go there, however, had been finally turned down. Every one of his letters to Gwyn at that time made some reference to his dilemma:

[T]he lots of tiny stories without continuity will have to stop before long. I have to have some kind of movement and I'm working on a method for that and that will require a little horse trading. (JS/GS 7/21/43)

You can see how nilly-willy my mind is going today and I'm a guy who is supposed to write three thousand words today. And I will but they won't be good. But good or not they have to come out. That is the fine thing about this job. It makes me write whether I want to or not. (JS/GS 7/22/43)

He had, however, hit upon a foolproof scheme to get himself sent to Africa:

The six articles a week are tiring me badly now. The trouble is lack of continuity, so I am going to start something more continuous, which is the supply story from receipt here to battlefield. I'm also going to make a motion picture for Services of Supply. It is a trade. I've been refused permission to go where I want to go as a correspondent so I'll go as a picture maker and do both jobs at once. I might as well work really hard. ... My cameraman is coming to see me at noon. Strange how I keep running into moving pictures and I don't even like them. But this time I'm held down unless I do. The camera is my passport and I've tried just about everything else. (JS/GS n.d. July 1943)

In partial justification for having wangled the assignment, he wrote an article about the massive buildup of supplies in England in preparation for the anticipated Second Front. It was published in the *Herald Tribune* on 5 August. In the article, he suggested that a German prisoner of war should be shown the overwhelming mass of arms and materials being accumulated all over the southern English countryside, and then allowed to escape to Germany. If the enemy realized what they were up against, he argued, they would assuredly lose the will to fight. He was, however, overlooking one of the basic realities of war: that most soldiers — and the Wehrmacht was no exception — fought all the more ferociously the more the odds were seen to be stacked against them. The article was nevertheless good propaganda, both for the consumption of the folks back home and for boosting the morale of the men and women engaged in supply depots and motor pools by making them realize that the overriding importance of the frequently boring work they were doing had not been overlooked.[25]

9

All this time, fantastic though it may seem, the investigation by Army Intelligence into Steinbeck's political background, activated at the beginning of the year by his application for a commission, had been steadily and remorselessly proceeding on the West Coast. During the period Steinbeck had been in England, Army intelligence agents Charles O. Shields and Martin Frankel had been visiting Los Gatos, Saratoga, San Francisco, Monterey, and Carmel, interviewing the author's friends and neighbors.

Many of those interviewed did not know Steinbeck personally or were, at best, merely acquaintances, so most of the so-called "evidence" they were prepared or eager to impart must have been nothing more than hearsay. The man who had purchased the Los Gatos ranch revealed to Shields that mail addressed to Steinbeck was still being delivered there, much of it second class mail of a communistic or radical nature, and that many of the books left behind by the author when he moved out were on radical subjects. When, however, Frankel interviewed Carol, she stated that her ex-husband had been definitely apolitical, and had never been a communist or even a party sympathizer. She had been the one who had subscribed to all the radical pamphlets and journals, and she admitted that while on one occasion she had registered as a communist she had done so merely out of curiosity. She further added that she regretted her past actions, for they seemed to have rebounded so unfortunately on her ex-husband. All Steinbeck's friends of long-standing, such as Webster Street and the professional vintner Martin Ray, also attested to the fact that Steinbeck had never been a communist and was simply interested in people in the lower working class, without regard to any political creed they might have, and specifically for the purposes of obtaining background material for his 1936 strike novel *In Dubious Battle*.

Shields, for one, became convinced of Steinbeck's innocence in the matter. His final report stated: "Although Subject exercised poor discretion during his early days of writing by associating with some elements of the Communist Party, he was not interested in advancing the cause of the party but in gathering material for his writings on certain social conditions existing in this country at that time." Such a conclusion from one of their agents did not have a great deal of influence on the Washington bureaucrats who, it can be safely assumed, had already made up their minds that Steinbeck was a dangerous Red. Their view had been amply substantiated by other reports from Navy intelligence, which had noted that the author had subscribed to the Communist Party's newspaper *People's World* as recently as 1939, and from the American Radical Research Bureau, which reported that he had contributed articles to the *Pacific Weekly* ("a Red publication of Carmel") and had acted as chairman of the Committee to Aid Agriculture Organization (a "very Red outfit"). On 27 July Lieutenant-Colonel Boris T. Pash, the chief of the Counter-Intelligence Branch, sent his recommendation to the War Department: "In view of substantial doubt as to Subject's loyalty and discretion, it is recommended that Subject not be considered favorably for a commission in the Army of the United States." The little big men of Washington and California had scored their final victory, for what it now mattered, although they still had not completely wound up their campaign against him, as he was to discover the following year.[26]

Even if in some circles his loyalty and discretion were being fundamentally questioned, he was still in other circles held in high esteem, and in response to a request from the United States he wrote a piece in support of the Third War Loan Drive. He wrote about the G.I.s who landed in England from the troopships that had brought them across the ocean from their homeland, the shiploads of supplies that followed them, and the dedicated flyers who manned the Flying Fortresses. He ended on an impassioned plea for humanity:

I have seen the hospitals with the mauled men, the legless and blind, the fingerless hands and the burned faces — all the destruction that steel and fire can do to a man's body and mind. I have seen children hauled out of a blasted building: lumps of crushed, dirty meat in pinafores, and dead — boxed and buried carrion. In God's name, what is it for except to get this horrible thing over with as quickly and as thoroughly as possible? And if this is true, it should not be a matter of "Who will lend his money?" but *"Who dares not to?"*[27]

This was written more than a week before the authorization for him to go to Africa was at last issued. When the call came, he was given only a few hours to get ready and pack. He had arranged for Eugene Solow to take over occupancy of the apartment while he was away. Reporting to the transportation office at seven-thirty in the evening, he was taken by truck, overnight train, and then another truck to an unnamed airfield, where eventually, after many hours of waiting, he boarded a C54A transport plane for the long and none-too-comfortable flight to Algeria.

10

His initial overpowering impression of Africa was the intense heat. The temperature when he stepped from the plane was 140 degrees. Although he had from time to time in his letters complained of the heat in London, he looked back now with some sense of nostalgia at the comparative coolness of the English summer with its occasional spells of rain. He had never been at his best in hot weather. The "terrible searing heat" of North Africa all but knocked him out until he became a little better acclimated to it.

He stayed for two nights and a day at the inland town where he had landed before being transported to Algiers. On the coast, the temperature was only 115 degrees during the day and was more or less bearable at night. The city was full of soldiers and all the hotels had been taken over by the military. The correct procedure he should have followed, so he later discovered, was to apply to the military for a billet, after which, following a wait of several hours while the administrative wheels slowly revolved, he would have been allocated a room that he would have to share with many others. Instead, having been told that most correspondents stayed at the Aletti Hotel, overlooking the waterfront, he marched up to the hotel's reception desk, asked for a room, and was given one. The Army was nonplussed: nobody had ever thought to try that one before. It was practically unknown for anyone to enjoy the luxury of a room of one's own. In his ignorance of protocol, he had obtained far better accommodation and consequently a greater degree of privacy than that enjoyed by most high-ranking officers.

For all that, it was not a very prepossessing room. He described it as being "like a set for a Maxim Gorki play," adding that it needed "only water dripping from the walls to make it perfect, that and the screams of the tortured in some sub cellar" (*Adventures* 526). The room displayed all the peripheral effects of the bombing that the city had endured: the wallpaper had been loosened by blast, and there were no windows or mirrors. The large window, in fact, had been bricked up with only two small holes near the top for ventilation. He was therefore denied whatever views there may have been of the harbor. Two narrow beds stood in the room, incongruously covered with Mexican serapes.

Within a short time of being in Africa, he had assumed the hue of a boiled lobster and was smothered with insect bites that made him look as if he were suffering from a bad case of smallpox. He was also, inevitably, constantly troubled by the "skitters." The heat made him dizzy and made the physical task of typing out his stories that much more difficult, for he had to stop every so often to wash his hands, which kept sticking to the paper and the keys. His feelings about his work in these conditions were becoming increasingly ambivalent: "Old deadline is riding me this afternoon and I am going to try to get out some copy. This is really very good for me and I hate it. But good or bad, I get lots of words out and I guess it doesn't matter whether they are good or not" (JS/GS 8/5/43).

It was not only that the heat was so oppressive, but he was also depressed and demoralized by the realization that, in coming to Africa, he had, by his own actions, effectively distanced himself even further from the woman he loved. A fortnight had passed since he had received a letter from Gwyn. The fact that he heard, almost every day, of people going back to the States deepened his sense of loneliness and homesickness. He knew, too, that he would have to go out on field trips with his camera crew to work on the film he had undertaken to do. These trips could last several days and would only aggravate the situation, with his mail possibly never quite catching up with him. On top of everything else, he was still the continuing target of petty professional jealousy from a minority of the journalist fraternity.

The type of story he had crossed the Atlantic with the avowed intention of writing, and which with great success he had been writing, was clearly wearying him. The human stories he wrote at this time and which were to appear in the *Herald Tribune* three or four weeks later were becoming rather commonplace in their content: "Steinbeck Says Greatest Plaint of Soldiers Is Lax Mail Service," "Steinbeck Tells About M.P.s Catching Army Watch Chiseler," "Steinbeck Tells of Soldier Who Went Over the Hill at Algiers," "Steinbeck Finds Short Snorter Is Developing Into War Menace," "Steinbeck Tells How the Senator Posed at the 'Palookas' Graves," and "Steinbeck Sees Wrecked Tanks Salvaged in Africa Bone Yard."[28] While, with their different slant on the war, they were dispatches the people at home obviously liked to read, he was painfully aware that the kind of material he sought was more and more difficult to find and that, unlike so many other war correspondents, he had not been obliged to put his person at risk, other than on the cross-Channel raid from Dover, to obtain it. The film job, too, had become something of a burden. The old story was being repeated, the whole project being made almost impossible by small-minded officers filled with a sense of their own importance, bent on foiling his every move.

Although his heart was no longer in the work, he stubbornly soldiered on with his cameraman, traveling as far west as Oran. He did not know it at the time, but General Eisenhower had issued a directive to him, ordering him to make the film, and armed with this he would have been assured of every facility and cooperation. He would never have had to stand for any nonsense from the officers who were now making everything so difficult for him. But it would seem that somewhere along the line the directive had been "lost" or "mislaid" or "misdirected." At any rate, it did not reach him until late in September.

A month had now passed without a letter from Gwyn. Thoughts of her dominated his mind. His principal aim now became getting the film job completed as soon as possible, escaping back to London from the African heat, and once there arranging for his return to New York. He knew that some of his letters had definitely been getting to her during the past few weeks, for he had asked various people bound for the States to deliver them to her personally, although strictly, of course, this was a practice that was forbidden. Everybody did it, however. He was concerned, obsessed even, by all the accounts he had been receiving both from her and from friends of the social life she had been leading from the moment he left New York, and his imagination had taken such a hold that he had begun to suspect she might be taking advantage of his absence to indulge in a string of affairs. It would seem that he had no real evidence to make him think this, but, on the other hand, the tone of Gwyn's letters obviously did nothing to allay his doubts. It was all part and parcel of her subtle campaign of revenge. While she, in his imagination, was living it up in New York, he was having to endure the North African heat and squalor. In his letters to her, he never failed to stress the adverse conditions under which he was existing, and to impress on her over and over that he had always remained faithful to her and was leading a blameless sex life:

It is almost impossible to keep clean here. The water is cold and dribbles and the soap doesn't seem to take hold. I think I am getting dirtier and dirtier but it isn't quite so noticeable since my complexion is getting darker and darker every day. Two weeks back in England will remove that, of course. But it is very sticky and unpleasant just the same here.

I have with me a camera man and an enlisted man and we have been jogging about the country seeing a great deal and taking some pictures for the film. . . . Isn't it strange how I always get mixed up with moving pictures. And I don't even like them. But I do seem to be able to make them. (JS/GS 8/19/43).

11

By the third week of August, the film assignment either completed or abandoned, he was back in the "Maxim Gorki" bedroom at the Aletti Hotel. This time, however, he was not to enjoy the luxury of having the room to himself. There had been an influx of newspapermen during his absence, all readying themselves for the expected invasion of the Italian mainland. The campaign in Sicily was by then virtually over. Palermo had fallen on 23 July, Catania on 5 August, and Messina on 16 August. Only the narrow Straits of Messina lay between the Allied troops and the tip of the toe of Italy.

He shared the room with Quentin Reynolds, who was writing for *Collier's*, H. R. Knickerbocker of the *Chicago Sun*, Clark Lee of I.N.S., and Jack Belden of *Time* and *Life*. "A ruffian gang," as Steinbeck later referred to them, "gallant and gay, and better reporters we will not see in our lifetime."[29] A British Vice-Consul named William Parisian also moved in with them while waiting for a room of his own.

They all took turns sleeping in the beds or on the floor. The telephone was constantly ringing. There was little or no opportunity for Steinbeck to find the peace he needed in order to work. Other newspapermen kept putting in an appearance, including Robert Capa and Ernie Pyle, whom Steinbeck was to describe as the "best and sweetest of them all."[30] Pyle had long admired Steinbeck's work and, hearing from Reynolds that Steinbeck was staying at the Aletti, decided to call. Sure that Steinbeck would never have heard of him and fearful of interrupting him in a busy moment, Pyle was nervous about meeting the author. He need not have worried. Steinbeck was similarly an admirer of Pyle's work and just as anxious to meet him when he heard Pyle was in town. Steinbeck and Reynolds happened to be alone in the room when Pyle arrived, so Reynolds was able to effect the introductions. Steinbeck and Pyle took to each other immediately, were soon talking nineteen to the dozen, and exchanging praise of each other's work. The three of them were invited as guests to dinner at the country villa of a British official. As Reynolds has recalled, Steinbeck and Pyle sat talking on the terrace of the villa until almost dawn, and "acted like a couple of lovebirds courting each other."[31]

Sadly, Steinbeck's friendship with Pyle was fated to last less than two years. During those two years, they were to see little of each other, but Pyle recorded his view that Steinbeck had carried to the war "a delicate sympathy for mortal man's transient nobility and beastliness that I believe no other writer possesses. Surely," he went on, "we have no other writer so likely to catch on paper the inner things that most people don't know about war — the pitiableness of bravery, the vulgarity, the grotesquely warped values, the childlike tenderness in all of us."[32] Pyle was to leave Algiers for the States the day after he and Steinbeck met. He flew from Rabat by clipper to New York, arriving there on 7 September. One of the first calls he made was on Gwyn, delivering letters from her husband and giving her firsthand news of him.

12

There were other visitors to the room in the Aletti, including Bob Hope and, on another occasion, two naval officers, Lieutenant Douglas Fairbanks, Jr., and Lieutenant Commander John Kremer. Reynolds again acted as intermediary. He recalled how almost the first words Kremer spoke to Steinbeck were to tell him how bad he thought the play *The Moon Is Down* was. While everyone present held their breaths, Steinbeck rose to his feet, laughed, and shook Kremer's hand, admitting he had never liked the play himself and was glad to meet someone who agreed with him. The two men became firm friends. Kremer was one of the top Navy experts on mines of every description, as well as a devotee of chamber music. "He and Steinbeck," Reynolds recalls, "often argued for hours about which was the most important instrument in an orchestra. Kremer held out for the violin; Steinbeck was a firm believer in the piano. Kremer talked of warfare in terms of music."[33]

On the evening of 24 August, Steinbeck accompanied Fairbanks and Kremer to a monastery in the country. They stood in the choir loft of the huge, darkened church and looked down on the monks at evening prayer. There were only two candles burning. The monks were singing Gregorian chant, and Steinbeck was overcome by the beauty and solemnity of the moment. "[I]t was very wonderful," he wrote to Gwyn, "the sound bellied up with great fullness" (*SLL* 260). After evensong, they conversed with some of the brothers and discovered they came from all over the world — Massachusetts, Germany, Holland, and France. There were also a few emotionally battle-scarred Allied officers staying at the monastery, sent there for the peace, quiet, and solitude they needed to recuperate.

The cruelty of war was again thrust upon him personally. He had been devastated when, two months earlier, Maurice's bomber had been shot down, and then overjoyed for Annie Laurie Williams when recently the news had come through that Maurice was safe, although a prisoner of war in German hands. Now, even closer to home, came word that Bill Dekker, the husband of his younger sister Mary, had been reported missing on 17 July.

Steinbeck had been eagerly anticipating a happy family reunion with Bill, and had been unsuccessfully endeavoring to contact his brother-in-law from the moment he had arrived in Africa. Bill, who had recently been awarded the Distinguished Flying Cross and promoted to the rank of Lieutenant Colonel, had participated in the Sicily invasion. About a week into the campaign, he had gone out on an operation and had not returned. Like many such happenings in wartime, it was all something of a mystery. In a letter to Gwyn on 28 August, Steinbeck sent a reassuring message to his sister that he believed that Bill was still alive. But he had no real basis for saying that, and, try as he may, he could not ferret out any further information — probably because nobody had any to give anyway. All he could do was to write as reassuringly as he could to Gwyn and leave it to her judgment what she passed on to Mary. "I think I know what happened," he speculated, but without saying what. "He might turn up. I really didn't have much hope for Maurice but he got out and Bill may well have escaped. Stranger things have happened here" (JS/GS 9/1/43). He told Gwyn he was now unfortunately cut off entirely from carrying out any further investigation into Bill's fate, but that he would resume his inquiries as soon as he could.

What he did not tell her was that he had decided, after all, not to ask to be sent back to London for the time being, and that, after having managed to get himself assigned to a fighting unit, he was expecting to be in the thick of action himself within the next few days.

The reason he had changed his mind about returning to London and thence back to the States are probably not too difficult to appreciate. The news about Bill would have had an unsettling effect on him, persuading him to hang around a little longer in the hope he might find out exactly what had happened to his brother-in-law. Then, additionally, despite being on friendly terms with most of the correspondents at the Aletti — those who understood and respected what he had set out to achieve in his unconventional dispatches — he knew that, before he could regard himself as a full-fledged war correspondent and their equal, he would have to undergo, as they all had, his own further baptism of fire. In a way, it was form of macho-challenge he felt necessary to put to the test before going home. No longer was it enough for him to be able to say that he had been in the war zone "somewhere in England and Africa."

13

He had got himself attached to a secret, recently-formed special operations unit designated Task Group 80.4, and had to thank his new friends, John Kremer and Douglas Fairbanks, Jr., for recommending that he should accompany the Group. Kremer and Fairbanks were, respectively, the Chief Staff Officer and the Assistant Chief Staff and Operations Officer of the Group, under the overall command of Captain C. L. Andrews, USNR. The Task Group's mission, working in conjunction with commando and paratroop units and O.S.S. personnel, was to cause general confusion among the enemy in the Gulf of Gaeta area during the days immediately leading up to Operation Avalanche, the code name for the landing at Salerno. The idea was that the Group would create a diversion by the simulation of impending landings on the Italian coast north of Naples, capture the island of Ventotene and its radar station, and subsequently carry out bombardment of the enemy coastal batteries in support of the actual landings on the Salerno beaches. Once the landing, planned for 9 September, had been successfully accomplished, the Task Group was to reform and raid enemy coastwise convoys to the north of Naples, and to occupy the islands—Ischia and Procida to the north, and Capri to the south—covering the approaches to the Gulf of Naples. The group consisted of the destroyer *Knight*, on which Captain Andrews had established his headquarters, two Dutch gunboats (one of which, owing to steering problems, had to return to harbor before actual operations commenced), and a bevy of smaller craft, including troop carriers and two Royal Navy flotillas, one of motor launches and the other of motor torpedo boats.[34]

The idea of this near-buccaneering-type series of operations was exactly what would appeal to Steinbeck's sense of adventure and his penchant for the unusual. Also, he knew he would have exclusive coverage of the Group's activities. Joining the rest of the team in Bizerte, he sat in on the conferences and briefings while final plans were formulated. Even so, he could not have imagined what he was letting himself in for.

He did have a slight foretaste of what was to come when, on 5 September, he embarked on one of the motor torpedo boats bound for Palermo, the port from which operations were to begin. They hit heavy weather on the way over, and were thrown about mercilessly. By the time they reached Palermo the following day, everyone on board, including the seasoned sailors, had been sick. They had a couple of days in which to recover and look around the city while they waited for the slower craft, which were being escorted by the *Knight*, to arrive. Steinbeck took the opportunity to write another letter to Gwyn before he went into action:

> Another chance to get a small note off to you. It will probably be a week or so before I am able to get another one. This is a beautiful place this X. I am always talking about it and it is a change from another X, which was not beautiful. But sometime we will come to this one. Just in here for the day and then out again. Still no forwarded letters from you from London. There will be a pile of them when I finally do connect with them. I hope so anyway. This is the strangest thing not to know a thing that is happening at home. ...
>
> I wish you would talk to George Cornish [of the *Herald Tribune*] about the advisability of coming home to do the work I have accumulated and will have accumulated when the next period is over. I will have a great deal of writing to do and I think some superb stuff some wonderful stuff if I can only put it down. It is truly picaresque. I'm sorry not to have been able to send stuff but it just can't be done and it doesn't matter because the sort of thing I am getting is not news at all but I think some great stories. (JS/GS 9/7/43)

Steinbeck did not, in fact, return to Palermo until the spring of 1957, and then not with Gwyn but with his third wife, Elaine, and his sister

Mary. They had come by cruise ship to Italy so that he could carry out research in Florence on Sir Thomas Malory. En route, they called at Lisbon, Gibraltar, Algiers, and Palermo, before disembarking at Naples to catch the train to Florence. As they had entered the harbor of Palermo, memory came flooding back — memory, he admitted, so dreamlike that he wondered if perhaps he had dreamed it after all, and wished that he had:

> Night and a blasted, deserted city — not a soul moving in the streets among the spilled rubble and the dead donkeys rotting in the alleys. And this pretty harbor — night and black water, oily and thick, and the red keels of sunken ships rising above the surface and some ships skip-bombed right up on the embankment.
>
> There was a dead woman floating face down in the black water. Her hair spread out around her like kelp, and she rocked a little on the oil-heavy tide-ripples of the harbor. It can't be true, but it was.[35]

It was true, but he had never set eyes on the dead woman. He had been told about her, as he reported in his dispatch published in the *Herald Tribune* on 11 October, by the captain of the motor torpedo boat in which he had sailed from Bizerte to Palermo. In the dispatch, Steinbeck recounts how the captain told him that when the city fell in July his boat had been on patrol nearby and, when he received the signal that the Seventh Army had secured the port, he had taken his boat in to have a look. One of the first sights he had seen as they nosed into the devastated harbor was the "dead woman floating on the oily water, face down and with her hair fanned out and floating behind her." He described to Steinbeck how the body had "bobbed up and down" as the wake of the boat hit it.[36] Steinbeck's memory of the blasted, deserted streets also sounds suspiciously like the recollections of the motor torpedo boat captain, as recounted in the 11 October dispatch. By 6 or 7 September, when Steinbeck arrived in Palermo, more than a month had elapsed since the city had been occupied by the Allies, and dead donkeys, on the grounds of basic hygiene alone, would surely by then have been long cleared from the streets. The "memory" clashes oddly with the possible facts and with the reference he made to the "beautiful place" he was in when he wrote to Gwyn from Palermo in 1943. Steinbeck, looking back over fourteen years, was nearer the truth when he wrote that the memory was so dreamlike that perhaps he had dreamed it. Certainly, it would seem that the captain's experience of seeing the woman's body floating in the water became so vivid and so real to Steinbeck that he, almost as if by some strange form of symbiosis, appropriated it as one of his own. The image also seems to have engraved itself to such a degree on his mind that he was to use it, or one very similar, to startling, disturbing, and poignant effect in his next work of fiction.

14

Although Steinbeck was with Task Group 80.4 during the whole period of its existence from the first days of September until it was disbanded on 18 September, he did not take part, indeed could not have taken part, in all its diverse actions and activities, many of which were carried out concurrently by various units within the Group. Obviously, while most of the dispatches were based on his firsthand knowledge, some were inevitably based on eyewitness accounts related to him by other members of the Group, accounts which, because of their immediacy, he could retain in his mind as vividly as if he himself had experienced them. It was not, however, always clear from a comparison between Andrew's official report and Steinbeck's dispatches in which actions Steinbeck became personally involved.

For instance, the events relating to the capture of the island of Ventotene, described so graphically by Steinbeck in his seven dispatches published in the *Herald Tribune* over the period 1—15 December, and the story of the secret mission undertaken by the "Plywood Navy," which he recounted in the dispatches published on 15, 17, and 19 November, were two of the operations carried out, at least in part, concurrently by different units within the Group. The landing on Ventotene took place shortly after midnight on 9 September. The Italians on the island promptly surrendered, but the German garrison manning the radar station held out. The Task Group's staff was withdrawn from the island after four hours, leaving a small force of paratroopers behind to hold the positions they had established, while the *Knight* proceeded to the Gulf of Salerno for reinforcements. The destroyer returned to the island that evening with further troops, only to discover that in the meantime the paratroopers ashore had managed to bluff the Germans into thinking they were facing an overwhelming Allied force. Consequently, the enemy had been persuaded to surrender, and the total capture of the island had already been achieved. Less than one hour before the midnight landing on Ventotene, however, Kremer left the *Knight*, taking two motor torpedo boats (the "Plywood Navy"), with the objective of landing two O.S.S. agents ashore northwest of Gaeta, north of Naples. Kremer and the two motor torpedo boats did not rendezvous again with the *Knight* in the Gulf of Salerno until the morning of the 9th. Clearly, it would have been impossible for Steinbeck to have witnessed and participated in (as he did) the first stage of the capture of Ventotene *and* have joined Kremer on the secret mission to Gaeta, and this is borne out by Quentin Reynold's account of his meeting with Steinbeck, Andrews, Kremer, and Fairbanks when, two days later, they came aboard the *USS Ancon*, the headquarters ship of the commander of the Western Task Force.[37]

Task Group 80.4 was temporarily dissolved on the morning of 10 September, its various units being ordered to report for duty under the direction of the Naval Commander Western Task Force. On the morning of the 11th, Andrews was ordered to collect landing craft from Salerno's Red Beach and to move reinforcements to the small village and seaside resort of Maiori, on the northern coast of the Gulf of Salerno. Maiori had a marina which was ideal as a base for motor torpedo boats and other small naval craft. It was felt that the place was under some threat of recapture by the enemy. This minor operation having been completed during the forenoon, Andrews, Kremer, and Fairbanks, accompanied by Steinbeck, went aboard the *Ancon* to receive further orders.

What now seems clear is that the only time Steinbeck spent on Red Beach was an hour or two during the morning of 11 September (D plus 2), as recorded in his dispatch published on 4 October (when he reported in detail what the soldier he met on the beach had told him about the actual landing), and that his dispatches on 3 October (account of what it felt like aboard an L.C.I. waiting for H-hour) and 6 October (the scenes of actual battle) were written from the eye-witness accounts of soldiers and, possibly, other correspondents, like Reynolds. Even looked at in the light of these revelations, it can be seen that Steinbeck does not compromise his integrity in any of the four dispatches covering the Salerno landings. In the two dispatches of 3 and 6 October, he does not present himself in any way as playing an active role, and in the dispatch of 4 October and another published on 6 October (clearly based on his visit aboard the *Ancon* on the afternoon of 11 September) he presents himself only in the role of a passive observer. There is none of the "I was there" attitude in any of the dispatches. Indeed, in the 4 October dispatch, the soldier asks Steinbeck when did he come ashore, then, without waiting for a reply, launches into his own story of how he came ashore with the second wave of troops. Right at the very end of the dispatch, his story finished, the soldier repeats his question: "When did you say you came ashore?" (*OTWW* 156). These are, in fact, the very last words of the piece, so we are not told how Steinbeck replied.

One can make whatever inference one chooses from the manner in which Steinbeck carefully slanted that dispatch and the manner in which he ended it. Similarly, one can, if one feels so inclined, question the validity of the references to "the correspondent" in the dispatch of 6 October, although nowhere in that dispatch does Steinbeck suggest that he is the correspondent concerned. He never uses the expression "this correspondent" or "your correspondent," always "the correspondent," so that this whole dispatch can be read as Steinbeck's sincere tribute to all those dedicated newspapermen who did venture into the front line to report the war. What is absolutely certain is that in respect of 99 percent of everything he wrote about the war − and we should remember, too, that in many respects he was the servant of the national propaganda machine − Steinbeck's integrity remained, and still remains, intact. We are all prone, perhaps entitled, to embroider our wartime experiences a little, and, without exception, we do − most of us to a far greater extent than Steinbeck ever permitted himself to do.

We can gather some idea of what Steinbeck actually experienced on that Salerno beach in September 1943 − and it should be remembered that the beach was then still being heavily strafed by the enemy − from the account he gave in a letter dated 1 December 1954 to Covici, toward the end of a nine-month stay in Europe and shortly after he had revisited Red Beach. His memory of that day eleven years before may well have been colored by thoughts of his good friend Robert Capa, who had been killed only six months earlier while reporting on the war in Indochina. Red Beach "still had a kind of horrid charge . . . like a remembered nightmare" for him and he felt some regret that he had not at the time written what he "really thought of the war," although, had he done so, "it wouldn't have been encouraging to those who had to fight it" (*SLL* 501).

While he was on the *Ancon* that September afternoon in 1944, or possibly a little later when he was back on the *Knight*, he found time to write a hasty note to Gwyn:

> I have a magnificent story and I should complete it within a week or ten days. Then I'll go back to London to clean up my job there and then if the H-T doesn't object I may go home to do the writing. It is just impossible to write in the circumstances under which I am now living. Sorry if they are disgruntled but they'll get better work for it in the end. (JS/GS 9/11/43)

That evening, Task Group 80.4, once more reorganized but now as a slightly smaller unit, set sail for the island of Capri. However, before the capture of that prize could be accomplished, the Group was ordered to return to Ventotene to investigate a request for additional troops. The Group then proceeded to the Gulf of Gaeta. The *Knight* fired star shells over the beaches, and Fairbanks, assisted by another member of the crew and employing all his considerable skills as an actor, conducted a verbal "landing operation" over the high-frequency RT. This seemed to create the desired degree of confusion and panic among the enemy ashore, before the Group retired from the area, returning to Maiori by forenoon the following day.

The delayed capture of Capri was duly effected later that day. Andrews sailed to the island with three motor torpedo boats, and at half past eight in the evening the Italian authorities on Capri officially surrendered the island to him. When Andrews returned to the *Knight* at Maiori, he discovered that a representative from Command was aboard and a conference in progress discussing plans to take the island the next day. He was pleased to be able to send an immediate signal to the Naval Commander Western Task Force reporting that the job had already been done.

The following day, the Group had to abandon Maiori as a base because enemy troops had launched a counterattack and were threatening to recapture the town. By this time, all the small craft were running dangerously short of fuel, thus endangering the success, or even the feasibility, of some of the planned future operations. Transferring its base to Capri, the Group turned its attention on the 14th to the two islands that lay to the north, Ischia and Procida, both of which, like Capri, commanded the approaches to the Bay of Naples.

At four o'clock in the morning, John Kremer and a small force consisting of ten British commandos and a British naval officer who spoke Italian left Capri for Ischia in a P.T. boat, accompanied by two small, captured Italian naval vessels. Although they had been informed, ostensibly on the best authority, that no Germans remained on the islands, they could not be sure of this until they had actually landed and the surrendering Italians had confirmed no Germans were there. Kremer stayed on the island, in overall charge of both civil and military matters, until an Allied military unit could take over. The British naval officer and the commandos also remained on the island, while the three craft returned to Capri.

The occupation of Procida, which lies inshore of Ischia and only two miles off the mainland, was achieved without incident late that same evening, although the local authorities had on this occasion sent word that they suspected that the Germans were planning to reoccupy the island. The following evening, owing to the island's too-convenient proximity to the mainland, the Allied garrison on Procida was reinforced by parachute infantry transferred from Ventotene.

On the 16th, the *Knight* made a sweep along the coast beyond Naples to a position approximately four miles north of Rome's seaside resort of Ostia. The destroyer was unescorted, for the motor torpedo boats that should have accompanied her had insufficient fuel for such a trip. Later, after managing to locate fuel, the motor torpedo boats made a sweep of their own into the Gulf of Naples, without encountering any opposition. After dark that same day, a small party of commandos raided the island of St. Martino, just north of Procida, which was the location of an Italian torpedo factory and was connected to the mainland by a bridge. The commandos were put ashore by rubber dinghy from a motor torpedo boat, took out the guards on the bridge, and disconnected the wires planted by the Germans for the purpose of blowing up the factory. The commandos also rescued an interned Italian admiral and his wife. Their getaway was delayed to some extent, since the admiral's wife insisted on packing her bags before leaving.[38]

Earlier that same day, the island of Procida was further reinforced by 150 airborne troops. The Germans had become convinced by all the Group's undisguised movements and by the judicious spreading of rumor that large Allied forces were in the area. The enemy opened fire on Procida, tragically killing an Italian political prisoner who, after having been incarcerated in prison for ten years following an assassination attempt on Mussolini, had just been released by Allied troops. A number of other released prisoners were also wounded during the bombardment. All the surviving prisoners were evacuated to Capri and from there to Palermo on the following day.

On the 17th, the *Knight* and two P.T.s carried out another sweep along the coast north of Naples, this time as far as the Argenterio Promontory, in search of an enemy convoy reported as sighted in the area. They were unsuccessful in finding it, but opened fire on an inquisitive Junkers bomber. The sweep had to be curtailed, since there was a danger from mines and also since one of the P.T.s had insufficient fuel for the return trip had they gone further. The destroyer and the two escorts reached Capri safely the next morning. That was the last operation carried out by Task Group 80.4. It was finally disbanded shortly after the *Knight* returned to base.

As already noted, it is not entirely clear which of these many diverse operations Steinbeck was directly involved in. There is, however, no doubt whatsoever that he went ashore with Fairbanks and the initial raiding party on Ventotene, and that he was present when Andrews accepted the surrender of Capri.[39] On the other hand, his description of the raid on St. Martino makes it obvious that he knew the details only secondhand, for there is no possibility that he would have been allowed to join the commandos on what was potentially a very dangerous mission — although he may have been aboard the motor torpedo boat from which the commandos had rowed ashore.

In a 1944 letter to Carlton Sheffield, he refers to being for a time with British motor torpedo boats raiding enemy shipping "at Gaeta and Genoa and over between Corsica and Sardinia before they were taken." The likelihood is that he was being guilty here of the 1 percent embroidery referred to earlier, for Task Group 80.4 never operated as far north as Genoa, nor as far west as Corsica and Sardinia. He gave Sheffield a vivid account of the occasion on one night "off Genoa," when he was on the upper deck as a flak ship began firing at them. He flung himself down as the tracers came toward them and the boat started taking violent evasive action. During the confusion, he lost the little notebook he had been carrying. It was returned to him via the Ministry of Information in London about a year later. "I suppose it got stuck in the slats some place and the skipper sent it in," he told Sheffield. "Now I remember that skipper. He was twenty-six and his name was Greene-Kelly. He was killed eight months ago ..." (*SLL* 273).

It is a nice story and, apart from the location, there is again little doubt that it is absolutely true. It seems likely that Steinbeck lost his notebook during the operations in the Gulf of Gaeta on the night of 11–12 September. Certainly, the commander of the 32nd Motor Torpedo Boat Flotilla, which played a leading part in those particular operations, was a Lieutenant-Commander Green-Kelley, R.N.R.

15

As soon as it became apparent that there was no chance of Task Group 80.4 being resurrected, Steinbeck applied to be sent back to Algiers. Before leaving the battle zone, he dashed off a hasty letter to Gwyn to put her mind at rest that he was safe, for he knew she must have heard now from other correspondents who had been to see her or who had telephoned her when they arrived back in the States that he had got himself involved in the invasion of Italy "I have been very lucky so far," he wrote. "And I think it is about time to leave here because anything now will be a repetition of what I have already seen" (JS/GS 9/18/43). Battle weary, somewhat deaf after his experiences under bombardment on Red Beach, dazed from lack of sleep, and covered with mosquito bites, he was nevertheless buoyed up by the thought of the exclusive material he had gathered during his time with the Group, and, more particularly perhaps, by his satisfaction with the way he had reacted under fire. "I do know those things about myself that I had to know," he told Gwyn. "I know that I can take it as well as most and better than some and that is a reassuring thing to know. And there is no way of knowing it until it happens" (JS/GS 9/18/43).

He had, of course, known fear during the ten days or so of intermittent action. As he told a friend in 1950, fear's physical manifestation had made itself disturbingly and embarrassingly apparent on the night he went ashore on Ventotene with Fairbanks and the scouting party, when, upon going to the head before boarding the landing craft, he discovered that his penis had retracted into his abdominal cavity. "I don't know whether this is common or not," he wrote. "Anyway it is a really shivery feeling" (*SLL* 416).

Talking to Michael Ratcliffe of the London *Sunday Times* in 1962, he saw himself as being in good company: "One of the most moving passages in all ancient literature comes when Hector faces Achilles, turns, and runs. It is an admission of cowardice, and it is of great comfort, for it has happened to every man."[40]

Steinbeck's own courage in the face of the enemy has never been in question. Typically, he did not publicly talk or write about his own most hairy experiences under fire. Whenever possible, his reports are written from an objective standpoint. For instance, when he was on Red Beach on the morning of 11 September, a shell from a German 88 "had come in nearby, blowing a stack of fifty-gallon oil drums every which way, one of which was thrown up in the air, hit the ground, and then rolling, slammed against his head, neck, and back" (*Adventures* 540). Nothing of this is mentioned in the 4 October dispatch. For his part in the landing on Ventotene, he had been recommended for the Silver Star, but was not awarded it, not being a member of the armed services (*Adventures* 533).

By 20 September, two days after Task Group 80.4 had been disbanded, he was on a ship bound for Algiers. He felt that at long last, after being as far away from Gwyn as he was ever likely to be, he was now on the first leg of his return journey to her. When he arrived in Algiers, he found that a packet of letters from Gwyn had been forwarded from London during his absence. He arranged the letters in chronological order. There were letters from throughout July, one from August, and even one dated 1 September. Then, getting into bed for the first time in three weeks, he settled down to spend the rest of the evening reading and rereading them. "I've had a charmed life these last three weeks," he wrote her on the 22nd, "or someone had me in prayers or something. . . . I haven't a scratch and my ears are coming back so I can hear quite well again" (*SLL* 263).

The following day, he drafted a letter to Frank Knox, the Secretary of the Navy, urging that the example set by the exploits of Task Group 80.4 be followed by the setting up of similar groups in the Pacific, and commending Captain Andrews and all his officers for the magnificent and imaginative manner in which they had performed their duties. Whether or not Steinbeck actually sent the letter is not known, but certainly he publicly acknowledged the work of the Group and its officers and men in an open letter to the Navy published as a dispatch in the *Herald Tribune* on 26 November. Under the heading, "Steinbeck Sees a Task Force [sic] Do Its Job the Old Navy Way," the letter had, of course, been duly censored, all references to the actual number designated to the Group being deleted, even though the Group had ceased to exist two months before the letter was published. The names of the officers also did not appear, but Steinbeck, anticipating the censor's blue pencil, had not, in any case, mentioned them in his original text.

16

The day after he drafted the letter to Frank Knox, Steinbeck was back in London, and had reoccupied his apartment overlooking Green Park. Eugene Solow, who had still been using and looking after the apartment, moved into the apartment next door. Steinbeck's luggage, including his clothes, typewriter, and notes had gone astray on the journey over from Algiers. Luckily, he had left some clothes behind in the apartment when he had left for Africa. The loss of his baggage was not the only minor disaster to have occurred, for he discovered, when he reported to his London office, that only a day or two earlier another batch of letters from Gwyn had been redirected to Algiers and that it would take a week or so before he could expect them back. His baggage, typewriter, and notes, however, caught up with him within two or three days.

One of the first things he did was to cable the *Herald Tribune* office in New York and, referring to all the unused material he had at hand, suggest it might be a good idea for him to return home to write his remaining dispatches. Dominating his thoughts was the need to be back with Gwyn without further delay, for he had begun to fear that if he were not he might lose her. He was, moreover, consumed with jealousy, even more convinced from the tone and content of her more recent letters that she was being unfaithful. Almost by return, however, came an answering cable from his editor at the newspaper, asking him to stay where he was. Clearly, high importance was being placed on his London dateline.

Nearly four months had passed since he had left Gwyn, and to him it seemed like forever. His original agreement with the *Herald Tribune* provided that he should complete a six-months' tour overseas, and, after receiving the cable he momentarily resigned himself to the fact that he would not be able to get home before Christmas. He would simply have to lose himself in work again and trust that the time would pass quickly. There were still many — too many, perhaps — stories to write, and he had also committed himself to finishing the work he had started, shortly before his departure for Africa, on the Army film Burgess Meredith was making. He put all this in his letters to Gwyn, assuring her that all he truly wanted was to be with her, but that he had obligations to honor. He promised her: "I SHALL be home by Christmas if I have to crawl home" (JS/GS 9/25/43). Meredith, he told her, was also pining for home, disillusioned because the closest he had been to the war was London, and there seemed no prospect of his ever getting anywhere else. "I don't want to be a glutton about it," he wrote, "and I will give my share to anyone who wishes it. But it is strange how you must do it. No one can do it for you. And the dark gentleman was very near" (JS/GS 9/25/43).

Out of the blue, there came a possible solution to all his problems. A

British film company proposed that he make a movie about a bombed town, and offered him all facilities and complete control in its making. When he refused outright, saying he wanted to be home with his wife by Christmas, the company suggested that Gwyn might be brought over to England. He broke the news to Gwyn in a letter he hoped would reach her quickly by diplomatic pouch, and urged her to accept the British invitation if it were offered. He assured her she would like it in England and that with her beside him he would be whole again. In case the letter missed the diplomatic bag, he also sent her a cable, pressing her for an early reply.

What he had in mind was for Gwyn to work with him on the film as screen editor and help with the music, but the whole project fell through a couple of days later without Gwyn ever sending a reply. Although the British authorities cleared everything so that Gwyn could be brought over, the State Department in Washington ruled that it was against policy to allow a husband and wife to be in the same area, as this could cause jealousies and other complications. After all the high expectations he had entertained, this further put-down by the bureaucrats at home was the final straw. In a letter on 29 September, he poured out all his feelings of frustration and bitterness to Gwyn, complaining that, whereas only a short time ago he had been unable to get anyone to give him a job, now there were not enough hours in the day to accomplish what seemed to be expected of him. On top of all that, he was still running up against the pettymindedness of staff officers who seemed to take great delight in continually blocking his path.

Even work on the dispatches had become extremely distasteful to him: "I don't like my work. I don't like sitting here doing work I could just as well do in New York. I do have to finish the army picture [with Meredith]. But after that I can't see much sense in it. It is just repetition. Most wars are repetition" (JS/GS 10/1/43). He went down with a fever. It was not malaria, but some infection "from bug bites" (JS/GS 10/2/43). He brooded more and more, maintaining that his work had gone "dry and dull," but forcing himself to carry on. "It is really tough to work now. Like pushing a great weight ahead of me" (JS/GS 10/2/43). Boredom with his work and worry about Gwyn were reaching an impossible pitch. He applied again to the *Herald Tribune* to be returned home.

This time, he extracted a positive response. A few days later, having in the meantime pulled out all the stops to finish the work he had promised Meredith he would do, he was on his way back to New York.

17

According to Gwyn, Steinbeck arrived home at the East 51st Street apartment early in the morning, and as unexpectedly as he had departed four and a half months or so before. There was a ring on the doorbell. When she answered it, she found him standing there, loaded down with assorted packages and surrounded by his kit, portfolio, briefcase, and attaché case. He was, she immediately noted, far from sober. After he had soaked in a hot tub and had some food, the two of them sat talking and drinking almost nonstop for the next forty-eight hours.[41]

Gwyn's reminiscences of her life with Steinbeck are notoriously unreliable and markedly one-sided, but, even so, it is plain that the reunion must have been a completely happy one, no matter how they may have felt about each other during the months of separation. Writing to Street about a week after his return, Steinbeck told his friend that he was "beginning to breathe freely again," and added: "We had vegetable soup last night and a woman was murdered right across the street Sunday morning, so you see the world is settling down to normal again" (JS/WFS late Oct. 1943).

They did not often join the New York social whirl, but mostly stayed at home, talking endlessly, regaling each other with stories of what they had been doing during the summer, both of them no doubt now stressing that fidelity had been strictly maintained throughout the time they had been apart. Even so, it is clear that their relationship had been permanently damaged. Overjoyed though they were to be together again, Gwyn still nursed a certain residue of the resentment she had felt from the way her husband had found it so easy to take off at a moment's notice to what he wanted to do, without any apparent thought for her feelings; and Steinbeck, remembering what she had written in her letters, possibly still suspected he might never again be able to trust her completely, the deep and consuming jealousy he had experienced overseas not being entirely abated by all the solicitude and loving she was heaping on him now.

He had not been home more than a few days before he received a request from the Navy to cover the war in the South Pacific. He demurred. There had been enough war to last him for quite a while, if not forever. In any case, not only was there no question of his leaving Gwyn again so soon, but he was in a state of nervous exhaustion, his nervous system shredded, his hearing still deadened from the effect of gunfire. He was later to discover that both his eardrums had been burst. "I've found there are only two kinds of people who aren't afraid of tracers — liars and people who haven't seen them," he wrote to Street, reliving recent nightmares. "A tracer has a way of coming right between your eyes and only turning aside in the last two feet" (JS/WFS late Oct. 1943).

In the same letter, he told Street:

My house is so comfortable here and my Gwyn is so nice. I just want to stay here a while and do some writing but not too hard and try to find out what happened to me in the last five months. I have some very curious ideas. Having it is very different from imagining it. (JS/WFS late Oct. 1943)

He had decided he would, for the time being, stay with the *Herald Tribune* until he had written up all the dispatches from his notes. Now that he was back with Gwyn, he discovered, as he had hoped, a renewed liking for the work, and, indeed, some of the dispatches he wrote after returning to America, including those describing the capture of Ventotene, were among the better ones of all the eighty-five he published. Probably, too, he did not exactly relish the idea of returning to his former post at the OWI, which had, after all, become a writing factory of sorts. Moreover, since he had been abroad and seen firsthand how the soldiers, sailors, and airmen lived, heard what they thought, and listened to their grousing, the churning out of basic propaganda seemed that much less worthwhile, to say the least, and considerably more distasteful than it had begun to seem before he had left on the troopship. As he wrote to Louis Paul: "People here at home like to think of the war as a heroic thing where nobody gets hurt, whereas it's a dirty thing where everybody gets hurt in one way or another" (JS/Paul c. Dec. 1943).

18

The troops in their thousands sit on their equipment on the dock. It is evening, and the first of the dimout lights come on. The men wear their helmets, which make them all look alike, make them look like long rows of mushrooms. (*OTWW* 3)

This, surely one of the most enduring images of World War II, is contained in the first three sentences of Steinbeck's first dispatch, sent by cable from London in the second week of June 1943, and published in the *New York Herald Tribune* on 21 June. It is an image at once poignant and shocking, an image of that vast gathering of men reduced and dehumanized into row after row of lower plant life, ripe for the plucking. It is an image evoking the memory of those long hours of mind-killing inactivity and boredom experienced all too frequently in camp, in transit, and even in the front line by everyone who has served in the armed forces. But, above all, it is an image that sets the tone of the underlying rationale of the dispatches that were to follow, dispatches concerned not with descriptions of great battles or analyses of stratagems and field tactics, but with the impact of modern war on the men and women who have been drawn into its maelstrom, those whose work necessitates their being based unglamorously in comparative safety and comfort far from the action, as well as those whose lot it is to engage in the actual fighting.

This human side of existence as a serviceman is what Steinbeck brings so vividly to life in his eighty-five dispatches.[42] He brings to the fore matters that, though small in themselves within the tremendous scheme of logistics and the context of the momentous events occurring at the time, take on an immense importance for the individual serviceman: the need, for example, to receive letters from home on a fairly regular basis; the neverending worry about loved ones left far behind across the ocean; the anger felt at the sometimes incomprehensible antics and decisions of Washington bureaucrats; the doubts about and hope for the quality of life in the postwar world. Steinbeck observes and minutely records the war in all its human aspects through the restricted vision of those anonymous "mushrooms" sitting patiently on the dock. While, as is only to be expected, he frequently expresses his own viewpoint, he does not allow it to dominate. It is ostensibly what the soldiers, sailors, and airmen think and talk about that he records so carefully.

There is always the possibility that not all the dispatches Steinbeck wrote were actually published. Some may have fallen afoul of the censor, who in any case did use his blue pencil on some of those that did appear; some may in fact have been rejected by the *Herald Tribune*'s editor for one reason or another; and others could conceivably have been killed by Steinbeck himself. What is remarkable about the dispatches, taken as a whole, is their high quality. There is perhaps a degree of falling off in this quality in the African and Italian dispatches, just as there was a slowing down in the frequency with which he cabled his stories to New York, both symptoms of his old problem of flagging interest in work that was continuing for too long and his impatience to progress to new projects. He had also, it should not be forgotten, to contend with chronic homesickness, an increasingly obsessive jealousy so far as Gwyn was concerned, and the oppressive heat and humidity of the Mediterranean climate, all of which were by no means conducive to work.

An analysis of the content of the eighty-five dispatches shows that sixty-three of these fall squarely into nine major story cycles. The first cycle (six dispatches) describes the Atlantic crossing on the troopship. The second cycle (nine dispatches) describes Steinbeck's visit to the bomber station, his meeting the crew of the *Mary Ruth*, and the two days he spent in London with Crain. Three of these dispatches were not reprinted in *Once There Was a War*. The third cycle (five dispatches) describes what he saw on his visit to Dover and nearby military establishments. The fourth cycle (four dispatches) describes his encounters with Big Train Mulligan. One of these dispatches was not reprinted in the book. The fifth cycle (eleven dispatches) describes his flight to Africa and his experiences in the Aletti Hotel and elsewhere. Three of these dispatches were not reprinted. The sixth cycle (four dispatches) relates to his visit to Sicily. Two of these dispatches were not reprinted. The seventh cycle (six dispatches) describes the rehearsals for the invasion of Italy and conditions on Red Beach during and after the landings. The eight cycle (eleven dispatches) describes the various activities of Task Group 80.4 to the extent the censor would allow. Three of these dispatches were not reprinted. The ninth and final cycle (seven dispatches) concerns itself solely with the capture of Ventotene. One of these dispatches, the very last in the series, was not reprinted. The remaining twenty-two dispatches, six of which were not reprinted in *Once There Was a War*, cover a wide range of subjects. In all of them, Steinbeck's insatiable curiosity seems to know no bounds. No subject is too insignificant for him to consider, and to most of these pieces he brings a freshness of approach, a more than occasional touch of humor, and an enormous sense of humanity.

The first six dispatches and the following eight dispatches (plus one further, later dispatch), the series of reports that comprise the first two major story sequences — which for the sake of convenience can be referred to as "Troopship" and "Bomber Station" respectively — contain some of the best work Steinbeck was to accomplish between 1939 and 1945, *Sea of Cortez* and *Cannery Row* excepted. In "Troopship," as Louis Owens has observed, Steinbeck mythologizes the voyage on the now-anonymous liner across the Atlantic from peace to war into "a ritual severence which allows men to cross the threshold of transformation which will take them from citizen to soldier," while at precisely the same time "he is introducing us once again to the oldest travel theme of all — the quest."[43]

The six dispatches in the "Troopship" sequence constitute a magnificent piece of writing: minute observation, understanding of human nature, and compassion, all knit together by an underlying and not over-obtrusive symbolism, transcending by far mere reportage. In "Troopship" — and for not the only occasion in the dispatches — Steinbeck reveals his own emotions, masked though they may be by a carefully manipulated, objective viewpoint, but mirrored in the thoughts and actions of the men he writes about.

In "Bomber Station," he at last tastes the realities of war firsthand. He had, in *Bombs Away*, recorded the training of the bomber crews back home: now he could record the end product of that training. Again, however, he is merely the objective observer. He does not accompany the Fortress crews on their raids, and he allows his own personality to intrude only in the last of the dispatches (not reprinted in *Once There Was a War*), the one in which he recounts how Crain spent his forty-eight-hour pass with him in London. The airmen answer his questions, but the questions are never actually stated. All we get in the first seven of these dispatches are the reactions of the men, both air crew and ground crew. In the second of the dispatches (also not reprinted), Steinbeck employs the Ernie Pyle format, and we are introduced, by actual name and identity of hometown, to the members of the *Mary Ruth* crew. It was a practice Steinbeck was quickly to abandon, presumably when, just about the time the earlier of the "Bomber Station" dispatches began appearing in the *Herald Tribune*, he had been given the news that Maurice and the crew of the *Mary Ruth* had failed to return from a mission.

If in *Bombs Away* Steinbeck had witnessed the coming together of the individual members of the trainee bomber crew into "a tight unit, a jealous unit," that "will plan together and eat and sleep together on mission," and finally will perhaps even die together, he finds that here on the bomber station the crew of a bomber is bonded even more intimately by the reality of war than was ever possible during the weeks of training and simulated missions. Now they are bound together "by a terrible experience."[44] "And it is a terrible experience," he adds. The men profess to have no hatred for the enemy, and are frequently frightened, though not too proud to admit it. The unspoken tension before a mission is almost unbearable. Defensively, the men make light as much as possible of their fear, in the hope they will conquer the anticipation of it. One tail gunner quips: "If anything should happen today, I want to go on record that I had prunes for breakfast" (*OTWW* 34). Superstition is rife. One of the crew misplaces his lucky medallion and, instead of trying to sleep, spends the whole night searching for it. After the ships have taken off, the ground crews, their work completed, retire to the barracks to get some sleep, but congregate on the field in good time for the homecoming, anxiously checking off the bombers as they land.

Talking to these men, Steinbeck discovers that what also troubles many of them are the lies, both of commission and omission, being fed to the folks back home. One gunner complains of the extent to which the air losses are being covered up for fear that the nation would lose heart if the truth were told. Another gunner, similarly contemptuous of a magazine article he has recently read, castigates the idea that the article posits that all fliers have "nerves of steel" and have only one thought — "to fly all the time and get a crack at Jerry" (*OTWW* 28).

These comments, and others like them, must have sounded oddly familiar to Steinbeck, for in many respects they echoed some of the ideas and opinions about the war he had long held himself and had already touched upon in such works as *The Moon Is Down*, and more particularly in the unpublished *A Medal for Benny* and *Lifeboat*. While he had thrown his energies wholeheartedly into his work for the OWI, he had never been unmindful of its overriding, sometimes blatant, propagandist nature.

There was in his mind a very real distinction to be drawn between propaganda for consumption by the enemy and propaganda for home consumption. He had frequently expressed the view, both in conversation and in correspondence with friends, that the public should, so far as possible, always be told the truth — indeed, was entitled to know the truth, no matter how unpalatable that truth might sometimes be. He professed having enough faith in the American people to believe that national morale would not collapse if the truth were told, opining rather that there was an insidious immorality on the part of the government in concealing it. While he had no alternative but to accept the decisions that had been made, he remained convinced long after the war was over that his two projected works dealing with the invasions of small American towns by German and Japanese forces were not against the interests of the war effort, but that they would have had the converse effect of energizing and strengthening it.

There is little doubt that within defined parameters he seized the opportunity to use the dispatches — through the mouths of the servicemen he met, or sometimes writing himself on their general behalf — to draw attention to many matters he felt needed publicity and urgent rectification. In the dispatches, he never criticizes the conduct and prosecution of the war by the military and political establishments. Such criticisms, as he well knew, would never pass the censor. His ends are more effectively achieved by the manner in which he confines himself to publicizing the small but important issues that affected the morale and comfort of the average serviceman, and by subtle (and sometimes not all that subtle) satire attacking hated bureaucracy.

Some of the dispatches clearly came straight from his own bitter experience. Two of these (neither of which was reprinted) concern, first, the effect on the morale of troops of the receipt or nonreceipt of letters from home, and second, the inexcusable length of time mail was taking to reach the men overseas. One could almost be forgiven for imagining that these two particular dispatches are, in part at least, personal messages to Gwyn. In the first, Steinbeck observes of one soldier whose wife had written to say she did not know how much longer she could bear the loneliness of their being parted:

> She was threatening him and he knew it. . . . He was putting in tremendous days of work and at night he had to go to bed with the picture of his wife going off with another man. She had the knife in him and she knew it. And he would get no rest and after a while his stomach would go to pieces and he would be hospitalized. . . . For all the talk about what soldiers do they want terribly to be related to one woman. They build a sort of image of perfection that couldn't possibly have been true, and they hold on to it as long as they can, and they will only abandon it when they have to.
>
> Good food can be given to a man, and entertainment and hard work, but nothing in the world can take the place of the letters. They are the single strings and when they are cut the morale of that man is shattered.[45]

In the second of these two dispatches, Steinbeck voices the rumors that abound among the men overseas that some mail bags are left to lie on the

New York docks for weeks before being shipped abroad, so that, after it has been written, a month or so can pass before a letter eventually reaches the man anxiously awaiting the latest news from home. Even if the sender pays airmail rates, it is unlikely, Steinbeck notes, for the letter to take anything less than three to four weeks, and he recommends: "It would seem that the mail system to the armed forces needs an overhauling."[46]

The majority of the dispatches Steinbeck wrote in London prior to leaving for Africa cover a multitude of disparate subjects: stories of the London Blitz, anecdotes about wounded servicemen, a ghost story centered on a bombed country cottage, Bob Hope entertaining the troops, and several examining the question of Anglo-American understanding and misunderstanding (the diversities in language and attitudes, the friendship-making properties of chewing-gum where children were concerned, the difference between the American and British methods of cooking vegetables.)[47] The dispatches, too, are redolent with the sound of the popular songs of the day: the favorite old-timers, like "Shine On Harvest Moon," "When Irish Eyes Are Smiling," "When the Saints Go Marching In," and "Home on the Range," as well as such contemporary songs as "Lili Marlene," "As Time Goes By," "Mr. Five by Five." and, most potently nostalgic to anyone who remembers those days, "You'd Be So Nice To Come Home To," which, recorded by Dinah Shore, was *the* song in London during the months of June through August 1943.

Then there are the four pieces Steinbeck wrote about his driver, Private "Big Train" Mulligan. Three of these were written in London, one of which was not really about the "Big Train" himself, but was the recounting of "one of Mulligan's lies" he had told Steinbeck about a memorable crap game on a troopship in the Pacific. The fourth piece was not written until Steinbeck returned to London in late September. The "Big Train" is surely one of most engagingly roguish characters Steinbeck ever captured on paper, all the more so perhaps for being based on a real-life character. After the first three pieces had appeared in the *Herald Tribune*, Steinbeck was advised to register the title of "Big Train Mulligan" because of the extreme popularity of the character among the newspaper's readers, and he was warned that if he failed to do so someone else would most certainly purloin the "Big Train" for his own.

While in the main the dispatches published in the *Herald Tribune* during the period 21 June through 12 August are in chronological order and relate specifically to what Steinbeck saw and heard and did during the first of his two periods in England, the chronological sequence of the dispatches published thereafter in the paper does become somewhat erratic. Furthermore, there are some pieces among these later dispatches that do not belong to either the African or Italian periods. The fourth Mulligan episode, published on 29 October, relates to events occurring in England after Steinbeck's return from the Mediterranean. Another dispatch, more an indulgent fantasy, telling the story of a girl named Barbara who supposedly invents a wonder weapon that will win the war, is set mostly in the Pentagon. In addition, the dispatches dated 19 October and 1 November, published within the series dealing with the Italian campaign, relate in fact to the period Steinbeck spent in North Africa — specifically Algiers — before he became involved with Task Group 80.4.

The African dispatches, as a collection, are arguably the weakest of all the pieces that Steinbeck turned in during his time as war correspondent, although some of them do possess a certain charm and humor and occasional fantasy, such as the four originally published between 31 August and 3 September, the last being the infamous (and not reprinted) saga of the Senators, and the one published on 1 November, which tells of the "elf" in Algiers.[48] The other displaced North African dispatch, that published on 19 October, describes Steinbeck's visit with Kremer and Fairbanks to the monastery on 24 August, when the three of them stood in the gallery gazing down on the brothers celebrating evensong. It is a moving passage:

> Over the rail and below was the body of the church, only you could not see it, for only one candle was burning, and it merely suggested the size and height. It picked out a corner and an arch and a point of gold, and your mind filled in the rest. Lined below, just visible were the rows of the white brothers. And then their voices came softly and swelling, singing the ancient music, of which Mozart said he would rather have written one chant than all his own. The evensong rose higher and higher, and it was rather like the dimness of the arched roof overhead. The great, vague room swelled and pulsed with the sound, and then it died and one single voice took it up and the others joined in and the candle flame darted about on its wick. (*OTWW* 182—83).

In many respects, although out of sequence, this episode is ideally placed, providing as it does a moment of serenity, of humanity, and of sanity coming after the violent scenes of battle that have preceded it and that are to follow it.

Three years earlier, when the *Western Flyer* had pulled into San Diego, en route to the Gulf of California, Steinbeck and Ricketts had met a naval gunnery officer who had recently won a target competition. Out of curiosity, they asked him if he could imagine what happened when one of his shells landed and the human consequences resulting from his order to fire. He replied almost matter-of-factly that the distances involved were so great that it was not possible to see what happened. As Steinbeck and Ricketts concluded, it was possible that if he could see the devastation wreaked he would be unable to perform his duties. "He himself would be the weak point of his gun. . . . The whole structure of his world would be endangered if he permitted himself to think" (*SC* 40—41).

Steinbeck, of course, knew all too well what would happen in that little street when the shell exploded. There had already been too many newsreels, too many photographs, too many vivid dispatches in newspapers for him not to picture the death and destruction the shell would wreak. Whereas the naval officer did not want — and, indeed, was seemingly unable — to accept the inevitability of his simple action, Steinbeck's curiosity as a writer and a humanitarian compelled him to ponder on the reality. It was, however, a reality that in 1940 he could only visualize either second-hand or in his imagination. In the streets beyond the beaches of Salerno, he came face to face with the reality at last, and witnessed for himself what the naval officer had refused to contemplate:

[T]he splash of dirt and dust that is a shell burst ... a small Italian girl in the street with her stomach blown out ... many dead mules, lying on their sides, reduced to pulp ... the wreckage of houses, with torn beds hanging like shreds out of the spilled hole in a plaster wall. (*OTWW* 158).

But the reality also had the smells that probably would not have been part of his imagination:

The burning odor of dust ... the stench of men and animals killed yesterday and the day before ... a whole building is blown up and an earthy, sour smell comes from its walls (*OTWW* 158)

Although, as already discussed, there is clearly some doubt whether or not Steinbeck underwent all the experiences attributed to "the correspondent" in this 6 October dispatch, there is contrariwise the certainty that "the correspondent" is a composite figure and that some of the experiences *were* Steinbeck's own. If he did not write about tactics and strategy, name generals, or decorate heroes in print, he did, as this composite correspondent did, sprain his knee when leaping ashore. As he admitted in his Introduction to *Once There Was a War*, all correspondents developed their own "coy little tricks with copy." His was never to admit having seen anything himself: "In describing a scene I invariably put it in the mouth of someone else. I forget why I did this. Perhaps I felt it would be more believable if told by someone else" (*OTWW* xvi). In many ways, the dispatches can be considered the first manifestation of the literary form in which the author appears as one of the characters, shadowy and circumspect though he may be — a form that was to attain its richest expression in novels like *East of Eden* and *Sweet Thursday*.

Just as "the correspondent" is a composite, so the operation carried out by the "Plywood Navy," as described in the dispatches published on 15, 17, and 19 November (that of 17 November was not reprinted in *OTWW*), is patently a composite of the operation carried out by Kremer on 8–9

September (while Steinbeck was on Ventotene), and the one carried out on the night of 11–12 September (while Steinbeck was aboard Green-Kelley's motor torpedo boat).

When, after he had returned to New York, Steinbeck came to set down his accounts of the composite motor torpedo boat operation and the capture of Ventotene, he complained that the Navy was "cutting the hell" out of his dispatches and even correcting his grammar (*Adventures* 541). Although only one line was cut from his dispatch of 15 November, thirty-two lines were cut from the dispatch of 17 November, and twenty from that of 19 November. Steinbeck was clearly so incensed by these excisions that he indicated in the published text all the places where lines had been cut. He refers to this matter in his Introduction to *Once There Was a War* when, with the passage of time, he could afford to feel more charitable toward the censors, accepting that they had a difficult task and had to be on their guard against letting anything slip through that might land them in trouble. It was, for them, he recognized, principally a matter of self-preservation, and so it was understandable if, to be on the safe side, they used the blue pencil liberally.

The final seven dispatches Steinbeck published in the *Herald Tribune*, the last of which was not reprinted in *Once There Was a War*, contain his account of the landing on Ventotene, initially by five men — of whom he was one — in a whaleboat, subsequently backed by a force of forty American paratroopers (fifty, according to Andrews's official report), plus three officers. The amazing story of how these forty-eight (or fifty-eight) men fooled an unspecified number of Italians and the eighty-seven (ninety-one in Andrews's report) Germans on the island into surrendering without a shot being fired in anger is beautifully and economically told by Steinbeck, and almost reaches the high quality of "Troopship" and "Bomber Station."

19

When sixty-six of the eighty-five dispatches were reprinted in *Once There Was a War* in 1958, they were, without any explanation, identified by reference to the dates they appeared in the *New York Herald Tribune*.[49] Any reader of the book who relies on these dates will therefore be grossly misled and confused if he assumes that the dates relate specifically to the events being described in the dispatches. He will be given the erroneous impression not only that the capture of Ventotene occurred long after the landings at Salerno and the captures of Capri and St. Martino, but also (if he has no knowledge of the Italian campaign) that Steinbeck was in the battle zone for approximately two and one-half months, whereas it was actually more like two weeks or so. These factors may or may not be of much significance, but they do help to throw both the book itself and the rather haphazard manner of its publication into perspective.

In his Introduction to the volume, Steinbeck justifies the form in which the dispatches have been reprinted:

> My first impulse on rereading them was to correct, to change, to smooth out ragged sentences and remove repetitions, but their very raggedness is, it seems to me, a parcel of their immediacy. They are as real as the wicked witch and the good fairy, as true and tested and edited as any other myth, (*OTWW* xxi)

That is all well and good as far as it goes, but there does seem, on the other hand, no reason at all why the import of the dispatches was not rationalized by their being reprinted in true chronological order, with the irrelevant and misleading dates omitted altogether.

There is, in fact, some evidence to suggest that Steinbeck himself may have had little or no say in the manner in which the pieces were reprinted, and had to tailor his Introduction to correspond to a text presented to him more or less as a *fait accompli* (see Fensch 202). It is not altogether clear how the concept of the volume originated, although, according to Benson, Carl Sandburg planted the idea in Covici's mind as far back as 1950 (*Adventures* 660). It would also seem that Steinbeck had no authorial control over the final selection of the pieces to be included, for in a letter to Covici at the time the book was being prepared for publication, or even shortly after it was published, he wrote bitterly to his editor, complaining that the two dispatches relating specifically to Henry Maurice Crain (those of 30 June and 17 July) had been omitted. He demanded to know why these had been thrown out and who was responsible. "I would like the pieces put back in," he told Covici. "They mean something to me" (Fensch 202). It may be that he did not approve other omissions, although it must be said that it had been a wise decision on someone's part not to reprint the last dispatch of all that the *New York Herald Tribune* published, even though, had it received different treatment from Steinbeck, it could have given a final thematic and emotional shape to the collection.

This last dispatch tells the pathetic story of the German corporal (warrant officer, in Andrews's report), who, when the preliminary landing force of five men approaches Ventotene's little harbor, has been detailed to destroy an E-boat (a small gunboat, in the official report) lying alongside the pier, to prevent its falling into Allied hands. Steinbeck unfortunately allows the propagandist in him to come to the fore, and treats the incident in what now seems an unnecessarily facetious manner. He nicknames the German "Corporal Bumblefoot," and makes fun of him generally for being "a failure" and "a dope." There is a complete absence of compassion. The corporal, if one thinks about it, and as Steinbeck knew full well, is a brave man. He has been assigned to blow up the boat, believing that a large Allied invasion force is imminent and knowing that, in carrying out his orders on the exposed pier, he stands a very good chance of being killed. For all that, he stands his ground long enough to toss three grenades into the boat and throw his Luger into the sea before surrendering. Later, the backup, invasion force of paratroopers having arrived, he stands with hands above his head and Tommy guns pointing at his midriff while being frisked by a sergeant who, leafing through the papers from his pockets, finds a photograph of the corporal's wife. She was, Steinbeck observes,

> a big, tough woman, and you could see that the corporal had not even been master race in his own home. The piercing eye and great folded biceps of his amazonian wife must have been things of terror to him. They should have drafted her, not her husband. It was apparent in her face that she thought him a dope, too.[50]

When he is told by the sergeant that he can put his hands down, the German fails to do so, possibly because he doesn't understand English. Even this small matter attracts Steinbeck's scorn:

> ... [The German] even resisted a little when the sergeant took him firmly by the wrists and put his hands down for him. His eyes rolled with terror. Perhaps he thought it was a trap or just possibly he remembered things his people had done to prisoners.
>
> He wasn't a very big prize. The four paratroopers looked a little embarrassed when they escorted him to the boat and helped him in. And as he stepped over the side he tripped and fell on his back in the bottom of the whale boat. Poor Corporal Bumblefoot! He had probably always been like that. They had tried to make of him the lean and tigerish soldier that all the posters show, that Dr. Goebbels talks about. He had been given the best training and the best indoctrination and he had emerged just what he was, a dope. Lying in the bottom of the boat, blushing a little, he was the perfect example of the failure of master-race conceptions. In him and probably in many thousands like him was the predestined failure of the whole Hitler concept. After years of the best they could do, he was still a human dope.
>
> With an apologetic grunt he scrambled up and seated himself. ... [A]nd he put his head down in his hands and began to cry.[51]

That final image is one that is representative of the futility and the utter madness of war. The German, failure and dope though Steinbeck may make him out to be, was not by any measure the only soldier in the history of World War II to have put his head in his hands and weep. This gesture of human vulnerability made by a soldier at the end of his tether is fitting counterpoint to that opening image in the first dispatch of the rows of nonhuman figures, as yet untouched by battle, sitting on the dock. They were the collective processed and packaged raw material. The German is the individual, disintegrating end product.

In his Introduction, Steinbeck presents an ambivalent and sometimes dismissive attitude toward his dispatches. After a period of fifteen years or so, he finds that "[r]eading these old reports sent in with excitement at the time brings back images and emotions completely lost" (*OTWW* ix). He is made to realize that they "are period pieces, the attitude archaic, the impulses romantic," and comes to suspect that "in the light of everything that has happened since, perhaps the whole body of work [is] untrue and warped and one-sided" (*OTWW* xi). Ultimately, he sees the dispatches as no more than "half-meaningless memories of a time and of attitudes which have gone forever from the world, a sad and jocular recording of a little part of a war I saw and do not believe" (*OTWW* xx).

The critical response to the reprinting of the dispatches was, predictably, mixed. In the *New York Herald Tribune Book Review*, Herbert Kupferberg considered that "these samples of Steinbeck's journalism decidedly do have validity, both as memory joggers and as artistically wrought pictures of the war that are often quite moving."[52] Herbert Mitgang's review in the *New York Times Book Review* compared *Once There Was a War* with Ernie Pyle's *Brave Men* and Bill Maudlin's *Up Front* ("two truly great books"); and adjudged Steinbeck's dispatches as being "not so good," while nevertheless conceding that "they do hold up today."[53] The *New Yorker* reviewer, however, dismissed the dispatches as "thin feature stories — 'human interest' without re-creating human beings."[54]

One gains the overall impression that most of the reviewers in 1958 were being carefully guarded in their remarks and their judgments. Time, as Steinbeck himself had discovered, gave a different and perhaps in many ways false perspective to the pieces, and it was difficult to project back to the atmosphere and emotions of those days in 1943. One can, for example, still berate Steinbeck for his treatment of the unfortunate German soldier in the eighty-fifth dispatch and for his similar satirical and condescending portraits of Italian prisoners of war in earlier dispatches, but it again has to be stressed that in 1943 such vignettes as these were what the general public and the Allied propaganda machine wanted. There is nothing more reassuring to a nation at war than to have the enemy look ridiculous. The Bumblefoots and their ilk are always preferable in wartime to the puzzling Lansers and the fanatical Prackles and Corells. If occasionally Steinbeck abandoned his high standards and ignored his sane appreciation of the reality that the majority of the enemy were no worse and no better, no braver and no more cowardly than the Allies, and indulged instead in propagandist drivel, he did have the good sense (or someone did on his behalf) to drop the worst of these satirical pieces from *Once There Was a War*.

If the essential worth of Steinbeck's dispatches can only be truly assessed were it possible to achieve the miracle of traveling back in time to 1943, then perhaps the author's own comments, made shortly after his arrival back in New York, can be regarded as a more trustworthy representation of his views than the retrospective comments he makes in the Introduction. He told John Cahill Oestreicher: "Some of the stuff that the other boys have written under fire and dashed off in a matter of minutes has been magnificent. I can't do it and there's no use kidding myself." He added "Tell you one thing, though. I was a good war correspondent in one respect. I could hit a foxhole quicker than anyone else on the front. And that's something."[55] With Webster Street he could afford to be more direct: "I know I write a lot of crap but at least I write" (JS/WFS Oct. 1943). A year later, after he had been able to distance himself a little from his experiences, he confided to Carlton Sheffield: "The crap I wrote over seas had a profoundly nauseating effect on me. Among other unpleasant things modern war is the most dishonest thing imaginable" (*SLL* 273).

Steinbeck was, however, being unduly harsh on himself and his achievement as a war correspondent.[56] "Troopship" "Bomber Station," "Ventotene" (except the final dispatch), as well as several other pieces, are of very high quality indeed, and eminently worthy of preservation as literature. Taken as a whole, though, it has to be admitted that the dispatches, hastily conceived and written under the most unpropitious circumstances, do not significantly enhance Steinbeck's literary reputation. On the other hand, following closely on the heels of *Sea of Cortez* and *Bombs Away*, they do point to his increasing involvement in nonfiction and journalism — ultimately, some have argued, to the detriment of his principal creative work as a novelist.

20

With the last of the dispatches written, Steinbeck deliberately turned his back on the war. "This has been a strange time," he wrote Ritch Lovejoy. "I'm forgetting it very quickly. Guess that is normal. I seem to react normally to everything" (JS/RL c. Dec. 1943). He had told Oestreicher: "A couple of years from now I think I am going to be able to write a book about the war, based on the things I've seen. It takes a year or two for things to percolate through me and then I can write about them."[57]

His head teemed with a confusion of other plans. He was considering putting the Eardley Street house in Monterey up for sale, principally to simplify his state income tax position by giving up his residential status in California. He began making arrangements for a two-month visit to Mexico with Gwyn. The trip would be mainly a vacation, but he also wanted to carry out some research for the short novel he had first had in mind to write in October the previous year. This was to be based on a story he had heard in La Paz while on passage aboard the *Western Flyer* to the Gulf of California in 1940, and concerned a poor Indian boy who found an enormous pearl. He was also perversely toying with the idea of returning to England for a while, but only on the understanding that he could take Gwyn with him. The British government, so he told his friends, had invited him to make a film there — almost certainly the same project he had been offered in September. For some reason or other, he seemed to imagine there was a real chance of the war being over by the spring, but, having regard to his current feeling about the war and anything to do with the war, it is probable that this idea about returning to England simply provided yet another temporary and almost ephemeral focus point on which to fix his restless sights. That he thought about it at all seriously is belied by the fact that by mid-December he had completed the necessary specific arrangements for the trip to Mexico — anticipating that he and Gwyn would leave New York in early January and stop off in New Orleans on the way. He had also by mid-December started on his first attempt to return to the writing of fiction with a "funny little book" titled *The Good Little Neighbor*, a novella-length work with a Mexican setting.

The feeling of restlessness was not entirely assuaged by thoughts of the Mexican trip. The cozy evenings with Gwyn, chatting in front of the fire, had blossomed into a period of general party-giving and party-going. But he was already tiring of the East Coast life style, which he had, in any case, always thought rather superficial, for all the good and lasting friendships he had made and was to make there. Despite his earlier idea about selling the Eardley Street house, he told Max Wagner that he hoped to move back to Monterey eventually.

7

1944: A New Masterpiece

1

NEW CONTROVERSY WAS INEVITABLY JUST AROUND THE CORNER. A FEW DAYS into 1944, the movie *Lifeboat* opened at the Astor in New York. When he saw it, Steinbeck was appalled and incensed to discover what had been done to his original script.

When, the previous March, Hitchcock had received Steinbeck's story treatment, he handed it over to the novelist MacKinley Kantor to produce a workable screenplay. After two weeks, however, Hitchcock decided he did not like the work Kantor was turning in, any more than he had liked Steinbeck's original treatment. Kantor was paid off, and the material reworked, this time by the professional Hollywood scriptwriter Jo Swerling. Even then, Hitchcock was still not satisfied, and worked over the script again himself. In the end, what Hitchcock had essentially engineered by all these processes was to take Steinbeck's basic situation, jettison most of the realism and all but the merest hint of the political content, create several new characters, change completely the characters of Bud Abbott, Albert Shienkowitz, Joe, and the German, and concoct an entertaining movie that owed very little to Steinbeck's original work, and, more importantly, effected a radical change in its whole artistic, philosophical, and psychological concept. The film had become nothing more nor less than a travesty of Steinbeck's intentions and achievement.[1]

In the movie, the principal character becomes Connie Porter, magnificently played with sardonic panache by Tallulah Bankhead. She and the German dominate the movie. Bud Abbot is reduced, as Kovac (John Hodiak), the engine-room oiler with communistic leanings, to a supporting role. Kovac, after an extended abrasive thrust-and-parry relationship, falls in love with the imperious Connie, who, in her turn, visibly softens in her attitude toward him. Albert Shienkowitz is barely recognizable in the guise of Gus (William Bendix), the seaman from Brooklyn whose main purpose in life seems to be to demonstrate his prowess on the dance floor with his sweetheart Rosie, and who, assuming some of the character of Steinbeck's Bud Abbott, has suffered a wound in his leg. In Gus's case, however, the wound turns gangrenous, necessitating an immediate amputation. An additional character, the ship's second radio operator, Stanley Garrett, (Hume Cronyn), is introduced, among other reasons, to replace Albert in a pairing off with the Red Cross nurse. In the movie, the nurse's name has been changed from Alice Both to Alice Mackenzie

(Mary Anderson), and she has been upgraded from second lieutenant to lieutenant. It is she, in the Hitchcock version, who, despite Joe's efforts to hold her back, leads the attack on the German when he is pushed over the side. Afterwards, in a passage in Swerling's script cut in the final editing of the film, Joe accuses the others of being a mob and tells Alice reproachfully, "And you're the ringleader."[2] Joe, nevertheless, has been turned into the Hollywood stock-Negro type, nicknamed "Charcoal" with condescending affection by Connie. It is established that he was once a very competent pickpocket. Although he saves the Englishwoman with her dead baby at the beginning of the film, he does not dive into the sea in an attempt to save the German, as he does in Steinbeck's script. As played by Canada Lee, he is suitably servile for most of the time, whereas Steinbeck's Joe never loses his innate sense of pride in his race nor the implied respect the others — particularly Bud — show toward him. Steinbeck's Joe would never have allowed anyone else to play his flute, as he allows the Brennan character in the film to do. Brennan becomes Charles J. Rittenhouse (Henry Hull), and remains very much the same character Steinbeck depicted, as does the pathetic Englishwoman (Heather Angel), who, while having no name in Steinbeck's script, is called Mrs. Higgins in the film.

The most radical deviation from Steinbeck's original story, however, lies in the treatment of the German, nicknamed "Willi" in the film. In the person of chubby Walter Slezak he is portrayed as sometimes sly, sometimes ebullient, sometimes disturbingly engaging, and endowed with many outstanding abilities, including that of speaking perfect English. It is he who amputates Gus's leg, claiming to have been a surgeon in civilian life, and it is he who finally takes over command. While the Americans slump exhausted in the bottom of the boat, he displays immense strength and stamina by rowing the heavy vessel singlehandedly — ostensibly showing himself to be the epitome of the Nazi superman. After all the furor generated by Steinbeck's unconventional portrait of Colonel Lanser in *The Moon Is Down*, it was unavoidable that a renewed attack would be mounted against this transformation of Steinbeck's German.

The attack was not long in coming, but even before the reviews began appearing Steinbeck, on January 10, had sent a letter of protest to the studio. His main areas of concern at that time were, however, not so much the ludicrous Hitchcockian version of the German as what he saw in the movie as slurs against organized labor and the misrepresentation of the Joe character, who had been reduced to "the usual colored travesty . . . half comic and half pathetic," instead of the "Negro of dignity, purpose, and personality" in his original script. "Since this film occurs over my name," he wrote, "it is painful to me that these strange, sly obliquities should be ascribed to me" (*SLL* 266).

One of the first public shots in anger was fired by Bosley Crowther in the *New York Times* of 13 January. Beginning with the assessment that *Lifeboat* was "a tremendously provocative film," he homed in on the character of the German, referring to him as the "personification of the Nazi creed, who proves to be the only competent leader in a boat full of ineffectuals," and noting that "at no time in the picture do Mr. Hitchcock and Mr. Steinbeck depart from that theme." He ended his review questioning whether such a picture, with such a theme, was judicious at that time.[3] He returned to the attack ten days later, on this occasion pulling no punches:

> Unless we had seen it with our own eyes, we would never in this world have believed that a film could have been made in this country in the year 1943 which sold out the democratic ideal and elevated the Nazi 'superman.' ... Is this a picture of civilians which we want our soldiers on the fronts to see? Is this, in short, an honest symbolization of our democratic strength? In the reasoned opinion of this writer it definitely is not.[4]

In the same issue of the paper, *Lifeboat*'s producer, Kenneth MacGowan, defended the film's theme, which he saw as the awakening of the trusting and unprepared democracies to the unscrupulous resourcefulness and viciousness of the Nazis, and the final victory of a "civilized people pressed too far" in polishing off the German who has been revealed "as just as thorough a scoundrel and just as 'ersatz' a superman as his own Hitler." MacGowan concluded his apologia of sorts by stating that the filmmakers (of whom, by implication he included Steinbeck) had not set out to make a symbolic film and had never allowed the possibilities of the theme to divert them from their principal object, which was "the shaping of a film with as much excitement and reality as we could summon under challenging technical limitations"[5] Such a misrepresentation of Steinbeck's original intention in writing *Lifeboat* seems almost indefensible.

Commenting on the rumpus, *Life* observed that most of the critical blame had fallen on Steinbeck as the author, and recalled that *The Moon Is Down* had also been interpreted in some quarters as being pro-German. *Life* noted: "Steinbeck, however, disclaimed any responsibility for Director Hitchcock's and Scenarist Jo Swerling's treatment of his material. Others professed no surprise at Hollywood's passion for tampering with writers' scripts."[6] This last was the point considered at some length by Bosley Crowther in his third article on the movie. Crowther, to his credit, had been doing his homework, having obtained the loan of a copy of Steinbeck's original script from Annie Laurie Williams, and he was now ready to lay the blame where it was due. "The fact is now plain," he wrote in the *New York Times* on 31 January, "that the film to be seen at the Astor has not the same story that Mr. Steinbeck wrote. . . . Mr. Hitchcock and Kenneth MacGowan, the producer, . . . changed the basic character—the original concept—of the author's work. They preempted his creative authority. We are told they had the right to do so."[7] With a detailed analysis of the many differences in character and plot between Steinbeck's original story and the film, Crowther did more than set the record straight. He stressed that it was only right and proper that the writer should receive equal authority in the making of a film as the producer and director, but, on the other hand, opined that it was, after all, the writer's responsibility to protect his brainchild and that, if he failed to do so, he had no one to blame but himself for any misrepresentation of his work. He advocated that screenwriters should collaborate in drawing up a standard contract to protect the integrity of their work, and not rely on critics fighting their battles for them.

2

The whole episode had been another salutary lesson for Steinbeck. By the time all this hullabaloo was in progress, however, he and Gwyn were in Mexico, having left New York on 10 January, spent a week or so in New Orleans as they had planned, and then flown from there to Merida in Yucatan on the 22nd or 23rd. They made Mexico City their base. Steinbeck did no writing, content for the moment to do "completely tourist things." They both relaxed and generally enjoyed themselves, sightseeing among the ruins of Mitla and Monte Alban near Oaxaca, and spending a few days in Cuernavaca and San Miguel de Allende. The country was awash with Americans, restricted by the war from traveling further afield and taking advantage of the absence of rationing. It was not until he had enjoyed several long stretches of deep sleep that he realized how tired he must have been. Although he had planned to write some articles for the *Herald Tribune*, he could not be bothered. "Newspaper work is not natural to me," he told Covici. "And while I could turn out the wordage, it wouldn't be worth printing, like so much of my work overseas" (*Adventures* 543).

By mid-February, he had still done hardly any work on *The Good Little Neighbor*, although knowing perfectly well, or so he thought, that he could sit down then and there and do it if he wanted to. He considered the title of the projected work even better in Spanish: *El Buen Vecinito*. However, feeling at last his own man again and without professional commitment to anybody, he decided he would let the book mellow a while longer in his head before putting pen to paper.

Mail took from ten to twelve days to arrive from America, and he was only now beginning to catch up with the developing *Lifeboat* controversy.

The news, reaching him via Annie Laurie Williams, disturbed him greatly. Echoing some of the sentiments he had expressed following the publication of *The Moon Is Down*, he told Covici:

> It occurs to me that critics now have a deadly weapon in their hands, whereas before it was a blunt weapon. Now, by calling names, they can really injure a man, and they are using this power with pleasure. Some of them have indeed constituted themselves the mind and conscience of the American people. And these are dangerous. A critic with a mission plus a daily column can become a danger. (JS/PC 2/15/44).

Possibly, when he wrote that letter, he had not seen the copies of *Life* and the *New York Times* containing the articles that generally and specifically exonerated him from the blame erroneously attached to him as author of the script. Four days after his letter to Covici, he sent a telegram to Annie Laurie Williams, asking her to send notice of his displeasure to Twentieth Century-Fox and to demand that his name "be removed from any connection with any showing of this film" (*SLL* 267). If his agent passed on his request to the studio, his wishes were ignored. The one aspect that had particularly annoyed him was that Hitchcock had publicly maintained he had not changed the·original script in any way.

Gwyn was by now more than three months pregnant. Steinbeck's feelings about this seem to have been rather mixed, although he did often express the desire for a settled life back in California. His dream was to buy fifteen to twenty acres of land straddling the Carmel River, not too far from the ocean, and spend an indefinite amount of time getting everything just the way he wanted.

The frenetic tempo of their social life had tailed off considerably since they first arrived in Mexico, apart from accepting an invitation to attend a reception at the Russian Embassy in Mexico City on 23 February to celebrate the twenty-sixth anniversary of the founding of the Soviet Army. His attendance at this function was duly logged in his security files in Washington. Gwyn had sworn off liquor for the period of her pregnancy, and Steinbeck too seemed temporarily to have lost the taste for it — because, so he said, of the altitude or the climate. They were both experiencing pangs of homesickness for their New York apartment and for Willie.

While in the Mexican capital, Steinbeck had renewed acquaintance with some of the film people he had met there nearly four years previously when he was working with Kline on *The Forgotten Village*. One of the people he met was the up-and-coming film director Indio Fernandez, an ex-cowboy and ex-revolutionary, of whom great things were being predicted. Fernandez had taken under his wing the fading film star Dolores del Rio, persuading her to eschew all her glamorous makeup and long eyelashes, and had made her into a considerable emotional actress. He worked with a cameraman, Gabriel Figuroa, who was achieving remarkable photographic effects. In the eyes of many, the films they were producing together possessed the flavor of the notable French auteurs of the thirties, like Renoir and Carné, and Steinbeck was convinced that Fernandez was destined to become one of the leading directors in the world.

He told Fernandez the parable of the Indian boy and the great pearl, and the director showed interest in making a film based on the story. It was more or less immediately decided that Steinbeck would write a script and that the two of them would collaborate on making the film without any concessions to Hollywood whatsoever. Fernandez had recently completed *Maria Candelaria*, a film that had attracted a great deal of attention in Mexico, and he was currently riding high on a wave of critical approbation. He told Steinbeck that he saw no difficulty in obtaining financial backing for any new film he might want to make.

Before leaving Mexico, Steinbeck had committed himself to having the script of *The Pearl*, as the film was to be called, ready soon after Christmas, when Fernandez would be free to work with him on the preparation of the shooting script. The intention was that Steinbeck would then return with the director to Mexico and assist in the day-to-day making of the film.

3

Steinbeck and Gwyn arrived home in mid-March. He had at last recommenced work on *The Good Little Neighbor* and was hoping to have the book finished by the summer. He was, however, still feeling below par, and a visit to a doctor revealed that both his eardrums had been burst, and moreover that little vesicles all over his body had also been ruptured. This legacy of action in Italy, he was informed, would take from one to two years to clear. His hearing was slowly improving, but he still suffered from unaccustomed nervousness, bad dreams, and insomnia.

A month later, he was able to report to Sheffield that the medical treatment he had been receiving was working well and he was sleeping much better. He told Sheffield that he did not care if he never heard another gun as long as he lived. "I think the things that hurt the worst are the five-inch guns," he contended. "The big ones don't hit so hard. We sailed under some 16 inchers on a British monitor that were firing one day and they didn't seem to hurt nearly so badly. But the five-inchers or the British nine-pounders seem just literally to take the skin off" (JS/CAS 5/10/44).

The previous month he had told Sheffield he was "working every day on a silly book that is fun anyway" (*SLL* 269). This was *The Good Little Neighbor*. But in his letter of 5 May he reported that he had abandoned the work, which "just wasn't any good and woudn't jell" (JS/CAS 5/10/44).

It was only a temporary setback, however, and he was soon working on another short novel, *Cannery Row*. Viking provided him with a small room at their offices and, clearly with Covici's on-the-spot encouragement, he began making excellent progress. As he told Street on 4 July: "It has been hard to do a book because I've had to work for the treasury and the army too and it's kind of sneaking a book out. But it is a kind of a fun book that never mentions the war and it is a relief to work on" (JS/WFS 7/4/44). It is not clear what work Steinbeck was doing at that time for the Treasury and the Army, but it obviously did not constitute a long-term commitment. What had been established is that he did provide drafts for at least two political statements used by Roosevelt during the course of the 1944 Presidential campaign.[8]

He completed *Cannery Row* in six weeks, before the end of July. He had made a lighthearted bet with Gwyn that he would produce his book before she produced her baby, and he collected twenty dollars from her. Writing a few days later to Ritch and Tal Lovejoy, he told them:

'I just finished a crazy kind of book about Cannery Row and the lab etc. All fiction of course but born out of homesickness. And there are some true incidents in it. And some of it is a little funny I think. Also I have an idea for a musical comedy and if I have time or inclination I might do it before we start home. (JS/RL end July 1944).

He had by then definitely made up his mind that they would return to Monterey as soon as possible after the baby was born. He had purchased a secondhand station wagon, and was proposing to drive it cross-country, taking Gwyn and the baby with him, always assuming they would be fit enough to make the journey. If they were not, he planned to send them by train and make the trip alone with just Willie as company.

4

When in May Steinbeck abandoned the unsuccessful novel-in-progress, *The Good Little Neighbor*, he obviously decided not to commence work immediately on *The Pearl*, but instead began searching around for another possible subject for a new novel. It seems he may have chanced upon the unfinished manuscript of *The God in the Pipes*, the play-novel he had finally put aside in midsummer 1941. If this is indeed the true sequence of events then it is clear that, after reading through the old manuscript, he not only found the setting for the new novel but also realized that he could adapt some of the unused material, minor characters, and situations from *The God in the Pipes* in writing it.

There is no possibility that he would have contemplated finishing the original play-novel. As well as recognizing the basic flaws in the work, too much had happened in the interim for him to recapture its fragile essence as he had conceived it those several years ago. Retaining but a few pages of the manuscript, he threw away all he had written, and started over.

If the location of his new book was the same as that of the earlier work, the story he had to tell, his viewpoint, and his whole approach to the material became vastly different. He abandoned the rather gentle, whimsical satire and allegory of *The God in the Pipes*, replacing it with a far more abrasive brand of satire that he channeled into a biting commentary on contemporary mores. In its simplest and most obvious form, his thesis contrasted the carefree existence of the debased modern counterparts of the noble savage, living on their wits and whatever they can scavenge, with the sterile respectability of the bigoted middle and upper classes he had so effectively satirized in the recent *Lifeboat* and *A Medal for Benny*.

In recycling his material, Steinbeck, jettisoned the central characters of Cameron, the rather insipid stranger from "far Salinas," and Mr. Boss, the self-appointed landlord of the pipes, although some aspects of the Mr. Boss character survive in the new work in the minor character of Mr. Malloy. As his new principals. Steinbeck installed the more vibrant characters of Mack and the boys, and Doc, the thinly-disguised portrait of Ed Ricketts. It had been Steinbeck's longtime wish to write a full-length work in which to celebrate Ricketts, the man, as he really was. He had, of course, several times in earlier works introduced a Ricketts-like character through whose mouth he had disseminated some of Ricketts's theories and philosophies: for instance, Dr. Burton in the 1936 novel *In Dubious Battle*, Jim Casy in *The Grapes of Wrath*, and Dr. Winter in *The Moon is Down*. But in only one previous work, the early (1935) short story "The Snake," had he committed to paper anything like a recognizable physical portrait of his friend. In "The Snake," based on an actual incident that had occurred in Ricketts's laboratory, Ricketts appears under the guise of "young Dr. Phillips."[9] In *Cannery Row*, the portrait was to be undeniably recognizable, and all the kaleidoscopic events of the novel would be set in motion by and revolve around the almost fabulous figure of Doc.

If Steinbeck himself wrote the disclaimer printed in the preliminaries to the published text, he must surely have done so with tongue in cheek: "The people, places, and events in this book are, of course, fictions and fabrications." Although on the surface he continued to promote the idea that the book was completely fiction, the truth was, as he had explained to the Lovejoys, that there were "some true incidents in it." After the book was published, anyone who had the slightest knowledge of the Monterey scene could have been under no illusion about that. Not only did they find that Steinbeck had described in exact detail the physical appearance and most of the salient features of Ricketts's character, as well as the precise layout of the Pacific Biological Laboratory (renamed Western Biological in the novel), but that he had encapsulated within the covers of the book the vital ambience of Ocean View Avenue, Monterey, and the immediate surrounding vicinity, whether it be thinly disguised — Flora Adams and her Lone Star Cafe (Dora Flood and the Bear Flag Restaurant in the novel) and Wing Chong's Market (Lee Chong's Grocery) — or by actual name — the La Ida Cafe, the Halfway House, Jimmy Brucia's Bar, the San Carlos Hotel, Holman's Department Store, and the Scotch Bakery.

In a very real way, what Steinbeck was attempting to do in this book (at least while writing it) was nothing short of working out his need to obliterate the war. Nine years later, he would claim that he wrote the book as "a kind of nostalgic thing . . . for a group of soldiers who had said to me 'Write something funny that isn't about the war. Write something for us to read — we're sick of war.'"[10] Shortly afterward, he reiterated to Peter Lisca that he had written the book "as a relaxation from the war, which had depressed him, and that he wanted the troops to read it and enjoy it."[11] But the real truth undoubtedly was that he wrote the book because *for him* at that particular time its creation constituted a very necessary trip back into the past, an imaginative return to a period (as perhaps he came to realize more and more as the writing progressed) that had disappeared forever.

If, however, his main motivation in writing the book was indeed a compulsive desire to escape from present day reality into the past, then he surely did not entirely succeed. *Cannery Row*, for all its rambunctious humor and its sentimentality, possesses an undercurrent of darkness, a preoccupation with loneliness and death. He had, after all, only recently returned from the war zones of Britain, Africa, and Italy, and no matter how much he might have liked to think that by writing this nostalgic book he would be able to release himself from the experience of the realities he had witnessed and the emotions he had felt while overseas — the images of pain and mutilation, and the aching sense of aloneness, the uncertainty, the jealousy at being separated from Gwyn — they were all still imprinted on his mind and could not be completely eradicated. But while he was actually writing the book, he could — or so he thought — effectively hold present-day reality at least at arm's length. With the penultimate chapter completed, he wrote at the head of the next page of his manuscript: "Last chapter and how I dread it."[12] Three pages more, and it was done. Shortly afterward, he told Joseph H. Jackson: "[I]t's a book I enjoyed writing very much and the war is never mentioned in it" (JS/JHJ Aug. 1944).

Part black comedy, part farce, part scientific treatise, part penetrating comment on the human condition, part joyous celebration of the "simple life" of those who have discarded many of the social conventions that burden modern man, *Cannery Row* represents Steinbeck's first tentative testing of the water of metafiction he had anticipated, but in somewhat different terms, when he had set out to write *The God in the Pipes* four years earlier. This novel—"if," as Benson has suggested, "one can call it that" (*Adventures* 555)—is written in a gritty and freewheeling prose style and literary structure. Critics have devoted much space in their attempts to endow the book with some sort of rational structure, but, as Benson has pertinently pointed out, one factor "that makes the book so attractive is the fact that it has been such a puzzle."[13] After noting Steinbeck's comments in letters to his editor soon after the book's publication that "no critic has stumbled on the design of the book" (letter dated 5 January 1945), and that "no critic has discovered the reason for those little inner chapters" in the book (letter dated 15 January 1945), Benson observes:

> No magic key to the novel has been found, however, and the reason, I suspect, is that no key of the sort that critics are inclined to look for actually exists. I am relatively certain that the problem of interpreting *Cannery Row* depends upon adjusting our perspective rather than discovering an elaborate literary apparatus.[14]

In *Cannery Row* there are several chapters, the "inner chapters" to which Steinbeck referred, that are undoubtedly similar in the purely literary sense to the intercalary chapters of *The Grapes of Wrath*. In the earlier novel, such interchapters served the double purpose of extending the Joad experience into an overview of the universal human experience of the Okies and of providing the necessary historical and sociopolitical backgrounds and perspectives against which the saga of the family unfolds. In *Cannery Row*, on the other hand, Steinbeck does not employ the interchapters with the same purpose in mind, but uses them simply to develop and simplify a mood or to complement and reinforce a particular theme. In *The Grapes of Wrath* there is, with two exceptions, a strict alternating pattern of expository and narrative chapters, but in *Cannery Row* the actual (and even underlying) pattern created by the introduction of interchapters is by no means clear-cut. Indeed, over the years there has been some measure of disagreement among several distinguished Steinbeck scholars, not only as to which chapters should properly be designated interchapters, but also as to the exact nature and purpose of each interchapter.[15]

An examination of Steinbeck's original holograph manuscript and the original typescript prepared from it demonstrates that there is no small measure of difficulty in attempting to impose and sustain a satisfactory alternating chapter/interchapter design on the book in the way some scholars have maintained exists,[16] and that the possibility remains that Steinbeck never did in fact seek to impose any preconceived structural pattern on the book in the conventional sense, although it is evident that some sort of pattern must have emerged in his mind at an early stage in the writing.[17] After all, the brief opening section of the book, preceding the numbered chapters, suggests that this may well have been the case. In the holograph manuscript, this section was given the heading: "Concerning the difficulties involved in writing such an account as this————". The section begins with a description of Cannery Row as "a poem, a stink, a grating noise, a quality of light, a tone, a habit, a nostalgia, a dream" (CR 1), and concludes with the rhetorical observation:

> How can the poem and the stink and the grating noise — the quality of light, the tone, the habit, and the dream — be set down alive? When you collect marine animals there are certain flat worms so delicate that they are almost impossible to capture whole, for they break and tatter under the touch. You must let them ooze and crawl of their own will onto a knife blade and then lift them gently into your bottle of sea water. And perhaps that might be the way to write this book — to open the page and let the stories crawl in by themselves. (CR 3)

The first five numbered chapters, together with the opening section, can be regarded as constituting the preliminaries to the narrative proper by introducing the reader to all the principal characters in the ensuing narrative (Lee Chong, Mack and the boys, Doc, and Dora Flood and her girls), as well as to some of the minor characters who are to make frequent appearances throughout the book (Alfred, the old Chinaman, and Henri the painter). They establish the environment in which these characters act out their lives. They set out, particularly in Chapters 2 and 4, the rationale and the thematic concerns of the book. They reveal in the last sentence of Chapter 2 the well-spring of the whole action of the story in Mack's comment: "That Doc is a fine fellow. We ought to do something for him" (CR 13), a voiced expression of love and gratitude subsequently widened into the universal desire felt throughout the Row in the very last sentence of Chapter 5: "And everyone who thought of him thought next, 'I really must do something nice for Doc'" (CR 29). The implication of these two statements is, of course, reflected in the ensuing narrative by contrasting the disastrous first party, planned in somewhat haphazard fashion by Mack and the boys, with the successful second party, carefully and lovingly planned by the whole community—albeit with some unobtrusive assistance from Doc himself.

The book, as Steinbeck explained to Joseph H. Jackson, "is written on several levels of understanding and people can take out of it what they can bring to it but even on the thinnest level of understanding I think it is fun" (JS/JHJ Aug. 1944). While he did not make it clear to Jackson just how many levels of understanding he was referring to, he did subsequently reveal to Sheffield that he considered there to be four, although he did not say what they were. Various critics have expressed their own opinions about his claim, and some have even themselves claimed to have discovered more than four levels. It will, however, be sufficient here to take Steinbeck at his somewhat ambiguous word and confine discussion to the four he possibly had in mind. First, pure narrative: the recounting of the events leading up to the first and second parties thrown in Doc's honor. Second, the underlying thematic structures: the recurring contrasts between the bums and respectable society, the essential loneliness of the individual, and, as Warren French has noted, the proposition that "love does not always bring joy and that pain does not result only from spite."[18] Third symbolism: the concept that the tidepool represents a microcosm of humanity, and the examination of human behavior through animal analogies (the frog community, the puppy, the gopher). And lastly, social comment: as, for example, in the Josh Billings and Mary Talbot chapters, and perhaps most tellingly and poignantly in the Frankie chapters.

The basic plot of *Cannery Row*, as already noted, is simplicity itself: the idea initiated by Mack that he and the boys should throw a party for Doc, because he is such a "fine fellow"; the haphazard planning of the party; the realization of the problems inherent in funding such an event when you are indigent; the arrangement the boys come to with Lee Chong by trading the sackful of frogs they have caught for Doc, on the basis that Doc will then pay Lee for them; the disastrous outcome of the party that begins spontaneously before Doc has returned from La Jolla, that gets completely out of hand and results in the wrecking of the lab; the gloom and bad luck that descends on the Row following this debacle, until Dora eventually instils a sense of purpose in the whole community, dispelling the blanket of unhappiness and adversity, by suggesting to Mack that the solution is to organize another party for Doc and to ensure that this time he is there to enjoy it; the concerted planning that proceeds ostensibly in secret; and finally the party's rip-roaring celebration.

Like the panoramic shot at the beginning of a movie, the whole physical landscape of the Row is established in the book's opening section, and we see, as from above, the daily routine of the fishermen and the cannery workers. Finally, we briefly glimpse the principal characters: the bums emerging from the shade of the black cypress tree to sit on the disused pipes in the vacant lot; the girls from the Bear Flag enjoying whatever sun there is before the evening's work begins, Doc strolling across the road from the lab to Lee Chong's for groceries and beer.

At the beginning of Chapter 1, the "camera" tracks down into Lee Chong's Grocery, an establishment of which it is said that "within its single room a man could find everything he needed or wanted to live and to be happy" (CR 5), with the sole exception of that certain commodity that could be obtained just along the street at the Bear Flag. Lee Chong is presented as not only a temporary benefactor to his customers by allowing them credit, but also a respected, astute businessman who almost invariably collects his debts by the simple expedient of cutting off further credit once those debts have reached an undesirable level. He may occasionally be duped by Mack and the boys, but only when it serves his purpose to be duped. When he comes into the ownership of the old Abbeville building beyond the cypress tree and the railroad track, he agrees to let Mack and the boys occupy it for a stipulated rent he knows they will never pay and have no intention of paying. But he knows too that they will ensure that the property is protected against marauding children and that not only will they spend at his store whatever money may from time to time come their way, protecting the store itself from the unwelcome attention of drunks and foraging kids from town, but will also avoid his store when they carry out their own pilfering expeditions. All in all, Lee eventually decides with some degree of satisfaction that the pros outweigh the cons.

The boys, who had previously lived under the black cypress tree, retiring temporarily in wet weather to the discarded cannery pipes on the vacant lot, take pride in their new home. The building has been used for the storage of fish meal and consequently is far from sweet-smelling when they take it over. But the boys clean out all the remaining vestiges of the fish meal, furnish the place, and call it the Palace Flophouse Grill.

Mack is "the elder, leader, mentor, and to a small extent the exploiter" of the others in the group: Hazel, "a young man of great strength"; Eddie, "who [fills] in as a bartender at La Ida"; and Hughie and Jones, "who occasionally [collect] frogs and cats for Western Biological" (CR 10—11). The five boys are joined, as the story begins, by Gay, a married man tired of having to beat up his wife, a woman who persistently hits him while he is asleep, only stopping when he overreacts in his own defense, but who refuses to take out a warrant against him, having realized that he now prefers the amenities to be enjoyed at the new Salinas jail to those offered at home. By rejecting his wife and home for the Palace Flophouse Grill, Gay contrives to become one of that "little group of men who had in common no families, no money, and no ambitions beyond food, drink, and contentment" (CR 10), the disguised envy of "a generation of trapped, poisoned, and trussed-up men," who regard them as "no-goods, come-to-bad-ends, blots-on-the-town, thieves, rascals, bums" (*CR* 15). While Mack and the boys are all these things, they are also, as Steinbeck suggests, "the Beauties, the Virtues, the Graces" (*CR* 15). They may be seen by the majority as bums, but like every other human being on the face of the earth there is good as well as bad in them. Inevitably, Steinbeck tends to sentimentalize them, as he does every other character who lives on the Row. As he points out on the very first page of the book, the inhabitants of the Row are,

> as the man once said, "whores, pimps, gamblers, and sons of bitches," by which he meant Everybody. Had the man looked through another peephole he might have said, "Saints and angels and martyrs and holy men," and he would have meant the same thing. (*CR* 1)

Certainly, like the Arthurian knights of old, many of whom were rogues and rascals to be sure, Mack and the boys have their own strict rules of honor, obliging them to help those less fortunate than themselves whenever they feel such assistance is deserved, to remember (if not always to repay) their debts, to avoid ruining their reputation by working when it is not absolutely essential, and never to roll a drunk.

If Steinbeck tends to sentimentalize Mack and the boys, he also makes "saints and martyrs," if not "holy men," out of Dora Flood and the girls of the Bear Flag Restaurant. Dora is yet another in the long line of Steinbeck's "happy hookers," as Robert E. Morsberger has referred to them. With the exception of Kate in *East of Eden*, all the madams and whores in Steinbeck's fiction are endowed with oversized hearts and oversympathetic natures. Dora and her girls fit snugly into the pattern. Dora is "a great big woman with flaming orange hair and a taste for Nile green evening dresses," and she runs "a decent, clean, honest, old-fashioned sporting house," a one-price house where no hard liquor is sold and where no loud or vulgar talk is allowed (*CR* 16). She named the house the Bear Flag Restaurant "in a moment of local love," and by so doing misled many people into entering it for a sandwich. Dora cherishes her girls, even when they are not fully active owing to age or infirmity. She keeps them under her roof, even though "some of them don't turn three tricks a month ... but go right on eating three meals a day" (*CR* 17). Generosity is both forced upon her and given freely by her. Threat of legal closure obliges her to contribute far above the recognized average to police and Chamber of Commerce funds and other charities. On the other hand, during the Depression she almost bankrupted herself by paying the grocery bills of needy families.

One member of the community who never avails himself of the services of the Bear Flag is Doc. As Doris, one of the girls, observes, "He never comes in here for a trick." Phyllis Mae, another of the girls, comments, "Lots of guys don't want to pay. Costs them more but they figure it different" (*CR* 190).[19] Doc, so it is said, is never short of female company. Earlier in the book, Mack and the boys are discussing what would be the best way of doing something nice for Doc, something that would please him:

> "He'd like a dame," said Hughie.
> "He's got three four dames," said Jones. "You can always tell — when he pulls them front curtains closed and when he plays that kind of church music on the phonograph."
> Mack said reprovingly to Hughie. "Just because he doesn't run no dame naked through the streets in the daytime, you think Doc's celebrate."
> "What's celebrate?" Eddie asked.
> "That's when you can't get no dame," said Mack.
> "I thought it was a kind of a party." said Jones. (*CR* 44)

There is, of course, no question of Doc being "celebrate," it having already been established that he is as "concupiscent as a rabbit" (*CR* 29), and that he has "helped many a girl out of one trouble and into another" (*CR* 28). Mack's malapropism and Jone's comment do, however, serve to instill the idea in the minds of the boys that they should organize a party for Doc.

Physically, Doc is described as "rather small, deceptively small, for he is wiry and very strong and when passionate anger comes on him he can be very fierce" (*CR* 28). In this respect and in his facial appearance he closely resembles Ed Ricketts: "He wears a beard and his face is half Christ and half satyr and his face tells the truth" (*CR* 28). Over the years, just as Ricketts had done, he has become on the Row "the fountain of philosophy and science and art" (*CR* 28).

Just as in Lee Chong's Grocery it is said that a man could obtain everything with which to live and find happiness, so in Western Biological it is possible to "order anything living" and to be sure, sooner or later, of getting it (*CR* 25–26). The wares of Western Biological and the interior of the building are described in loving detail, as Steinbeck, while writing the book, relived the many happy hours he had spent with Ricketts within the four walls of Pacific Biological; closely working with the biologist on marine scientific investigations; helping to prepare specimens for sale; engaging in long, philosophical discussions; and joining Ricketts and other friends in marathon sessions where both drink and conversation flowed freely. Steinbeck's deep affection for the man and for the real-life laboratory, which for him from time to time had become a sort of refuge from everyday cares, radiates uninhibitedly from the printed words on the page.

It is the interaction between all these characters — Lee Chong, Mack and the boys, Dora and her girls, and Doc — that provides the excitement, the tension and the impetus within the exuberant narrative, in which (though it may be argued that very little happens) everything happens. These vividly evoked characters from the author's past exist in a strange harmony, sometimes in uneasy acceptance of one another, but always with a great deal of love as well as sentimentality. Only once is a truly discordant note struck — when Doc, returning from La Jolla, walks in upon the ruin of his lab, hits Mack, and calls him a "dirty son of a bitch" (*CR* 136). So interlocked is the relationship between the denizens of the Row that this event temporarily throws the whole ordered tempo of the community out of kilter, resulting in that period of gloom, studded with a series of misfortunes.

Underpinning the basic narrative structure are the various thematic structures, of which probably the most important is introduced in Chapter 4, the chapter describing the boy Andy's encounter with the mysterious old Chinaman. This Chinaman, one of the survivors from *The God in the Pipes*, walks every evening at dusk down the hill, past the Palace Flophouse, across the vacant lot and the street, through the opening between Doc's lab and the adjacent Hediondo Cannery, traverses the beach beyond, and finally disappears beneath the pier. He carries a covered, wicker basket, and wears an old flat straw hat, blue jean jacket and trousers, and "heavy shoes of which one sole was loose so that it slapped the ground when he walked" (*CR* 22). At dawn he emerges from under the pier and with his basket now full of whatever it is he has been collecting during the night, retraces his steps of the previous evening, this time disappearing through the gate in a high board fence up the hill behind the Palace Flophouse.[20] Although he has been following this same routine each evening and each morning for years, nobody seems to know who he is:

> Some people thought he was God and very old people thought he was Death and children thought he was a very funny old Chinaman, as children always think anything old and strange is funny. But the children did not taunt him or shout at him as they should for he carried a little cloud of fear about with him. (*CR* 23)

Only one boy, the ten-year-old Andy from out of town, plucks up sufficient courage to challenge the old man. One evening, in a spasm of bravado, he marches behind the old man, singing 'Ching-Chong Chinaman sitting on a rail — 'Long came a white man an' chopped off his tail" (*CR* 23). The Chinaman turns and faces him and stares into his face:

What happened then Andy was never able either to explain or to forget. For the eyes spread out until there was no Chinaman. And then it was one eye — one huge brown eye as big as a church door. Andy looked through the shiny transparent brown door and through it he saw a lonely countryside, flat for miles but ending against a row of fantastic mountains shaped like cows' and dogs' heads and tents and mushrooms. There was low coarse grass on the plain and here and there a little mound. And a small animal like a woodchuck sat on each mound. And the loneliness — the desolate cold aloneness of the landscape made Andy whimper because there wasn't anybody at all in the world and he was left. (*CR* 23—24)

The passage, unbearably terrifying in its implications, mirrors one of the most potent of all human fears. Ricketts rightly adjudged *Cannery Row* "an essay in loneliness."[21] Indeed, Doc himself is described as being "in spite of his friendliness and his friends ... a lonely and set-apart man" (*CR* 104). In the ultimate resolution of the narrative, the one service that Mack and the boys, Dora and the girls, and everyone else on the Row cannot give Doc, no matter how many parties they may throw in his honor, no matter how many "dames" may spend the night at the lab, is a cure for that sense of loneliness and apartness that is a fundamental element in his psychological makeup.[22]

The basic reason for the Chinaman's self-imposed loneliness remains a puzzle. The answer seems unlikely to have ethnic origins, for there are other Orientals living contentedly on the Row with whom he can, if he so wishes, mingle. The reasons for the loneliness experienced by other characters are not, however, shrouded in mystery: William, the watchman at the Bear Flag, finds himself rejected even by those bums whose company he courts with bottles of the cheap whiskey known affectionately as Old Tennis Shoes and guaranteed four months old; the Captain whom Mack and the boys meet on the frog hunt pines for the marital warmth and companionship his wife withholds; Henri the painter cannot find any girl willing to share her life with him in the makeshift cabin on his unfinished boat; Mary, the party-loving wife of the indigent writer and cartoonist Tom Talbot, is reduced to entertaining the neighborhood cats rather than the neighbors themselves; and Frankie, as a consequence of is impossible love for Doc, is shut away in an institution for the mentally retarded. Even Mack and the boys and Dora and her girls are not immune from the scourge of loneliness. After the wrecking of the lab, for which they bear full responsibility, Mack and the boys taste the bitterness of temporary ostracism. Dora and her girls are, of course, condemned by the very nature of their profession. As Morsberger has pointed out: "Prostitution may be casually accepted in the world of Steinbeck's fiction, but it's ultimate name is loneliness."[23] And loneliness is the note on which the book ends. The saga of the lonely gopher serves to emphasize the final image of Doc, alone in the lab the morning after the second party, weeping as he reads aloud to himself the verses of the Sanskrit poem "Black Marigolds," while in their cages the white rats scamper and scramble and "behind the glass the rattlesnakes lay still and stared into space with their dusty frowning eyes" (*CR* 208).

In the same way that the gopher, the rats, and the rattlesnakes can be seen as symbols for human loneliness, so the tide pool, the source of Doc's interest and income, and incidentally the source of all human life, is a symbol of contemporary human society, its inherent savagery a metaphor for the human condition:

> A wave breaks over the barrier, and churns the glassy water for a moment and mixes bubbles into the pool, and then it clears and is tranquil and lovely and murderous again. Here a crab tears a leg from his brother. The anemones expand like soft and brilliant flowers, inviting any tired and perplexed animal to lie for a moment in their arms, and when some small crab or little tide-pool Johnnie accepts the green and purple invitation, the petals whip in, the stinging cells shoot tiny narcotic needles into the prey and it grows weak and perhaps sleepy while the searing caustic digestive acids melt its body down. . . . On the exposed rocks the starfish emit semen and eggs from between their rays. The smells of life and richness, of death and digestion, of decay and birth, burden the air. (*CR* 30–32)

Certainly, *Cannery Row* contains its full quota of death and violence. There are four suicides. Horace Abbeville shoots himself after relinquishing ownership of the fish-meal storage place to Lee Chong in settlement of his large, accumulated debt. Because he cannot find a job, the father of the young boy Joey drinks rat poison and suffers a painful, lingering death. William, the watchman, stabs himself with an ice pick after he overhears Mack and the boys voicing their deep contempt for him. The young girl whose body Doc discovers on the reef at La Jolla has, one assumes, drowned herself on account of unrequited love or perhaps an unwanted pregnancy. There are other deaths: Josh Billings, who passed away in a hotel room while on a visit to Monterey in 1885; and the imagined murder of a baby witnessed by the hallucinating Henri as he sits in solitary drunken stupor in his cabin. Elmer Recheti loses both his legs when he falls asleep on the railroad track. Alfred, William's successor at the Bear Flag, ejects a drunk too violently, and breaks the man's neck.

The Josh Billings interchapter, with its morbid recounting of the fate of the dead humorist's "tripas," is undoubtedly the most distasteful episode in *Cannery Row*. On a first reading, it appears to have no relevance whatsoever to the rest of the book. It is not even contemporaneous with the narrative, in the way other interchapters are. So why did Steinbeck include it? Apparently, the Josh Billings incident was one he had been wanting to write for several years. He first heard the tale in 1938 from the lips of a Monterey resident, Mrs. Harriet Gragg. He mentions it in a letter he wrote to Elizabeth Otis in February 1939, shortly after finishing the revision of *The Grapes of Wrath*, and in another letter, probably written in 1938 or 1939, to Jane Grabhorn of the Colt Press.[24] Having regard to the haphazard surface structure he had devised for *Cannery Row*, he clearly decided that he had at last found a place for the story. What is more, he realized it would in fact demonstrate to perfection the sort of views he held on the current social scene, and furthermore allow him to have a very personal dig at the respectable citizens of the Monterey draft board who had not only made life so difficult for him but had pronounced so slightingly on his literary standing. If there is some evident relish in the telling of the tale of how Josh Billing's carelessly discarded "tripas" were recovered and given a decent burial, there is even more relish in the ironic final sentence of the interchapter: "For Monterey was not a town to let dishonor come to a literary man" (*CR* 75).

In *Cannery Row*, as in his other work, Steinbeck uses every opportunity, by way of social comment, to take a swipe at hypocritical respectability and that broad element of philistine thinking that poisons society. How typical, he suggests, is the interest occasioned in town by the flag-pole skater, who, as well as boosting the business of the local department store, gives many passers-by pause for thought — not, as one might imagine, to marvel at the skater's skill and endurance or to contemplate the essential pointlessness of the whole exercise, but simply to wonder how he manages, high above the town, to cope with the problem of his normal excretory functions.

Steinbeck shows himself time and time again to be on the side of the bums, the underdogs, the outcasts, the underprivileged, the losers, Not only are Mack and the boys ("the Beauties, the Virtues, the Graces") compared favorably with those who hold them in contempt, but they are celebrated as having discovered the ideal way of life. As Doc observes:

"There are your true philosophers. I think . . . that Mack and the boys know everything that has ever happened in the world and possibly everything that will happen. I think they survive in this particular world better than other people. In a time when people tear themselves to pieces with ambition and nervousness and covetousness, they are relaxed. All of our so-called successful men are sick men, with bad stomachs, and bad souls, but Mack and the boys are healthy and curiously clean. They can do what they want. They can satisfy their appetites without calling them something else. . . . They could ruin their lives and get money. Mack has qualities of genius. They're all very clever if they want something. They just know the nature of things too well to be caught in that wanting." (*CR* 148—49)

But, of course, it is not so simple as all that. In some ways—in many ways—such a philosophy is a cruel illusion, as Doc surely knows. As Steinbeck himself surely knew. Certainly, Mack and the boys, for all their rascally scheming, do not have and cannot have the completely carefree existence Steinbeck suggests. Their acquisition of the fish-meal shed and the loving way in which they transform it into the Palace Flophouse Grill and a home can be seen as marking their first step toward a possible future respectability. Even Mrs. Malloy can hanker after the additional social kudos that curtains would give her windowless boiler home.

For all that it is rooted in remembered reality, *Cannery Row* is a fable, or perhaps more precisely a series of fables, impressively conveying all of Steinbeck's anger and disenchantment on his return from the war. Intended as an exercise in escapism, he was unable to prevent its humor being lethally double-edged, so that the book turned out in the end, as John Timmerman has called it, "surely one of the darkest [novels] in Steinbeck's canon."[25] Timmerman goes on to observe: "*Cannery Row* is a novelistic probing of the dark, subconscious urges in humanity, based upon the metaphorical alliance with the sea and its violent subsurface world."[26] By means of such images, Steinbeck was clearly endeavoring to eradicate, perhaps even in a strange way to justify, by the imposition of a form of scientific objectivity on his narrative, the subjective experience of his months overseas and the memory of the shattered cities and the mutilated bodies he had seen.

He may very well have confidently told Jackson that the war was never mentioned in *Cannery Row*, but its presence is nevertheless there, lurking in the book's dark underside. It is there in the mutilation of Elmer Recheti. It is there in the slitting of the baby's throat during Henri's hallucination. It is there in every example, great or small, of pain given or indifference displayed. It is there most obviously perhaps in Chapter 18, in the image of the drowned girl at La Jolla:

Between two weeded rocks on the barrier Doc saw a flash of white under water and then the floating weed covered it. He climbed to the place over the slippery rocks, held himself firmly, and gently reached down and parted the brown algae. Then he grew rigid. A girl's face looked up at him, a pretty, pale girl with dark hair. The eyes were open and clear and the face was firm and the hair washed gently about her head. The body was out of sight, caught in the crevice. The lips were slightly parted and the teeth showed and on the face was only comfort and rest. Just under water it was and the clear water made it very beautiful. It seemed to Doc that he looked at it for many minutes, and the face burned into his picture memory. (*CR* 114)

The image of the girl's face precedes Doc as he makes his way back to the beach. He sits on the sand. Music sounds in his ears, "a high thin piercingly sweet flute carrying a melody he could never remember, and against this, a pounding surf-like wood-wind section." The sound of the flute rises "into regions beyond the hearing range and even there it [carries] its unbelievable melody." He cannot get the girl's face out of his mind. "The girl's eyes had been gray and clear and the dark hair floated, drifted lightly over the face. The picture was set for all time" (*CR* 115). The dead girl is the dead girl who floated in the harbor of Palermo, only this girl at La Jolla is floating face upward and not face downward. Doc is to be spared nothing, but is forced to experience Steinbeck's own night-marish recollection of the sight he never saw, the imagined sight that became akin to an obsession, written about not only in the original *New York Herald Tribune* dispatch, but also here in *Cannery Row* the following year, and yet again in the 1957 newspaper article for the *Louisville Courier-Journal*.

If indeed Steinbeck had begun writing *Cannery Row* as an exercise in escapism and nostalgia, it had become in the writing something much more — not only an attempt to exorcise the demons of war by confronting them in symbolic terms, but also an opportunity to express once again his anger and bitterness against all those in New York and Washington who in his eyes were having a good time, thank you very much, living it up and raking in the profits, without thought to all that was going on overseas. It was a subject, as we have seen, he had touched upon in his *Lifeboat* script, although when he had written that he had not experienced for himself the true meaning of war, "that dirty thing," as he had told Louis Paul, "where everyone gets hurt in one way or another" (JS/Paul c.Dec. 1943). His bitterest attack against those of his fellow-countrymen who were sitting out the war at home was contained in the discarded interchapter subsequently published as a short story, "The Time the Wolves Ate the Vice Principal." As Warren French was the first to suggest:

> Since this tale is one of Steinbeck's most gruesome ones, I suspect publishers omitted it not as irrelevant but as too grisly for American readers who like to hear about death only when they have not been responsible for it. The chapter tells of the gathering of a pack of wolves on the Salinas courthouse lawn, their ranging about the town, and their finally eating the ailing vice-principal of the local high school on the steps of the house of a woman who sleeps through the episode. Like Chapter 18, it emphasizes people's ignorance of what is happening on their own doorsteps.[27]

As French goes on to say, in this discarded interchapter Steinbeck is not only commenting, in memorable fashion, on the general complacency of the American people who were, to a significant degree, responsible for creating the conditions in which the outbreak of World War II became inevitable, but also is attacking "respectable society's insensitivity to the truth about what's happening and its complacent complicity in unchecked violence."[28]

While its surface structure may be episodic and seemingly random, *Cannery Row* is, in fact, as French and other scholars have demonstrated, thematically very tightly structured. Although a short book, it is nevertheless extremely rich in texture, far more impressive in the ideas it propounds than many a book two or three times its length. The imposition by Steinbeck of the objective nature of his tide pool observations on the teeming community of the Row has resulted in the creation of some of the more memorable characters in all his fiction.

In addition to being the fictive medium for the expression of many of his own and Ricketts's pet philosophical and biological theories, *Cannery Row* is also the medium (to be explored more deeply in his next work, *The Pearl*) for the expression of his continuing interest in the cinema. His last sustained work of fiction had, after all, been the film script *Lifeboat*. The cinematic qualities of the opening paragraphs of the novel have already been commented upon. In the same way, the last paragraph of all is like the final close-up shot in a movie, so that one can almost visualize the camera iris closing on the "dusty, frowning eyes" of the snakes in Doc's laboratory, while the Gregorian melody accompanies the fade-out and the credits. In between, we are given the quick cutting techniques, the flashbacks, and in several places (the frog hunt, the gopher) the artificial (to the human eye) extremely low camera angles. And at La Jolla, the emotional impact of Doc's discovery of the dead girl is heightened by a very effective piece of "background music," a device Steinbeck was to use more frequently but with far less subtlety in *The Pearl*.

When Malcolm Cowley read *Cannery Row* he found it "bland, carefree and very entertaining," but on a second reading he became aware of the "undercurrent of morbidity" that had been undetected by most other critics of the day. "It isn't a cheap book," Cowley wrote, "but the writing is cynical as if the author were trying to protect his emotions, which nevertheless escaped him. The aftertaste is a little unpleasant, as if you had eaten a poisoned cream puff."[29] When he read the review, Steinbeck commented that if Cowley had read the book a third time he would have discovered how very poisoned it was.[30]

Steinbeck could have meant many things by that remark, but it is possible that Stoddard Martin put his finger precisely on the crux of the matter when he offered the observation that "*Cannery Row* is ... the creation of a man disappointed in marriage. No extended male-female relationship is depicted as successful."[31] If by writing the novel Steinbeck did not entirely succeed in the impossible task of exorcising the remembered horrors of war, he also did not wholly exorcise his disillusionment with marriage. Not only was the pain of the divorce from Carol still very much on his conscience, but he had been unable to free himself completely from the suspicion that while he had been overseas Gwyn had been cheating on him. The streak of misogyny that had always been evident in his work surfaced undisguised in *Cannery Row* in the references to the terminated marriages of Mack and Henri, and in the accounts of the unhappiness prevalent in the marriages of Gay, Richard Frost, and, to a lesser degree, Sam Malloy and Tom Talbot. Only Dora and her happy hookers are fully exempted from the latent antagonism directed against the book's other female characters.

In no way can *Cannery Row* be categorized as a featherweight work. In retrospect, it can be seen as the direct bridge, via *The God in the Pipes*, between *The Grapes of Wrath* and the postwar works. It is Steinbeck's last fictive masterpiece, and can take its place unchallenged alongside *In Dubious Battle* and *The Long Valley* snugly behind *The Grapes of Wrath*.

5

The musical comedy he had mentioned in his July letter to the Lovejoys was to be called *The Wizard of Maine*. It was an idea he and composer-lyricist Frank Loesser had dreamed up that summer in New York as a vehicle for comedian Fred Allen. The show became a project that was to occupy Steinbeck's time and thoughts on and off over many months during 1944 and 1945. Like so many other projects he contemplated or even embarked on around this time it eventually came to nothing, even though, in this case he did end with a rough outline script.

During the spring and summer, Steinbeck and Gwyn resumed the round of party-going and the constant meeting of friends, among them, as well as the Frank Loessers and the Fred Allens, other people from the entertainment world, like dramatic author and director Abe Burrows, folk singer Burl Ives, and film actor Humphrey Bogart; magazine and newspaper celebrities like photographer Robert Capa, columnist Leonard Lyons, and *Life* article writer George Frazier; and authors Vincent Sheean, John Hersey, Robert Ruark, and John O'Hara.

By the end of July, the baby had still not arrived and was four or five days overdue. They were then more or less confined to the apartment. Gwyn was taking regular doses of castor oil in the hope of helping nature along, but nothing happened. In the New York heat, they became both tired and irritable. People were constantly ringing up for the latest news, and this friendly concern became in its way an additional burden. Steinbeck spent the days writing letters. He sent a copy of the manuscript of *Cannery Row* to Ed Ricketts, wanting his friend's reactions before he finally submitted it for publication.

A few days later, on 2 August, at 7:30 in the evening, Gwyn was delivered of a son weighing six pounds ten ounces. It was not an easy birth. They named the boy Thom.

"Thom seems to be a baby-shaped baby and I like him very much," the new father informed Street three weeks later (*SLL* 271). Shortly afterward, writing to Joseph Jackson, he again endeavored by adopting a deliberately facetious attitude to play down the burst of paternal love and pride he felt for his first offspring:

> Any rumors you hear about [the baby's] good looks are overdrawn. But he has a good head and good eyes and is strong and healthy. Gwyn claims he is beautiful but she is nuts. But he seems to be going to have very red hair and very blue eyes and it is all pretty exciting and that's the report on young Red Tom [sic]. (JS/JHJ n.d. Fall 1944)

Fatherhood seemed to have a rejuvenating effect on him. He declared himself full of energy and anxious to begin further projects, more specifically *The Pearl*. But before he could start work, he had to find a new home for himself, Gwyn, and Thom. The lease of the New York apartment had expired and he did not wish to renew it, for the idea of returning to the West Coast had become fixed in his mind. He was fired with tremendous excitement at the prospect of going back to his roots, where he had done so much good work in the past, and he hoped that nothing would spoil it for him.

The baby had been delivered by Caesarian section and Gwyn had to stay in the hospital for two weeks. She was still so weak after she came home that she was unable to nurse the baby. The services of a professional nurse, a Miss Diehl, were engaged. There was, of course, no possibility of their going to California until Gwyn was stronger, and the scheduling of the move was postponed until early October. The plan was that Steinbeck would make the journey by station wagon, taking Willie and a load of household goods with him, leaving Gwyn, Thom, and Miss Diehl to follow by plane.

Before leaving New York, Steinbeck saw Ernie Pyle, recently returned from Europe following coverage of the liberation of Paris. Pyle was physically exhausted and totally war-weary. Although joyful at seeing Pyle again, Steinbeck was troubled by the awareness and expectancy of death he saw mirrored in his friend's eyes.

The move to California was a nightmarish experience for all of them. Gwyn, Thom, and the nurse were obliged to change planes a number of times. The baby was taken ill. By the time they arrived in Dallas, he had developed prickly heat and was vomiting. Some friends of Gwyn's came to the rescue, but it was several days before Thom was well enough for them to resume the interrupted journey. Meanwhile, in California,

Steinbeck was almost out of his mind with worry as he waited for them to arrive.

The house that a friend had found for them was in the Highlands and about eight miles outside Monterey. There was no bus service, and because of gas rationing — they were allotted a mere two gallons a week — they were practically marooned in the house and rarely able to get into town. It was a modern-style house perched on the cliffs overlooking the sea. There were no less than one hundred and forty-two steps down to the beach. They suffered from the cold the whole of the time they were there, for the walls of the house consisted almost entirely of large picture windows. Gwyn hated the place, referring to it as "a hunk of shit." In the end, after a comparatively short time, they decided that enough was enough, and took up temporary quarters in the tiny family cottage on Eleventh Street, Pacific Grove, where Steinbeck and Carol had lived for a time during the thirties.

Using the cottage as a base, they continued their search for a new home, and were eventually rewarded by finding exactly the sort of place they wanted — a white adobe at 460 Pierce Street, Monterey, a property Steinbeck in fact had had his eye on for many years. The house had been built by a family named Soto in the early 1830s, and was known locally as "the Soto House." To all intents and purposes, it had been carefully maintained over the years, with good foundations and air vents preventing dampness. There was no sagging in the walls, which were three feet thick. All it apparently needed was a fresh coat of whitewash. If the house itself was not large, the garden was huge, the size of eight city lots. The whole property was surrounded by an adobe wall, and the street outside was unpaved and devoid of traffic. Their nearest neighbors were never all that much in evidence. Best of all, while they could enjoy a sense of isolation whenever they wished, they would be only three blocks from the town center and within walking distance of the wharves and Ricketts's laboratory.

Ricketts had by now been discharged from the army, and Steinbeck visited him as often as he could. Indeed, it had been one of Gwyn's gripes when they had been marooned out in the Highlands that all the gas ration had been used on his trips into town to see his friend.

In October, an overseas French edition of *Bombs Away* (*Lachez les Bombes!*) was published by Viking Press. For this edition, Steinbeck's original preface was discarded altogether and he revised somewhat the latter part of his introduction, converting this revised introduction into a new and enlarged preface. The changes he made to the text reflected the turning of the tide of war in favor of America and her allies, as well as his own attitude toward the conflict. To the recently liberated peoples of Europe, Steinbeck reaffirmed his purpose in writing the book, and re-affirmed his faith in the airmen of whom he had been writing. He was painfully aware, however, that many, if not all, of those Bills and Als and Abners and Joes and Allans and Harrises, those physically perfect young men with their assured futures in aviation, had by then been killed in action, or been physically or psychologically maimed. In his revised text, there is no sweet-talk dismissing the "myths" about the vulnerability of air gunners. Randall Jarrell's "The Death of the Ball Turret Gunner" had already been published in *Partisan Review*, and, the previous year, when Steinbeck had been visiting United States air bases in England, he had seen for himself the B-17s and B-24s flying off on their daily missions over Germany, and had watched the survivors limping back home after enduring the hell of enemy skies. No longer was it possible for the War Department to conceal completely the truth about the horrendous losses of planes and men that had become an almost day-to-day occurrence. Although in his revised preface Steinbeck still continued to proclaim that the "young people of today are the equals of young Americans in every period of our history," and that "these young people have cleared the European sky of the so-called invincible Luftwaffe ... pounded Hitler's armies and razed to the ground the factories which equipped those armies,"[32] his closing sentences, repeating the closing sentences of his original preface and explaining the significance of the words "Bombs Away," seemed now an expression of war weariness, a desire for it to be over for once and for all, rather than, as it was in 1942, a clarion call to arms.

6

Work on *The Pearl* had to be delayed until after the move into the new house had been made. Steinbeck was spending all his available time repainting the exterior and carrying out whatever small repairs were found necessary, while Gwyn busied herself organizing the decorations. It was, he averred, "a laughing house" (*SLL* 274), and they both had ideas about extending it later as their needs demanded and of planting walnut and almond trees in the garden. They planned to move in around the 10th of November.

By then, the country was in the final throes of the Presidential Election campaign, with Roosevelt fighting for his fourth term in office. His Republican opponent was Thomas E. Dewey, Governor of New York. Steinbeck was disgusted by the manner in which certain politicians seemed to be trying to blame Roosevelt for their own inadequacies and stupidities. "This," he wrote to Covici, "has I am sure been one of the dirtiest of all political campaigns. I'm glad it is over. I worked up a really personal dislike for Dewey" (JS/PC late Oct. 1944). On election day, 7 November, Roosevelt won by 25,610,946 popular votes to Dewey's 22,018,177. Dewey even failed to carry his own state of New York. Commenting on the result, Steinbeck wrote: "The election was good all except Clare Luce. I hoped she would be dumped. That's a bad woman. But you can't expect everything and quite a few bad ones were dumped" (JS/ERO 11/11/44).

The Soto House proved not to be in so good a condition as they had first thought, and he hired an old friend from way back to help him with the enormous amount of painting that needed to be done. By 11 November, he and Gwyn were able to bring in some of their possessions, but their furniture had not yet arrived from New York, and it was another couple of weeks or so before they could actually move in.

The editors of *Life* offered him a fee to collaborate with the magazine's photographers on a feature article about Cannery Row to tie up with the book's impending publication. He was by no means sold on the idea, being inherently suspicious of the magazine's politics and the way in which its editors retained the right to cut and rearrange texts, often, so he felt, changing the meaning and intent of an article. He however mentioned the proposal to Ricketts, who also expressed a mild distaste for the project.

Advance orders for the book were exceeding all Steinbeck's expectations. Covici reported they were 60 percent higher than the sixty-five thousand advance orders that had been received for *The Moon Is Down*. Viking had in fact ordered paper for a quarter-million copies, even then anticipating that further paper would eventually be needed. Copies of the galleys were sent to Nunnally Johnson and Carlton Sheffield. Johnson showed great interest in the book's potential as a movie. "I don't know whether it is effective or not," Steinbeck had admitted to Sheffield. "I would be anxious to know what you think of it" (*SLL* 273). Sheffield's response was less than enthusiastic:

> My feelings are so mixed about it that I hate to put them down on paper. It is almost the book that I hoped you would have written when I heard the title. In its own right, it is a swell book, and it's one which I enjoyed thoroughly. ... I must admit that I haven't identified the "four planes" of which you speak — I can pick out at least 16 planes or things which could be identified as such, but I don't know which ones you meant. Certainly, the wolf pack will not bother about such considerations: its members will say with extreme cleverness that Steinbeck, California white hope, has at last started to repeat himself, and that they had suspected as much for a long time. (CAS/JS Nov. 1944)

One cannot avoid the suspicion that Sheffield was not being entirely truthful in setting out his views for fear of hurting his old friend, that he had been more disappointed by the book than he cared to admit, perhaps even to himself. There is little doubt that in the hypersensitive state he was in, Steinbeck was upset by Sheffield's letter. He did not reply to it, and in fact it was to be another eight years before he resumed correspondence with Sheffield.

Ricketts had been more carefully ambivalent in his reaction after Steinbeck had given him the typescript to read. Ricketts's opinion and approval were more important to Steinbeck than those of any other single person. Ricketts's spontaneous verdict had been: "Let it go that way. It is written in kindness. Such a thing can't be bad" (*Adventures* 560).

By now, very conscious of the passage of time and of the commitment he had made to Fernandez and his associates, Steinbeck was uncomfortably concerned that he had not even started work on *The Pearl*. In some ways, the script had become almost an encumbrance. As he told Elizabeth Otis, he realized now that he might have been ill-advised to have become involved in the project. "Some time maybe I'll learn not to contract to do jobs," he added (JS/ERO 11/6/44). He knew it was going to be difficult, if not impossible, to find during the coming weeks the necessary peace in which to write. Even after they had moved into their new home, they would still be far from settled. Gwyn would be busy planning and putting the finishing touches on the decorating. Thom would be a distracting presence, and Miss Diehl had not from the very beginning shown herself to be the most unobtrusive of people to have around the house. She had displayed an irritating propensity for taking over at the slightest provocation, and frequently without any excuse at all. Steinbeck only tolerated her because, all said and done, she was a good nurse.

He began looking around for a small office to rent, where, as he had been able to do at Viking earlier in the year, he could shut himself away and concentrate on his work. He found a room nearby, in the only office building in Monterey, but when he telephoned the owner he was asked what line of business he was in. Replying that he did not run a business, that he was a writer, he was then asked if he owned a business license. Upon pointing out that a writer did not require a license, he was told that only professional people, such as doctors, dentists, and insurance agents, were welcome in the building. After this snub, Steinbeck decided to clean out the woodshed at home and do his writing there. Covici's comment when he heard of the incident was suitably scathing: "That's a wonderful story — a world-famous author but not in Monterey, a town of a handful of people. I bet there isn't a village in Norway or Sweden where you are not known" (PC/JS 12/1/44).

There had been no rest or relaxation since they had arrived back on the West Coast. Gwyn had valiantly been trying to keep up, but she had still not recovered anything like her old strength since the birth. Covici, concerned also for Steinbeck's health, counseled him to take a few days off before embarking on *The Pearl*: "Quietly soak in some ocean breezes and let your mind dwell in the depths measureless to man, then cover yourself with the hills and the dreams will come. The Pearl should be pure fantasy and imagination, grounded on reality" (Fensch 37). Steinbeck asked him to send some long yellow legal pads and a pencil sharpener, as these were unobtainable in Monterey. "I'll let you know how The Pearl goes," he wrote. "It will probably take me several days to get started or several false starts" (JS/PC 11/25/44).

Two days later, in a letter to Annie Laurie Williams, he declared his intention of starting work on *The Pearl* the following day. "It will probably take some time to get started but maybe not. I get very nervous about starting—a kind of stage fright I guess. It always happens. I'll get over it as soon as I start" (JS/ALW 11/27/44). When he did at last sit down to begin writing in the woodshed, he set off at too fast a pace and had to throw the first day's work away. He was happier with his second attempt at writing the opening paragraphs. "Don't know that it is any good," he told Covici, "but it moves so far and sticks together and that's all I can expect of it. But at first I got off on the wrong foot entirely. Anyway, it is moving along and will probably pick up momentum" (Fensch 37).

Covici had managed to find a pencil sharpener for him, in spite of the fact that it seemed for some reason as difficult to come by in New York as in Monterey. He sent it, together with all the yellow pads he could lay his hands on, and enclosed a note of caution: "Now that you are late with Pearl what is happening with your trip to Mexico? I hope you won't hurry with the story" (PC/JS 12/1/44).

There were still more minor irritations to be coped with. The *Christian Science Monitor* telephoned long distance from Boston, disturbed by reports that half the whores in *Cannery Row* were to be portrayed as Christian Scientists. Could one of their representatives in San Francisco come to Monterey to discuss the matter? An appointment was fixed for the following Sunday. Steinbeck initially anticipated the encounter with some amusement, telling Covici that he would try to arrange it so that the book would be banned not only in Boston but by the Christian Scientists as well. Better still, he suggested, if everybody banned it sales would rocket. The Christian Scientist duly arrived, his main concern being that people would get the wrong impression about Christian Science from the book. Just before he left, the man suggested that if Dora Flood's whores were practicing prostitution as well as Christian Science then they were not good Christian Scientists. "Well, that's all right," Steinbeck replied, "because they weren't very good prostitutes either." The meeting ended ostensibly on a friendly note. As Steinbeck reported to his agents: "He said they would have to make a statement and I said I would be upset if they didn't" (JS/ML 12/2/44).

The first of the prepublication reviews of the book had begun to appear, and these seemed to echo all Sheffield's reservations about it.

Steinbeck vented his sense of frustration in a letter to his editor on 3 December:

> There is a time in every writer's career when the critics are gunning for him to whittle him down. This is my stage for that. It has been since the Grapes of Wrath. I see it all the time. The criticism is good but what saddens me is the active hatred of most of the writers and pseudowriters around here. It will not be terribly long before we will be associating only with fishermen, which is the best thing of all. There is a deep and active jealousy out here that makes me very sad. I haven't mentioned it before. It is a natural reaction of course but I don't like it any the better for that. (Fensch 39)

He was beginning to appreciate the truth of Thomas Wolfe's adage: "You can't go home again." It was nothing he could specifically put his finger on, but simply an attitude he sensed being adopted against him, an atmosphere in which he was made to feel unwelcome. The put-down from the owner of the office building had been one example. For all that, the manager of the Monterey County Trust and Savings Bank offered to rent him a small office in the bank building, and so, thankfully, he was able to move out of the cold woodshed. The office was quiet and warm, and he decided he would keep it on a permanent basis until such time as he was able to have a separate study built at home. That proved easier said than done. Permission for building work had to be obtained from the local authorities. When he made inquiries, he was informed he would have to wait until after the end of the year before his application could even be considered. From the overall tone of the response, he gained the impression that he should not hold out any high hopes of permission being granted even then.

After having made a good start at the second attempt, work on *The Pearl* hit a "slump." He just could not get going for some reason — possibly because he was conscious of working to order yet again, to a schedule not of his making: a situation he had always hated and endeavored to avoid, even though it may have had in the past a questionable beneficial effect of ensuring he applied himself to work. There may also have been at the back of his mind the thought that this particular work was not going to advance in any way his search for the new form that he had begun exploring so satisfactorily in *Cannery Row*. If anything, he surely must have felt that *The Pearl* was shaping up to be a return to the style and content of the sort of work he was doing in the thirties, the sort of work he was no longer really interested in doing. Certainly, when the book was published in 1947, it was greeted with a more generous critical response than he had experienced for many a year, principally, one may hazard a guess, because the reviewers found themselves safely once more on familiar Steinbeckian territory.

RKO had been in touch with him, interested in taking on the world distribution of *The Pearl*, but he told the studio he could not abandon the work he was at present doing on the script to provide them with the synopsis they requested, while being perfectly prepared to discuss the story with them over the telephone. RKO was anxious to open up Latin America and felt that such a movie, made with an all-Mexican director, cast, and crew, would boost their prestige in the south. As well as being willing to offer financial assistance toward the making of the film, their distribution know-how would ensure it received very wide circulation in both America and overseas. Although the studio guaranteed not to interfere in any way with the script, Steinbeck remained open-minded about the proposed RKO involvement. Under the terms of the commitment he had made to Fernandez, he had agreed he should received nothing from the film other than his expenses and 10 percent of the gross. While distribution by a large Hollywood studio would undoubtedly increase the gross take to an appreciable extent, his main concern was, whatever the extent of the studio's involvement, that nothing should be allowed to prevent the film being made straight, as Fernandez and he had always intended.

Once again, Covici was urging caution, counseling him not to rush his story in order to sell it to RKO or any other studio, but to wait until he had finished it as he wanted it.

> You conceived your story beautifully with poetry and a universal philosophy — all of which I am sure no movie enterprise, certainly no Hollywood studio, would ever dream of reproducing on the screen. They will maim, torture and destroy what is most precious about it. (Fensch 40)

Covici did not seem to appreciate fully the extent to which Steinbeck had already made commitments to Fernandez, who was still aiming to come to California early in the new year, as had been arranged between them, to work on the shooting script.

Another studio — Warners — was interested in buying *Cannery Row* for the screen. In Steinbeck's view, Warners had been turning out some of the very best of recent movies, and he was willing to sell to them, provided the right terms could be negotiated. After some of his experiences with Hollywood during the past few years, he was determined not to enter into any agreement that did not allow him control over the final script. "No more Lifeboats for me," he declared. "Maybe I could act in some sort of script advisory capacity. Not that some changes mightn't be made but I want to OK them and possibly work on them" (JS/ALW 12/8/44). Within a few days, however, after consultation with Annie

Laurie Williams, he decided that perhaps, after all, he did not want to sell the book to the movies for the time being.

As well as the consideration that he could spread his income for tax purposes, it may have been a visit by Jack Wagner that finally made him change his mind. Wagner had been in attendance at the Paramount studios during the shooting of *A Medal for Benny*, but had been allowed no say in the making of the movie. He regaled Steinbeck and Gwyn with a fund of stories, some hilarious and some sad, all of which confirmed Steinbeck's opinion that the Hollywood studios were not to be trusted and that watertight agreements relating to scripts, as advocated by Bosley Crowther, were absolutely essential. For all that, when one of the heads of RKO telephoned a few days after Wagner's visit and stated that the studio was willing to put up as much as half the money for *The Pearl*, as well as undertake worldwide distribution, Steinbeck was clearly convinced by the reiterated assurances then given that the studio would guarantee not to interfere with the script. He asked the studio to prepare a written proposal and submit it to Annie Laurie Williams. He advised her by letter of what had transpired, and told her he thought the deal could be a good one.

Work on the script meanwhile was going in fits and starts. Covici continued to give his support from afar, endeavoring to alleviate some of the guilt he suspected Steinbeck must be suffering for being so disastrously behind schedule. The urgency, as it happened, had been relieved to a certain extent by the news that Fernandez did not now propose traveling to the States until around the 1st of February, giving Steinbeck the best part of another month in which to get the script completed.

Almost immediately, with the immediate pressure off, he found himself able to work with greater fluidity. By mid-December, he was able to report to Covici:

> The Pearl moves slowly and I think pretty well. Just have to finish it and see. Toni Jackson is typing from my handwriting so that I will have a correction copy as soon as I finish the first draft. I haven't much idea of how good or how well done it is but I do think it moves. I have about 40 pages done now, maybe fifty. It might run a little longer than I thought. (JS/PC 12/15/44)

The productive spell soon petered out. A few days later, with the approach of Christmas, he took time off to help around the house, although it seems likely that Christmas was the excuse rather than the cause for not working. He confessed to Elizabeth Otis on 27 December:

> I took nearly a week off to help around the house but this morning I'm back at work, at least I hope I am. This Pearl moves on very slowly. I'll try to speed up

the output from now on. I've just been lazy about it and haven't disciplined myself. I'll try to do better from now on. (JS/ERO 12/27/44)

His resolution lasted no longer than two days. On the 29th, he wrote to Covici:

I've gone into a slump on the Pearl and that bothers me even remembering that I always go into two or three slumps on every book. But it always worries me. . . . You know I can inspect my slumps pretty well. I go grey in the head and then I begin to worry about not working. Then I get disgusted with myself and when this disgust grows big enough the whole thing turns over like an iceberg and I go to work again. It's always the same and it's always new. I never get used to it. (JS/PC 12/29/44)

The real trouble was, of course, that there had been and still were too many convenient distractions. Even if the room over the bank provided him with all the isolation he needed in which to write, he still had half his mind on the work that remained to be done on the house. Gwyn continued to be far from well, and had been ordered by the doctor to rest as much as possible. Even though the nurse was taking care of Thom, Gwyn was quite unable to cope with the housework, and there had been some difficulty in finding someone suitable to come in and do the work for them. Consequently, Steinbeck was himself obliged to take over some of the chores. There were, too, so many other jobs that had to be done before they had the house as they wanted it. They planned to add a wing, containing a guest room and a bathroom, as well as the study, but there was still the uncertainty of their being allowed to go ahead with the building work. Tentative approval had been granted by the authorities, but the recent German counterattack in the Ardennes threatened to prolong the war and induced a certain sense of panic in the local establishment, with the Army having first call on available materials. Until all the building work was completed, there was little point in developing the garden, although he did go ahead and plant some cypress trees to replace others that had died.

They had a tree-decorating party on the 23rd, with a Mexican orchestra in attendance, and invited a whole host of guests. Burgess Meredith, now out of the Army, and Paulette Goddard suggested that the four of them spend the holidays together, but that was out of the question. They would not have been able to take Thom and Miss Diehl along, and, in any case, Gwyn was not really fit enough. It was just as well, as it turned out, that the arrangement was not made, for, after spending a quiet Christmas Eve, Gwyn went down with a bad cold. She was confined to bed all Christmas Day, while Steinbeck went off to visit his sister Esther in Watsonville. In her memoirs, Gwyn bitterly recalls that Christmas of

1944, accusing her husband of leaving her when she was suffering with a temperature of 106 degrees. She maintained that she did not even get a present from him. His letters of those days, however, reveal that her memory—as on a number of other occasions—was faulty, for he had given her a little Ford convertible, and he goes into raptures over the early American glass she gave him—decanter, six sherry glasses, and a goblet. Disapproving of the manner in which American children were acquiring a frightening greed for possessions, he bought Thom a five-thousand-dollar bond toward his future education.

While in Watsonville, his sister had given him an olive wood box that once belonged to their father. It contained his grandfather's civil war papers, marriage license, and citizenship papers, as well as many other items, including deeds to property in Palestine and Florida, and a bill for a headstone for the grave of his grandfather's brother, murdered by the Bedouin in Jaffa in 1853.[33]

Thom had been making good progress and, under Miss Diehl's supervision, had been little trouble, despite the usual teething problems. By the year's end he weighed eighteen pounds and, according to his father, was "getting to be very agreeable" and was crying "less and less" (JS/ERO 12/27/44).

Ricketts called in fairly frequently, and Steinbeck returned his visits by going to the laboratory for long talks with his old friend about the progress of the war, the fishing situation, and more or less everything under the sun. Jack Wagner stayed at the Soto House for a while during December. He clearly had the idea that he and Steinbeck should get together and collaborate on another original movie story, but for the time being this, of course, was out of the question.

Preparations for the publication of *Cannery Row*, fixed for 2 January, were proceeding apace. Covici had the original manuscript of the book, the typescript, and the corrected galley each bound separately, then placed in a case in the form of a big book, together with the page proofs and a copy of the published book itself. He presented these as a gift to Gwyn. "It is a beautiful thing," Steinbeck commented. "I had never seen anything like it" (JS/ERO 12/27/44).

Rumors began circulating in the papers that advance sales of the book had reached a staggering 150,000 copies. Covici, however, set the figure at a more conservative 90,000–95,000, while still maintaining that the book would assuredly sell at least a quarter-million copies. By Christmas, without waiting for the official publication date, the book was already being sold surreptitiously in California bookstores. Jack Wagner telephoned to report that, while browsing in a Hollywood bookstore, he had seen fifty copies sold from under the counter. It seemed, then, there was a good chance of Covici's prediction being proved correct, and that the book would indeed be a runaway best-seller.

8

1945: More Filmmaking in Mexico

1

On 5 January, Steinbeck received from Covici the early reviews of *Cannery Row* from the *New York Times* and the *New York Herald Tribune*. Replying to his editor the same day, Steinbeck observed:

> The reviews are wonderful. They are almost identical with the reviews of *Tortilla Flat*. Gwyn is saving the most savage of them to put in with the mss that you sent her. What a humorless crowd they are. And I love that man who stumbled on the heat wave theory. He was so delighted with his own cleverness in thinking that one up. (JS/PC 1/5/45)

He was referring to Orville Prescott's review in the *New York Times*. Recording that Steinbeck had written the book in an air-conditioned room in the Viking offices during six sweltering weeks in the summer, Prescott had suggested that it was, so far as he was aware, "the first novel ever to have been written in a publisher's office by a refugee from a heat wave." He had gone on to note that Steinbeck had returned to California, where heat waves like the one in New York the previous summer were unknown. "Perhaps," Prescott concluded, "in his own country [Steinbeck] will find again the power and the passion of his best books and escape the confusion of thought and artistic futility that weaken *Cannery Row*."[1]

Most critics at the time of the book's publication missed the underlying darkness in *Cannery Row*. It was regarded by the majority of reviewers as a disappointing, featherweight work. "This," wrote Prescott, "is John Steinbeck in an off moment. There is no driving idea, no creative energy, no living juice in *Cannery Row*."[2] F. O. Matthiessen likened the story to a "Grade-B scenario," and pondered on the reason "why Steinbeck should have wanted to write or publish such a book at this point in his career."[3] C. G. Paulding was cruelly dismissive. "Is there any use in reading this book?" he asked, noting: "It is as sentimental as a book can be. It oozes sentiment."[4]

Whatever the majority verdict of the critics, Steinbeck defiantly predicted that *Cannery Row* would be "one of the best liked and most reread" of his books (JS/PC 1/5/45). He had heard that many local people were buying it to send to troops overseas, regarding it as escapist literature. One Monterey bookseller had sold his entire stock of the book by the end of publication day, and was complaining that he had received only fifty

250

copies, although having ordered five times that number. From New York, Covici reported that the American Express Company had exhausted its initial order of twenty thousand copies and was now calling for a further twenty-five hundred. Moreover smaller shops with initial orders of between twenty-five to fifty copies were already urgently wiring duplicate orders. Covici cautioned Steinbeck against reacting badly to the reviews, arguing that there would always be a certain critical element willing at every opportunity to hurl "poisoned javelins" for his being not only a successful writer but also one who commanded serious critical attention.

Covici was clearly concerned that the adverse reviews would have a detrimental effect on progress on *The Pearl*, but if Steinbeck's "slump" showed no sign of ending, this was more likely caused by other factors. Steinbeck himself was not overlyworried by his lack of progress. There had been no news from Mexico for a while, and at the back of his mind he persuaded himself that the whole Fernandez project would come to nothing. This sort of thinking was probably more a measure of the temporary guilt he was feeling, and he continued to declare that, whatever happened in Mexico, he was determined as a matter of self-discipline, if nothing else, to finish the work.

His disinclination to write in fact stemmed in large part from the atmosphere of dissension pervading the home. Although Gwyn had more or less recovered from the influenza that had laid her low on Christmas Day, she still nursed a grudge against him for the manner in which he had left her bedside to visit his sister. To assuage some of his guilt, he decided to take Gwyn, Thom, and the nurse on a three-day trip to San Francisco. It was a break they all needed.

They saw a number of friends in the city, including Joseph Jackson and Ernie Pyle. Pyle was on his way back to the war. The Navy had persuaded him to report on operations in the Pacific, although he had been most reluctant to accept any further assignments, having decided, as Steinbeck had done, that he had seen more than enough war, death, and destruction. Steinbeck and Gwyn spent most of 11 January with him at his hotel. They invited him and his liaison officer, a Commander Max Miller, to have dinner with them, but Pyle was so tired that he made his excuses. The other three went out, while Pyle ate alone at the hotel and had an early night. He was probably grateful to the Steinbecks for taking Miller off his back for the evening.

On returning to Monterey the following day, Steinbeck found letters from Annie Laurie Williams, Elizabeth Otis, and Covici awaiting him. Annie Laurie Williams had enclosed a letter she had received from Maurice, now in a prisoner-of-war camp. The letter was noncommital, and she was worrying in case, as she had begun to convince herself, her husband was trying to hide the fact that his legs had been badly injured when he had bailed out of the plane. Steinbeck assured her that had Maurice been as seriously injured as all that, he would almost surely have been repatriated. The likelihood was that he had perhaps been slightly injured, and had decided to play it down for fear she would imagine his wounds were far worse than they actually were.

In his letters to all three, Steinbeck promised that he would now apply himself to serious work on *The Pearl*. He still anticipated that Fernandez would be arriving in Monterey around 15 February, and he planned to have the first draft completed by then. Even so, he reiterated his suspicion that the whole project would fall through, particularly as, within the last few days, rumors had reached him of a rift between Fernandez and Dolores del Rio, in both their personal and professional relationships. "That won't make for good things," he commented to Annie Laurie Williams. "But I'm damned well going to finish this script anyway. But I don't much think it will be a play. It's made for a picture because of the possibility of space — although so far it hasn't moved about very much" (JS/ALW 1/12/45). If he had not altogether changed his mind about selling *Cannery Row* to the movies, he nevertheless gave Annie Laurie Williams *carte blanche* to act as she thought fit. He was still heavily in favor of Warners as the most suitable studio for any such sale.

He had become involved in another project that had been interesting him for some time. This, an offshoot of research he had volunteered to carry out for the War Food Administration, was to write an article for *Collier's* magazine on his theories relating to the possible link between the type, quality, and variety of food served in factory canteens and the corresponding incidence not only of high or low production levels but also of absenteeism among workers.

Covici had enclosed another batch of *Cannery Row* reviews. Steinbeck wrote: "They are really furious, aren't they. It would make me sadder if I didn't remember that they have panned me all along. . . . The tendency in reviewers always to like the book before is very apparent. Sure I knew the book would be panned but I didn't know they would be so emotionally angry" (JS/PC 1/12/45). Three days later, he again wrote bitterly to Covici, stung over and over by the adverse reviews:

> . . . It is interesting to me, Pat, that no critic has discovered the reason for those little inner chapters in C.R. You would have known. Nearly all lay readers know. Only critics don't. Are they somehow the lowest common denominator. If in pictures, the thing must be slanted for the 9 year old mind, in books they must be slanted for critics and it seems to amount to the same thing. Far from being the sharpest readers, they are the dullest. You say I am taking it philosophically. I am not and I feel wonderful. Don't you remember the years when these same critics were sneering at every book — the same books incidentally that they now remember with awe. No I feel all of the old contempt for them and it is a good feeling. I *know* C.R. is a good book. (JS/PC 1/15/45)

He was, on the other hand, amused to discover that the critical malice directed at *Cannery Row* had "aroused a defensive state of mind in readers," who, on the West Coast at least, had begun "attacking the critics" (JS/ERO 1/17/45). Indeed, he was amused generally by local reaction to the book. The local bookstore owner told him that his profits from the sale of *Cannery Row* had been the first real money to come his way for a considerable time. Monterey seemed to be adopting a proprietory interest in the book, considering a bad review to be, in some way, a slur on the town itself. The local policeman professed a hatred for Joseph H. Jackson for categorizing the book as fantasy. The policeman swore it was the literal truth. "Why," he declared, referring to the characters portrayed in the book, "I've taken them all to jail in my time" (*Adventures* 561). The real-life Mack disclosed that the feelings of many people on the Row had been hurt—but only because they resented having been left out of the book. On the other hand, it appeared that the more respectable people in town were uncertain whether the book was in good taste or not and were reserving their opinions until they were able to discover what the majority thought. Steinbeck found it all immensely amusing.

He heard from Covici that a new edition of *The Red Pony*, illustrated by Wesley Dennis, that Viking was to bring out later in the year, had been selected by the Book-of-the-Month Club as a dividend book, from which he would receive a minimum of sixteen thousand dollars. He was astonished by the news. "How did you promote the Red Pony deal?" he asked. "Boy have you milked that one. That's an incredible amount of money for a story that has been reissued a dozen times" (JS/PC 1/22/45).

Despite the fact that Miss Diehl had succumbed to a bad throat infection, leaving Gwyn, still not in the best of health, to take care of both Thom and the nurse, with Steinbeck "helping around the edges" and fighting off a cold of his own, some solid work was at last achieved on *The Pearl*. On 17 January, he reported to his agents that he was writing one thousand to fifteen hundred words a day, and that he hoped to have the script completed in approximately one month. He was working in close detail, for effectively what he was writing, he said, was a shooting script for the camera. By 22 January, he had finished 80 of an estimated projected total of 125 to 130 typed pages. He was working in what he considered a particularly successful way. First, he wrote his holograph draft, then dictated the text on a record, making changes as he read. Toni Jackson then transcribed the recording into a typed draft, which he proposed to use as the second draft, and this would eventually be corrected to obtain the final draft. As was normal with him, he was not at all sure the work he was doing was any good, although Gwyn had read some of it and liked it. He figured he needed only another ten working days to finished it. "It's a strange piece of work full of curious methods and figures," he told his agents. "A folk tale I hope. A black-and-white story like a parable"

(JS/ERO & ML 1/22/45). Announcing that he would now have to delay work on the factory-feeding article for *Collier's*, he wondered if the magazine might be interested in publishing the *Pearl* script in the meantime.[5]

The editors of *Life* had been in touch again and made it known they were still anxious to publish an illustrated article on *Cannery Row*. Both Steinbeck and Ricketts maintained their opposition to the idea. Having been unsuccessful in eliciting the cooperation of not only Ricketts but also George Frazier and Annie Laurie Williams in their attempts to persuade Steinbeck to change his mind, the *Life* editors approached Ritch Lovejoy, then employed on the *Monterey Peninsula Herald*, to write the article. It was an assignment that Lovejoy, always desperately in need of cash, could not refuse, and straightaway began playing on Ricketts's legendary generosity of spirit by asking him to help on the project. If Ricketts felt obliged to assist an old friend, Steinbeck made it known in no uncertain terms that he would not allow any shots of him to be taken by *Life*'s photographers and, furthermore, refused to have anything to do with the project. To some people, no doubt, his attitude smacked of sour grapes, but he had been incensed by what Lovejoy had done, and charged that Lovejoy would have sneered had he himself been guilty of the same sort of wheeler-dealing, as he saw it, to make a fast buck. A coolness developed between the two men that was never to be entirely dissipated.

On 23 January, he reached that section of *The Pearl* where the poor fisherman, Kino, and his family have been forced to flee into the mountains. As he embarked on the last few pages of his manuscript, he now knew that he would not only meet his deadline but have time to spare. He planned to complete the draft within a week or so, and Fernandez was not due to arrive until sometime between the 1st and the 15th of February to work on the shooting script. One matter was certain, he told Max and Jack Wagner—he would not go to Mexico until he was sure that filming had begun. He hoped that Gwyn would spend some time with him in Mexico, and, although nothing had yet been decided, his sister Beth had volunteered to look after Thom while they were both away.

Plans, as it turned out, were to be changed in quite a radical manner. At the end of the month, when Steinbeck had only one day's work remaining on the script, Fernandez phoned from Mexico, urging him to come down as soon as possible to assist in the casting of the film, the finding of suitable locations, and the commissioning of an appropriate musical score. This meant that any idea he had of working on the *Collier's* article before going to Mexico would have to be dropped. He wanted Gwyn to accompany him to help with the music, and she agreed to go, while Thom and Miss Diehl, as had been tentatively arranged, went to stay with his sister Beth in Berkeley. The intention was that both he and Gwyn would stay in Mexico for two weeks. If it then seemed that production of the film was imminent, he would stay on, and Gwyn would return home alone. Despite her continuing health problems, he still regarded it essential that she, possessing the degree of musical knowledge he himself did not have, should be involved at least in the preliminary discussions with Fernandez. "When you read the script," he told Covici, "you will see how important the music is" (JS/PC early Feb. 1945).

Now that it was apparent that the Mexicans were taking some definite steps to get the production under way, some of the old enthusiasms for the project were revived. "This can be a very fine film," he wrote Elizabeth Otis, "and I want to help to make it one. ... I think the story ended pretty well. ... Worked very hard to finish and it was a devilish hard story to do. One of the hardest I have ever tried" (JS/ERO & ALW early Feb 1945).

2

The Pearl, however, represents a regression after the brilliance of *Cannery Row*. On the surface one of the most simple — one might even say simplistic — stories Steinbeck ever wrote, the book probably has, as Louis Owens has pointed out, "generated more contradictory criticism than any other work by Steinbeck."[6] This divergence of critical opinion rarely extends beyond the conflicting interpretations of the book's inner message. Most scholars are agreed on its intrinsic literary worth. Howard Levant, for example, boldly asserts that *"The Pearl* is a success," while conceding that it is flawed by an unconvincing ending.[7] Richard O'Connor had referred to it as "a short novel almost as perfect as a real pearl";[8] the Indian scholar Sunita Jain has called it "a model of economy";[9] Lester Jay Marks sees it as "a beautifully written parable";[10] and Lawrence William Jones has written that in his opinion "this well-made parable exemplifies all that is best in the fabulist's art."[11] On the other hand, Warren French offers the dissenting view when he records that, when it first appeared, *The Pearl* was a "disappointment" to Steinbeck's many admirers, and contends that rather than simply being flawed, *"The Pearl* proved to be paste."[12]

French's judgment, it must be said, seems to be a minority one. The book has proved over the years to be one of Steinbeck's most enduringly popular works. It has become an all-time favorite among the set books of many a high-school literature course, and certainly is eminently suited to that particular role by virtue of its aforesaid simplicity of style, content, and language, not to mention its comparative brevity and its moral message.

In any discussion of *The Pearl*, it is imperative to bear in mind its provenance and the circumstances under which it was written. Steinbeck's first recounting of the legend of the Indian boy of La Paz who discovers "a pearl of great size, an unbelievable pearl" (*SC* 102) occupies something less than a page of text in *Sea of Cortez*. According to the legend, as Steinbeck then told it, the boy is astute enough to realize that this fabulous object can provide the means not only to satisfy all the desires and needs of the flesh in this life (by providing him with the wherewithal to give up work, to be drunk as often and as long as he might wish, and to take a wife and as many mistresses as he might covet), but also to ensure that in afterlife he would be popped "out of Purgatory like a squeezed watermelon seed" (by his being able to guarantee his own salvation by the purchase of sufficient masses during the remainder of his earthly life) (*SC* 102). But he soon comes to realize that possessing the means of acquiring such joys is altogether a different matter from actually converting those means into the desired ends. When he approaches the pearl dealers with his treasure, they act concertedly to cheat him. Angered by their greed and collective duplicity, he refuses to sell, and hides the pearl under a stone on the beach. He is attacked, hunted, and tortured, until eventually he retrieves the pearl from its hiding place and throws it back into the sea from whence it came. By this action, he makes himself "a free man again with his soul in danger and his food and shelter insecure" (*SC* 103). Steinbeck comments:

> This seems to be a true story but it is so much like a parable that it almost can't be. This Indian boy is too heroic, too wise. He knows too much and acts on his knowledge. In every way, he goes contrary to human direction. The story is probably true, but we don't believe it; it is far too reasonable to be true. (*SC* 103)

In fleshing out the basic story to provide sufficient narrative content to sustain a full-length feature film, Steinbeck transformed the character of the Indian boy into the poor fisherman Kino, complete with common-law wife Juana and a baby son Coyotito, as well as a brother and sister-in-law. After discovering the great pearl, Kino's immediate thoughts are properly not of the carnal joys that could be his. Rather, he contemplates the joy of being able to pay for his union with Juana to be blessed in the eyes of God by marriage in the church, of buying new clothes, of acquiring a new rifle, and of sending his son to school to learn to read and write and do sums. Coyotito's knowledge, Kino predicts, will "make us free because he will know — he will know and through him we will know" (*TP* 38). But in addition to changing the character and status of the principal protagonist, Steinbeck also sensationalized the events following Kino's proud and angry rejection of the dealer's derisory monetary offer. His canoe, the sole means of carrying on his livelihood, is smashed, his house burned to the ground. Not only is he attacked, wounded, and hunted, like the boy ·in the original legend, but he succeeds in killing four of his attackers and suffers the death of his baby son before he throws the pearl back into the sea.

If Steinbeck encountered creative difficulties, particularly in the form of "slumps," while writing *The Pearl* these are not immediately apparent from an examination of the extant holograph manuscript.[13] This, unfortunately incomplete, consists of sixty-eight foolscap sheets, the first twenty-one being written in pencil, and the remainder in ink. The first page of the manuscript is headed: "Trial sheet To be thrown away." The notation would, on the face of it, seem to accord with Steinbeck's statement in the letter he wrote Covici on 30 November 1944 recording his dissatisfaction with the first day's work. On the other hand, it implies that he had second thoughts, for the ensuing holograph text is virtually identical (subject to later minor revisions of spelling, syntax, punctuation, and paragraphing) with the opening paragraphs of the published book. There are two lacunae in the manuscript. The first covers several pages of the printed text toward the end of Chapter 3 and the beginning of Chapter 4. The second is of a few lines only at the beginning of Chapter 5. The manuscript does, however, also break off just prior to Kino's attack on the three trackers, and a single note relating to the fight sequence — "The barrel flame made a picture on his eyes." — is tacked to the end of the manuscript text. As with the first page, the whole of the surviving manuscript text, suitably refined and paragraphed, is almost exactly as published.[14] The process of initial creation through to ultimate publication can therefore be seen as following the pattern achieved with the realization of *The Grapes of Wrath* (and, incidentally, of *Cannery Row*), with the sole exception of the extended time lag between completion of the manuscript and publication of the book — two years in the case of *The Pearl*.

The holograph manuscript indicates conclusively that Steinbeck wrote the piece with the double intention of providing Fernandez and the film backers with a detailed concept of what the finished film would be like and at the same time producing a narrative that could be published in its own right as a work of literature. While in a similar fashion the manuscript of *Lifeboat* could quite easily be published as a novel, Steinbeck had not, at the time he wrote that earlier work, fully mastered film technique as a method of telling a story and creating atmosphere, as he was later to do when he came to write *Viva Zapata!* (released in 1952). The *Lifeboat* manuscript is essentially a literary work, merely providing the story line for the projected film. *The Pearl* stands at a midway point, as it were, between *Lifeboat* and *Viva Zapata!*, not only chronologically but also in terms of Steinbeck's development as a writer for the cinema. As Joseph R. Millichap had observed of *The Pearl*:

> Steinbeck's prose in the novel often takes a cinematic point of view. Scenes are presented in terms of establishing shots, medium views, and close-ups. In particular, Steinbeck carefully examines the natural setting, often visually contrasting human behavior with natural phenomena.[15]

The trouble is that *The Pearl* suffers as a novella because of the cinematic point of view imposed on it, which is, here and there, too intrusive.

Most of the action of the novella is seen through Kino's eyes, and almost the whole of the book's emotional thrust is expressed through Kino's simple and limited conscious thoughts. At the very beginning of the story, for example, there is a description of Kino awakening in his hut in the morning. Kino's eyes become the camera lens through which the reader sees precisely what Kino sees, in the same way that the audience in the cinema sees precisely what the director of the film wants it to see:

> Kino's eyes opened, and he looked first at the lightening square which was the door and then he looked at the hanging box where Coyotito slept. And last he turned his head to Juana, his wife, who lay beside him on the mat, her blue shawl over her nose and over her breasts and around the small of her back. Juana's eyes were open too. Kino could never remember seeing them closed when he awakened. Her dark eyes made little reflected stars. She was looking at him as she was always looking at him when he awakened. (*TP* [3])

The Kino viewpoint is not, however, uniformly sustained throughout the book. There are occasions when intentional digressions are introduced — such as, to quote two examples, the scene in the doctor's bedroom in Chapter 1, and the second paragraph of Chapter 2 with its description of the tiny marine life of the beach — but there are also those other occasions when Steinbeck slips awkwardly from the subjective viewpoint of Kino to an objective authorial viewpoint, as in the scene when the trackers and the horseman stop in the road opposite the spot where Kino is hiding:

> When the trackers came near, Kino could see only their legs and only the legs of the horse from under the fallen branch. He saw the dark horny feet of the men and their ragged white clothes, and he heard the creak of leather of the saddle and the clink of spurs. The trackers stopped at the swept place and studied it, and the horseman stopped. The horse flung his head up against the bit and the bit-roller clicked under his tongue and the horse snorted. Then the dark trackers turned and studied the horse and watched his ears. (*TP* 101—2)

Although perfectly acceptable in cinematic terms, such an abrupt switch from subjective to objective viewpoint, when the reader has been conditioned to the idea that Kino's range of vision is severely restricted so that he can see only the legs of the trackers and of the horse, is momentarily distracting and ruptures our complete identification with Kino, if not our continuing awareness and appreciation of his predicament.

While most of the cinematic techniques reflected in *The Pearl* are perfectly acceptable, and in some cases work wonderfully well, the use of "theme music" as a means of pointing to a mood or to an emotion or to concentrate on a particular object does seem rather artificial on the page. The aural repetition of certain musical themes by way of background music is markedly more unobtrusive but more insidiously effective in registering on the subconscious of the individual members of a cinema audience than is the stark repetition of printed words on the eyes of the reader. As Steinbeck had told Covici, he laid great emphasis on the importance of the musical score, and in *The Pearl* he introduces the Song of the Family, the Song of Evil, the Song of the Enemy, the Song of the Pearl That Might Be, the Song of the Undersea, and, of course, "the music of the pearl" itself. This use of "music" is a re-use of the experimental device Steinbeck had employed far more subtly in *Cannery Row* during the episode when Doc discovers the drowned young girl in the La Jolla tide pool. It was a device he was to use again in the "tones" or "voices" that Doc hears within himself in *Sweet Thursday*.[16]

Despite these reservations, *The Pearl* works more successfully as a novel in its own right than does either *The Moon Is Down* or his third published play-novel, *Burning Bright*. The confinement to stage setting interiors that bedevil those two books disappears in the far-ranging outdoors action of *The Pearl*. Yet the freedom Steinbeck enjoyed to open up the original basic parable posed its own problems, and these problems he did not entirely solve. He weighed himself down with so much specific action, so much elaboration of character, not to mention metaphor and inner meaning, that the simple storyline became perilously overburdened.

The elimination of stagecraft artificiality does not, on the other hand, automatically ensure that a more realistic atmosphere will pervade a work. It should be borne in mind that Steinbeck consistently referred to *The Pearl* as a parable. Any attempt to consider the book solely as a work of realism presents immediate difficulties, for arguably there is some justification in contending that Steinbeck failed to establish his characters in a completely believable set of circumstances. To believe in the reality of the whole, it is necessary to believe in all, or (at the very least) most of, the component parts. In short, it has to be accepted without question that, against all odds, Coyotito would have survived the scorpion sting, that Kino could so successfully and easily have attacked and killed the four men hired to rob and murder him, and that one bullet fired more or less blindly toward the cave entrance from thirty feet or so below could have blown off the top of Coyotito's head as he lay under a blanket close against his mother's back.

Perhaps even more importantly from the realistic point of view, the principal problem Steinbeck did not and could not solve was to reach a credible ending for the book. He was, of course, saddled with that ending, for it does provide the whole *raison d'être* of the story. But what has been altered disastrously in Steinbeck's overelaborated version are the events leading up to the casting of the pearl back into the sea. In the original legend, the Indian boy did not kill anyone. He had no wife, no child, no house, no boat. Indeed, he had no identifiable position in the community. He existed conveniently as a single human being without apparent family ties and without possessions. After he had been attacked and beaten and tortured, there was a simple logic to his gesture in throwing the pearl, the cause of all his troubles, back into the sea: he just wanted to be left alone and to return to his old, uncomplicated, peaceful, if poverty-ridden, way of life. But, as French has pointed out, in Steinbeck's version "too many loose ends remain unresolved."[17] Steinbeck has encumbered Kino with so many possessions at the beginning of the story, has established his position in the tiny fishing community so firmly, that it has become impossible for Kino, by the simple act of returning the pearl to the sea, to regain the dubious "Eden" of his former way of life. It cannot be ignored that his boat, his "bulwark against starvation" (*TP* 22), has been destroyed, his baby is dead, and his relationships with his wife and his brother and the other villagers have been radically and irretrievably altered by what has happened. Although the implication is that Steinbeck wants his readers to accept all this as a satisfactory, if not a happy, conclusion to the story, it is, as French has maintained, no ending at all. It does not seem possible that Kino would be content to return to the environment from which he imagined he had escaped, nor can it be accepted that he would have been welcomed back unreservedly by those whom he had, in his briefly assumed position of superiority, been forced to leave behind in his obstinate search for wealth. And what of the four men he has killed? Are not the pearl dealers going to exact some sort of revenge, even if they cannot now get their hands on the pearl by fair means or foul? It is surely significant that at the conclusion of the book of all the things Kino desired when he first held the pearl in his hand there is only one that he now possesses—indeed, it is his only possession: a rifle, a symbol of violence that he has acquired by violence. Kino will have to defend himself with it. There is more blood to be shed—ultimately, some time or other, inevitably Kino's own. The logical ending of the story is in that future tragedy and death.

It follows that if, after due consideration, the book does not convince as a work of realism, it should be accepted as the parable Steinbeck says it is. Here, again, is another problem. In its purest form, a parable (or fable) expresses a single moral truth. In *The Pearl* there is a multiplicity of possible moral truths or quasi-moral propositions: that, in the words of St. Matthew, "What is a man profited, if he shall gain the whole world, and lose his own soul?"; that one should accept one's preordained social station in life and not presume to aspire above it; that pride goes before a fall; that greed is never rewarded; that happiness cannot be achieved through material wealth; and so on. Because Steinbeck has so loaded the story with detail, with various examples of human behavior, any one of these questionable conclusions, or any combination of them, can be regarded as equally valid. Steinbeck has left the reader with an open-endedness that is not only unsatisfactory on the realistic level but on the fabular level as well.

Steinbeck's own subsequent ambivalent attitude toward *The Pearl* is clearly expressed in the brief introductory note to the published book. "If this story is a parable," he suggests, "perhaps everyone takes his own meaning from it and reads his own life into it" (*TP* [2]). It is possible that Steinbeck did consciously set out to make the work mean all things to all men. On the other hand, there could have been a confusion of intent in his mind, so that when the work was finished, as a letter to his agents at the time implies, he felt that he had failed in what he had set out to do.[18]

If he did fail, he certainly did not fail because *The Pearl* is too simple a work, but because it is too complex a work. In it, he tried to encompass not only three quite-disintinctive narrative forms (cinematic, realistic, and fabular), but also an overwhelming preponderance of identifiable symbols, metaphors, and philosophies for so slight a tale. There are strong echoes of the Bible, Greek tragedy, and Faustian legend all present in the manner of the telling. If Steinbeck *has* succeeded, as most critics would maintain, in creating a considerable work of art, he has possibly done so by default. What, above all, is certain is that a work that can raise so many passions in its critics, generate so many contradictory interpretations, elicit so much praise for the beauty and clarity of its prose, and give immense pleasure to countless millions of discerning readers cannot be judged a failure.

3

There was suddenly a renewed urgency about life. Steinbeck hoped that while he and Gwyn were in Mexico some work could be done to the house, but they were informed that their application to the Housing Association had still not been processed. A week before their departure, Thom's christening took place in the Episcopal church.

After staying a day with Jack Wagner in Hollywood, they flew from Los Angeles to Mexico City, arriving there on 9 February. All in all, it proved to be a fairly successful trip. Steinbeck and Fernandez completed the first shooting script. Gwyn became absorbed in working with others to devise the form of the musical score, based entirely on traditional Indian music. On the debit side, both she and Steinbeck contracted severe colds. There were, too, the inevitable major and minor squabbles that always seemed to surround the process of filmmaking in Mexico. The local RKO representative in Mexico City apparently claimed that the studio had a fifteen-day clause that enabled it to approve or veto the cast selected by Fernandez, and some mention was made that a "big name," like Dolores del Rio, should play the female lead. That, however, was out of the question, for there was no possibility that she and Fernandez would be able to work together. Although until recently they had been lovers, their relationship had deteriorated to the stage where they literally hated each other. Added to which, the idea of a forty-two-year-old actress playing the part of the eighteen-year-old heroine seemed somewhat ludicrous. As if that were not enough, del Rio had made it palpably clear that she did not wish to play opposite Pedro Armendariz, the actor Fernandez had chosen for the male lead.

The RKO representative was also proposing that an overseer technician appointed by the studio should be present throughout the making of the picture and have the right to cut any scenes he decided he did not like. When news of this turn of events was passed on to Annie Laurie Williams, she was able to assure Steinbeck that with the release of the film already arranged and the contract being crystal-clear and watertight in all specifics there was certainly no provision for this sort of interference from RKO.

Other problems reared their heads. On 28 February, shortly before leaving Mexico City for home, Steinbeck sent the only spare copy he had of *The Pearl* manuscript to his agents in New York. It did not arrive, having presumably been either held up by the censors or lost in the mails. When, a week or so later, he and Gwyn returned to Monterey, he was not only informed that the gas rationing board had withdrawn his supplemental gas ration but also found that during his absence the Housing Association had returned his petition to carry out plumbing work on the house because a signature had been entered on the wrong line, an error that would retard the commencement of the work for at least another six weeks. The authorities, in fact, subsequently changed their minds about allowing any work of whatever nature to be carried out on the house. He was beginning to become paranoid again over the whole business. "There seems to be a profound enmity toward me from the local businessman who are on boards," he complained to Annie Laurie Williams. "They've never had any power over me but now that they have it they are using it to the hilt" (JS/ALW 3/18/45).

It was altogether an unsettling time. Gwyn took Thom to Los Angeles to show him to his grandmother. While there, she took the opportunity to visit her old music teacher, Sandy Oliver, and seek his advice about the music for the film. Jack Wagner came up to Monterey to stay for a couple of weeks. The intention was now for Wagner, who could speak Spanish like a native, to accompany them when they returned to Mexico about the first of May. With work on *The Pearl* for the moment in abeyance and his research for the War Food Administration and the *Collier's* article sabotaged by the withdrawal of his supplemental gas ration and his consequent inability to travel freely to widely scattered companies, he resorted to writing a series of testimonials for the Red Cross, War Bonds, and the Merchant Marine. He also attempted, toward the end of March, to begin work on the script of the projected musical comedy, *The Wizard of Maine*. He did not progress very far, as he revealed in a letter to Annie Laurie Williams:

> I made a start on the Wizard and tossed it out yesterday but that is normal. Got off on the wrong foot. I'll make another try today. It will be a loose long short story just trying to convey the framework within which a show could be built. I won't do it in terms of scenes or anything. ... It's a kind of natural and funny frame for a good variety show and a satiric story. And while there isn't a lot of book at least it is fresh and not the hackneyed thing that has been done so often. (JS/ALW 3/22/45)

Unable to settle into any solid work and distressed by the antagonistic attitude of the people of Monterey, he experienced the old feeling of restlessness. When Gwyn and Thom returned from Los Angeles on 28 March, he talked the situation over with her and Wagner. He wanted to get away. It was decided almost there and then that the three of them, together with Thom and Miss Diehl, would clear out and head down to Cuernavaca. He and Wagner and the dog Willie departed by train from Los Angeles to Mexico City on 6 April, leaving Gwyn and Thom and the nurse to follow by plane on the 10th.

He left Monterey in a cloud of bitterness, unsure even if he would ever want to return. He had been made to realize how much of a mistake it had been for him to go back there in the first place and imagine that he would be welcomed and be able to make a home for Gwyn and Thom and himself there. The sense of persecution he had felt had been almost overwhelming. All his friends, Ed Ricketts excepted, had seemed to have deserted him. He expressed some of his emotions in a long letter to Covici, writing a few days before leaving for Mexico:

It really seems to me that you can't go home again. . . . You see this isn't my country anymore. And it won't be until I am dead. It makes me very sad. There's no one to talk to or associate with. And I'm so glad to be going back to Mexico and I'll probably be back in the east next winter.[19]

4

Once all the members of the Steinbeck entourage had met up after journeying to Mexico City by train or air, they stayed a few days in the capital before traveling the fifty miles or so south to Cuernavaca. Steinbeck had decided to make his base there for as long as it took to see the filming through to its completion.

In Cuernavaca, they established themselves temporarily in the Hotel Marik, while they looked around for more permanent and less expensive accommodation. Through some relatives of Gwyn's in the real-estate business there, they found a beautiful, pleasant house, and rented it for six months. The house ideally suited their purpose, being only half a mile out of town (for convenience, they continued to use the Hotel Marik as a mailing address) and no more than an hour-and-a-half's drive to the capital and the headquarters of the film people with whom Steinbeck and Wagner would be working. The house, although not large, had sufficient rooms to allow them to entertain house guests, and Steinbeck was soon urging both Covici and Street to come and stay. There was a commodious porch, and an extensive garden with a sloping lawn and a sixty-foot swimming pool. The garden was filled with exotic flowers, and there was a large bougainvillea, in the shade of which, seated at a rickety table, Steinbeck would do much of his writing during the ensuing weeks.

In his letters to New York, he rhapsodized in his descriptions of the house and the life they were leading in Cuernavaca. The sun was warm but not too hot, except at midday. The mornings and the evenings were perfect and the heat was dry, not sticky as it was in New York. Within a few days of their moving in, a high wind shredded the leaves of the banana trees, and shortly afterward the rainy season began—but this, so far as he was concerned, was even better. The rain and the thunderstorms seemed to occur always at night, and in the mornings the country was washed and fresh in the sun.

Gwyn was kept busy getting the household routine organized and in brushing up her Spanish for her dealings with the Mexican houseman, Victor, who had no English. Thom's skin turned copper-colored in the sun. His father showed unnecessary concern over the child's progress, because Thom was not yet walking and, although he could stand, would not crawl. Willie, after the long journey confined to the boxcar of the train and the subsequent limitations imposed by hotel life, was in his element in the large garden. He was known all over town and was nicknamed "El Oso" ("The Bear"). Only the firecrackers the locals set off at every conceivable excuse for a celebration disturbed Willie's idyllic existence.

Following all the hostility they had left behind in Monterey, Steinbeck was deeply touched by the warmth and the apparent genuineness of the welcome they encountered from the moment they had arrived in Mexico. He wondered again if he would ever want to return to the West Coast. The extent of the welcome in Cuernavaca did, however, have its disadvantages. During the first weekend they were there, they had so many callers that eventually the place became, as Steinbeck put it, "a kind of a mad house" (JS/WFS 4/30/45). Every weekend thereafter they had visitors from Mexico City, but during the week they were left more or less in peace.

The war seemed very remote, for in Cuernavaca they were not being bombarded with daily news reports. They could not rely on the Mexican newspapers, which carried mainly national and local news. Only by listening to the short wave radio at night, although atmospherics were bad, were they able to keep fairly abreast of international events. The announcement of the president's death on 12 April shocked them all. Steinbeck, especially, felt it an almost personal loss. Roosevelt, he wrote Covici, "left a profound mark on his times all over the world. For one thing, he is the first president since Lincoln with a sense of humor" (JS/PC mid-Apr. 1945).

Six days later, Steinbeck received the news that Ernie Pyle had been killed by a Japanese sniper on Ie Shima, the ten-mile-square island west of Okinawa. Pyle's death affected him as greatly as had the president's, perhaps more so when he recalled his last meeting with Pyle three months before in San Francisco and how, even then, the man had the aura of death about him and seemed aware of it himself. He could not get it out of his head that his friend had been sacrificed on an assignment he had never wanted. Possibly at the back of Steinbeck's mind was the thought that had he not turned down the Navy's request to report on the Pacific war he might also have met the same fate. He received a number of telegrams, asking him, as a friend and fellow war correspondent, to write an appreciation, and while he felt it an indelicate assignment and would have preferred not to do it he eventually gave in when he had a wire from Pyle's employer, Scripps-Howard. As soon as he had written the piece, he wired Scripps-Howard and asked how he should deliver it to them. As he reported disgustedly to Elizabeth Otis: "They replied by wire that it was too late. This was ten days after his death and he was no longer news to Scripps-Howard whom he had been practically supporting. *Sic* etc." (*SLL* 282). Conceivably Scripps-Howard had not liked some of the truths Steinbeck had written:

It's a hard thing to write about a dead man who doesn't seem dead to you. Ernie Pyle didn't want to go back to the war. When he left France, he set down his disgust and fear and weariness. He thought he could rest a little, but he couldn't. People told him what to do and what he should do. He could have overcome that but he couldn't overcome his own sense of responsibility. . . . War was everything Ernie Pyle didn't like. He hated filth and he hated cruelty.[20]

The war in Europe was fast approaching its inevitable end. On 29 April, the news came through that Mussolini, the ex-dictator of Italy, had been captured by Italian partisans and that he and his mistress had been summarily executed, their bodies publicly strung up by the feet in the main square of Milan. When the news of the German surrender was announced, Steinbeck could get no sense of elation at all, rather a sense of overwhelming sickness that the war should have happened. Unable to conceal his bitterness, he wrote to Street the day after the news broke: "I suppose there was celebration at home, mostly, I'll be [bound], by people who hadn't been involved in it" (JS/WFS 5/7/45). Although there were parades in Mexico City, there had been no V.E. Day celebrations in Cuernavaca: "The people who got drunk are the ones who get drunk every day anyway. But the poison fringe and the pansys [sic] and their elderly consorts just drank the usual cocktails and had the usual fights. We had one toast and that was all" (JS/ERO 5/10/45). He delighted in the report of the capture of Hermann Goering, and suggested that the Nazi leader should, as the inventor of city bombing, be made to stand trial in London before a jury of Cockneys in a tribunal set up within the ruins of the Temple or Inns of Court. He predicted that the Pacific war would not last long now that the full might of the European bomber force could be diverted against the Japanese mainland. He also predicted the fall of the Churchill government in Great Britain.

The news that Annie Laurie William's husband had been found in Austria provided the occasion for much personal rejoicing between New York and Cuernavaca. Maurice was safe but apparently in a rather sorry condition, weary and half-starved after having been, together with hundreds of other Allied prisoners of war, forced by the Germans to march westward away from the advancing Russians. Annie Laurie Williams had heard he was resting in a hospital, regaining his strength and awaiting passage home.

5

The manuscript of *The Pearl* lost in February between Mexico City and New York had been located. It had not, after all, been held up by the censors, nor had it been lost in the mails as Steinbeck had feared, but had, owing to some incredible misunderstanding, been in New York all the time. Apparently, some clerk in the McIntosh & Otis office, not realizing what it was, had marked the package for return to Mexico. Fortunately, the error had been discovered and the manuscript retrieved from the Post Office, where it had been languishing.

Having now had the opportunity to read the manuscript, Covici and Elizabeth Otis were at last able to convey their long-awaited opinions. Covici was typically enthusiastic about the work, declaring it to be "as tense and compelling a story as I have read in years." He told Steinbeck: "This undoubtedly contains some of your best prose" (Fensch 47). The author was, however, more concerned to have Elizabeth Otis's judgement, and after she had written to tell him how good she thought the book was, he replied:

> Naturally I am very glad and frankly relieved that you like the Pearl. It was so full of experiments and I had no idea whether they would come off at all. Also the thing seemed doomed never to get there. It was all ominous. (JS/ERO 5/3/45)

He was at that time very conscious of the fact that this was the third in an unbroken series of short books he had completed — four, if the unpublished *Lifeboat* were included. The time was ripe, he knew, for a more substantial work. There had been enough little books. He feared that, with the publication of *The Pearl*, he would become established in the minds of his readers as a writer of novellas and that his critical reputation, shaky as he felt it then to be, would be further damaged in the absence of another work on the same scale as *The Grapes of Wrath*. He already had plans for another novel, *El Camion Vacilador*, which he was eager to begin, and with which — at fifty thousand to sixty thousand words, about twice the length of *The Pearl* — he hoped to break the chain of very short books.

Covici and Elizabeth Otis were of similar mind on the matter. Covici's solution was to propose that *The Pearl* should be published either in a limited edition, or in an omnibus volume with two other short novels, ideally also with Mexican themes. Not only, Covici argued, would such a volume represent a complete departure from anything Steinbeck had ever published before, but it would be certain to sell extremely well. He suggested that Steinbeck might consider completing *The Good Little Neighbor*, the story he had abandoned in the early part of the previous year, and that the new story, *El Camion Vacilador*, could be the third component of the volume.

Steinbeck, however, had no intention of going back to *The Good Little Neighbor*. The story had got out of hand, he said, and had soured on him permanently. Nor did he go along with Covici's suggestion that *The Pearl* be issued in a limited edition. On the other hand, he approved the idea of publishing *The Pearl* jointly with *The Wayward Bus*, the approximate translation of *El Camion Vacilador*. The two, he pointed out, would make a sizable book of about one hundred thousand words.

There, for the moment, the matter stood. In the meantime, he was not averse to his agents selling *The Pearl* for magazine publication. He would have preferred *Collier's* to take it, but appreciated it would probably be too long for that magazine. When it eventually appeared in the December issue of *Woman's Home Companion*, he liked the new title the editors had given it: "The Pearl of the World." He did however think the repetition of sound rather irritating. It would have been much better, he contended, had the title been in Spanish: "La Perla del Mundo." He told Elizabeth Otis he would suggest that as the title for the movie.

6

When the movie would be made was another matter entirely. Although Steinbeck's main motivation for the early move to Mexico had been to escape the poisonous atmosphere of Monterey, both he and Jack Wagner — and to a lesser degree Gwyn — expected to begin work on the movie, if not immediately, at least within a week or so of their arrival. Gwyn, with Sandy Oliver's assistance, had already made some recordings of the Family and the Pearl themes based on ancient Indian music, and had also made some progress on the Evil theme. Steinbeck declared himself very pleased with the results. But when they arrived in Mexico City, they discovered that Fernandez had become involved in directing another film, *Pepita*, said to be based on a Spanish classic, and that, as a consequence, he would not be free until the end of July, three months away.

While Steinbeck may undoubtedly have felt the now-familiar sense of frustration at this news, it is also possible that he may have been secretly relieved to find he had some time of his own before immersing himself in the pressures of Mexican film production. He was at that time experiencing the "mental and moral tailspin" that seemed to follow his completion of every major piece of work (JS/PC 5/3/45). On the other hand, he was still very much aware of the heavy schedule of work facing him in the months ahead — *The Pearl* movie, *The Wizard of Maine*, and *The Wayward Bus*. He had planned to begin work on *The Wayward Bus* that fall. There was no time for relaxation.

So, soon after they had moved into the house in Cuernavaca, and leaving Wagner to scout around for suitable locations for the movie, he settled down to the composition of *The Wizard of Maine*. In many ways, it was an ideal work for him at that time, for it was a light piece of nonsense he had no intention of publishing. As he told his agents, he regarded it as no more than "a kind of prospectus to write a musical comedy from and probably no good anyway" (JS/ERO 5/10/45).

Within days, he had established a pleasant routine, writing his two thousand or so words in the morning (except on those days when the exuberant setting-off of firecrackers disturbed the peace and his concentration), then having a swim and going for a walk in the afternoon. By the end of the month, he was deep into the work. By 3 May, he had completed ten thousand words and was declaring that he found it "rather fun to write in a time when if one didn't keep busy he would go nuts" (JS/ALW 5/3/45). He estimated he would have the job done within two to three weeks. He told Covici: "It seems silly to work on manuscript in the face of these earth shaking events and yet that is exactly what people do. The death of Hitler and I write 2000 words on the Wizard of Maine" (JS/PC 5/3/45). On 7 May, he wrote to Elizabeth Otis: "It is amusing and that is all and it keeps my pen point damp. The world is blowing up so completely, that's the best I can expect" (JS/ERO 5/7/45). By 10 May, he had written approximately twenty thousand words and was perhaps two-thirds finished.

Three days later, he was contacted by a young public relations man named Alfred Katz he had previously met in New York. Katz was on a business trip to Mexico, and phoned from Mexico City, saying that he had heard about the musical comedy project and would like the opportunity of getting it produced on Broadway. Steinbeck told him that he hoped to have the synopsis (as he now referred to it) finished within a few days, and it was arranged that Katz should come down to Cuernavaca on the weekend. When he had completed the manuscript, Steinbeck rated it "not very good," but suggested it "could be amusing if made satiric" (JS/ALW 5/21/45).

7

Steinbeck's original holograph synopsis is approximately sixteen thousand words in length (he seems uncharacteristically to have overstated the word-count in letters to his editor and agents), and is divided into seven numbered sections. It is an unusual piece of work and is not wholly a synopsis as such. In addition to a detailed summary of the action of the play, complete with extensive dialogue, it contains in the first and second of its sections particularized material relating to past events — material that could not be enacted on stage and could only have been incorporated in any production by way of explanatory dialogue, or song delivered in front of the curtain, or through the medium of a "stage manager" figure. The story seems now as hackneyed and of as little significance as the book of most musical comedies, providing merely the peg on which to hang the musical numbers, the dancing, and the spectacular routines and set pieces, and consists of the usual comedy of errors involving unforeseen and improbable twists of plot and the ups and downs of young love. The main action is contained in the first and fourth through seventh sections of the work. The second section is pure unactable narrative, and the third section is an extended authorial aside that has nothing to do with the actual plot of the play itself.[21]

According to Jackson J. Benson, when Steinbeck and Frank Loesser first hit on the idea during the summer of 1944 of writing a musical for Fred Allen, the story they conceived at the time was to be about "a snake-oil salesman, a genial humbug who travels from small town to small town doing magic tricks — and doing good, although he pretends to be indifferent to everything but profit and expresses a cynical view of human nature" (*Adventures* 551).

However, by the time he sat down in the garden in Cuernavaca to begin sketching out the synopsis for the play, Steinbeck's own concept of the principal character, old Doctor Thorne, seems to have undergone something of a change. No longer does the doctor profess to be interested only in profit, but is motivated by the entirely altruistic desire to spread the postulated benefits of his "Powhatan's Secret Herbal Elixir, Painkiller, and Deodorant" far and wide across the eastern states. While being a self-styled "doctor," old Doctor Thorne truly believes himself to be a bona fide medical man, a dedicated professional, and considers the Elixir to be the philosopher's stone among medicines. He regards the juggling, magic tricks, banjo playing, and ritual selling homilies he performs in his show, which have been handed down to him from his father, as chicanery and quackery, justified only to the extent to which they ensure both a good sale of the Elixir and the success of his crusade to spread the medical benefit it provides around the countryside. He is, indeed, a dedicated man, no swift-talking, glib-tongued rogue.

In essence, the plot consists of two parallel story lines: the first the love story of Pocahontas ("Nan"), the doctor's daughter, and Rainfield Lightner ("Rainey"), an itinerant songster, and the second the story of the efforts of four purple Tibetan lamas to retrieve a lost magic wand. The lamas brought the wand to New York for repair, but, by a strange and ludicrous sequence of events, it has been erroneously packed in a box of magic tricks Rainey has ordered in order to enhance Doctor Thorne's amateurish conjuring. The love affair between Nan and Rainey is disrupted by the machinations of Rainey's rival, Horace, a young man who, before Rainey joins up with the show, has inveigled his way into the doctor's confidence, persuading him to reveal the secrets of the Elixir. Horace has set his sights on marrying Nan and taking over the show for his own unscrupulous ends. The wand summons the services of the Billy Rose figure, Abe

Blossom, who transforms the doctor's modest entertainment into a series of stupendous production numbers (that incidentally would have cost a small fortune to stage), and attracts not only national radio coverage but also the attentions of big business anxious to invest in the show and provide the doctor with a percentage. When, however, the lamas appear on the scene and make known the identity of the miraculous wand, the good doctor hands it over to them immediately. All ends happily, with Horace arrested, Nan and Rainey free to marry, the lamas returning to Tibet with the wand, and Doctor Thorne reconciled to resuming the previous pattern of his life, but with the added anticipation of grandchildren.

It is obvious that at the time he was writing the synopsis Steinbeck was enjoying himself immensely, devising the trite and improbable plot and letting his mind run riot, safe in the knowledge that the work was not for publication. Indeed, he harbored no illusions or pretensions concerning its worth, and was at root indifferent to its ultimate fate. His attitude was: If someone might wish to use the idea as the basis for a full-blown production, all well and good; if nobody was interested, then there was no skin off his nose. It is true that when other people did become interested in the project, he also put forward suggestions of his own as to who might produce it, develop the bare synopsis into a book, compose the music and lyrics, and play the leading role, but it is doubtful that he was at any time totally committed to it. Certainly, whatever interest he may briefly have shown in its fate was all but completely dissipated by his involvement in the filming of *The Pearl* and his impatience to begin work on *The Wayward Bus*.

The trite musical comedy plot outlined by him is only part — although, measured by length, the main part — of this inconsequential work. The most interesting aspects of the manuscript are the extended authorial asides comprising the whole of the third section and a substantial portion of the seventh, for these asides, if nothing else, serve to expose Steinbeck's attitude toward the work and to the New York social scene.

"In musical comedy," he begins the third section, "it is just as well to know what you are doing and why. This is not often practiced but there is no harm in it. Let's consider our audience" (*Wizard* 15). For this purpose, Steinbeck concentrates on two imaginary people sitting in the second row of the stalls: a fat man named Henry Hampton, who is in the auto loan business, and his wife Hope:

> Henry can't get into his dinner jacket with ease. His war effort has made him run to fat. He has been so afraid of a famine (predicted by Louis Bromfield) that he had been overeating for three years. Hope ... studied the dark streak in her blonde hair so long that she was late for dinner. She has been dieting on martinis and couldn't get an appointment with her hairdresser. They aren't

really friends yet. Hope hates Henry's belches and he says it was because he had to eat too fast because she was so fucking long getting dressed. But here they are twisting their programmes. They want to see a musical comedy. Henry doesn't want to be disturbed except below the belt. As the great Eddie Cantor once said, "Crotch and tits and mother—that's good entertainment." Let us not then outrage these good people with thought. ... There must be no ideas because they are always red. You take a man with ideas and why he's nearly always a new dealer or a red or both. That's been Henry's experience. Henry believes in individual enterprise except in competitors. Right and virtue are going to triumph and don't let us forget it for a moment. We're going to send Henry and Hope to 21 on a pink cloud after the show. (*Wizard* 15—16)

Henry and Hope represent exactly the people Steinbeck most despises, but, with tongue in cheek and with bitter cynicism, he sets out in the synopsis to ensure they will have an enjoyable evening in the theater. It is, one can hear him saying, all reduced to that sort of level for that sort of person—the lowest common denominator. The whole work is designed to please the Henrys and the Hopes of this world, to make them feel good by vicarious identification with the handsome juvenile lead and the lovely young soubrette. If it can, at the same time, be made into what is called "great theater," so much the better. "For," as Steinbeck comments, "the American theater is a great art and we must approach it humbly" (*Wizard* 16).

Steinbeck returns to the attack in the seventh section. As the section opens, he contemplates whether or not he has contrived a sufficiently insoluble situation for his principal characters to escape from; whether or not Rainey has contributed enough to the plot; whether or not Nan and Rainey should have a big misunderstanding, with Nan stamping her feet and refusing to speak to him; whether or not there should be a lady comic character who falls in love with Rainey but finally teams up with Abe; whether or not Horace has been painted black enough as the villain of the piece. "We must not forget," Steinbeck muses,

that Horace must be enough of a rat so that Henry can feel virtuous by contrast. And that is quite an order. And Hope who got rid of her last maid (without paying her two weeks in advance) by claiming the maid had stolen some earrings which Hope herself had hocked. Hope has to feel young and virtuous, albeit hotpantsed. So Horace has to be a proper son of a bitch because competition in the audience is pretty tough. (*Wizard* 28)

Time is taken out to lunge at Hollywood:

I remember when a famous Hollywood producer said to me, "I got a great idea for that story of yours (Mice and Men). That guy that kills that girl," he said. "He don't do it. Somebody else does it and he gets the blame."

"Wonderful," I said. "I spend 30,000 words to establish an inevitability and you knock it over with an idea."

"Yeah! Good, ain't it?" he said. "In this business you got to have ideas." (*Wizard* 28)

When all the trivial threads of the trivial plot have at last come together satisfactorily and the curtain has finally descended, Hope leaves hotfoot for the theater lobby so that, out of sheer cussedness, she can get in the way of those people endeavoring to get a cab, and so play her part in "the beautiful after theater pageant of New York" (*Wizard* 30).

The reviewers, too, are not forgotten as they make their way back to the newspaper offices to pound out their vitriolic notices for the early morning editions. "The critics dust off the crack they were saving for the next musical. I have an idea about critics. Give each one of them 100 dollars worth of stock." Steinbeck goes on to reflect: "It would be interesting anyway" (*Wizard* 30).

He checks that he has followed to the letter the conventions of the genre: "Now, let's see — is there anything we have neglected to steal from 'Oklahoma' or that 'Oklahoma' forgot to steal from Victor Herbert — no — I guess not" (*Wizard* 30). And finally, he is able to congratulate himself on what he has achieved for Henry and Hope: "And so we end a glorious night in the theater."

Despite its relative unimportant status in the Steinbeck canon, *The Wizard of Maine* manuscript does reflect in many ways the author's state of mind at the time he was writing it. As much as anything else, it is clear that had he not been on an emotional rebound from all the anger and sadness he had felt from having to leave Monterey, and had he not had time on his hands after arriving in Mexico, he would probably never have wasted his time and energy on writing such a piece of trivia (in which he patently did not believe). The imbalance of the structure and nature of the synopsis — the first long section, which is detailed in its descriptions of setting and action and which has an almost old-fashioned, folksy atmosphere, followed by the less explicit sections in which he allows his thoughts to meander on paper — is clear evidence that Steinbeck had either run out of ideas how to keep the original theme moving along, or had simply become bored with the whole work and had decided to spice it up with the introduction of Henry and Hope, and three impossibly extravagant production scenes. Even so, it cannot be denied that the synopsis *does* possess a certain charm and wit, which, as in the case of *Cannery Row*, presumes to conceal the poison lurking in the cream puff.

8

Katz took copies of *The Wizard* typescript back with him to Mexico City. From there he mailed one copy to Annie Laurie Williams. He then left for San Francisco for an emotional reunion with his parents and his sister, all of whom had recently arrived there after being in Japanese hands in Santa Tomas for three and a half years. Recalling the confusion that had occurred over the manuscript of *The Pearl*, Steinbeck did not want to take any chances of *The Wizard* becoming mislaid, and so he arranged for Katz to send another copy of the typescript to New York once he had reached the West Coast. After spending some time with his family and subsequently concluding some business in Los Angeles, Katz planned to return to New York within the next few weeks. There he hoped to begin negotiations with Williams for an option on the work. Advising her of all this, Steinbeck again warned Annie Laurie Williams that *The Wizard* was not worth much, and went on to assure her he would not be disappointed if nothing were done with it.

With Jack Wagner now in Acapulco, continuing his search for locations, and Fernandez now anticipating he would not be free of *Pepita* until the end of August, Steinbeck decided he would turn his attention immediately to *The Wayward Bus*, believing he could get it written before he became involved in the serious work on *The Pearl*. No sooner was the decision made than a bout of dysentery, probably brought on from eating too much fruit, laid him low and made work out of the question. Gwyn and Thom, fortunately, were not affected. Thom had at last started to crawl. His father joked that he was "a backward child," being that, to begin with, he could only crawl backwards. Steinbeck, for all his joking, was unable to resist playing the role of proud father, reporting to his agents that Thom had "hands as big as barns and feet like violins." He added: "He is going to be huge. He weighs over 25 pounds" (JS/ERO 5/22/45).

9

Katz was due to arrive in New York on 11 June, and Annie Laurie Williams had fixed a meeting with him on the 13th to discuss his ideas with regard to *The Wizard*. Although Steinbeck had once again expressed his doubts about the worth of the synopsis, urging his agent to throw it out the window if she thought it no good, he became interested in the fate of the work once she had indicated she considered it had real potential. By 14 June, he was already opining that with the right people something quite nice could be produced from it. He kept in close touch with Annie Laurie Williams by letter and occasionally by telephone with both her and Katz, intently following the course of their negotiations, and constantly offering his own suggestions and expressing his own wishes as to who might be invited to become involved in the production of the work. His dream combination was S. J. Perelman for the book, and Rodgers and Hammerstein for the music and lyrics. He was fully aware that this dream was an impossible one, and, in a more practical vein, favored Frank Loesser as composer and lyricist. For the leading role of old Doctor Thorne, he proposed Fred Allen as his first choice and the actor for whom the play had been originally conceived, then veteran Broadway star Victor Moore, and finally folksinger Burl Ives.

Steinbeck became extremely upset upon discovering that Annie Laurie Williams had sent a copy of the synopsis to George S. Kaufman. Not only did he and Gwyn consider that Kaufman had become "a hard-luck child" in recent years and that there were far better and fresher talents in the field, but they also knew that Kaufman's wife, Beatrice, had been spreading unpleasant gossip about him. There is no record of Kaufman's reaction to the synopsis, but certainly from then on his name drops completely from the correspondence between New York and Cuernavaca.

Having more immediately pressing matters on his mind, Steinbeck was content to leave the thinking about *The Wizard* to his wife and Annie Laurie Williams. Gwyn, he pointed out, knew so much more about the theater and loved it more than he did anyway. There was even some talk of Gwyn taking a trip to New York for a few days to consult personally with Annie Laurie Williams and participate in negotiations with Katz, but on 20 July the agent wired them that she had already signed an agreement with Katz and the stage designer Stewart Cheney, giving them an option as coproducers of the show, an arrangement that Steinbeck and Gwyn fully approved. The two men represented in their eyes the vanguard of the kind of fresh, young talent they had always hoped would help to steer *The Wizard* to its realization on stage. Steinbeck, while content that the matter was in good hands, was still unable to prevent himself from making the occasional suggestion, and he proposed that George Frazier should be invited to write the book. Frazier had never done such work before and, inevitably, there was a great deal of opposition from the other parties involved.

Much else had been happening in the meantime. Steinbeck had definitely decided by then to postpone any plans he may have had to begin work on *The Wayward Bus* until his commitment with the movie was concluded. He realized how impossible it would be to divide his attention and energies between the two projects. In any case, he and Wagner had made up their minds that they should not wait around any longer, but go ahead without Fernandez to prepare a full shooting script. They argued that this would not only save considerable time once the director was available but also that, if as a *fait accompli* they could produce a tight shooting script, there was less danger of anyone messing around with it afterward. They estimated it would take them four weeks, and that they would thus have the job wrapped up by the middle of July. Had it not been for Wagner taking a trip to Hollywood in the last week of June, they may very well have accomplished this. Wagner had been obliged to take the trip north for the purpose of making a formal reentry into Mexico, after having his status changed in the United States so as to bring his presence in Mexico in line with the labor laws designed to protect Mexican workers from being ousted by foreigners. These rules did not affect Steinbeck since he was not, unlike Wagner, receiving a salary for the work he was doing on the movie. Wagner expected the business to take about a week to complete in Hollywood, and they agreed that during his absence Steinbeck would soldier on alone with the preparation of the script.

At the time Wagner departed, they had seen nothing of Fernandez for over three weeks. They anticipated still being able to start filming in August, provided always that *Pepita* kept to its last adjusted schedule and a current threat of strikes in the industry did not materialize.

The cards, however, seemed to be stacked against them. Steinbeck was again being troubled with dysentery, and this time Gwyn too was affected. They had both suffered from what they thought was a bout of food poisoning earlier in the month, and this had progressively worsened, both of them losing weight and energy. Even the mere act of standing up caused Steinbeck to sweat. Eventually, they were forced to consult a doctor. No amoebic infection was detected, but they were told they were both suffering from severe gastroenteritis. They were given treatment and put on a diet. As if that were not enough, Willie was stolen. The dog was not recovered until, over a week later, the thieves contacted them and a reward was paid for his return. To add even further to their problems, Jack Wagner reported from Los Angeles that he had become entangled in a web of red tape and that his return to Mexico was going to be delayed. It was almost a month before he obtained the necessary clearances. Then, to cap it all, in the last two weeks of July, Webster Street and his wife arrived for a ten-day visit.

In Wagner's absence, Steinbeck found work on the shooting script not made any easier by the chronic lack of facilities. The Mexican company, Aguila Films, which would be making the film, was operated from an office in Mexico City by producer Oscar Dancigers, with a total production staff consisting of himself and two assistants. Dancigers was unable to provide Steinbeck with a stenographer, or even with a typewriter. Wagner had been gone for less than a week before Steinbeck began expressing his extreme irritation over the way in which he was expected to work, and frustration at the delay in getting the picture started. As he told Katz at the beginning of July:

There are rumors of trouble in the pic industry. If that comes to a head I will clear out. Oscar also couldn't get me a dictaphone. I had to borrow one. I wonder whether he will be able to supply sandwiches. We're getting pretty bad cabin fever. We sit down here while they fart around with Pepita, which from all I can hear is pretty bad. But you know the story. A young priest walking in the woods and praying to get rid of an erection instead of taking the simple way out. Ten reels of that. But they say it is a classic of Spanish literature. Emilio hates it. And the actors are fighting each other pretty badly. . . . There's going to be trouble. Twice Indio has tried to get out of it. (JS/Katz c.7/5/45)[22]

In all probability it was only his conviction that Fernandez was a filmmaker of genius and would do a magnificent job of directing *The Pearl* that kept him from packing his bags and leaving Mexico there and then. He was becoming impossibly bored with working on the shooting script, reducing the emotion of his story into a series of explicit camera shots. He declared that he would never again agree to do another shooting script. It was not his kind of work at all—"this moving a camera around from place to place" (JS/ERO 7/9/45). He referred to it as "plumber's work" (JS/ALW 7/12/45).

For all that, when he was approached by another company calling itself Pan-American Films with the proposal that he might consider writing a script for a movie dealing with the life of Emiliano Zapata, he thought it perhaps too good an opportunity to be missed, and wrote to Annie Laurie Williams, informing her of the project. While telling her that he would very much like to do such a film, he made it clear that he was not prepared to commit himself until *The Pearl* was completed. Indeed, he indicated that it might be fifteen months or more before he was free to begin work on the Zapata film, for work on *The Wayward Bus* would also have to take precedence. Aware that there were still men in high places who had been involved in Zapata's downfall and assassination, he stressed that if he did embark on the project he would require cast-iron assurances that there would be no governmental interference in the making of the film. Furthermore, he would consider doing the film only on the under-standing that Fernandez would be directing it. As a final matter, remem-bering what the studios had done to *Lifeboat* and *A Medal for Benny*, he again stipulated that the terms should provide for his retention of the right to withdraw from the production and have all mention of his con-nection with it also withdrawn if he found himself dissatisfied with the veracity of the picture. Although he did, with some assistance from Gwyn, carry out certain initial research on Zapata's life (see *Adventures* 570), he did not enter into any specific undertaking to do the movie.[23]

Early in July, he received news from Elizabeth Otis of yet another possible project. The *New York Herald Tribune* had floated the idea that he should cover the war crime trials of the Nazi leaders in Nuremburg.

His first reaction was to accept. Gwyn, too, thought he should go. "It's a little like finishing the story," he admitted to his agent, "and this time without censorship. I saw what these men did when they were in power, I'd like to see their finish" (JS/ERO 7/9/45). He even toyed with the suggestion, providing that Gwyn could accompany him to Germany, that he should, after the trials were over, travel with her through Denmark, Sweden, Norway, and Russia, and send back dispatches from each country reporting on how its people were coping in the postwar world. But there was, of course, no way he could go. Apart from anything else, he was determined to see *The Pearl* through to the bitter end, even through the cutting room. Although he advised Elizabeth Otis to inform the paper he would not be free from his Mexican commitments until October, he knew that even this was unlikely.

10

It was not simply the schedule of work still to be done on *The Pearl* that was the cause of his turning down the newspaper assignment. *The Pearl* was simply the excuse. The real reason was his anxiety not to have anything else stand in the way of his starting work on *The Wayward Bus*, a book that, as he had told Elizabeth Otis, was to be "quite different not only from the Pearl but from anything I have ever done" (JS/ERO 5/22/45).

In Covici's opinion, Steinbeck should have been devoting his time to the new novel rather than puttering around on the continually delayed movie. Understandably, he felt impatient with the author for involving himself yet again in projects that were constantly diverting him from his true role as a novelist. So far as Covici was concerned, Steinbeck, in writing *The Pearl*, had produced a beautiful and brilliant piece of fiction and should have left it at that: let someone else — someone he nevertheless implicitly trusted — to see the movie through to fruition.

Above everything else, Covici and Viking were naturally eager for Steinbeck's name to be kept before the reading public, while agreeing that it would not be propitious to publish *The Pearl* at that time. They had it in mind that, in everybody's interest, it would be probably more advantageous to wait and bring the book out to coincide with the release of the movie. There was no question that a longer book — as *The Wayward Bus* was obviously shaping up to be — was needed to break the run of short books. In an attempt to encourage Steinbeck to leave Mexico, Covici offered him the same facilities he had enjoyed while writing *Cannery Row* by putting a room at the Viking offices at his disposal for as long as took to complete the book.

In the meantime, it was proposed to schedule for early publication after the New Year a revised edition of *The Portable Steinbeck*, dropping one of the three episodes from *Sea of Cortez* included in the 1943 edition, and adding the short story "How Edith McGillcuddy Met R. L. S.," five war dispatches from the *New York Herald Tribune*, and Chapters 13 and 15 ("Frog Hunt") from *Cannery Row*. Covici asked Lewis Gannett to write a long biographical and critical introduction to the new collection. With the additional material, the volume would, with the exception of any extracts from *Cup of Gold* and *To a God Unknown*, present to the reading public (and the critics) a concise overview of the Steinbeck canon to date. Steinbeck surely welcomed the inclusion of a lengthy extract from *Cannery Row*. He had been somewhat disturbed by the manner in which the magazine *Coronet* had edited his text for a condensed version of the novel, cramming it into a mere sixteen and a half of the small double-column pages of its June issue. As he commented to Covici: "I've heard a lot of discontented talk about the job of cutting Coronet did on Cannery Row." Then he added with some satisfaction, recalling the treatment the book had suffered at the hands of the critics at the beginning of the year: "That's a funny book. It is attracting its devotees who defend it like a religion and take it very seriously" (JS/PC 7/10/45).

During the weeks since he had left the West Coast, his bitter feelings toward Monterey had not decreased, in fact, if anything, they had deepened. He had decided to sell the Soto House, the house he had purchased with such high expectations of having found the perfect, permanent place to set down his roots again. It was arranged that Webster Street would dispose of the property and oversee the removal and storage of its contents. He still felt so badly about the way he had been treated by the people of Monterey that he did not want to return there even for the purpose of supervising the operation himself.

He was again aware that in many ways his career was possibly at another crossroads. "I don't have the sense of rush I used to," he wrote Covici at the time he was briefly contemplating acceptance of the *New York Herald Tribune* proposal to send him to Nuremburg:

In fact sometimes I seem to be waiting maybe for a design or a shadow or something to indicate a future. I don't know what it will be. I know the lines are down but the accidental historical direction is not sketched yet and no party line or theory is likely to give us the direction. Everything takes so long and I want to see everything and then I want to think about it and there doesn't seem to be the time for all of that. That's where a reporter has the edge. He doesn't have to think about it and let the pieces fall into place. He just has to set it down. (JS/PC 7/12/45)

Gwyn's medical condition was showing little signs of improvement. He became very concerned about her, and ruled that she, taking Thom and

Miss Diehl with her, should fly to New York to seek further medical advice and receive whatever hospital treatment might be deemed necessary. She left with Thom and the nurse on the last day of July, shortly after the Streets returned home to California, and two days before Thom's first birthday.

11

Once they had left, Steinbeck felt desolate, worried sick about Gwyn's state of health, and incidentally not a little concerned about his own. He was also upset that he would not be with his son on his birthday. At least Max Wagner had returned at last from Los Angeles, and, as a temporary measure, the two of them moved into the Hotel Marik, leaving Victor in charge of the house and Willie, although they still returned to the house from time to time each day to work on the script. This new arrangement meant that Steinbeck would be on the spot if any message came through from Gwyn. He occupied a ground-floor room in the hotel, overlooking the garden and swimming pool. Thom's birthday was suitably celebrated on one of their visits to the house. A small but enthusiastic group of friends and neighbors was invited and there was much drinking and many loud and near-lethal fireworks were set off in Thom's honor.

Some of Steinbeck's cares were dissipated when he received Gwyn's telegram informing him of her safe arrival in New York, and the subsequent news that she had entered the hospital and was undergoing tests. His attempts to telephone her were unsuccessful. In his letters, he kept her fully up-to-date with all that was happening, although to begin with almost nothing was happening. All he could give her were snippets of local gossip and report how well Victor was looking after Willie, taking great pride in keeping the dog's coat well-groomed. Willie was, Steinbeck opined, beginning to look like a show dog.

There continued to be no hard news from either Fernandez or Dancigers as to how near *Pepita* was to completion. The stage had been reached where it was essential to have Fernandez's active collaboration on the shooting script. Steinbeck, indeed, had again convinced himself that there was not the slightest chance of *The Pearl* ever being made. He was now on a very short fuse indeed, ready at the slightest excuse to walk out on the whole business and be where he felt he should be — with Gwyn and Thom in New York, and writing *The Wayward Bus*. An imminent visit from Peter Rathvon, RKO's president, from Los Angeles was, however, expected. "We'll maybe have a few things out in the open then," Steinbeck wrote Gwyn. "I'm tired of the skulking. And I'm not going to be away from you unless I am very sure we've got a picture and right now I'm not sure we have. But I'll know soon" (JS/GS 8/4/45).

In fact, he discovered the following day, when at last he managed to make telephone contact with someone at the Aguila Films office in Mexico City, that Fernandez had finished shooting *Pepita* two days earlier. On the other hand, no one he spoke to at the office seemed to know of the elusive director's whereabouts. Steinbeck did at least extract an assurance that Fernandez would be left in no doubt that he and Wagner were waiting for him to put in an appearance. Steinbeck made up his mind at that point that he would wait only two more days for some firm news to come through, then, if nothing happened, he would send a message to Dancigers that the end of the road had been reached and that he was leaving the country. Later that day, Dancigers telephoned to report that Fernandez was already on his way to Cuernavaca.

The director turned up the following day, and the three of them were finally able to begin concentrated work on the definitive version of the shooting script. Steinbeck and Wagner decided that it would be more convenient, now that Fernandez had joined them, to work in the hotel. The three-way collaboration began with an altercation. On the very first day, Fernandez took five hours for lunch. By the time he eventually showed up again, Steinbeck was ready to explode and threatened to catch the next plane to New York. Fernandez was suitably contrite, and promised it would not happen again. He kept his word, and from that time on the work proceeded amicably and at an incredible pace, Steinbeck writing and rewriting dialogue, and Fernandez and Wagner working on the storyboard and fixing camera angles and cuts. They all worked "like fiends," often from seven-thirty in the morning through until quite late in the evening. By 10 August, they had finished the new drinking scene that had been introduced to follow Kino's discovery of the great pearl. They estimated that at the rate they were going they should have the whole script completed within two weeks.

The previous day, the news broke that Japan had sued for peace after the dropping of the second atomic bomb on Nagasaki. "I can't get it yet," Steinbeck confessed to Gwyn.

My stomach is all upside down and churning. Jesus I don't feel like getting drunk at these things. I feel more tearful than anything else. There will be terrific changes in everything now. And what a scramble. By the time you get this it will be old news. (JS/GS 8/9/45)

On that day, they wrote thirty-five scenes. In the evening, he received a wire from Mildred Lyman, telling him that the hospital had diagnosed Gwyn's illness: It was, after all, amoebic dysentery. He wrote Gwyn a commiserating but encouraging letter early the next morning. He had been up since four o'clock in order to finish a scene before he, Wagner, and Fernandez traveled to Mexico City to attend a party, where they were to meet Rathvon for the first time and confer with him and the local RKO representative, George Whittaker.

The party was a success and both Rathvon and Whittaker seemed pleased at the way everything was going. The only cloud on the horizon was an ongoing distributors' strike, which from all accounts was going to be a hard one to crack. However, they all agreed that it was a matter that did not greatly concern them at this stage—it was to be hoped that by the time the shooting of the movie was completed the strike would be over. The party went on into the small hours. Dancigers had booked Steinbeck into a hotel, but it was after three o'clock before he eventually checked in, only to be told that his room had been given to someone else. The receptionist even denied that any room had been reserved for him. He decided it was too late to bother seeking alternative accommodation, roamed around the silent city until seven, then attended mass in a little church where the congregation was composed entirely of servants on their way to work. By the time he returned to Cuernavaca he was very tired indeed, and he discovered moreover—most probably as a direct result of the partying—that he had been unduly optimistic in boasting to Gwyn that his own stomach problems had cleared up.

By 14 August, the day of the Japanese surrender and the official ending of World War II, work had started on the chase sequence of the script. He reported to Covici that once the script was finished they would be going to Mexico City again for the casting of the picture, and then on to Acapulco to begin filming. He was content now that he and Fernandez were working so well together, but he was also anxious to begin writing *The Wayward Bus*. "I think Pat it might be the long serious book we have talked about only it won't be in necessarily serious terms. I want to have fun and be happy while I'm doing it" (JS/PC 8/15/45).

While work continued to go well on the script, it did nevertheless slow up for a while to enable Fernandez to make occasional trips to the capital to supervise the editing of *Pepita*. Both he and Dancigers were in a happier frame of mind now that the emotional stress of completing that picture had been virtually lifted. On the other hand, it would be true to say that in normal circumstances Fernandez could have expected a short rest before plunging into work on *The Pearl*. Steinbeck's impatience and understandable demands had made such respite impossible. Fernandez's unbelievable energy, however, saw him through, and, after the initial contretemps with Steinbeck, it was he who set the pace and, by so doing, was in real danger of running his collaborators out of steam. "The work slowed the last couple of days," Steinbeck admitted to Gwyn on 17 August "just as long hours but not as many scenes. Maybe we are getting tired" (JS/GS 8/17/45). Fernandez had gone back to Mexico City the previous night to work on *Pepita* and was expected back later that day. The following day, a Sunday, they completed nearly sixty scenes. "We're going like hell on the story and I am a little pooped but not completely. We'll finish my part in a few days now, and I think good" (JS/GS 8/18/45).

He planned to take a break from the grind and go hunting near Tampico in two weeks' time. His stomach had settled down again, but he still lacked a certain energy. He asked Gwyn to get in touch with the *New York Herald Tribune* and advise them that he had definitely decided not to take up the war trials assignment, but that he would, as he had previously suggested, still be interested sometime in touring Europe and reporting on the postwar Continental scene.[24] He was feeling very lonely without her and Thom. There was a void that not even participation in the nightly social gathering on the hotel porch could fill. The news that Webster Street had taken the first steps toward putting the Soto House on the market did nothing for his sense of restlessness and isolation. He was very conscious of the fact that shortly he would be without any fixed home base.

The best news to come through was that Gwyn was making a good recovery in the hospital. He spoke to her by phone on 19 August and was reassured by her obvious cheerfulness. The hope that she might soon be able to rejoin him in Mexico buoyed up his flagging spirits for a while, but he told her he did not want her to contemplate the journey if this was to be at the expense of her health. If she could not come to him, he would join her in New York for a few weeks once the actual production of the movie was under way. His main concern was that he should be in the studio for the editing. There was some talk of George Frazier and his wife giving up their New York apartment, and he suggested to Gwyn that she might explore the possibility of their taking over the apartment when the Fraziers moved out. By this time, in the face of Covici's misgivings, it had been agreed that Frazier should be given a crack at producing some sort of commercially viable script from the *Wizard* synopsis.

That day, the 19th, Steinbeck, Fernandez, and Wagner worked on the shooting script most of the time at the house, having apparently found too many distractions at the hotel, where everyone seemed to be in the throes of an extended celebratory mood following the ending of the war. They managed to complete a great deal of work, including five entirely new scenes. "It seems to be going very well," he reported to Gwyn,

but the bottom is dropping out of my disposition and for no reason. ... We came in to eat at the hotel and afterwards we'll work a few more hours, then home and to bed, and I'll be a little tired and woozy. Saturday Peter Rathvon asked us up for a conference. I'm pretty sure we'll get some kind of action. Meanwhile if the work should go as well as it has today, I shall be very happy about both its speed and its quality. (JS/GS 8/19/45)

The next day, he wrote the dialogue for two scenes and, with these done, his part in the preparation of the script was concluded, apart from a measure of "filling-in," as he called it.

Three days later, the script was finished, and the three of them moved to the capital to finalize casting arrangements and to attend to other preproduction matters. Steinbeck closed up the house in Cuernavaca. Dancigers had found an apartment for the two Americans, but they never moved in, for at the last moment they discovered that the owner would allow no dogs on the premises. So while Victor took Willie with him to stay with his mother, Steinbeck and Wagner took a hotel room for a few days, in the hope of finding an alternative apartment. "Mexico City is just the same only more so and I am tired of it," Steinbeck told Gwyn (JS/GS 8/26/45). He had abandoned the idea of going to Tampico and now had only thoughts of flying to New York for a couple of weeks to be with her and Thom. Gwyn had left the hospital on 22 August, and he received a letter from Covici counseling him not to allow her to return south to join him. Three weeks later, having satisfied himself that filming was safely in progress, and leaving Wagner to keep an eye on things, he took the plane to New York. He spent more than a month there.

He took the opportunity to confer with Annie Laurie Williams and Katz and his partner about the possible production of *The Wizard of Maine*, but, according to Frazier, it was almost impossible to persuade him to work on the playscript in even the most uncommitted manner. While quite willing to offer suggestions, he seemed to draw the line at involving himself in any actual work on the piece. His attitude was very much to treat the whole project as a sort of pastime. Even Covici's proddings drew only a negative response from him. Frazier was particularly aggrieved at his attitude, for he had put his job with *Life* on the line in order to devote himself full-time to the playscript. In fact, Frazier did eventually lose his job. Steinbeck, when told of this, expressed sorrow that Frazier had been sacked, but went on to point out that *Life* had lost John Hersey in similar circumstances, and he predicted that in the long run Frazier would not regret what had happened. To Steinbeck's way of thinking, anyone who severed ties with the hated Luce organization was to be congratulated.[25]

By mid-October, Steinbeck was back in Mexico with Fernandez and Wagner on location in Acapulco. He had left Gwyn behind in New York, with the understanding that she would join him later in the month. The heat in Acapulco was insufferable, but he was enormously pleased with the way the filming was going. He saw the first rushes on 20 October. "They look beautiful," he reported to Gwyn.

> Too many long walking shots but that is for cutting. No dialogue in yet. Then last night we helped the crew celebrate the 12th anniversary of the forming of

the syndicate. It was quite a brawl, ending with guitars and complaints from many guests of the hotel. It was a lovely night. Full moon. ... Heard the Banda Sinfonica de los Chiles Refritos this morning. They are more wonderful than ever. (JS/GS 10/21/45)

The "Banda Sinfoncia de los Chiles Refritos" was the nickname Steinbeck and Gwyn had given the Mexican musical group they had come across some months earlier. The musicians were so bad that Steinbeck had hit on the happy idea of using them in the film to give authentic color to the village scenes. The leader of the little group had some strange ideas about musical theory, explaining one day to Steinbeck that all music was "all the same except for the twiddleys on the edges" (JS/GS 10/22/45). The musicians, however, began to take their playing too seriously and became so good that Steinbeck changed his mind and decided he did not want them after all. But they redeemed themselves unwittingly a few days later when, the evening before they were to be recorded for the sound track, they all went to a party, got well and truly drunk, and played all through the night. By the time they came to do the recording they were "their old dear selves." Steinbeck commented: "They couldn't tell a note from a hole in the ground and I think it is going to be wonderful" (JS/GS 10/24/45)

He continued to suffer from the heat. The glare of the sun was giving him headaches and he invested in a pair of dark sun glasses. He was so badly bitten by mosquitoes on his hands that it became difficult for him to write. The bites eventually became infected and he had to take a course of sulpha to clear the infection. His neck was also giving some discomfort and pain — a legacy from the injuries he had suffered at Salerno two years before — and he was unable to obtain proper medication. Fernandez's brother, a fireman, offered to give him massages, but they, perhaps not surprisingly, did not seem to do much good.

Gwyn flew down to Mexico City at the end of October. She was pregnant again, the baby due in June. Steinbeck, thankful for the excuse to escape the coastal heat, joined her in the capital, and they returned to Cuernavaca. The food he had been eating in Acapulco, like the sun, had not agreed with him. He had convinced himself that he had contracted scurvy, or something similar, and was taking vitamins in the hope of regaining his strength. "It was pretty awful down there," he wrote Annie Laurie Williams. "And here it is wonderful. I'll get some rest" (JS/ALW 11/6/45). He was once again tired and disillusioned with the whole business of film-making. He told Covici: "The picture is coming well I guess. I just don't like pictures. I hope this is the last one I get intimately mixed up in" (JS/PC 11/15/45).

Early in November, Covici sent him a newspaper clipping that listed his name among four candidates being considered for the 1945 Nobel Prize for Literature, the other three being Jules Romains, C. F. Ramuz, and Gabriella Mistral. No awards had been made for 1940 through 1943 because of the war. Although Steinbeck might reasonably have hoped to receive the award in 1944 for *The Moon Is Down* by virtue of the high esteem in which it was held in the Scandinavian countries and by resistance fighters in the occupied countries, the Danish novelist Johannes Vilhelm Jensen had been chosen as that year's Nobel Laureate. While Steinbeck had tended always in the past to belittle the Nobel Prize, he nevertheless admitted to Covici that it was the only literary prize he would like to have.[26] He added that he did not think he would get it, however, predicting that the prize would go to the French novelist Jules Romains. A few days later, it was announced that the Chilean poet and educator Gabriela Mistral had been awarded the prize. In a consoling letter on 20 November, Covici ventured his own prediction that Steinbeck was certain to win the prize within the next three years.[27]

Gwyn stayed for three weeks only, before returning to New York by air, flying first to the West Coast to see her mother and Webster Street. While in Monterey, she took time out to settle up affairs with regard to the disposal of the Soto House.

Once more on his own, Steinbeck became more and more frustrated with every small delay preventing the completion of the film on schedule. He had vowed to remain in Mexico until such time as the editing had been carried out to his satisfaction, but his general low state of health and morale, coupled with his itch to be back in New York with his wife and son, brought about a change of mind.

Since arriving back in Mexico, he had purchased a secondhand automobile, which he had christened "Blue Baby." He gave Victor driving lessons, and early in December he and Victor and Willie drove from Mexico all the way to New York. The car was of extremely uncertain reliability and, even though it had ostensibly undergone a thorough overall before they set out, it broke down before they had gone even a hundred kilometers. They had to coax it along for nearly two thousand miles before they were able to find someone with the capability of carrying out effective repairs. The whole journey was a disaster. It was bitterly cold, snow lay on the ground, and at times Steinbeck must have doubted if they and the car would reach New York in one piece. But they did, and by the middle of the month he had joined Gwyn and Thom in a furnished apartment on East 37th Street.

They spent Christmas among friends and anticipated the first year of peace. As Steinbeck had told his editor a month or so before: "I am looking forward to such a good year of work and pleasure. Hope it may be so. I don't think I will be deflected again" (JS/PC 11/15/45). He was determined that just as soon as the seasonal festivities were out of the way he would commence serious work on *The Wayward Bus*, the book that had, in so many respects, become of overriding importance to him and on which so many of his hopes were now centered.

9

The Bus That Failed

1

As Steinbeck had intimated to Covici, he was determined that with the coming of the new year he would allow nothing to interrupt the work he had planned on *The Wayward Bus*. Once he arrived in New York, he effectively closed his mind to the fact that he had left behind in Mexico City much work undone; work he had always insisted he must carry out personally. He was just as ruthless in his attitude toward *The Wizard of Maine*, for despite the fact that Frazier and all the other interested parties were making loud noises that he should involve himself more actively in bringing the musical comedy to fruition, he had already decided in his own mind that the work no longer played any role in his future plans. As he was to tell Street in mid-March, after he had finally killed the project: "I didn't like it and didn't know what was the matter with me. I thought I just had a continual stomach ache from something else, but that was it" (*Adventures* 576–77).

He and Gwyn continued living in the rented apartment on East 37th Street, while a house they had purchased on East 78th Street was being remodeled for them. They were still living in this temporary accommodation when, in mid-February, he received a disturbing "progress report" from Fernandez. The director's letter made it clear to him that work on the movie had ground almost to a standstill. Matters at the studio were apparently in a parlous state. Fernandez and Dancigers had quarreled and were no longer talking to each other. There were fundamental differences of opinion as to how the picture should be edited and what music should be used. Fernandez warned Steinbeck that unless he came back to Mexico City to help defend their picture everything they had worked for together would be lost.

The letter could not have come at a worse time. Gwyn was by then five months pregnant and going through a very difficult period directly stemming from her illness of the previous year. Not only would he not consider for a moment leaving her at this juncture, but he was now far too preoccupied with the writing of *The Wayward Bus*. The book was not going well. By the end of January, he had been forced to throw out twenty thousand words and begin again. Determined that all his creative thoughts and energies should be concentrated on the novel, he told Fernandez he was sorry but there was no possibility of his returning to Mexico at this time.

The move into the new house was effected shortly afterward. Taking over a room in the basement, he worked doggedly on his manuscript throughout the spring and early summer. The baby—a second son, John Steinbeck IV—was born on 12 June 1946. By the next month, he realized that it had obviously become imperative for him to set aside temporarily *The Wayward Bus* and go down to Mexico City to see what could be done to sort out the mess there. The deciding factor, so far as he was concerned, had been a recording Dancigers had sent him of the music for *The Pearl*. He expressed his opinion of it very forcibly in a telegram to the producer: "This music is the poorest, weakest, most undistinguished faeces I have ever heard. Suggest you go back to Dominguez themes or send picture here to be scored. This is disgraceful" (JS/Dancigers 7/15/46). A fortnight later he was in Mexico City. He reported back to Gwyn that nothing had changed:

> Emilio is out of town, Oscar is feeling terrible. I am going to see the Pearl today. There has been a campaign against it among the local press as well as a whispering campaign. ... The film has not been finished in cutting. I'm going to rush it through. ... Jack did the narration and it isn't good. I'll do it myself. ... Without having seen the picture—I don't think there is anything insuperable about this nor do I think it will take me long. (JS/GS 7/30/46)

In fact, it took him nearly a month to sort it all out. By that stage, the best he could do, particularly as his heart was not really in the job, was to paper over the cracks, reconcile differences, and ultimately once more leave someone else to put the finishing touches on the work.

The film was not released by RKO until mid-February 1948, opening at a small art house, the Sutton Theater, in New York. Some kudos were claimed for the picture as the first Mexican film to receive first-run release in the United States. On the whole, the critics were not impressed, although most remarked favorably on the beauty of the photography and the landscape. "[T]he finely filtered cameras of Director Emilio Fernandez have filmed an arresting drama of man struggling against inevitable fate," wrote Bosley Crowther. "Photographing in vivid outdoor settings against the sea, the mountains, and the sky and at a rhythm in movement and rhetoric that conveys the legendary idea, he has caught precisely the quality of the story's simplicity and strength."[1] It was, however, the preciseness and simplicity of the acting of the main characters that drew forth adverse comment from other critics, such as Robert Hatch. "The way they interpret roles pitched at a level just above aborigine is to move very slowly, to look bewildered and to strike picturesque attitudes," Hatch wrote in the *New Republic*. "The effect is less simple than simple-minded."[2] *Time*, inevitably it seems, printed arguably the most savage review of all, declaring that "too often the film's makers confused genuine artistry (which requires a clear, tough sense of reality) with the woozily 'artistic'."[3]

It is, of course, not difficult to diagnose what had gone wrong. The conflict between an excess of ingrained Mexican artistry and Hollywood commercialism had produced the worst of all possible worlds. No matter what he may have wished to believe while he was in Mexico, Steinbeck had not exercised anything like effective control over his material, although it is extremely arguable if this failure on his part was indeed a vital factor in the overall failure of the film. Admirers of Steinbeck's novella would have noted, as Charles R. Metzger has pointed out, the omission of two important characters from the book: the priest and Kino's elder brother, Juan Tomas. These admirers would also have been distracted by the uncharacteristic handsomeness and beauty of the film's Kino and Juana, as well as by their well-fed and well-clothed appearance. They would also have been disturbed by the unnecessary interpolation of the fiesta and drinking scenes, clearly inserted (incidentally by Steinbeck himself) to give some contrast to and relief from the somber main action of the story and perhaps also as an excuse to capture the "Banda de los Chiles Refritos" on film. Metzger's fine exposition of the movie reveals just how much Steinbeck's simple but striking fable in *Sea of Cortez*, already diluted by its treatment in the novella, was further weakened by the additional material introduced in the movie.[4] This is also exactly the point subsequently made by Joseph R. Millichap. Millichap detects the influence of RKO in understandably tailoring the movie for American audiences, charging that "the director's cinematic pretensions and the producer's commercial compromises confused its purposes, converting the movie into little more than a curiosity of Mexican studio production."[5]

It cannot be denied that Steinbeck must himself share a large part of the responsibility for the disastrous way the film turned out. He was, after all, very closely involved in the writing of the shooting script, was present at much of the actual shooting on location in Acapulco, and pronounced himself extremely pleased when he saw the rushes. To what extent he was ultimately involved in or responsible for the editing while he was in Mexico during the summer of 1946 is unclear, but what is certain is that he did not see the process through to the bitter end. If on-the-spot decisions were made without his knowledge or approval then he had only himself to blame. When, just prior to the movie's United States release, he viewed it again, he was, according to Gwyn, aghast at the excruciating slow pace of it all (*Adventures* 629).

2

Viking Press published the novella version of *The Pearl* in November 1947, in time to catch the last-minute Christmas trade and as a tie-in with the forthcoming New York opening of the movie.

There was a sharp divergence of opinion between those reviewers who, like Orville Prescott, thought it "much the best book which Mr. Steinbeck has written since *The Red Pony* and *The Grapes of Wrath*,"[6] and John Farrelly who found only "a lackluster, almost iambic, prose, which suggests, more than anything else, the boredom of the writer."[7] While the *New Yorker* critic saw "the distinction and sincerity that are evident in everything [Steinbeck] writes,"[8] Maxwell Geismar considered that the book "raises some serious questions about almost all Steinbeck's recent books and his work as a whole," and ended his longish critique in the *Saturday Review* with a statement that seemed both a warning and an admonishment to the author, and an attempt to place Steinbeck's waning critical reputation into some sort of perspective:

> The most important point in Steinbeck's earlier career was the change, around 1935, from such pagan excursions as *To a God Unknown* or *Tortilla Flat* to the novels of social criticism, *In Dubious Battle* and *The Grapes of Wrath*. It is interesting to speculate on the reasons why Steinbeck has now returned to this earlier and less satisfactory vein of his work. And, without stressing the fact that our national history did not end with the Second World War, one would like to remind this gifted and volatile American novelist that his recent works do mark a sort of reversionary tendency in his career.
>
> One might say that the artist, too, must discover and cherish his own pearl — he cannot reject it for a state of false innocence.[9]

3

Chronological parameters arbitrarily imposed are seldom convenient finite boundaries. Such is the case here. As a prelude to this survey of Steinbeck's life and work during the period 1939—45, it was appropriate to touch briefly on the circumstances relating to the writing of *The Grapes of Wrath* in 1938 before considering the ramifications of the critical and popular response to that book when it appeared in the spring of 1939. In the same way as it has been appropriate to consider the 1947 critical response to the novella *The Pearl*, the last of Steinbeck's works to have been completed during the relevant period, so it is also appropriate to touch briefly on the circumstances relating to the writing of the full-length novel that first germinated in the author's imagination as *El Camion Vacilador* in the spring of 1945 and postdated *The Pearl* in composition, together with the critical response to it when it was published in February 1947, nine months prior to the appearance of the novella.

If Steinbeck had hoped that *The Wayward Bus* would restore him in the eyes of his peers as a writer of substance, he must surely have been shaken to the core by the ferocity with which so many critical piranhas did their level best to strip the remaining vestiges of flesh from his literary reputation. While most critics praised the quality of the prose and welcomed the return of the striking descriptive passages — so conspicuously absent from both *The Moon Is Down* and *Cannery Row* — evoking the bucolic beauty of the California landscape, the reviews were, as Benson has noted, "better called 'contradictory,' rather than 'mixed'" (*Adventures* 593). Some critics were by no means circumspect in expressing their opinions, calling the book "trite and meaningless," "tedious," "insignificant," "familiar, flat and trivial . . . sordid, petty, and vulgar."[10]

Writing in the *New York Times Book Review*, J. Donald Adams put his finger perceptively on the crux of the matter when, at the same time as expressing his admiration for the descriptive and storytelling powers Steinbeck displayed in the book, he wondered if there was in the work as a whole "a wide gap between [Steinbeck's] intention and accomplishment."[11] Undoubtedly, the novel had not been an easy book for Steinbeck to write. There had, in addition, been too many distractions, not the least being the move into the new house, the vexatious and time-consuming interruptions connected with the completion of *The Pearl* movie, and Gwyn's ill health and increasing demands for his attention prior to and following the birth of their second son. With his publishers pressing him for the delivery of the new work, Steinbeck had hurried the writing of the later chapters, then realized that the whole text needed radical revision before he could consider releasing it for publication. According to one of Steinbeck's biographers, he was, however, persuaded otherwise by Covici. Steinbeck was subsequently to regret that he had failed to veto the too-hasty publication. Ten years or so later, he openly admitted that the book had been "a paste-up job" and that he "should never have let it go out the way it did."[12] As one critic put it: "The publication of this latest work of Steinbeck does raise a very grave question: why do so many of our serious American writers deteriorate?"[13] In his withering review in the *New York Times*, Orville Prescott pondered on the possibility that Steinbeck was in fact merely "a one-book author whose reputation has been so inflated that it has intimidated critics and readers alike into a mood of respectful admiration which his books do not deserve."[14]

These and similar judgments, coming as they did after the many indifferent and often antagonistic reviews that greeted *Cannery Row*, were not entirely expunged in the minds of the critical fraternity by the generally more favorable reviews accorded *The Pearl*. Indeed, it was from this point on, while the reading public remained faithful and appreciative, that a large and influential faction among critics tended to adopt a campaign to decry everything Steinbeck was to publish thereafter and to minimize his continuing artistic achievement: a campaign that became almost self-perpetuating and was, as we have seen, to reach its infamous peak with the announcement of the Nobel Prize award in 1962, shortly after the publication of his penultimate book, *Travels With Charley*.

Afterword

1

THE SEVEN YEARS 1939 THROUGH 1945 WERE, IN MANY RESPECTS, A PERIOD that was to determine the pattern of much that was too follow, both in terms of Steinbeck's creativity and of the critical reaction to his work. It was, too, a period that brought into being two novellas, *Cannery Row* and *The Pearl*; one play-novel, *The Moon Is Down*; the opening sections of another play-novel, *The God in the Pipes*; two full-length works of nonfiction, *Sea of Cortez* and *Bombs Away*; at least eighty-five war dispatches for the *New York Herald Tribune*; a large number of film synopses, scenarios, and shooting scripts, *The Forgotten Village*, *The Red Pony*, *Lifeboat*, *The Pearl*, as well as various assorted unfinished film work for the Army; an untold multitude of articles and broadcast talks for the FIS, OWI, and other government propaganda agencies, and several drafts for presidential speeches.

Overall, it may seem a most impressive output, but a large proportion of the work was of inferior quality, ephemeral in content, its provenance dictated more by outside influence than by Steinbeck's own creative impulses. While in terms of creativity the period was one that did not begin until 1940 with the writing of the aborted *The God in the Pipes* and ended with the writing of the ultimately unrealized *The Wizard of Maine*, in publishing terms the period opened with the appearance of one master-piece, *The Grapes of Wrath*, and concluded with the appearance of another masterpiece, *Cannery Row*, the latter book marking the first manifestation in print of the "new form" Steinbeck mentioned to Street in 1939. If *Cannery Row*, by way of the unfinished and unpublished experimental *The God in the Pipes*, can be seen as providing the direct link between *The Grapes of Wrath* and Steinbeck's postwar work, then, regarded solely in that light, the intervening wartime work can arguably be categorized as the product of a period of stasis in Steinbeck's develop-ment and logical progression of his career as a writer. One can therefore possibly speculate how Steinbeck's canon might now be viewed if there had not been the intervention of *The Moon Is Down*, *Bombs Away*, the war dispatches, *Lifeboat*, and *A Medal for Benny*. How different, we perhaps are entitled to ask ourselves, would Steinbeck's literary standing be today if those wartime works did not exist, and, even more to the point, if he had not drained so much of his creativity in writing them?

But the wartime works do, of course, exist and cannot be ignored. Both the work and the events of the war years — including *The Pearl*; all the work he did for the FIS, OWI, and the Army; his scientific research with Ricketts; and his various excursions into the world of movies — all contributed to make Steinbeck the writer he became during the postwar years, and in the same way that this is true so it is also true that everything that happened during the war years can be seen as flowing directly from the composition and publication of *The Grapes of Wrath*.

The Grapes of Wrath was an exceptional work, written in exceptional circumstances and published in exceptional circumstances: a novel composed at white-hot speed, rushed into print in what was virtually first-draft form, and immediately hailed as the masterpiece that it is by the majority of contemporary critics. It was a process and an outcome that could never be duplicated. *Cannery Row*, to be sure, was also published in what was virtually first-draft form, but that book, unlike *The Grapes of Wrath*, attracted little critical approval at the time it came out. The next book Steinbeck published, *The Wayward Bus*, was also rushed into print, but with the disastrous results related in the preceding chapter. It was neither critically acclaimed (far from it), nor was it the important work it might have been.

Steinbeck often referred to the Nobel Prize as an award that took the form of an epitaph on a writer's career and had noted that few writers so honored ever went on to write anything of worth after receiving it. If *The Grapes of Wrath* was a milestone in Steinbeck's career, then it was also, as it were, a sort of metaphorical tombstone that cast its shadow, so far as his critical reputation was concerned, over the subsequent works that were to come from his pen. He had always been aware of the danger. He had known success previously with *Tortilla Flat* and even more substantially with the novel and play versions of *Of Mice and Men*, but he had always somehow contrived, more or less successfully, to keep himself out of the public eye, insisting that he remain as far as possible the faceless author. Only by protecting his anonymity did he believe that any decent work would be produced. The publication of *The Grapes of Wrath*, however, finally catapulted him protesting into the public domain, and from then onward his public persona all too often seemed to become more important to many of the commentators of the day than did his writing.

The vilification was extreme. The adulation was extreme. But the adulation also evolved, at least so far as many critics were concerned, into a gathering antagonism. It all followed an age-old pattern. He whom the gods love, the gods destroy. *The Grapes of Wrath* was to be the pinnacle of Steinbeck's achievement, the triumphant curtain at the end of the first brilliant act of his literary career. F. Scott Fitzgerald, incidentally one of Steinbeck's most virulent detractors, had been ironically perceptive when among the notes for his unfinished novel, *The Last Tycoon*, he had suggested: "There are no second acts in American lives."[1] If that is admittedly not an absolute truth, there have not been many American writers who were able to surmount or even satisfy critical expectation during the second acts of their careers. So it proved in Steinbeck's case. While reader popularity continued unabated, critical acclaim in the coming years was to waver, flicker, and all but die.

The trend was set during the war years. In exactly the same way as, after *The Grapes of Wrath*, the critics had been expecting another massive, "proletarian," realistic novel and were given the short and, to their eyes, completely atypical *The Moon Is Down*, so, after the *New York Herald Tribune* dispatches, they had been expecting Steinbeck's great war novel and were nonplussed and angry when presented with the apparent inconsequential series of episodes that constituted what they saw as the lightweight, antisocial, and somewhat bawdy *Cannery Row*. Never has any important twentieth-century American work of fiction been so misunderstood and undervalued at the time of its publication. Only much, much later was its true quality appreciated and its success as a work of art duly acknowledged.

Steinbeck was never to write his great novel of the war. *The Moon Is Down* remains the only work of fiction with an explicit war theme he was ever to publish, and it has to be admitted that, as literature, it is a minor work. It brilliantly served its purpose during the war by extolling the courage of the patriots in the occupied countries of Europe and by helping to comfort and inspire those members of the Resistance fortunate enough to read clandestine copies of the book circulating under the noses of the Germans. If, as has already been noted, the distinguished Swiss critic and scholar Heinrich Straumann regarded *The Moon Is Down* as "the most powerful piece of propaganda ever written to help a small democratic country to resist totalitarian aggression and occupation," it is also arguable that it is only this particular aspect that constitutes the work's principal continuing claim to fame.

The Grapes of Wrath also marked a watershed in Steinbeck's career for being the last work in which Carol had a direct and significant involvement. Her assertion that when she first met Steinbeck he had been "a bad Donn Byrne," and that by the time of their separation she had made him "a good writer," is one that cannot be entirely discounted, although the extent of her influence on his writing is not always altogether easy to judge. While Carol was never directly responsible — as has been claimed or suggested by certain of Steinbeck's detractors — for any of the writings attributable to her husband, what is certain is that she *did* indeed have an influence on his achivements in the 1930s, the period during which, as most scholars would agree, he did his best work.[2]

Carol's role, however, was not that of a teacher as such, but rather that of advisor, initial editor, and sales promoter. Clearly, she did persuade him to abandon the rococo style of *Cup of Gold*, and, from *The Pastures of Heaven* onward, to write in that freer and more simple style which, with its subtle rhythms, distinguishes his best prose. Indeed, it would not be too fanciful to suggest that, on the whole, the advice she gave him was as important, if not more important, than any Covici gave him. The discipline she imposed on his writing, the honesty of her criticism, the instinctive appreciation of where perhaps he was going wrong, all stemming from her penetrating aesthetic awareness, were in complete contrast to Covici's sometimes over-the-top enthusiasms, stemming all too often, it seems, from a commendable desire to encourage, but also to a great extent, and understandably so, with commercial considerations in mind.

2

Steinbeck had more than once declared that all the work he produced before 1938 had been a preparation for the writing of *The Grapes of Wrath*. With that book written, he had been suddenly faced, for the moment at least and until he discovered the "new form" on which to center his creativity, with the fact that there was, so far as novel-writing was concerned, nowhere to go. His search for new beginnings, as has been seen, culminated in his embarking on *The God in the Pipes*, but that too, in its turn, proved at the time to be a dead end, an experiment that was unfortunately, or perhaps fortunately, not carried out with any consistency and eventually abandoned. There were, in addition to all the turmoil of his emotional life, too many diversifications arising from ill-conceived (in terms of his literary career) projects involving collaborations with others.

In later years, he was to declare that there are "no good collaborations" (*JN* 58), a belief he expanded in *East of Eden*:

> Our species is the only creative species, and it has only one creative instrument, the individual mind and spirit of a man. Nothing was ever created by two men. There are no good collaborations, whether in music, in art, in poetry, in mathematics, in philosophy. Once the miracle of creation has taken place, the group can build and extend it, but the group never invents anything. The preciousness lies in the lonely mind of a man. (*EE* 132)

Not everyone might agree unreservedly with that thesis, but that is the way it seemed to Steinbeck. He had certainly gained sufficient experience in the matter to speak with personal authority. The collaborations that are an essential prerequisite of filmmaking exerted an intermittent and malignant fascination over him, although he constantly griped about the restrictions they imposed upon him and the frustrations they engendered. During the period 1939−45, he frittered away (even though it did not always appear so then) too much of his time in the movie world and in making his services available to others in cinematic projects that did nothing to enhance his literary reputation — such as the assistance he gave to Lorentz and Chaplin, *The Forgotten Village*, the work he did for the OWI and the Army Air Force, *Lifeboat*, *A Medal for Benny*, and *The Pearl*, not forgetting, in another entertainment genre, *The Wizard of Maine*. He was, possibly in the worst sense, the inspired amateur when it came to filmmaking, and proved to have neither the expertise nor the long-staying temperament for such work. He should instead have been concentrating on pursuing his search, via *The God in the Pipes* and other experimental work, for his literary Grail. As it was, his love affair with the movies, his on-off fascination with the process of writing film scripts in which he described everything the camera would record and transfer to the screen, permeated his postwar fiction. Although the influence was by no means all bad, to the larger extent it gave rise to the accusation that he was writing with one eye on Hollywood.

Many of the projects of the war years, not only in filmmaking but in other areas as well, were the direct consequence of Steinbeck's intense patriotic zeal — and even that ironically was to be misunderstood and belittled by the many enemies he had in the establishment. Because of way in which he was obliged so often to write at the drop of a hat and in the most unpromising of conditions, and, more importantly, forced to relegate his own creative work to second place, his patriotism was also responsible for an overall deterioration of his prose style. All his wartime work during the years 1942 and 1943, the vast quantities of it that he produced during those two years, was written quickly and with a minimum of revision, if indeed there was any revision at all. Much of it was composed directly on a typewriter or into a dictaphone, bypassing that essential and mystical chemistry brought into play when pen or pencil touches paper and (particularly so in Steinbeck's case) is part and parcel of the whole mysterious process of creation. He was naturally aware of what was happening when he wrote the letter to Mildred Lyman in November 1942 bewailing the fact that any prose style he ever had had already gone to pieces.

The tragedy is that he was right. He never really regained his distinctive prewar prose style in his postwar work, other than here and there in such books as *The Wayward Bus* and *East of Eden*. Some indefinable element was almost invariably missing. When he was writing well, he was in a class of his own, but too often for comfort in the postwar work his prose tended to become somewhat wooden, and lose its immediacy and vitality. One cannot entirely brush aside the disparagements of the French critic Claude-Edmonde Magny concerning the "limited vocabulary" of many of Steinbeck's characters and the "scarcely more extensive vocabulary" present in narrative passages.[3]

Yet it would be as well to consider if the answer is the one Magny arbitrarily rejects — that Steinbeck in fact deliberately chose to employ a Racine-like "deliberate poverty" of vocabulary. The extreme simplicity of language was not, after all, a factor that manifested itself only in the books Steinbeck published after *The Grapes of Wrath*, and it can be argued that, in some respects, Steinbeck's use of the "limited vocabulary" was always, in a strange sort of way, a possible strength rather than a deficiency in his art. In the rhythms, the tones, the cadences of simple words and the simple sentence constructions are echoed and preserved the simplicity and the music of human speech, allowing readers across the whole spectrum to identify with what Steinbeck is saying and the ideas he is propounding. Each reader is given the opportunity to impose his own individual vision of beauty and wonder, joy and sorrow, pain and loss, and in so doing endow a universal verisimilitude to the narratives. Steinbeck's prose at its best, before overexplicitness and a vague return to his early rococo style in some of his later work devalued it, is rather like that candle in the North African monastery, whose tiny light was sufficient to suggest the whole magnificent edifice of the church. Steinbeck's aim, as he had told Kline, was to attempt to write on two distinct levels at one and the same time:

> On one top level for our peers, those who know as much as we like to think we know — and on another level to keep it simple and true for people with little or no education so they can understand and be moved by our story.[4]

In 1951, when he was writing *East of Eden*, he told Covici he was trying to keep the whole book "in an extremely low pitch and to let the reader furnish the emotion." He added significantly: "If I can do that I will have succeeded" (*JN* 49). In 1961, after the publication of *The Winter of Our Discontent*, his last novel, he declared that his whole writing life had been "aimed at making people understand each other."[5] What cannot be denied, whatever the alleged limitations of his vocabulary, is that Steinbeck remained to the very end a communicator of the first order.

The far-reaching consequences to Steinbeck's art that had their origins in the tragic outcome of his return to California in 1944 have also to be recognized and acknowledged. While he was never simply a regional writer *per se* (like all regional writers of genius his themes transcend mere geographical boundaries), it is probably true to say that the mainspring of his art was, almost more than any other factor, deeply rooted in and dependent upon the ambience of the central California valleys.[6] Just how much his native environment meant to him can be gauged from a letter he wrote his publisher Robert Ballou in late 1932 or early 1933:

... My country is different from the rest of the world. It seems to be one of those pregnant places from which come wonders. Lhassa is such a place. I am trying to translate my people and my country in this next book [*To a God Unknown*]. The problem frightens me, when I let myself think of it. Jeffers came into my country and felt the thing but he translated it into the symbols of Pittsburg. I cannot write the poetry of a Jeffers but I do know the god better than he does for I was born to it and my father was. Our bodies came from this soil — our bones came originally from the limestone of our mountains and our blood is distilled from the juices of this earth. I tell you now that my country — a hundred miles long and about fifty wide — is unique in the world. I'll write about it to the best of my ability and then some time I'll show it to you and that will be better.[7]

For many critics and scholars, Steinbeck's withdrawal from his natural roots was the single most important cause of what they saw as his "decline" as a writer. Elia Kazan has expressed the view very bluntly indeed, maintaining that when Steinbeck left California he "looked a fool in New York theater society and on the right bank of Paris."[8] This seems a rather overmelodramatic opinion, but it again cannot be denied that Steinbeck never felt entirely at ease among the people of his adopted environment on the East Coast. The tragedy was (and there were many tragedies in the course of his long literary career) that he would have felt even less at ease had he remained in California.

There is, however, another aspect to all this. Not only did Steinbeck finally lose in 1945 the ambience from which he drew the core of his inspiration and in which he was able to complete his best work, but he also lost his innate subject matter and, with it, much of the joy he had found in his writing — although he would always continue to aver in public to the very end that this last was not so. Regarded by many as a realist writer of fiction, he was in fact an incurable romantic who once delightedly proclaimed that he was "happy to report that in the war between reality and romance, reality is not the stronger" (*TC* 122). It was indeed a revealing admission for him to have made. While the experiences of war dampened the spirit of romanticism in him for a time at the war's end, he found it difficult as an individual to confront the reality of the postwar world, and almost impossible to do so as a writer of fiction. In the postwar literary scene, this vital writer who had written arguably the greatest of twentieth-century American novels of social protest became unfairly labeled by his detractors as something of an anachronism. For all that, he was still perceptive enough to admit in 1954 that he was not the only American writer who was failing to interpret the modern world and its problems, particularly insofar as they affected the common man. He told an interviewer:

> The novel in America is on a plateau. Outside of the neurotic crowd, none of us are digging into or writing about our present life or trying to look into the future. Instead we are seeking refuge elsewhere than America, or going into the past.[9]

Only in his final and one of his least impressive novels, *The Winter of Our Discontent*, published seven years after that interview, did he set his work in a truly contemporary postwar scene and endeavor to explore the current malaise he then saw infecting all levels of contemporary American society.

3

There is no single answer to the enigma of Steinbeck's postwar "decline," if indeed it can be described as such, either in the reality of his fall from critical favor or, as so many have maintained, in the evidence of the failing quality of his work. Harold Bloom has charged that Steinbeck's failure as a writer was that he "aspired beyond his aesthetic means."[10] That may be seen by some as true, but Benson's alternative explanation seems to be more to the point when he questions the extent to which Steinbeck's

> alleged decline in quality following *The Grapes of Wrath* was real and how much simply the expression of a lack of interest in Steinbeck's new subjects by critics who were disappointed that he didn't write the same book over and over again. (*Adventures* 496)

Steinbeck's searching and questioning mind was, in this respect, both an attribute and a disadvantage, a fact that was by no means lost on the author himself. As he told another interviewer in 1959:

> I once worked out a thing about criticism that it hates to change its mind. The only safe writer is a dead one for the critics. If he changes a writer confuses critics, and yet if he doesn't change he's really dead. I'm surprised there's been any continuity at all in my books. ... The critical attitude is too often static. Nobody complains that Picasso has painted in many different ways, but let a writer change a lot and he is supposed to be outraging himself.[11]

The argument is well-stated. It can be said to mitigate to an appreciable degree, at the same time as it substantiates, Alfred Kazin's rather dismissive opinion of Steinbeck as "a distinguished apprentice."

Certainly, to assert, as so many have done, that nothing Steinbeck wrote after *The Grapes of Wrath* bears rereading is as much arrant nonsense as it is to suggest that he did not continue writing in the mode of the thirties because he had lost his way. There is a world of difference between losing one's way like an aimless wanderer and deliberately seeking new ground, fully equipped and organized like an explorer. Steinbeck *did*, of course, consciously traverse new territory in *Cannery Row* and the postwar books. In doing this, he was simply doing nothing more than continuing the selfsame practice, interrupted during the years 1942 and 1943, that he had followed during the prewar years. As Edmund Wilson wrote in 1940: "[W]henever [Mr. Steinbeck] appears, he puts on a different kind of show."[12] Those two war years of 1942 and 1943, however, undoubtedly destroyed something precious and vital in his creative being, a certain element in the magic and in his instinctive mastery over his medium that he was never afterward quite able to recapture. W. M. Frohock has suggested that this element may have been wrath—"an emotion strong enough to hold his pages together"—and that it is this emotion that is lacking in the postwar books.[13] When broached on this very point a few years later, Steinbeck replied:

'I haven't lost capacity for indignation. What has changed is my expression of it. When you are young you feel that you must shout at everyone. When you are older you know that a whisper is more penetrating. ... [M]y approach to problems that move and distress me has altered. My convictions haven't.'[14]

4

In many ways, it has to be seen as regrettable that Steinbeck was not awarded the Nobel Prize in 1944 when he was first nominated and when his critical reputation was still mostly intact, for he would then unquestionably have been showered with the critical accolades of his fellow-countrymen that he so richly deserved. On the other hand, one can speculate that, had he received the prize then, might it not have been the "tombstone" he had always thought of it as being? Perhaps, after all, we should be grateful to the Swedish Academy for not seeing fit to honor him then. Had they done so, the world might never have had *East of Eden*, that sprawling monolith of a novel, regarded by many as Steinbeck's best work and the one he himself always regarded, despite his reservations about it, as his "big book." The world might never have had the endlessly underrated, exuberant *Sweet Thursday*, the delicate and delightfully frothy pseudo-Frenchness of *The Short Reign of Pippin IV*, or the structurally flawed, idiosyncratic but vastly entertaining *Travels With Charley*. Nor would we have had the two essential posthumous works: the fascinating and revealing *Journal of a Novel: The EAST OF EDEN Letters*, and the triumphant blend of scholarship and imagination that permeates the final two sections of the unfinished *The Acts of King Arthur and His Noble Knights*. This last work, surely, contains some of the most exciting pieces of writing Steinbeck ever did. "Gawain, Ewain, and Marhalt" and "The Noble Tale of Sir Lancelot of the Lake" can be seen as the final defiant rebuttal to all those critics who had written Steinbeck off as a writer of consequence.

When the war ended, Steinbeck was still a comparatively young man of forty-three, but no longer the brand of angry young man he had been when he had written *In Dubious Battle* and *The Grapes of Wrath*. By 1945, the world had changed, and his muse too had undergone a subtle metamorphosis. His natural subject matter had been taken away from him. Wrath had been converted into indignation, and compassion became frequently overwhelmed by the sentimentality that had always tended to mar the vitality of his fiction. Occasionally, too, in the search for the definitive "new form," for that literary Grail he never ceased seeking and that seemed always just to elude him, he wandered briefly off the path, as he did when he wrote *Burning Bright*.

Whatever view we may take of the work Steinbeck wrote and published from 1946 onward (the books from *The Wayward Bus* to *America and Americans* and the vast amount of journalism and other nonfictive short pieces) it should all be cherished, the superb and the not so good and even, let it be admitted, the occasional bad. For the work of the postwar years should be recognized for what it is—part of the essential and precious gift to the world from one of the greatest and, as importantly, one of the most *enduring* American writers of the twentieth century.

Appendix

Steinbeck's second marriage did not long survive the war years. In 1948, Gwyn told him she wanted a divorce. Although he was still deeply in love with her and tried in every way to dissuade her, she went to Reno with their sons and obtained a divorce on the grounds of incompatibility. She was given custody of the boys, with Steinbeck being granted visitation rights. The divorce plunged Steinbeck into a long period of terrible depression, which ended only after he met Elaine Scott in 1949. They were married in December 1950, following her divorce from stage and movie actor Zachary Scott. In later years, Thom and John IV spent much time with their father and Elaine, and both served with the Army in Vietnam. In 1969, John IV published *In Touch* (which he dedicated to his father, who had died two months before it came out), a book describing his experiences in Vietnam and his subsequent arrest in Washington on a drug charge from which he was eventually acquitted. Gwyn ended life an asthmatic and died in Montana in December 1975, aged 58. John IV died on 7 February 1991 from complications following back surgery. At the time of his death, he was writing his memoirs, titled *Legacy*. Thom lives in Austin, Texas, and is the chief executive of Steinbeck Films, Inc., the company he had set up with his brother to produce faithful movie adaptations of their father's works.

Most of those who were closest to Steinbeck during the war years are now dead. Two of the three friends and associates who in their different ways had the greatest influence on his life and career predeceased him: Ed Ricketts and Pascal Covici. Ricketts died on 11 May 1948, three days before his fifty-first birthday and four days after his car had been struck by the Del Monte Express on a crossing in Monterey, a stone's throw from Cannery Row. Of Ed Ricketts, Steinbeck wrote in 1950: "He will not die. He haunts the people who knew him. He is always present even in the moments when we feel his loss the most" (*LSC* xi). Covici died in New York on 14 October 1964 at the age of seventy-five after undergoing major surgery. "Pat Covici was much more than my friend," Steinbeck declared during a spoken tribute at the funeral service. "He was my editor ... my collaborator, and my conscience. He demanded of me more than I had and thereby caused me to be more than I should have been without him" (*Adventures* 961). Steinbeck's other great friend, his agent Elizabeth R. Otis, who always believed in his work and on whose advice he invariably acted, survived Steinbeck by thirteen years, dying in May 1981. Her colleague, Mavis McIntosh, died in August 1986, aged eighty-three.

Steinbeck's younger sister, Mary, with whom he had acted out the roles of King Arthur and Lady Guinevere when they played together as children and the fate of whose husband he had endeavored to discover while he was in the Mediterranean war zone in 1943, succumbed to cancer in January 1965. His two elder sisters survived him. The eldest of the Steinbeck siblings, Olive Esther, died in May 1986, aged ninety-four, and her younger sister, Elizabeth, was the last of all to die in October 1992 at the age of ninety-eight.

Steinbeck's first wife, Carol, married a Monterey business man, William Brown, in 1952 and outlived both Steinbeck and Gwyn. She died at the age of seventy-six in February 1983.

Notes

Introduction

1. "The Leader of the People" did, in fact, appear in the British short story magazine *Argosy* in August 1936. "Flight," on the other hand, had not been previously published anywhere prior to its appearance in *The Long Valley*.

2. "Steinbeck Busy Writing of Oklahomas In California," *Monterey Peninsula Herald*, 11 January 1938.

3. Dorothy Steel, "'Oklahomans' Topic of Steinbeck: Book Deals With Dust Bowl Refugees," *Los Gatos Mail News*, 4 November 1937.

4. Louis Walther, "Oklahomans Steinbeck's Theme: Author Says Migrants Altering California," *San Jose Mercury-Herald*, 8 January 1938. Reprinted *Conversations* 11–14.

5. Louis Kronenburger, "Hungry Caravans," *Nation* 148 (15 April 1939): 440–41.

6. Harry Thornton Moore, *The Novels of John Steinbeck: A First Critical Study* (Chicago: Normandie House, 1939), 96.

7. Ibid., 96.

8. James Gray, *On Second Thoughts* (Minneapolis: University of Minnesota Press, 1946), 139.

9. Maxwell Geismar, *American Moderns* (London: W. H. Allen, 1958), 155.

10. Alfred Kazin, *On Native Grounds* (New York: Reynell & Hitchcock, 1942), 394.

11. Alfred Kazin, "The Unhappy Man from Happy Valley," *New York Times Book Review*, 4 May 1958, 1, 29.

12. Stanley Edgar Hyman, "Steinbeck and the Nobel Prize," *New Leader* 45 (10 December 1962): 10–11.

13. Arthur Mizener, "Does a Moral Vision of the Thirties Deserve a Nobel Prize?" *New York Times Book Review*, 9 December 1962, 4, 43–45.

14. John Steinbeck, "Letters to Alicia," *Newsday*, 3 December 1966 through 20 May 1967.

15. Roger Sale, "Stubborn Steinbeck," *New York Review of Books*, 20 March 1980, 10–11.

16. John W. Aldridge, "Yokel Lancelots," *New York Times Book Review*, 30 September 1979, 12 & 22.

17. Thomas R. Edwards, "The Innocent," *New York Review of Books*, 16 February 1984, 25–27.

18. See the pioneering work of, among others, such distinguished Steinbeck scholars as Richard Astro, Jackson J. Benson, Robert DeMott, John Ditsky, Warren French, Tetsumaro Hayashi, Lawrence William Jones, Howard Levant, Peter Lisca, Louis Owens, and John Timmerman.

19. John Ditsky, "A Kind of Play: Dramatic Elements in Steinbeck's 'The Chrysanthemums'," *Wascana Review* 21 (Spring 1986): 62–72.

20. French 1, 171.

21. John Ditsky, *John Steinbeck: Life, Work, and Criticism* (Fredericton, N.B., Canada: York Press Ltd., 1985), 30.

22. Harold Bloom, *Modern Critical Views: John Steinbeck* (New York: Chelsea

House Publishers, 1987), 1.
23. French 1, 137.
24. French 2, 171.
25. Christopher Isherwood, "The Tragedy of El Dorado," *Kenyon Review* 1 (Autumn 1939): 450–53.
26. Wilbur L. Schramm, "Careers at Crossroads," *Virginia Quarterly Review* 15 (Autumn 1939): 630–32.
27. Fred B. Millett, *Contemporary American Authors* (New York: Harcourt, Brace & Company, 1944), 50.
28. J. Donald Adams, *The Shape of Books to Come* (New York: Viking Press, 1944), 139.

Chapter One. The Creation of a Twentieth-Century Masterpiece: *The Grapes of Wrath*

1. Steinbeck's original holograph manuscript of *The Grapes of Wrath* is in the Clifton Waller Barrett Library, University of Virginia Library.
2. For full details of these and other important variations between the holograph manuscript and the published text, see Roy S. Simmonds, "The Original Manuscript," *San Jose Studies* 16 (Winter 1990): 117–32 [special issue devoted to *The Grapes of Wrath*].
3. Jackson J. Benson & Anne Loftis, "John Steinbeck and Farm Labor Unionization: The Background of *In Dubious Battle*," *American Literature* 52 (May 1980): 194–223.
4. The passage Steinbeck originally wrote read as follows: "Every man will marshall his troops of hurt and the armies will march and there'll be a dead terror in it. And it will tramp out the sickly lines of the slaves of the monster. And the monster will collapse. You're buying bitterness from the driven men and you're foreclosing bitterness for the margin of profit" (*GOW* ms. 39). Alderman Library.
5. The new passage appears on pp. 612–13 of the Viking 1939 first edition.

Chapter Two. 1939: Into the Public Domain

1. Burton Rascoe, "But ... Not ... Ferdinand," *Newsweek* 13 (17 April 1939): 46.
2. Burton Rascoe, "Excuse It, Please," *Newsweek* 13 (1 May 1939): 38. Roscoe's niece, Judith Rascoe, has suggested that this second review resulted in possible irreparable damage to her uncle's reputation as a critic: see her letter "A Cautionary Tale for Reviewers" in *New York Times Book Review*, 14 May 1989.
3. Philip Rahv, "A Variety of Fiction," *Partisan Review* 6 (Spring 1939): 111–12.
4. Rev. Arthur Spearman, S. J., "Marxist Taint in Steinbeck Book," *Albany Times-Union* (NY), 11 June 1939, Sec. D, 7.
5. Pare Lorentz, *FDR's Moviemaker: Memoirs & Scripts* (Reno: University of Nevada Press, 1992), 130–31.
6. Aaron Copland, "The Aims of Music for Films," *New York Times*, 10 March 1940, Sec. 11, 7. See also Aaron Copland & Vivian Perlis, *Copland 1900 through 1940* (New York: St. Martin's Press, 1984), 297–300.
7. JS/Merle Armitage, 17 February 1939. Alderman Library.

8. Nunnally Johnson's screenplay of *The Grapes of Wrath* is reproduced in John Gassner & Dudley Nichols (eds.), *20 Best Film Plays* (New York: Crown Publishers, 1943), 333—77. For detailed accounts of the making of the movie and for scholarly appraisals, see: Frank Condon, "The Grapes of Raps," *Collier's* 105 (27 January 1940): 23, 64—65; Warren French (ed.), *A Companion to The Grapes of Wrath* (New York: Viking Press, 1963), 163—89; Warren French, *Filmguide to The Grapes of Wrath* (Bloomington & London: Indiana University Press, 1973); Sheridan, Owen, Macorie & Marcus, *The Motion Picture and the Teaching of English* (New York: Appleton-Century-Crofts, 1965), 103—11; Robert E. Morsberger, "Steinbeck on Screen," in *A Study Guide to Steinbeck: A Handbook to His Major Works*, ed. Tetsumaro Hayashi (Metuchen, NJ: Scarecrow Press, 1974); Russell Campbell, "Tramping Out the Vintage: Sour Grapes," in *The Modern American Novel and the Movies*, eds. Gerald Peary & Roger Shotzkin (New York: Ungar, 1978); Andrew Sinclair, *John Ford* (London: George Allen & Unwin Ltd., 1979), 95—100; Henry Fonda, *Fonda: My Life*, as told to Howard Teichmann (New York: New American Library, 1981), 128—31; and Dan Ford, *The Unquiet Man: The Life of John Ford* (London: William Kimber, 1982), 141—46.

9. Herb Caen, "Easy Come, Easy Go," *San Francisco Chronicle*, 30 March 1993, B1.

10. JS/Dan [James], c. late 1939. *Bradford Morrow Bookseller Catalogue Eight: John Steinbeck—A Collection of Books and Manuscripts (The Harry Valentine Collection)* (Santa Barbara, CA: Bradford Morrow Bookseller Ltd., 1980), 76.

11. These terms were to hold out for a grossly unrealistic price and that it would be a condition of the sale that the author should work on the picture on his own terms, even having charge as writer-producer-director, reserving the right to have his name deleted from the credits if he was not pleased with the completed picture.

12. Michael Mok, "Slumming with Zanuck," *Nation* 150 (3 February 1940): 127—28.

13. Franz Hoellering, "Films," *Nation* 150 (3 February 1940): 137—38.

14. Frank S. Nugent, "The Screen in Review," *New York Times*, 25 January 1940, 17.

15. "The New Pictures," *Time* 35 (12 February 1940): 70—71.

16. Otis Ferguson, "Steinbeck's Other Vineyard," *New Republic* 102 (19 February 1940): 247.

17. "The New Pictures," *Time* 35 (15 January 1940): 60, 62.

Chapter Three. 1940: The Search for New Beginnings

1. *New York Times*, 14 February 1940, 19.

2. Joe Klein, *Woody Guthrie: A Life* (London: Faber & Faber, 1981), 142. In 1940, Steinbeck wrote a brief appreciation of Guthrie: "Woody is just Woody. Thousands of people do not know he has any other name. He is just a voice and a guitar. He sings the songs of a people and I suspect that he is, in a way, that people. Harsh voiced and nasal, his guitar hanging like a tire iron on a rusty rim, there is nothing sweet about Woody, and there is nothing sweet about the songs he sings. But there is something more important for those who will listen. There is the will of the people to endure and fight against oppression. I think we call this the American spirit." The appreciation was written as an introduction to Guthrie's

album of dust bowl songs, *Hard Hitting Songs for Hard Hit People*, but not published until 1962. Quoted in Klein, p. 160.

3. Herbert Kline, "On John Steinbeck," *Steinbeck Quarterly* 4 (Summer 1971): 80—88.

4. Jimmy Costello, "Steinbeck, Ricketts Embark on Cruise: Author, Scientist & Crew Board Purse Seiner, Bound for Six Weeks' Voyage to Lower California," *Monterey Peninsula Herald*, 11 March 1940.

5. Untitled holograph manuscript, one page. Gwendolyn C. Steinbeck Collection, Bancroft Library.

6. For a comprehensive "insiders" memoir of the Steinbeck/Ricketts expedition to the Gulf of California, see Sparky Enea (as told to Audry Lynch), *With Steinbeck in the Sea of Cortez* (Los Osos, CA: Sand River Press, 1991).

7. *Saturday Review* 21 (11 May 1940): 8.

8. Kline, "On John Steinbeck," 84.

9. Addison Gayle, *Richard Wright: Ordeal of a Native Son* (Garden City: Anchor Press/Doubleday, 1980), 126—27.

10. John Steinbeck, "Foreword," *Speeches of Adlai Stevenson*, ed. Richard Harrity (New York: Random House, 1952), 5.

11. John Steinbeck, "A Primer on the '30s," *Esquire* 103 (June 1980), 85—93.

12. The untitled holograph manuscript fragment is in the John Steinbeck Collection, Stanford University Library. It is written on both sides of four sheets, folio numbers 167 through 174, detached from the same ledger in which Steinbeck wrote the manuscript of *The Grapes of Wrath*. The fragment was incorrectly identified by Mrs. Gwyndolyn Steinbeck as a "substantial portion of [a] chapter cut from *Cannery Row* before publication."

13. John Ditsky has suggested to me that not only might Mr. Boss's gun barrel be "a deliberate Westernish lance symbol," but that there is also the possibility Mr. Boss might originate in Mark Twain. On page 113 of his *Steinbeck's Reading*, Robert DeMott lists Twain's *A Connecticut Yankee in King Arthur's Court* as one of the books Steinbeck owned or borrowed. In that book, the protagonist is named "The Boss," or "Sir Boss."

14. Kline, "On John Steinbeck," 84.

15. Ibid., 87.

16. Ibid., 87.

17. Robert DeMott, "After *The Grapes of Wrath*: A Speculative Essay on John Steinbeck's Suite of Love Poems for Gwyn, 'The Girl of the Air'," in *John Steinbeck: The Years of Greatness, 1936—1939*, ed. Tetsumaro Hayashi (Tuscaloosa & London: University of Alabama Press, 1993), 20—44. The texts of all twenty-five poems can be found in an Appendix to "'The Closest Witness': The Autobiographical Reminiscences of Gwyndolyn Conger Steinbeck," edited and annotated by Terry Grant Halladay. MA thesis. Stephen F. Austin State University, May 1979.

Chapter Four. 1941: Conflict and Creativity

1. The music had been composed by Max Eisler, who had little experience in writing for the screen. See Theodore Strauss, "Musical Marathon," *New York Times*, 23 November 1941, Sec. 9, 5. Steinbeck's original choice as composer, Silvestre Revueltas, died while the film was being shot.

2. See Astro, 13 and Hedgpeth, Part II, 7.

3. Quoted in Astro, 14.

4. *New Yorker* 17 (7 June 1941): 77—78.

5. Margaret Marshall,"The Forgotten Village," *Nation* 153 (12 July 1941): 36.

6. Ralph Thompson, "Books of the Times," *New York Times*, 26 May 1941, 17.

7. Astro, 60.

8. Ibid., 59.

9. Hedgpeth, Part 2, 180.

10. See *Time* 39 (18 May 1942): 84, and Steinbeck, "My Short Novels," *Wings* (October 1953): 4—8.

11. It is noticeable that this quickening of pace toward the end of a full-length work, the abrupt resolution of plot, the too-rapid culmination of action, recurs time and time again in Steinbeck's work, with the notable exceptions of *Of Mice and Men*, *The Moon Is Down*, and *Burning Bright*, all of which are closely structured on dramatic considerations for stage presentation. The point should however be made that in the case of *Sea of Cortez* Steinbeck may have been obliged to resort to the quickening pace purely for structural purposes, as will be noted later in this chapter.

12. Quoted in Hedgpeth, Part 2, 7.

13. See Richard Astro, "Steinbeck and Ricketts: Escape or Commitment in *Sea of Cortez*," *Western American Literature* 6 (Summer 1971): 109—21; Richard Astro, *John Steinbeck and Edward F. Ricketts: The Shaping of a Novelist*; Betty L. Perez, "Steinbeck, Ricketts, and *Sea of Cortez*: Partnership or Exploitation?" *Steinbeck Quarterly* 7 (Summer—Fall 1974): 73—79; Richard Astro, "Travels with Steinbeck: The Laws of Thought and the Laws of Things," *Steinbeck Quarterly* 8 (Spring 1975): 35—44; and Betty Perez, "The Form of the Narrative Section of *Sea of Cortez*: A Specimen Collected from Reality," *Steinbeck Quarterly* 9 (Spring 1976): 36—44.

14. See Peter Lisca, *John Steinbeck: Nature and Myth* (New York: Thomas Crowell Company, 1978), 215—19. It is worthy of mention that in the third of Steinbeck's full-length "travel" books, *Travels With Charley*, there is a similar quickening of the narrative toward the end of the book. In this latter instance, however, it is clear that not only had Steinbeck abandoned for this or that reason the later stages of his projected itinerary but that, approaching the end of his illustrious writing career, had lost interest in the book.

15. Ricketts/Joseph Campbell, 31 December 1941. Quoted in Hedgpeth, Part 2, 11.

16. John Steinbeck, *Sweet Thursday* (New York: Viking Press, 1954), 1.

17. Hedgpeth, Part 2, 119.

18. Ibid., 146—47.

19. Webster F. Street, of course, also went on the trip on the outward passage as far as San Diego, but his time on board was so brief that his presence would have made very little difference to the provisioning requirements.

20. Joseph Waldmeir, "John Steinbeck: No Grapes of Wrath," in *A Question of Quality: Popularity and Value in Modern Creative Writing*, ed. Louis Filler (Bowling Green, Ohio: Bowling Green University Popular Press, 1976), 219—20.

21. Expanding on this answer, Steinbeck is reported to have said that not only had he gained intense satisfaction from the painstaking firsthand research that had preceded the writing of the book, but had been gratified by the discovery that this research had both confirmed and consolidated his own nonteleological worldview based on a system of the rhythmic ebb and flow rather than one of beginnings and

endings. He went on to explain that he had found his early scientific training had instilled in him a lifelong respect for accuracy, and had, moreover, forced him to research with immense care all that he wrote. Such research had sent him to the Sea of Cortez, and also, before that, on the long trek with the Okies. In his view, he added, a curious and inquiring mind has the potential for discovering many matters during its adventures that have the power to convert mere inquiry into research, and that, in turn, can stimulate or even order the creative process.

22. John Steinbeck, *East of Eden* (New York: Viking Press, 1952), 132.

23. Steinbeck's preliminary notes and the first version of the narrative film script of *The Red Pony* are in the John Steinbeck Collection, Bancroft Library, University of California, Berkeley. Another version of the narrative script is held in the John Steinbeck Collection, Stanford University Library. The two versions are very similar in most essentials, although it is clear from the manuscript emendations and deletions and inset additions that the Bancroft manuscript precedes the Stanford manuscript, which is a fair copy of a slightly different text. For purposes of clarity, all quotations have been extracted from the Bancroft manuscript only.

The working notes are contained in a carbon typescript of thirty-nine pages of standard typing paper, $8\frac{1}{2}$ by 11 inches. Black carbon paper has been used. The sheets are numbered 1 through 36 (two being numbered 17, two being numbered 29, and the final page being unnumbered). The first twenty-two sheets of the typescript are in large type, the next eight in small type, and the last nine in large type again, although the last two-line comment on the final page is in small type and has been typed directly onto the carbon copy.

The narrative manuscript itself has no title page, and is a ribbon copy. The emendations and additions in Steinbeck's hand are in black ink. There are one hundred eighty-four sheets, of which five are holograph inserts to pages 48, 62, 114, 151, and 171. There are two pages numbered 88 and two numbered 91. The page between pages 162 and 163 is numbered 162a. The remainder of the pages are numbered consecutively from 1 through 176, although the page after 135 has been incorrectly numbered 134 and that page and the subsequent six pages (134 through 140) have been renumbered in ink 136 through 142 to bring them into correct sequence. Pages 143 and 144, which contain inserted sections describing Billy Buck carrying Jody back to the farm after the death of the pony, are numbered in ink and the material on these pages follows on from approximately one-third of the way down the page numbered 142. The narrative at the foot of page 142 is continued on the page renumbered from 141 to 145, and pages 142 through 153 have been renumbered 146 through 157. The pages in large type are: 1 through 40, 44 through 65, and 85 through 95. The pages in small type are: 41 through 43, 66 through 84, and 96 through 176. Triple spacing has been used throughout. All the typewritten sheets are $8\frac{1}{2}$ by 11 inches in size. Pages 1 through 123 are on three-hole notepaper, but these holes do not match up on all sheets. From page 124 onward, standard typing paper without holes has been used.

Two of the holograph sheets (inserted at pages 48 and 62) have been detached from lined yellow legal pads. The sheet headed "Insert at p. 48" has been torn to size $8\frac{3}{8}$ by 10 inches. The sheet headed "Insert p. 62" is $8\frac{3}{8}$ by $9\frac{1}{2}$ inches. The remaining three holograph sheets are lined, 4-hole, yellow notebook paper measuring 8 by $10\frac{1}{2}$ inches.

There is a total of 124 scenes, numbered 1 through 116, but there are no numbers 15, 20, or 26, and there are two scenes each numbered 21, 25, 60, 61, 83, 87, 103, and 114. There are also three scenes that are unnumbered. Following

Scene 90, there is a note "End of Section II," and Scene 91 is preceded by the note "Section III." The end of Section I and the beginning of Section II are not, however, distinguished in the typescript.

24. In the movie version, all the characters retain the names given them in the narrative script, except for Jody. In the movie, he is called "Tom."

25. The story cycle itself, however, was fresh both in its narrative and emotional content when Steinbeck wrote the stories in the early 1930s. It is the plethora of similar, and lesser, stories since written that makes the cycle and the film script now seem somewhat hackneyed. For example, in 1938, Marjorie Kinnan Rawlings published *The Yearling*, the story of a young boy, also named Jody, and his tragic love for a fawn. *The Yearling* won the 1939 Pulitzer Prize for fiction, and in 1946 was made into a successful film. In 1941, Mary O'Hara published an extremely sentimental short story, again about a boy and a colt who gets sick, "My Friend Flicka," in the January-February issue of *Story* magazine. A novel version followed later that same year, and this, too, was made into a film in 1943.

26. For a comprehensive analysis and critique of the 1949 movie, see Millichap, 107—21. It should be noted, however, that some of Millichap's conclusions have apparently been reached without his having the opportunity of examining Steinbeck's 1941 narrative script.

27. I have relied on Clayton R. Koppes & Gregory D. Black, *Hollywood Goes To War: How Politics, Profits and Propaganda Shaped World War II Movies* (London: I. B. Tauris & Co. Ltd., 1988) for the information regarding the formation and purpose of the various government propaganda departments.

28. See Herbert Mitgang, "Annals of Government: Policing America's Writers," *New Yorker* 63 (5 October 1987): 47—90; Herbert Mitgang, *Dangerous Dossiers: Exposing the Secret War Against America's Greatest Authors* (New York: Donald I. Fine, Inc., 1988), 71—79; Natalie Robins, "The Defiling of Writers," *Nation* 245 (10 October 1987): 367—72; Jack Siraca, "The U.S. Army vs. John Steinbeck," *San Jose Mercury News*, 2 June 1984, 1A, 12A; and Jack Siraca, "FBI tracked Steinbeck's travels and friendships for nearly 30 years," *San Jose Mercury News*, 14 June 1984, 1A, 12A.

29. "Steinbeck Lashes Out at Bungled Goodwill Drive in Latin States: A Reply to American Censorship," *Carmel Cymbal*, 4 September 1941, 3.

30. John Steinbeck, "Reflections on a lunar eclipse," *NYHT*, 6 October 1963, Sunday *Book Week* section, 3.

31. Single page untitled statement, n.d. [c. May 1942]. Butler Library, Columbia University.

32. Ibid.

33. The original holograph manuscript and the first typescript of *The New Order* are in the Annie Laurie Williams Collection, Rare Book and Manuscript Library, Butler Library, Columbia University, New York. The holograph manuscript is contained in two spiral-bound notebooks measuring $10\frac{1}{4}$ by $7\frac{1}{4}$ inches. The first notebook contains pages 1—55 of the text (Act 1 of the published play version of the work), and the second notebook contains pages 56—100 of the text (Act 2 of the published play version). The text is divided into three acts and seven scenes, which compare with the published texts of the novel and play as follows:

Holograph Manuscript		Novel	Play
Scene Ia	pp. 1—17	Chapter One	Act I, Scene I
Scene Ib	pp. 18—37	Chapter Two	Act I, Scene 2
Scene IIa	pp. 38—55	Chapters Three & Four	Act I, Scenes 3 & 4

Scene IIb pp. 56–67	Chapter Five	Act II, Scene 1
Scene IIc pp. 68–81	Chapter Six	Act II, Scene 2
Scene IIIa pp. 82–92	Chapter Seven	Act II, Scene 3
Scene IIIb pp. 93–100	Chapter Eight	Act II, Scene 4

There are two additions to the original holograph text:

1. Twelves lines on reverse of page 35 substitute seven lines deleted from page 36.

2. Five lines on reverse of page 75 to be inserted on page 76.

The first typescript is 145 pages in length, although there is an error in the numbering of the pages, so that there is no page 81 and the last page is accordingly numbered 146. Pages 103–15 of the original typescript (the latter section of Chapter Six of the published text) were discarded and substituted by new pages 103–17. The pages originally numbered 116–21 have been renumbered 118–23. Pages 122–42 of the original typescript have been discarded and substituted by new pages 124–46 (in the text of the published novel being from page 153 through to the end of the book).

34. This version of the passage was carried over into the first typescript. The change of name of Captain Lunt to Captain Loft is one of the three name changes between the first holograph draft and the published text. In the manuscript, Colonel Lanser is named Colonel Gort, and Mr. Corell is named Mr. Curseling. It is interesting to speculate on the possible reasons for these name changes, which were effected late in the process of publication. The salesman's dummy, in fact, uses the names "Curseling" and "Gort" on the first eight pages of text that were reproduced. It is likely that the name "Lunt" was abandoned so as to cause no possible offense to the distinguished Broadway star of the day, Alfred Lunt. The name "Gort" was an unfortunate choice by Steinbeck, for he must have forgotten that the name of the commander of the British Expeditionary Force in France from the Outbreak of war to the Dunkirk evacuation was General Gort. "Curseling" has obvious (perhaps too obvious) metaphoric connotations, but perhaps the true reason was the similarity in the name with the name of the Norwegian traitor, Quisling.

35. Richard Watts, Jr., "The Wayward Steinbeck," *New Republic* 116 (10 March 1947): 37–38.

36. The invasion of Norway was launched by the Germans in April 1940. In *The Moon Is Down*, the invasion occurs in the early fall.

37. John H. Timmerman, *John Steinbeck's Fiction: The Aesthetics of the Road Taken* (Norman: University of Oklahoma Press, 1986), 183–87.

38. It is interesting to note that this image harks back to Steinbeck's first published novel. On page 183 of *Cup of Gold*, the Spanish cavalry defending Panama against Morgan's mauraders stumble into a marsh and are described as "flies caught in a green flypaper."

39. See also John Ditsky, "Steinbeck's 'European' Play-Novella: *The Moon Is Down*," *Steinbeck Quarterly* 20 (Winter-Spring 1987): 9–18, on page 12. The effective, but sparing use of the conjunctive "And" to begin a sentence can be observed, for example, in the opening words of Katherine Mansfield's short stories "The Garden Party" and "A Dill Pickle," where the "And" seems to convey with complete and satisfying conviction the essential prehistory of the narrative that ensues. I am indebted to Dr. Frances Garner of Mobile College, Mobile, Alabama, for drawing my attention to this.

40. Astro goes on to note: "In marked contrast with the efficacious effect of

Ricketts' way of seeing on the thematic materials in Steinbeck's greatest fiction, the overpowering force of Ricketts' thinking overwhelmed the novelist in *The Moon Is Down*, with fatal consequences to the quality of his art," (Astro 157).

41. See R. S. Hughes, *Beyond The Red Pony: A Reader's Companion to Steinbeck's Complete Short Stories* (Metuchen, NJ: Scarecrow Press, 1987), 77—80.

42. John Steinbeck, *Cup of Gold* (New York: Robert M. McBride & Company, 1929), 179.

43. John Steinbeck, *The Long Valley* (New York: Viking Press, 1938), 302.

44. Ibid., 302.

45. Mimeographed handout issued to reviewers by the Viking Press on 12 November 1941.

46. Charles Poore, "Books of the Times," *New York Times*, 5 December 1941, 21.

47. See Edmund Wilson, "The Californians: Storm and Steinbeck," *New Republic* 103 (9 December 1940): 784—87; reprinted in *Classics and Commercials* (New York: Farrar, Straus, 1950), 34—45.

48. Stanley Edgar Hyman, "Of Invertebrates and Men," *New Republic* 106 (16 February 1942): 242—44.

49. R. L. Duffus, "John Steinbeck Makes an Excursion," *New York Times Book Review*, 28 December 1941, 3.

Chapter Five. 1942: In Limbo

1. Book jacket, *The Moon Is Down* (1942).

2. Clifton Fadiman, "Two Ways to Win the War," *New Yorker* 18 (7 March 1942): 59—60.

3. James Thurber, "What Price Conquest?" *New Republic* 106 (16 March 1942): 370.

4. "Correspondence," *New Republic* 106 (30 March 1942): 431.

5. Ibid., 431.

6. Clifton Fadiman, "Steinbeck Again," *New Yorker* 18 (4 April 1942): 63—64.

7. "Correspondence," *New Republic* 106 (4 May 1942): 607—8.

8. John Chamberlain, "Books of the Times," *New York Times*, 9 May 1942, 11.

9. Winston S. Churchill, *The Second World War: Volume 4, The Hinge of Fate* (London: Cassell, 1951), Appendix C.

10. *Catholic World*, CLV (May 1942): 253—54.

11. John Gunther, "One of the Best Short Novels I Ever Read," *New York Herald Tribune Book Review*, 8 March 1942, 1.

12. Norman Cousins, "The Will to Live and Resist," *Saturday Review* 25 (14 March 1942): 6.

13. Margaret Marshall, *Nation* 154 (7 March 1942): 286.

14. Stanley Edgar Hyman, "Some Notes on John Steinbeck," *Antioch Review* 2 (June 1942): 185—200.

15. Donald V. Coers, *John Steinbeck as Propagandist: THE MOON IS DOWN Goes to War* (Tuscaloosa & London: University of Alabama Press, 1991), 43.

16. John Steinbeck, "Reflections on a lunar eclipse."

17. James W. Tuttleton, "Steinbeck in Russia: The Rhetoric of Praise and Blame," *Modern Fiction Studies* 11 (Spring 1965): 79—89. Reviewing the book on

21 December 1942, the Communist Party newspaper *Pravda* saw in Steinbeck's objectivity "not a sign of lack of hatred but solely the effect of his not having personally witnessed the events described." See "Pravda Likes Steinbeck: 'The Moon Is Down' Praised by Moscow Reviwer," *New York Times*, 22 December 1942, 23.

18. Heinrich Straumann, *American Literature in the Twentieth Century* (London: Arrow Books, 1962), 138—42.

19. "Baying at the Moon," *Time* 39 (22 June 1942): 88, 90.

20. "Divorces John Steinbeck," *New York Times*, 13 March 1942, 12; "Mrs. Steinbeck Gets Divorce," *Monterey Peninsula Herald*, 13 March 1942.

21. Brooks Atkinson, "The Play," *New York Times*, 8 April 1942, 22; Brooks Atkinson, "The Moon Is Down," *New York Times*, 12 April 1942, Sec. 8, 1.

22. "Steinbeck's Faith," *Newsweek* 19 (20 April 1942): 72—73.

23. "New Play in Manhattan," *Time* 39 (20 April 1942): 36.

24. "The Moon Is Down," *Commonweal* 36 (24 April 1942): 14—15.

25. *Newsweek*, 20 April 1942, 72—73.

26. Milton Bracker, "Note on Colonel Lanser: To Otto Kruger Falls the Wretched Role of an Agreeable Nazi," *New York Times* 19 April 1942, Sec. 8, 1—2.

27. For a detailed scholarly appraisal and analysis of the contemporary critical reception afforded the play, see Warren French, "*The Moon Is Down*: John Steinbeck's 'Times'," *Steinbeck Quarterly* 11 (Summer-Fall 1978), 77—87.

28. See, for example, Herbert Mitgang, *Dangerous Dossiers*, 72.

29. The whole story of this incident is recounted by Steinbeck in "About Ed Ricketts," *The Log from the Sea of Cortez* (New York: Viking Press, 1951), lviii-lxii.

30. Philip T. Hartung, "The Meek and the Masterful," *Commonweal* 36 (12 June 1942), 182—83.

31. Manny Farber, "Not by the Book," *New Republic* 106 (1 June 1942): 766.

32. John Mosher, "The Current Cinema," *New Yorker* 18 (23 May 1942): 63.

33. Millichap, 69.

34. John Ditsky, "Steinbeck's *Bombs Away*: The Group-man in the Wild Blue Yonder," *Steinbeck Quarterly* 12 (Winter-Spring 1979), 5—14. Ditsky's was the first published in-depth essay to consider *Bombs Away* and its implications both as propaganda and as an illustration of Steinbeck's confusion of mind at the time concerning the direction his writing was taking. Most other critics have shied away from such in-depth commentary. See, however, Astro and French 2.

35. *Bombs Away* is also one of the few of Steinbeck's books never to have been published in Britain. A French translation of *Bombs Away* (*Lachez les Bombes!*) was published in New York by the Viking Press in 1944, with a slightly revised introduction by Steinbeck.

36. Ditsky, "Steinbeck's *Bombs Away*," 13.

37. See Astro, 147.

38. Steinbeck had, however, already written a work not based directly on his own experience in *The Moon Is Down*, and he was to do so again in early 1943 when he wrote the original treatment for the movie *Lifeboat*.

39. Holograph manuscript, "Introduction" by "Pascal Covici." Harry Ransom Humanities Research Center, University of Texas at Austin.

40. Clifton Fadiman, "Books," *New Yorker* 18 (28 November 1942): 95—96, 98.

41. *New Republic* 108 (18 January 1943): 94.

42. "Brighter 'Moon'," *Newsweek* 21 (5 April 1943), 86, 88.

43. Copies of the synopsis of *A Medal for Benny* are in the Annie Laurie Williams Collection, Butler Library, Columbia University, New York. There are two copies of the work held: the first, a carbon typescript of fifteen pages, titled "Benny's Medal. Synopsis for a Motion Picture by John Steinbeck and Jack Wagner"; the second, a typescript of twenty pages (page 12, however, is missing), titled "A Medal for Benny. Synopsis for a Motion Picture by John Steinbeck and Jack Wagner." In the top right-hand corner of the first page of this second typescript is a handwritten note: "Sample script (sold to Paramount for $20,000)".

44. It is difficult to avoid the suspicion that Steinbeck was here again satirizing (as he had done in *The God in the Pipes*) the town of his birth. The similarity between the two names "Chilinas" and "Salinas" is, of course, patently obvious. The town was renamed "Pantera" in the movie.

45. The Frank Butler script has been published in *Best Film Plays of 1945*, ed. John Gassner & Dudley Nichols (New York: Crown Publishers, 1946), 589–648.

46. In the Butler script, Charlie says: "Maybe it is good for the country that she must depend for her life on all kinds of people—on men like my son—and on such women as their mothers, their wives—and their sweethearts ... " (*Best Film Plays of 1945*, 645).

47. It is possible that this could have been the chronicle of his family and the people of the Salinas Valley that was eventually to become *East of Eden*.

48. George Jean Nathan, "The Theatre," *American Mercury* 55 (December 1942): 738–44.

Chapter Six. 1943: European War Correspondent

1. A copy of Steinbeck's revised manuscript of *Lifeboat* was generously loaned to me by Twentieth Century-Fox Film Corporation. The manuscript bears the date "March 26, 1943." The pagination runs from page 1 through page 110, then page 197 through page 244. There is not, however, any break in the narrative.

2. Bud, of course, is also at root just as unsure of himself in this matter as Brennan. After the German has been killed, it is Bud who suggests to the others that perhaps they should have followed the German's advice after all, and steered east.

3. It is clear that, through the character of Connie Porter, Steinbeck was expending some of the bile he felt toward Henry Robinson Luce, the founder and president of the Time-Life publishing organization, which had consistently over the years given his work such a rough reception. Connie Porter seems to be fairly closely based on Luce's wife, Clare Booth Luce, the playwright and congresswoman.

4. "The New Pictures: *The Moon Is Down*," *Time* 41 (5 April 1943): 54, 56.

5. Hermine Rick Isaacs, "The Films in Review," *Theatre Arts* 27 (May 1943): 289–90.

6. *Time* 41 (19 April 1943): 42.

7. Quoted by C. Patrick Thompson, "John Steinbeck," *Good Housekeeping* (British edition) 44 (December 1943): 4–5, 64–65, 67.

8. "Steinbeck Here," *Evening Standard*, 8 June 1943, 2.

9. W. A. Darlington, "Deeply Moving War Play," *Daily Telegraph*, 9 June 1943, 3.

10. "Looker On," "Whispers from the Wings," *Theatre World* 39 (August 1943): 25.

11. Darlington, *Daily Telegraph*, 9 June 1943.

12. W. A. Darlingon, "London and 'The Moon Is Down'," *New York Times*, 11 July 1943, Sec. 2, 1.

13. By 2 September, *The Moon Is Down* had notched up its one hundredth performance at the Whitehall Theatre, but nine days later the play closed, to begin its post-London tour in Glasgow on 14 September. Several cast changes occurred for the tour, and Stepanek and Scofield, for two, did not stay with the play.

The most probable reason for the London closing would seem to be that the theater, noted for its short runs, had been booked for a limited period only by Wee Georgie Wood and his fellow-presenter, Basil C. Langton, who took over the role of Colonel Lanser during the subsequent tour. This possibility is borne out by the fact that when the play closed on Saturday, 11 September, Lydia Kyasht's Russian Ballet took over the theater for a new season, without any break whatsoever, on Monday 13 September.

The Whitehall run of the play lasted nearly fourteen weeks and played 111 performances, as against the New York run of nearly nine weeks and 71 perform-ances. It should be recognized, however, that the Martin Beck is a larger theater than the Whitehall. The New York production, it is recorded, was seen by approximately fifty-six thousand people. Even if the Whitehall had been fully booked for each performance — which is unlikely — the maximum number of people who could have seen the London production would have totaled only about sixty-two thousand. In terms of audience statistics, therefore, there was little in it. There is no doubt, on the other hand, that artistically the London production was the superior one.

14. *Evening Standard*, 8 June 1943, 2.

15. "Steinbeck Joins Daily Express," *Daily Express*, 25 June 1943, 1.

16. See Roy S. Simmonds, "John Steinbeck's World War II Dispatches: An Annotated Checklist," *Serif* 11 (Summer 1974): 21–30.

17. Thompson, "John Steinbeck," 64.

18. John Steinbeck, "Troopship," *Readers Digest* 44 (March 44): 67–70.

19. John Steinbeck, "Steinbeck Tells Story of Crain, Lost With Flying Fortress Crew," *NYHT*, 17 July 1943, 2.

20. See Steinbeck's dispatch published in the *NYHT* on 7 July, reprinted in *OTWW*, 49–52.

21. *NYHT*, 13 July 1943, reprinted *OTWW*, 65–68.

22. John Steinbeck, "Report on America," *Punch* 228 (22 June 1955): 754–55.

23. P. L. Mannock, "New Films," *Daily Herald*, 10 July 1943; Anthony Gibbs, "Drama of Europe's 'Little People'," *Sunday Chronicle*, 11 July 1943, 6.

24. Edgar Anstey, "The Cinema," *Spectator* 171 (16 July 1943): 59.

25. John Steinbeck, "Steinbeck Says This Is a War of Supply, Not Combat Services," *NYHT*, 5 August 1943, 17.

26. The detailed information about the investigations has been drawn from two sources: Jack Siraca, "The US Army vs. John Steinbeck," and Herbert Mitgang, *Dangerous Dossiers*.

27. "John Steinbeck Writes Appeal For Third War Loan Drive," *Monterey Peninsula Herald*, 17 September 1943. The reference to the dead children is taken from the dispatch published in the *NYHT* on 18 July 1943, and reprinted in *OTWW*, 78–80. The reference to the burned pilots is taken from the dispatch published in the *NYHT* on 11 July 1943, under the heading, "Steinbeck Finds Burned Pilot, Hands Gone, Eager to Fly Again." This dispatch was not reprinted in *OTWW*. Like so many other experiences he encountered during his time in the war zone, this image of the burned pilot was one that Steinbeck could never erase from his mind. In the dispatch, he wrote of the mutilated pilot:

His face is twisted and scarred by the flames, but he has a new nose built on with skin from his own chest. But his face is still twisted with fire and the skin is purple. His eyes are very sharp and blue and his teeth white."

When he was writing *East of Eden* in 1951, he recalled how he used to visit the burned British pilots:

It wasn't that they had no faces that was horrible; you could get used to the blob of flesh without lips, noses, eyelids or ears. The thing you couldn't get used to was the fact that behind that they were perfectly nice normal men with normal impulses. (*JN* 96—97)

28. See *NYHT*, 29 August 1943, 31 August 1943, 1 September 1943, 2 September 1943, and 5 September 1943.

29. John Steinbeck, "Welcome Parties Use Up 1st Half of a Voyage, Good-by Parties Rest," *Louisville Courier-Journal*, 21 April 1957.

30. Ibid.

31. Quoted in Lee Miller, *The Story of Ernie Pyle* (New York: Viking Press, 1950), 278—79. Reynolds himself gives a longer and somewhat different account of the meeting in *The Curtain Rises* (London: Cassell & Company Ltd., 1944), 225—29. Steinbeck's own account of the meeting is contained in his 21 May 1966 "letter" in the series *Letters to Alicia*.

32. Quoted in *The Ladies Home Journal Treasury*, ed. John Mason Brown & the editors of the *Ladies Home Journal* (New York: Simon & Schuster, 1956), 288.

33. Reynolds, *The Curtain Rises*, 221. See also John Steinbeck, "Steinbeck Hears Sea Warfare Compared to Chamber Music," *NYHT*, 19 October 1943, reprinted in *OTWW*, 180—83.

34. The details relating to Task Group 80.4 and its operations have been drawn from the declassified top-secret report titled "Task Group 80.4, Report of Actions during Operation *Avalanche* by," submitted by Captain C. L. Andrews. A copy of the report is in the possession of the John Steinbeck Library, Salinas.

35. Steinbeck, *Louisville Courier-Journal*, 21 April 1957.

36. John Steinbeck, "Steinbeck Tells of Weird Night of Two PT Men Alone in Palermo," *NYHT*, 11 October 1943, 17, reprinted in *OTWW*, 163—67.

37. Reynolds, *The Curtain Rises*, 271—72.

38. The story of this raid is told in Steinbeck's dispatch published in *NYHT* on 15 October 1943, reprinted *OTWW* 173—77.

39. See Betty Knox, "Over Here," *Evening Standard*, 15 October 1943, 5. During an interview that Steinbeck gave after he had returned to London from the Italian battle zone, he produced a ragged piece of paper on which were written the surrender terms for Capri. He claimed to have assisted in drafting them, and said that the surrendering Italian commanders had signed an extra copy for him. He quipped: "I guess I'm the only novelist who didn't go to Capri to write a romantic novel."

40. Michael Ratcliffe, "Cutting loose at Sixty: by John Steinbeck," *Sunday Times*, 16 December 1962, 20. Reprinted *Conversations*, 80—84.

41. See Halladay, "The Closest Witness," 140.

42. Steinbeck's eighty-five dispatches were published in the *NYHT* during the period 21 June through 15 December 1943. In one of these, the fifty-second in order of publication (17 September), he merely announces in a few lines that Capri, "famed in song and story and one of the outer defenses of the Harbor of Naples," surrendered on 12 September and that he was "the only newspaper man to make the island assault." Of the eighty-five dispatches, only seventy-two or so

were written while he was overseas, the balance being written up from notes after his October return to New York. Sixty-six of the dispatches were reprinted in *OTWW*. The remaining nineteen dispatches (including that of 17 September) have never been reprinted.

Having regard to the period over which the events described in the dispatches occurred (the early days of June through mid-September), it is obvious that the dates of their publication can be most misleading in pinpointing the actual dates on which those events took place. For example, the dispatches published from 1 December through 15 December, recounting the capture of Ventotene, have none of the immediacy of most war dispatches, for the simple reason that not only were they not written in the field but, by the time they appeared in the *NYHT*, the operations they describe were already part and parcel of recent history, having occurred three months or so previously on 8−9 September. Admittedly, none of the dispatches Steinbeck wrote after returning to New York is given a dateline or is in any way purported to have been written in the field. In fact, the dispatch published on 29 October was preceded by an editorial note explaining that Steinbeck had just returned to America and that this particular piece had been written in England immediately before he had left there for home.

To add to the confusion, as a result of Steinbeck's rather idiosyncratic way of working, the dispatches have no consistent chronological sequence, particularly the later ones dealing with the activities of Task Group 80.4. The dispatches relating to the landing on Red Beach at Salerno (covering the period 9−11 September) were published on 3−8 October, and preceded those relating to Steinbeck's visit to Palermo (6−7 September) which were published on 11−13 October and 22 November, as well as preceding those relating to the capture of Ventotene (8−9 September) which, as already noted above, were not published until 1−15 December.

43. Louis Owens, "The Threshold of War: Steinbeck's Quest in *Once There Was a War*," *Steinbeck Quarterly* 13 (Summer-Fall 1980), 80−86.

44. John Steinbeck, "Steinbeck Finds a Little Fear, No Ferocity in Bomber Crew," *NYHT*, 28 June 1943, 1, 7.

45. John Steinbeck, "Steinbeck Says Letters Are Center of Soldier's Lives," *NYHT*, 3 August 1943, 15.

46. John Steinbeck, "Steinbeck Says Greatest Plaint of Soldiers Is Lax Mail Service," *NYHT*, 29 August 1943, 10.

47. This last was a subject obviously dear to Steinbeck's heart, for he returned to it years later in an article for a British magazine: "Cooks of Wrath," *Everybody's*, 9 April 1955, 15. The article was reprinted under the title "The Vegetable War" in the *Saturday Review* 39 (21 July 1956): 34−35.

48. Quentin Reynolds has repeated the essentials of Steinbeck's story about Charlie Lytle (*The Curtain Rises*, 222−24), and verified its authenticity, although, of course, the description of the magical appearances of the crates of whiskey in puffs of smoke was whimsical embellishment by Steinbeck.

49. In actual fact, the dispatches published in the *NYHT* between 21 June and 3 July are antedated in *OTWW* by one day, i.e. 20 June to 2 July. The dispatches published on 4 July and 5 July in *NYHT* are both dated 4 July in *OTWW*. From then onward, however, the dates in the *NYHT* and *OTWW* coincide.

50. John Steinbeck, "Steinbeck Looks at Herrenvolk: Here's Corporal Bumblefoot, a Dope," *NYHT*, 15 December 1943, 23.

51. Ibid.

52. Herbert Kupferburg, "Correspondent Steinbeck," *New York Herald Tribune Book Review*, 8 February 1959, 10.

53. Herbert Mitgang, "Noble Men in Uniform," *New York Times Book Review*, 16 November 1958, 12.

54. *New Yorker* 34 (8 December 1958), 203.

55. John Cahill Oestreicher, *The World Is Their Beat* (New York: Essential Books, 1945), 27.

56. Steinbeck was by no means the only ex-war correspondent to decry his own reporting. As the Canadian Charles Lynch, who had been accredited to the British army for Reuters, observed thirty years after the event: "It's humiliating to look back at what we wrote during the war. It was crap—and I don't exclude the Ernie Pyles or the Alan Mooreheads. We were a propaganda arm of our governments. At the start the censors enforced that, but by the end we were our own censors. We were cheerleaders. I suppose there wasn't an alternative at the time. It was total war. But for God's sake, let's not glorify our rôle. It wasn't good journalism. It wasn't journalism at all." Quoted in Philip Knightley, *The First Casualty* (London: Andre Deutsch, 1975), 332—33.

57. Oestreicher, *The World Is Their Beat*, 26.

Chapter Seven. 1944: A New Masterpiece

1. As Joseph Millichap has put it: "With each rewriting Steinbeck's story was changed: Kantor heightened the allegory; Swerling provided the Hollywood gloss; and Hitchcock created a thriller" (Millichap, 79).

2. Jo Swerling, *Lifeboat: Screenplay with revisions 9/16/43* (Hollywood, CA: Script City, n.d.), 140.

3. Bosley Crowther, "The Screen in Review," *New York Times*, 13 January 1944, 17.

4. Bosley Crowther, "Adrift in 'Lifeboat'," *New York Times*, 23 January 1944, Sec. 2, 3.

5. Kenneth Macgowan, "The Producer Explains," *New York Times*, 23 January 1944, Sec. 2, 3.

6. "Movie of the Week: Lifeboat," *Life* 16 (31 January 1944): 76.

7. Bosley Crowther, "On Writing for the Screen," *New York Times*, 2 February 1944, 3.

8. See Cliff Lewis, "Steinbeck: The Artist as FDR Speechwriter," in *Rediscovering Steinbeck: Revisionist Views of His Art, Politics and Intellect*, ed. Cliff Lewis & Carroll Britch (Lewiston: The Edwin Mellen Press, 1989), 194—217.

9. In *In Dubious Battle*, *The Grapes of Wrath*, and *The Moon Is Down* the descriptions of the "Ricketts" characters bear no resemblance to the original. In *In Dubious Battle*, Dr. Burton is described as "a young man with golden hair," whose face is "almost girlish in its delicacy," and whose "eyes had a soft, sad look like those of a bloodhound" (129). In *The Grapes of Wrath*, Jim Casy has "a long head, bony, tight of skin ... set on a neck as stringy and muscular as a celery stalk," with protruding eyes, a "beaked and hard" nose, and "an abnormally high forehead" (25—26). In *The Moon Is Down*, Doctor Winter appears as "old" and "bearded and simple and benign" (14). In "The Snake," Dr. Phillips is described as having "the mild preoccupied eyes of one who looks through a microscope a great deal," and who wears "a short blond beard" (*LV* 74).

10. John Steinbeck, "My Short Novels," *Wings* (October 1953): 8.

11. Lisca, 198—99.

12. Holograph manuscript *Cannery Row*. Stanford University Library (see note 16).

13. Jackson J. Benson, "*Cannery Row* and Steinbeck as Spokesman for the 'Folk Tradition'," in *The Short Novels of John Steinbeck: Critical Essays with a Checklist to Steinbeck Criticism*, ed. Jackson J. Benson (Durham & London: Duke University Press, 1990), 132.

14. Ibid, 133–34.

15. It is arguable if the "little inner chapters" Steinbeck referred to in his letter to Covici are as frequent and their specific identity as apparent as some of the ongoing critical discussion over the years has suggested. If for the moment we disregard the first five numbered chapters, it can be seen that there are effectively only four true interchapters in *Cannery Row*: that is, chapters that are completely self-contained; that could, like the rejected wolves chapter, be published separately as short stories; that do not introduce characters appearing elsewhere in the book, but that nevertheless do have close thematic links with the narrative chapters. These interchapters are Chapter 12 (the death of Josh Billings), Chapter 24 (Mary Talbot and her craving for parties), Chapter 26 (the episode of the two little boys), and Chapter 31 (the sad saga of the gopher). The wolves chapter, of course, had it been retained, would have brought the total of true interchapters to five.

It can perhaps be argued that there are, in addition, six other chapters that can also be regarded as interchapters in that they do not serve to advance the plot in any material respect, although they do in fact mention characters who either play an integral part in the plot or who are mentioned frequently in the narrative chapters and thereby contribute toward the evocation of the overall ambience of the Row. These are Chapters 8 (Sam and Mrs. Malloy), 10 (Frankie and his love for Doc), 14 (the interlude describing early morning on the Row), 16 (the flashback to "the busiest time the girls of the Bear Flag ever had"), 19 (the flagpole skater), and 22 (Henri the painter). On the other hand, it might also be as convincingly argued that these six chapters are, in essence, little different from the occasional digressive sequences one would expect to find in most works of fiction.

While the time span covered in the book is rather vague, the action related in two of the six chapters mentioned above clearly occurs during the period in which the story line unfolds. The narrative proper probably begins in the month of May or June, with the first disastrous party described in Chapter 21 taking place in that latter month. The date of the party can be roughly fixed by reference to Doc's conversation with Richard Frost in Chapter 23, which takes place on the Fourth of July. The planning of the second party obviously spans the fairly long period from a time after the date of the County Fair until 28 October, the day following Doc's bogus birthday. The flashback in Chapter 16 is clearly to March of that year, "the March of the big sardine catch," when Eve Flanegan had gone on vacation to East St. Louis and Phyllis Mae had broken her leg. (These matters are, of course, resolved in Chapter 25, when Eve Flanegan returns from vacation and Phyllis Mae's leg is stated to be "knitting nicely"). Both Chapter 10 and Chapter 22 are also arguably outside the time span of the narrative proper, for there is no clue given as to when Frankie makes his first appearance at Doc's lab or when Henri's (ex-Doc's) girl leaves him after five months. Similarly, the timing of the flagpole skater's appearance at Holman's Store is a matter for conjecture. On the other hand, the quarrel between Sam Malloy and his wife over curtains clearly occurs immediately after Doc and Hazel return from their trip to the Great Tide Pool (see the exchange between Mack and Sam at the beginning of Chapter 9). The early morning idyll described in Chapter 14 also undoubtedly occurs during the time when Doc is in La Jolla and Mack and the boys are away on the frog hunt, for none of them is mentioned, although one of Dora's girls, Lee Chong, the old Chinaman, and Alfred, the Bear Flag watchman, are observed about their various businesses.

16. The holograph manuscript of *Cannery Row* is in the John Steinbeck Collection, Special Collections, Stanford University Library. It is bound in leather and buff linen. The text is written in pencil on one side of 143 sheets of yellow, legal-size, lined paper. The typescript is similarly bound in leather and buff linen and is 198 pages long. It bears Steinbeck's corrections to the text in both pen and pencil, as well as the editor's notations.

The manuscript and the typescript demonstrate that Steinbeck made two radical changes to the design of his book before it reached galley proof stage. In the holograph manuscript, the present Chapters 6 through 17 are numbered 7 through 18, the original Chapter 6 in the manuscript having been omitted from the published text. This chapter was subsequently published in March 1947 in *'47 Magazine of the Year* as the self-contained short story "The Time the Wolves Ate the Vice Principal." The decision to drop this particular chapter was obviously taken while Steinbeck was in the process of writing the first draft of the book. There is ample evidence to indicate that the preparation of the typescript was already proceeding while he was still at work on the holograph manuscript, and that this decision to drop the chapter was taken when Steinbeck was approximately halfway through the composition of the work. The wolves chapter does not figure at all in the typescript, and in the holograph manuscript the chapter following Chapter 18 (the present Chapter 17) has also been numbered 18 to correct the effect of the discarding of the original Chapter 6. The remaining fourteen chapters in the holograph manuscript follow the sequence of the chapters in the published book, with one exception, occasioned by the second of the two radical changes made. What was originally Chapter 19 in the manuscript (the episode of the two little boys, Joey and Willard) was switched to a later position in the book, becoming Chapter 26.

Another re-ordering of chapters as originally conceived in the holograph manuscript was also carried out at the time the typescript was prepared. This occurred at an early stage in composition. Clearly, Steinbeck underwent a change of mind before he had completed writing the third section of the manuscript. In the manuscript, these first three sections are unnumbered. The first section (which survives as the unnumbered opening section of the published book) is headed: "Concerning the difficulties involved in writing such an account as this———". The second section, which in the manuscript is given the heading, "Lee Chong and the Palace Flop House," contains the first half of what is Chapter 1 of the published text, ending on page 9, line 24 of the Viking first edition. The third section of the manuscript has no heading whatsoever, and continues the text of the published Chapter 1 from the point where the second section of the manuscript ended: "Now Lee Chong owned the Abbeville building . . ." (*CR* 9). It is obvious, having regard to the heading he had given the second section of the manuscript, that Steinbeck had intended to include in this section the taking over and the renaming of the Abbeville building by Mack and the boys, so the knitting together of the second and third sections into a single chapter was a logical, if not an inevitable, step. This intention on Steinbeck's part seems to be verified by the fact that when he had completed the third section he correctly numbered the fourth section "Ch II".

17. As Warren French has noted: "Steinbeck was a more self-conscious narrative architect than has always been recognized, but even he in his cyclical works, like *The Pastures of Heaven*, *Cannery Row*, and *The Red Pony*, created more subtle

patterns than he may have deliberately contemplated in providing an overall meaning for seemingly heterogenous elements in an episodic narrative" (Introduction to *Steinbeck's "The Red Pony": Essays in Criticism*, ed. Tetsumaro Hayashi & Thomas J. Moore [Muncie, Indiana: Steinbeck Monograph Series, No. 13, 1988], xii).

18. French 2, 122.

19. Mack also never visits the Bear Flag. "It would have seemed a little like incest to him" (*CR* 156).

20. In *The God in the Pipes*, of course, the Chinaman makes his appearance in the early morning walking down from behind the cypress trees at the back of the vacant lot toward the small wharf.

21. Lisca, 217.

22. Ricketts's comment is interesting, particularly from his viewpoint as the real life Doc. It should be noted that his marriage in 1922 lasted no more than a year and that it was not until 1941 (after the period in which *Cannery Row* is set) that he embarked on a steady relationship with Antonia ("Toni") Sexias Jackson, which lasted until late in 1947, shortly before his death.

23. Robert E. Morsberger, "Steinbeck's Happy Hookers," *Steinbeck Quarterly* 9 (Summer-Fall 1976): 101−15.

24. See *WD*, 30 & 141; *Letters*, 14; and undated letter to Jane Grabhorn in the Colt Press Papers, Stanford University Library.

25. John H. Timmerman, *The Dramatic Landscape of Steinbeck's Short Stories* (Norman: University of Oklahoma Press, 1990), 250.

26. Ibid., 250.

27. French 2, 119. French makes the same point in his first Twayne study of 1961.

28. Ibid., 120.

29. Malcolm Cowley, "Steinbeck delivers a mixture of farce and Freud," *Chicago (PM)*, 14 January 1945, Magazine Section, 15.

30. Antonia Sexias, "John Steinbeck and the Non-Teleological Bus," *What's Doing on the Monterey Peninsula* 1 (March 1947). Reprinted in *Steinbeck and His Critics*, ed. E. W. Tedlock, Jr. & C. V. Wicker (Albuquerque: University of New Mexico Press, 1957), 275−80.

31. Stoddard Martin, *California Writers* (London: Macmillan Press, 1983), 93.

32. John Steinbeck, *Lachez les Bombes!* (New York: Viking Press, 1944), vii. This translation by Stan and Alison Dex.

33. Steinbeck has recounted some of the history of his paternal grandparents in his *Letters to Alicia*, which appeared in the 12 & 26 February 1966 editions of the Long Island newspaper, *Newsday*.

Chapter Eight. 1945: More Filmmaking in Mexico

1. Orville Prescott, "Books of the Times," *New York Times*, 2 January 1945, 17.

2. Ibid.

3. F. O. Matthiessen, "Some Philosophers in the Sun," *New York Times Book Review*, 31 December 1944, 1.

4. C. G. Paulding, " More Books of the Week," *Commonweal* 41 (26 January 1945), 89−90.

5. The novella, under the title "The Pearl of the World," was eventually first published in the December 1945 issue of *Woman's Home Companion*. It was not

published by Viking Press until 1947.

6. Louis Owens, *John Steinbeck's Re-Vision of America* (Athens: University of Georgia Press, 1985), 35.

7. Howard Levant, *The Novels of John Steinbeck: A Critical Study*, with an introduction by Warren French (Columbia, Missouri: University of Missouri Press, 1974), 205.

8. Richard O'Connor, *John Steinbeck* (New York: McGraw-Hill Book Company, 1970), 94.

9. Sunita Jain, *Steinbeck's Concept of Man* (New Delhi: New Statesman Publishing Company, 1979), 78.

10. Lester Jay Marks, *Thematic Design in the Novels of John Steinbeck* (The Hague: Mouton & Co., 1969), 106.

11. Lawrence William Jones, *John Steinbeck as Fabulist*, ed. Marston LaFrance (Muncie: Steinbeck Monograph Series, No. 3, 1973), 22.

12. French 1, 137 & 142.

13. The manuscript of *The Pearl* is in the John Steinbeck Library, Salinas.

14. For a more detailed description of the holograph manuscript (and of the carbon copy of the typescript held by Harry Ransom Humanities Research Center, University of Texas at Austin), together with a comparison between the manuscript and the published text, see Roy S. Simmonds, "Steinbeck's *The Pearl*: A Preliminary Textual Study," *Steinbeck Quarterly* 22 (Winter-Spring, 1989): 16–34.

15. Millichap, 97.

16. In *Sea of Cortez*, Steinbeck writes; "Undoubtedly there are sound symbols in the unconscious just as there are visual symbols . . . If there be visual symbols, strong and virile in the unconscious, there must be others planted by the other senses" (*SC* 185–86).

17. French 2, 129.

18. In a letter dated 27 January 1945 to Mildred Lyman, Steinbeck confessed: "Still don't know if it is any good or a mess but I think it is certainly a good picture." Stanford University Library.

19. JS/PC, c. April 1945. Most of this letter has already been reproduced in *SLL*, 280–1, and in *Adventures*, 567–68.

20. Extracted from the unpublished holograph draft of Steinbeck's obituary of Ernie Pyle. Steinbeck Research Center, San Jose State University.

21. The holograph manuscript of *The Wizard of Maine* is held in the John Steinbeck Library, Salinas. It consists of thirty leaves, measuring approximately $13\frac{1}{4}$ by 9 inches, torn from a ledger. There are thirty-five lines to a page. The manuscript is written in ink on one side of each sheet. Steinbeck's handwriting is typically small and cramped (unlike the handwriting in *The Pearl* manuscript) and is occasionally difficult to decipher. There are few emendations. When the manuscript came on the market in 1980 as one of the items in the Harry Valentine Collection of Steinbeck Books and Manuscripts, the Bradford Morrow catalogue erroneously described it as being divided into six sections. The mistake clearly occurred as, by some oversight, Steinbeck had also numbered the seventh section of the manuscript "VI".

22. Steinbeck considered a dictaphone an essential tool, and told Covici: "When the army starts selling some of its thousands of dictaphones, I'm going to get one. They are marvellous for notes and transcriptions. And there will be plenty of them on the market" (JS/PC, 10 July 1945).

23. Steinbeck's fascination with Zapata remained however, and he contacted Pan-American Films again when he revisited Mexico in 1948. By then, the

company was no longer able to contemplate the project, owing to lack of funds. It was not until 1949 that Steinbeck at last completed a screenplay which was eventually produced by Darryl F. Zanuck for Twentieth Century-Fox, directed by Elia Kazan, and released to great acclaim in 1952.

24. Steinbeck did make a trip to Russia (with Robert Capa) for the *NYHT* in 1947. His dispatches, which appeared in that newspaper during the second half of January 1948, formed the basis of the subsequent book, *A Russian Journal*, published in 1948.

25. In his article, "John Steinbeck! John Steinbeck! How still we see thee lie, And lie and lie," *Esquire* 72 (November 1969): 150–1, 269, 271, 274–75, Frazier bitterly records how he attempted unsuccessfully to persuade Steinbeck to collaborate with him on the playscript.

26. See letter to Covici dated 15 November 1945. The *New York Times* the following day reported the award to Steinbeck on 15 November of King Haakon's Liberty Cross "for his presentation of Norway's resistance efforts to German occupation in his *The Moon Is Down*."

27. Romains never did win the Nobel Prize and Covici, of course, would have lost his bet. Steinbeck had to wait until 1962 before being awarded the Prize.

Chapter Nine. The Bus That Failed

1. Bosley Crowther, "The Screen in Review," *New York Times*, 18 February 1948, 6.

2. Richard Hatch, "Movies: Back to Adam," *New Republic* 118 (1 March 1948): 26.

3. "New Picture," *Time* 51 (1 March 1948): 84, 86.

4. Charles R. Metzger, "The Film Version of Steinbeck's 'The Pearl'," *Steinbeck Quarterly* 4 (Summer 1971), 88–92.

5. Millichap, 107.

6. Orville Prescott, "Books of the Times," *New York Times*, 24 November 1947, 21.

7. John Farrelly, "Fiction Parade," *New Republic* 117 (22 December 1947): 28.

8. "Briefly Noted: Fiction," *New Yorker* 23 (27 December 1947): 59.

9. Maxwell Geismar, "Fable Retold," *Saturday Review* 30 (22 November 1947): 14–15.

10. See: Eleanor Clark, "Infantalism and Steinbeck," *Nation* 164 (29 March 1947): 370, 372–73; J. M. Lalley, "A Sermon from Mr. Steinbeck," *New Yorker* 23 (22 February 1947), 87–88, 90; Elizabeth Hardwick, *Partisan Review* (March-April 1947): 198; and Orville Prescott, "Books of the Times," *New York Times*, 17 February 1947, 17.

11. J. Donald Adams, "Speaking of Books," *New York Times Book Review*, 2 March 1947, 2.

12. Thomas Kiernan, *The Intricate Music: A Biography of John Steinbeck* (Boston: Little, Brown & Company, 1979), 281.

13. Frank O'Malley, *Commonweal* 46 (25 April 1947), 43–44.

14. Prescott, *New York Times*, 17 February 1947.

Afterword

1. F. Scott Fitzgerald, *The Last Tycoon* (London: Grey Walls Press, 1949), 189.

2. There is an appreciable body of evidence that seems to substantiate Carol's importance in this respect. The painter Bruce Ariss who, with his wife Jean, knew Steinbeck well during the years of his first marriage, has recorded:

> There was no question in our minds that Carol had been responsible for much, if not most, of John's success. As Jean put it, Carol had 'goosed John up the ladder of fame by his bootstraps' ... she edited and typed John's manuscripts and made them ready for mailing to the publishers. ... I thought she was a damned good editor, too. She groomed John's sometimes sloppy and sentimental prose with a steel-bristled, intellectual, curry comb. (Bruce Ariss, *Inside Cannery Row: Sketches from the Steinbeck Era*, San Francisco: Lexikos, 1988), 96−97

Ed Ricketts's son, Ed Jr., has also acknowledged the editorial work carried out by Carol: "It's why my father thought of her as 'the backbone of John's writing,' and he referred to her that way. ... Everything that came out of him was scrutinized by her. Yes, Carol's eyes were the first to see his work. She would say what was good and what was bad" (Gene Detro, "Carol Steinbeck: Victor of a Dubious Battle," *Monterey Life*, January 1985, 83−84, 86−87). Steinbeck's elder son, Thom, has also praised Carol "without qualification," and is quoted as saying that "it was Carol who made my father. ... Carol knew what she was doing. Manuscripts would never have gotten to New York without her" (Ibid., 83).

3. Claude-Edmonde Magny, *The Age of the American Novel: The Film Aesthetic of Fiction* (New York: Frederick Ungar Publishing Company, 1972), 175.

4. Kline, "On John Steinbeck," 84.

5. Kenneth Allsop, "The wrath hasn't left Steinbeck," *Daily Mail*, 18 September 1961, 8.

6. As one critic has put it: "It is in these valleys of the imagination that one finds the roots of Steinbeck's art," Peter Shaw, "Steinbeck: The Shape of a Career," *Saturday Review* 52 (8 February 1969): 10−14, 50.

7. JS/Robert Ballou, n.d. [c. 1932−1933]. Harry Ransom Humanities Research Center.

8. Elia Kazan, *A Life* (London: Andre Deutsch, 1988), 273.

9. "Steinbeck on the Novel," *Carmel Pine Cone-Cymbal*, 10 March 1955, 6 & 7. The article reports the interview Steinbeck gave to Bill Pepper in Rome for his "It Happened in Italy" column in the *Rome Daily American*. The interview appeared a day or so after it had been announced on 28 October 1954 that Ernest Hemingway had been awarded the Nobel Prize for Literature.

10. Harold Bloom, *Modern Critical Views: John Steinbeck*, 4.

11. W. J. Weatherby, "Big Man from Monterey," *Guardian*, 13 October 1959.

12. Edmund Wilson, "The Californians: Storm and Steinbeck," 784−87.

13. W. H. Frohock, *The Novel of Violence in America* [2nd edition] (Dallas: Southern Methodist University Press, 1957), 140.

14. Kenneth Allsop, "The wrath hasn't left Steinbeck."

Select Bibliography

Abbreviations used:

NYHT   *New York Herald Tribune*
SJS   *San Jose Studies*
SNJS   *The Short Novels of John Steinbeck: Critical Essays with Checklist to Steinbeck Criticism*, edited by Jackson J. Benson. Durham: Duke University Press, 1990.
SQ   *Steinbeck Quarterly*
SQn   *The Steinbeck Question*, edited by Donald R. Noble. Troy, N.Y.: The Whitston Publishing Company, 1993.
YOG   *John Steinbeck: The Years of Greatness, 1936–1939*, edited by Tetsumaro Hayashi. Tuscaloosa: University of Alabama Press, 1993.

Primary Sources

Steinbeck's Major Works

Cup of Gold. New York: Robert M. McBride & Company, 1929.
The Pastures of Heaven. New York: Brewer, Warren & Putnam, 1932.
To a God Unknown. New York: Robert Ballou, 1933.
Tortilla Flat. New York: Covici-Friede, 1935.
In Dubious Battle. New York: Covici-Friede, 1936.
Of Mice and Men. New York: Covici-Friede, 1937.
Of Mice and Men: A Play in Three Acts. New York: Covici-Friede, 1937.
The Red Pony. New York: Covici-Friede, 1937.
Their Blood Is Strong. San Francisco: Simon Lubin Society of California, 1938.
The Long Valley. New York: Viking Press, 1938.
The Grapes of Wrath. New York: Viking Press, 1939.
The Forgotten Village. New York: Viking Press, 1941.
Sea of Cortez (with Edward F. Ricketts). New York: Viking Press, 1941.
The Moon Is Down. New York: Viking Press, 1942.
The Moon Is Down: Play in Two Parts. New York: Viking Press, 1942
Bombs Away: The Story of a Bomber Team. New York: Viking Press, 1942.
The Viking Portable Steinbeck, selected by Pascal Covici. New York: Viking Press, 1943.
The Steinbeck Pocket Book. New York: Pocket Books, Inc., 1943.
Cannery Row. New York: Viking Press, 1945.
The Portable Steinbeck (enlarged edition), selected by Pascal Covici. New York: Viking Press, 1946.
The Wayward Bus. New York: Viking Press, 1947.
The Pearl. New York: Viking Press, 1947.
A Russian Journal. New York: Viking Press, 1948.
Burning Bright. New York: Viking Press, 1950.
The Log from the Sea of Cortez. New York: Viking Press, 1951.
East of Eden. New York: Viking Press, 1952.
The Short Novels of John Steinbeck. New York: Viking Press, 1953.

Sweet Thursday. New York: Viking Press, 1954.
The Short Reign of Pippin IV. New York: Viking Press, 1957.
Once There Was a War. New York: Viking Press, 1958.
The Winter of Our Discontent. New York: Viking Press, 1961.
Travels With Charley in Search of America. New York: Viking Press, 1962.
America and Americans. New York: Viking Press, 1966.
Journal of a Novel: The East of Eden Letters. New York: Viking Press, 1969.
The Portable Steinbeck, revised, selected, and introduced by Pascal Covici, Jr.
New York: Viking Press, 1971.
Viva Zapata!, edited by Robert E. Morsberger. New York: Viking Press, 1975.
Steinbeck: A Life in Letters, edited by Elaine Steinbeck & Robert Wallsten. New
York: Viking Press, 1975.
The Acts of King Arthur and His Noble Knights, edited by Chase Horton. New
York: Farrar, Straus & Giroux, 1976.
Letters to Elizabeth, edited by Florian J. Shasky & Susan F. Riggs. San Francisco:
The Book Club of California, 1978.
Working Days: The Journals of The Grapes of Wrath, edited by Robert DeMott.
New York: Viking Press, 1989.
Zapata, edited by Robert E. Morsberger. Covelo, California: The Yollo Bolly
Press, 1991; reprinted together with screenplay *Viva Zapata!*. New York:
Penguin Books, 1993.

Steinbeck's War Dispatches Not Collected in *Once There Was a War*

"Steinbeck Finds a Little Fear, No Ferocity in Bomber Crew." *NYHT*, 28 June
1943, 1 & 7.
"Steinbeck Tells How Air Gunners Prepare Their Weapons for Raid." *NYHT*, 30
June 1943. 23.
"Steinbeck Finds Burned Pilot, Hands Gone, Eager to Fly Again." *NYHT*, 11
July 1943, 14.
"Steinbeck Tells Story of Crain, Lost With Flying Fortress Crew." *NYHT*, 17 July
1943, 7.
"Steinbeck Finds London Crowds Groping for Facts on Mussolini." *NYHT*, 30
July 1943, 13.
"Steinbeck Says Letters are Center of Soldiers' Lives." *NYHT*, 3 August 1943, 2.
"Steinbeck Says This Is a War of Supply, Not Combat, Services." *NYHT*,
5 August 1943, 17.
"Steinbeck Answers Air Fighter, Anxious Over Post-War World." *NYHT*,
10 August 1943, 21.
"Steinbeck Finds Flyers Show Little Feeling over Foe or War." *NYHT*, 27 August
1943, 13.
"Steinbeck Says Greatest Plaint of Soldiers Is Lax Mail Service." *NYHT*, 29
August 1943, 10.
"Steinbeck Tells How the Senator Posed at the 'Palookas' Graves." *NYHT*, 3
September 1943, 17.
"Steinbeck With Naval Force Invading Capri." *NYHT*, 17 September 1943, 3.
"Steinbeck Says Italians Resent Losing Status as Allied Captives." *NYHT*,
13 October 1943, 25.
"Steinbeck Sighs for Mulligan And £2 the Big Train Owes Him." *NYHT*,
29 October 1943, 17.
"Steinbeck Relates How Barbara Won the War From Home Front." *NYHT*,
8 November 1943, 17.

"Steinbeck Sees 'Plywood Navy' Take Part in a Secret Mission." *NYHT*, 17 November 1943, 17.

"Steinbeck Tells of Unfunny Joke: The Boat Never Left for Brooklyn." *NYHT*, 22 November 1943, 17.

"Steinbeck Sees a Task Force Do Its Job the Old Navy Way." *NYHT*, 26 November 1943, 21.

"Steinbeck Looks at Herrenvolk: Here's Corp. Bumblefoot, a Dope." *NYHT*, 15 December 1943, 23.

Steinbeck's Miscellaneous Shorter Writings Published During Period 1939 through 1945

"No Riders." *Saturday Review* 20 (1 April 1939): 13–14, 16. (A slightly abridged version of Chapter 2 of *The Grapes of Wrath*.)

"The Squatters' Camp." *The Progressive Weekly* 3 (6 May 1939): 3. (Reprint of second chapter of *Their Blood Is Strong*.)

"Two for a Penny." *Reader's Digest* 17 (August 1939): 9–12. (Abridged version of Chapter 15 of *The Grapes of Wrath*.)

John Steinbeck ... A Letter written in reply to a request for a statement about his ancestry. Stamford, Connecticut: The Overbrook Press, 1940. (Monograph containing the texts of an exchange of letters between the Reverend L. M. Birkhead, National Director of the Friends of Democracy, and Steinbeck.)

"Of Beef and Men." In *Famous Recipes by Famous People*, compiled and edited by Herbert Cerwin. San Francisco: Lane Publishing Company, 1940, 11. .

"How Edith McGillcuddy Met R. L. Stevenson." *Harper's Magazine* 183 (August 1941), 252–58.

"Steinbeck Lashes Out at Bungled Goodwill Drive in Latin States: A Reply to American Censorhip." *The Carmel Cymbal* 15 (4 September 1941): 3.

"'Our Best'—Our Fliers." *New York Times Magazine* 92 (22 November 1942): 16–17, 29. (Reprints excepts from *Bombs Away*.)

"The Bomber—Our Best Weapon." *Science Digest* 14 (July 1943): 62–66. (Abridged version of a chapter from *Bombs Away*.)

"John Steinbeck Writes Appeal For Third War Loan Drive." *Monterey Peninsula Herald*, 17 September 1943.

"The Aerial Engineer." *Scholastic* 43 (6 December 1943): 17–18. (Extract from *Bombs Away*.)

"Over There." *Ladies Home Journal* 61 (February 1944): 137, 139–42, 144–58. (Abridged version of six of the *NYHT* war dispatches.)

"Troopship." *Reader's Digest* 44 (March 1944): 67–90. (Condensed version of six of the *NYHT* war dispatches.)

"The Pearl of the World." *Woman's Home Companion* 72 (December 1945): 17–18, 85–86, 96–100, 104–105, 109–13, 120. (First publication of the novella *The Pearl*, published in 1947.)

Other Selected Steinbeck Miscellaneous Writings

"The novel might benefit by the discipline, the terseness of the drama ..." *Stage* 15 (January 1938): 50–51.

"The Time the Wolves Ate the Vice-Principal." *'47 Magazine of the Year* 1 (March 1947): 26–27.

"Critics, Critics, Burning Bright." *Saturday Review* 33 (11 November 1950): 20—21.
"The Secret Weapon We Were Afraid To Use." *Collier's* 131 (10 January 1953): 9—13.
"Reflections on a lunar eclipse." *NYHT*, Book Week section, 6 October 1963, 3.

Secondary Sources

Biographies and Memoirs

Benson, Jackson J. *The True Adventures of John Steinbeck, Writer*. New York: Viking Press, 1984.
————. *Looking for Steinbeck's Ghost*. Norman & London: University of Oklahoma Press, 1988.
Enea, Sparky. *With Steinbeck in the Sea of Cortez*, as told to Audry Lynch. Los Osos, California: Sand River Press, 1991.
Fensch, Thomas. *Steinbeck and Covici: The Story of a Friendship*. Middlebury: Paul S. Eriksson, 1979.
Hedgpeth, Joel W. *The Outer Shores. Part I: Ricketts and Steinbeck Explore the Pacific Coast. Part II: Breaking Through*. Eureka, California: Mad River Press, Inc., 1978.
Kiernan, Thomas. *The Intricate Music: A Biography of John Steinbeck*. Boston: Little, Brown & Company, 1979.
Parini, Jay. *John Steinbeck: A Biography*. New York: Henry Holt and Company, 1995.
Valjean, Nelson. *John Steinbeck, The Errant Knight: An intimate biography of his California years*. San Francisco: Chronicle Books, 1975.

Guides and Histories

Ariss, Bruce. *Inside Cannery Row: Sketches from the Steinbeck Era*. San Francisco: Lexikos, 1988.
Cannon, Ray. *The Sea of Cortez*. Menlo Park, California: Lane Magazine & Books Company, 1966.
Crouch, Steve. *Steinbeck Country*. Palo Alto, California: American West Publishing Company, 1973.
Hemp, Michael Kenneth. *Cannery Row: The History of Old Ocean View Avenue*. Monterey: The History Company, 1986.
Knox, Maxine, & Mary Rodriguez. *Steinbeck's Street: Cannery Row*. San Rafael, California: Presido Press, 1980.
Mangelsdorf, Tom. *A History of Steinbeck's Cannery Row*. Santa Cruz: Western Tanager Press, 1986.
March, Ray A. *A Guide to Cannery Row*. Monterey: Ray A. March, 1962.
Person, Richard. *History of Cannery Row*. Monterey: City of Monterey, 1973.

Criticism

Astro, Richard. *John Steinbeck and Edward F. Ricketts: The Shaping of a Novelist*. Minneapolis: University of Minnesota Press, 1973.

————. *Edward F. Ricketts*. Boise, Idaho: Boise State University Press, 1976.

Astro, Richard, and Tetsumaro Hayashi, eds. *Steinbeck: The Man and His Work*. Corvallis: Oregon State University Press, 1971.

Benson, Jackson J., ed. *The Short Novels of John Steinbeck: Critical Essays with Checklist to Steinbeck Criticism*. Durham: Duke University Press, 1990.

————. *Steinbeck's Cannery Row: A Reconsideration*. Muncie, Indiana: Steinbeck Research Institute, 1991. Steinbeck Essay Series, No. 4.

Benton, Robert M. "The Ecological Nature of Cannery Row." In *Steinbeck: The Man and His Work*, edited by Richard Astro & Tetsumaro Hayashi, 131–39.

Bloom, Harold, ed. *Modern Critical Views: John Steinbeck*. New York: Chelsea House, 1987.

————, ed. *John Steinbeck's The Grapes of Wrath*. New York: Chelsea House, 1988.

Brown, Alan. "From Artist to Craftsman: Steinbeck's *Bombs Away*." In *SQn*, 213–22.

Burns, Stuart L. "The Turtle or the Gopher: Another Look at the Ending of *The Grapes of Wrath*." *Western American Literature* 9 (Spring 1974): 53–57.

Coers, Donald V. *John Steinbeck as Propagandist: The Moon Is Down Goes to War*. Tuscaloosa & London: University of Alabama Press, 1991.

Davis, Robert Con, ed. *Twentieth Century Interpretations of The Grapes of Wrath*. Englewood Cliffs: Prentice-Hall, Inc., 1982.

Davis, Robert Murray, ed. *Steinbeck: A Collection of Critical Essays*. Englewood Cliffs: Prentice-Hall, Inc., 1972.

DeMott, Robert. *Steinbeck's Reading: A Catalogue of Books Owned and Borrowed*. New York: Garland Publishing Company, 1984.

————. "After *The Grapes of Wrath*: A Speculative Essay on John Steinbeck's Suite of Love Poems for Gwyn, 'The Girl of the Air.'" In *YOG*, 20–45.

Ditsky, John. "The Ending of *The Grapes of Wrath*: A Further Commentary." *Agora* 2 (Fall 1973): 41–50.

————. "Steinbeck's *Bombs Away*: The Group Man in the Wild Blue Yonder." *SQ* 12 (Winter-Spring 1979): 5–14.

————. *John Steinbeck: Life, Work, and Criticism*. Frederiction, N.B: York Press, 1985.

————, ed.*Critical Essays on Steinbeck's The Grapes of Wrath*. Boston: G. K. Hall & Company, 1989.

————. "Steinbeck's 'European' Play-Novella: *The Moon Is Down*." In *SNJS*, 101–10.

Donohue, Agnes McNeill. *A Casebook on The Grapes of Wrath*. New York: Thomas Y. Crowell Company, 1968.

Federle, Steven J. "*Lifeboat* as Allegory: Steinbeck and the Demon of War." *SQ* 12 (Winter-Spring 1979): 14–20.

Fontenrose, Joseph. *John Steinbeck: An Introduction and Interpretation*. New York: Holt, Rinehart & Winston, Inc., 1963.

French, Warren. *John Steinbeck*. Boston: Twayne Publishers, Inc., 1961.

————. *A Companion to The Grapes of Wrath*. New York: Viking Press, 1963. (A new edition published by Penguin Books in 1989.)

————. *Filmguide to The Grapes of Wrath*. Bloomington: Indiana University Press, 1973.

————. *John Steinbeck* (Second edition, revised). Boston: Twayne Publishers, Inc., 1975.

————. "After *The Grapes of Wrath*." *SQ* 8 (Summer-Fall 1975): 73–78.

————. "*The Moon Is Down*: John Steinbeck's 'Times'." *SQ* 11 (Summer-Fall 1978): 77—87.

————. "*The Red Pony* as Story Cycle and Film." In *SNJS*, 71—84.

————. *John Steinbeck's Fiction Revisited*. New York: Twayne Publishers, 1994.

Gannett, Lewis. "John Steinbeck: Novelist at Work." *Atlantic* 176 (December 1945): 55—60.

Garcia, Reloy. *Steinbeck and D. H. Lawrence: Fictive Voices and the Ethical Imperative*. Muncie: John Steinbeck Society of America, 1972. Steinbeck Monograph Series, No. 2.

Gladstein, Mimi Reisel. *The Indestructible Women in Faulkner, Hemingway, and Steinbeck*. Ann Arbor: UMI Research Press, 1986.

————. "*The Grapes of Wrath*: Steinbeck and the Eternal Immigrant." In *YOG*, 132—44.

Gray, James. *John Steinbeck*. Minneapolis: University of Minnesota Press, 1971.

Hayashi, Tetsumaro, ed. *Steinbeck's Literary Dimension: A Guide to Comparative Studies*. Metuchen, N.J.: Scarecrow Press, 1974.

————. "*The Pearl* as the Novel of Disengagement." *SQ* 7 (Summer-Fall 1974): 84—88.

————, ed. *A Study Guide to Steinbeck: A Handbook to His Major Works*. *Metuchen, NJ: Scarecrow Press, 1974.*

————, ed. *A Study Guide to Steinbeck (Part II)*. Metuchen, NJ: Scarecrow Press, 1979.

————. *Steinbeck's World War II Fiction, The Moon Is Down: Three Explications*. Muncie, Indiana: Steinbeck Research Institute, 1986. Steinbeck Essay Series, No. 1.

————, ed. *Steinbeck's The Grapes of Wrath*: *Essays in Criticism*. Muncie, Indiana: Steinbeck Research Institute, 1990. Steinbeck Essay Series, No. 3.

————. "Dr. Winter's Dramatic Functions in *The Moon Is Down*." In *SNJS*, 95—101.

————, ed. *Steinbeck's Literary Dimension: A Guide to Comparative Studies (Series II)*. Metuchen, NJ: Scarecrow Press, 1991.

————, ed. *John Steinbeck: The Years of Greatness, 1936—1939*. Tuscaloosa & London: University of Alabama Press, 1993.

Hedgpeth, Joel. "Genesis of *Sea of Cortez*." *SQ* 6 (Summer 1973): 74—80.

Hintz, Paul. "The Silent Woman and the Male Voice in Steinbeck's *Cannery Row*." In *SQn*, 71—83.

Hughes, R. S. *Beyond The Red Pony: A Reader's Companion to Steinbeck's Complete Short Stories*. Metuchen, NJ: Scarecrow Press, 1987.

————. *John Steinbeck: A Study of the Short Fiction*. Boston: Twayne Publishers, Inc., 1989.

————. "'Some Philosophers in the Sun': Steinbeck's *Cannery Row*." In *SNJS*, 119—31.

Jones, Lawrence William. *John Steinbeck as Fabulist*, edited by Marston LaFrance. Muncie, Indiana: John Steinbeck Society of America, 1973. Steinbeck Monograph Series, No. 3.

————. "Poison in the Cream Puff: The Human Condition in *Cannery Row*." *SQ* 7 (Spring 1974): 35—40.

Kline, Herbert. "'The Forgotten Village': An Account of Film Making in Mexico." *Theatre Arts* 25 (May 1941): 336—43.

Levant, Howard. *The Novels of John Steinbeck: A Critical Study*. Columbia, Missouri: University of Missouri Press, 1974.

Lewis, Cliff, and Carroll Britch. *Rediscovering Steinbeck: Revisionist Views of His Art, Politics and Intellect.* Lewiston: Edwin Mellen Press, 1989.
Lisca, Peter. *The Wide World of John Steinbeck.* New Brunswick: Rutgers University Press, 1958. (A new edition with an Afterword published in 1981 by Gordian Press, New York.)
———, ed. *John Steinbeck, The Grapes of Wrath: Text and Criticism.* New York: Viking Press, 1972.
———. *John Steinbeck: Nature and Myth.* New York: Thomas Y. Crowell Company, 1978.
———. "*Cannery Row*: Escape into the Counterculture." In *SNJS*, 111–19.
McCarthy, Paul. *John Steinbeck.* New York: Frederick Ungar Publishing Company, 1980.
Marks, Lester Jay. *Thematic Design in the Novels of John Steinbeck.* The Hague: Mouton, 1969.
Martin, Stoddard. *California Writers.* London: Macmillan Press Ltd., 1983.
Meyer, Michael J. "Precious Bane: Mining the Fool's Gold of *The Pearl.*" In *SNJS*, 161–72.
Metzger, Charles R. "The Film Version of Steinbeck's *The Pearl.*" *SQ* 4 (Summer 1971): 88–92.
Millichap. Joseph R. *Steinbeck and Film.* New York: Frederick Ungar Publishing Company, 1983.
Moore, Harry Thornton. *The Novels of John Steinbeck: A First Critical Study.* Chicago: Normandie House, 1939. (A second edition with a contemporary epilogue published in 1968 by Kennikat Press, Inc., Port Washington.)
Morsberger, Robert E. "Adrift in Steinbeck's *Lifeboat.*" *Literary Film Quarterly* 4 (Fall 1976): 325–38.
———. "Steinbeck and the Stage." In *SNJS*, 271–93.
———. "Steinbeck's War." In *SQn*, 183–212.
———. "Tell Again, George." In *YOG*, 111–31.
Nakayama, Kiyoshi. "The Artistic Design of *The Grapes of Wrath*: Steinbeck's Five Layers of Symbolism." *Essays and Studies* 34 (Fall-Winter 1982): 117–25.
Noack, J. S. "John Steinbeck." *Congregational Quarterly* (April 1941): 118–24.
Noble, Donald R., ed. *The Steinbeck Question.* Troy, NY: The Whitston Publishing Company, 1993.
Owens, Louis. "The Threshold of War: Steinbeck's Quest in *Once There Was a War.*" *SQ* 13 (Summer-Fall 1980): 80–86.
———. *Steinbeck's Re-Vision of America.* Athens: University of Georgia Press, 1985.
——— *The Grapes of Wrath: Trouble in the Promised Land.* Boston: Twayne Publishers, 1989.
Pauly, Thomas R. "*Gone With the Wind* and *The Grapes of Wrath* as Hollywood Histories of the Depression." *Journal of Popular Film* 3 (Summer 1974): 203–18.
Perez, Betty L. "Steinbeck, Ricketts, and *Sea of Cortez*: Partnership or Exploitation?" *SQ* 7 (Summer-Fall 1974): 73–79.
———. "The Form of the Narrative Section of *Sea of Cortez*: A Specimen Collected from Reality." *SQ* 9 (Spring 1976): 36–44.
Richards, Edmund C. "The Challenge of John Steinbeck." *North American Review* 243 (June 1937): 406–13.
Shillinglaw, Susan, ed. *San Jose Studies*, 16 (Winter 1990). Special issue containing essays based on presentations given 16–18 March 1989 at San Jose State

University: "*The Grapes of Wrath*: An Interdisciplinary Forum."

———. "California Answers *The Grapes of Wrath*." In *YOG*, 145–64.

Simmonds, Roy. "John Steinbeck's World War II Dispatches: An Annotated Checklist." *Serif* 11 (Summer 1974): 21–30.

———. "John Steinbeck, Robert Louis Stevenson, and Edith McGillcuddy." *SJS* 1 (November 1975): 29–39.

———. *Steinbeck's Literary Achievement*. Muncie, Indiana: John Steinbeck Society of America, 1976. Steinbeck Monograph Series, No. 6.

———. "Steinbeck and World War II: The Moon Goes Down." *SQ* 17 (Winter-Spring 1984): 14–34.

———. "Steinbeck's *The Pearl*: A Preliminary Textual Study." *SQ* 22 (Winter-Spring 1989): 14–34.

———. "Steinbeck's *The Pearl*: Legend, Film, Novel." In *SNJS*, 173–84.

———. "The Original Manuscript [of *The Grapes of Wrath*]." *SJS* 16 (Winter 1990): 117–32.

Tedlock, E. W., and C. V. Wicker, eds. *Steinbeck and His Critics*. Albuquerque: University of New Mexico, 1957.

Timmerman, John H. *John Steinbeck's Fiction: The Aesthetics of the Road Taken*. Norman & London: University of Oklahoma Press, 1986.

———. *The Dramatic Landscape of Steinbeck's Short Stories*. Norman & London: University of Oklahoma Press, 1990.

———. "The Shadow of the Pearl: Jungian Patterns in *The Pearl*." In *SNJS*, 143–61.

Watt, F. W. *Steinbeck*. New York: Grove Press, 1962.

Wyatt, David, ed. *New Essays on The Grapes of Wrath*. Cambridge: Cambridge University Press, 1990.

Index

premarital relationship with JS, 68, 69, 83, 93, 96, 110, 112, 122, 126, 127, 149, 151, 154; marriage to JS, 166; marital relationship with JS, 168–69, 186, 199, 200–201, 203, 206–7, 215, 224, 237–38, 241, 248–49; defense of JS in Nathan affair, 150; correspondence with JS overseas, 175, 176–78, 179, 180, 181, 185, 187, 188–89, 194, 197, 198, 199, 200; first pregnancy, 220, 222, 238–39; health problems, 239, 243, 248, 251, 255, 276, 279–80, 281, 283 284, 292; involvement in JS's work, 130, 139, 254, 262, 263, 268, 275, 277; in Mexico with JS, 264, 274, 285; second pregnancy, 285, 288, 289; divorces JS, 304; death, 304

Steinbeck, John: Army Intelligence, investigations by, 121, 129–30, 182–83; biographies of, contemporary reviews of, 6–7; Cannery Row, resistance to proposed *Life* article on, 242, 254; Carol, relationship with (*see* Steinbeck, Carol); censorship of and changes made to work, 13–15, 26, 95–96, 97, 138, 165, 203, 204, 206, 210, 216–19, 220, 247; Christian Scientists, objections to *CR* by, 244; cinematic techniques in work, 32, 98, 227–28, 237, 252, 253, 257–59; collaboration with Emilio Fernandez, 220–21, 243, 246, 247, 251, 252, 254–55, 257, 262, 275, 276, 280, 281–82, 283–84; collaboration with George Frazier, 275, 283, 284, 288; collaboration with Herbert Kline, 39, 43–45, 57–58, 61, 62, 64–65, 69–72; collaboration with George S. Kaufman, 22, 111, 121, 275; collaboration with Pare Lorentz, 21–22; collaboration with Lewis Milestone, 47, 84–86, 92, 94, 95; collaboration with Edward F. Ricketts, 34–36, 38, 40, 41–42, 63, 65–67, 74–84, 108–9; collaboration with Lee Strasberg, 111; collaboration with Jack Wagner, 146–49, 249, 263, 268, 274, 275, 276, 280, 281, 283, 284, 289,

collaborations, JS's view of, 297–98; communist loyalties, false accusations of, 14, 41, 121–22, 124, 150, 152, 182–83; critical predictions in 1939, 3, 9; critical reception of postwar work, 4–5, 291–93; critical reception of prewar work, 1–3; critical reception of wartime work, 4, 291, 295–96 (*see also under* individual titles); critical reputation at time of death, 5–6; critics, his reactions to and opinions of, 114, 220, 245, 250, 252–53, 273, 301; divorce from Carol, 166; Draft Board 119; Monterey, problems with, 128–29, 141–45, 149, 152, 165, 166, 168, 234; ecologist, as, 78–79; fatherhood, 239, 249, 274, 280, 289; FBI, investigations by, 18, 41, 121–22, 124, 128, 130, 220; filmmaking, antipathy toward, 22, 61–62, 181, 186, 243, 277, 285; flying lessons, 47; Gwyn, relationship with (*see* Steinbeck, Gwyndolyn Conger); health problems, 13, 16, 27, 59–60, 61, 63, 68, 185, 201, 221, 274, 276, 280, 285, 286; Hollywood, dealings with, 21, 25, 29–30, 31–32, 56–57, 61, 64, 73–74, 94, 95, 125, 137–38, 141, 148–49, 152–53, 216–20, 246–47, 262, 272–73; literary career in postwar years, 4–5, 302–3; literary career in prewar years, 1–3; literary career in war years, 294–95, 297–98; marine biology, influence on his fiction, 33, 48–49, 79–80, 233, 235 (*see also* Ricketts, Edward F.); marine biology, interest in, 34, 35, 36, 37, 78; marriage to Gwyn, 166; Mexico, visits to, 43–45, 57–58, 219–21, 262, 264–84, 284–86, 289; migrant situation in California, views on, 1–2; Monterey, homesickness for, 130, 215, 239; Monterey, makes home again in, 240; Monterey, disillusionment with, 243, 245, 262–64, 265, 273, 279; movies, his approval of *OMM* and *GOW*, 22–23, 25, 28–29; music, influence on his writing, 24, 34, 235–36, 254–55,